Business Elites and Urban Development

SUNY Series in Urban
Public Policy
Richard Rich and
Mark Schneider, Editors

Business Elites and Urban Development: Case Studies and Critical Perspectives

Edited by Scott Cummings

State University of New York Press

Published by
State University of New York Press, Albany

© 1988 State University of New York

For information, address State University of New York
Press, State University Plaza, Albany, N.Y., 12246.

Library of Congress Cataloging-in-Publication Data

Business elites and urban development.

(SUNY series on urban public policy)
Includes index.
1. Cities and towns—United States—Growth—Case
studies. 2. Businessmen—United States—Case studies.
3. Urban policy—United States—Case studies. 4. Urban
renewal—United States—Case studies. I. Cummings,
Scott, 1944–   . II. Series.
HT371.B79   1987   307.1'4'0973   87-6456
ISBN 0-88706-577-5
ISBN 0-88706-578-3 (pbk.)

10 9 8 7 6 5 4 3 2 1

Contents

Contributors

LARRY BENNETT is Associate Professor and Chairperson of the Department of Political Science at DePaul University. With Greg Squires, Kathy McCourt, and Philip Nyden, he is coauthor of *Chicago: Race, Class, and the Response to Urban Decline* (Temple University Press, 1987). His work has also appeared in several social science and urban affairs journals.

SCOTT CUMMINGS is Professor and Associate Dean of Urban Affairs at the University of Louisville. He has published numerous books and articles dealing with urban development, social problems, and minority relations. He is currently completing a book dealing with the political economy of neighborhood transition and change.

DAVID S. DAYKIN is currently a Development Associate for the Bilingual Foundation of the Arts in Los Angeles. He received a B.A. from Oberlin College and a Ph.D. in sociology from Vanderbilt University. His research interests include the study of urbanization and economic development in Latin America, mental health policy, neighborhood organization and change, immigration and labor markets and the evaluation of nonprofit organizations.

JOE R. FEAGIN is Professor of Sociology at the University of Texas at Austin. He specializes in urban sociology, and is the author of 90 articles and 18 books, the most recent of which is *The Capitalist City* (Basil Blackwell, 1987), with Michael Peter Smith.

RICHARD CHILD HILL is Professor of Sociology and Urban Affairs at Michigan State University. He is a co-author of *Restructuring the City* (Longman, 1983) and *Detroit: Race and Uneven Development* (Temple University Press, 1987), and author of numerous scholarly articles on urban theory, urban fiscal crises, race-relations, transnational corporations and industrial policy. He has been a visiting professor at the University of California, Santa Cruz; the Royal Danish Academy of Fine Arts, Copenhagen; and the Centre of Urban Studies and Urban Planning, University of Hong Kong. His current research includes studies of regional deindustrialization and industrial policy; and the social ramifications of global reorganization in the world automobile industry.

MICHAEL INDERGAARD is a doctoral candidate in the Department of Sociology at Michigan State University. He has co-authored "Labor Conflict and the Global Auto Factory," in Daniel Cornfield (ed.), *Workers, Managers and Technological Change* (Plenum, 1986). He is currently looking at the social response to deindustrialization in Downriver Detroit for his dissertation research.

THOMAS J. KEIL is Professor and Chair, Department of Sociology, University of Louisville. He recently completed a study of the Capital Cities strike in Wilkes-Barre. A monograph on this strike is forthcoming from the University of Alabama Press. He has published numerous articles dealing with urban problems, labor relations, and intergroup relations. Currently he is studying the martial arts as an example of ethnic entrepreneurship.

JOHN R. LOGAN is Professor in the Departments of Sociology and Public Policy, State University of New York at Albany. He is the author of a series of research articles on the patterns and politics of suburban development in the United States. Together with Harvey Molotch, he is also author of *Urban Fortunes: The Political Economy of Place* (University of California Press, 1987).

KATHLEEN McCOURT is Associate Professor of Sociology and Chairperson of the Department of Sociology and Anthropology at Loyola University of Chicago. Recently she has co-authored *Chicago: Race, Class and the Response to Urban Decline* (with Greg Squires, Larry Bennett, and Philip Nyden) and contributed to a study of fair housing in metropolitan Chicago sponsored by the Chicago Area Fair Housing Alliance. Her previous publications include *Working-Class Women and Grassroots Politics* and *Catholic Schools in a Declining Church* (co-authored with Andrew Greeley and William McCready).

HARVEY MOLOTCH is Professor of Sociology at the University of California, Santa Barbara. He has carried out research on mass media, interpersonal power, and racial integration. His most recent book (with John Logan) is *Urban Fortunes: The Political Economy of Place* (University of California Press, 1987).

THOMAS S. MOORE is an Assistant Professor of Sociology at Denison University. His current research is primarily concerned with the effects of industrial change upon social inequality. He has also published articles exploring the relationship of class and gender to work values and attitudes towards unions.

KENNETH J. NEUBECK is Associate Professor of Sociology at The University of Connecticut—Storrs. Professor Neubeck is the author of *Corporate Response to Urban Crisis* and *Social Problems: A Critical Approach.* He has contributed to anthologies on such topics as the impact of racism on welfare policies, and income maintenance experimentation and poverty politics. Additional articles have appeared in such journals as *Social Problems, Social Policy,* and *Teaching Sociology.* He is currently at work on analyses of political and economic factors influencing downtown city development, and exploration of data sets dealing with the consumer and investment behaviors of American families.

PHILIP W. NYDEN is Associate Professor of Sociology at Loyola University of Chicago. He is author of *Steelworkers Rank and File: The Political Economy of Union Reform Movement* and co-author of *Race, Class and the Response to Urban Decline.* He has recently completed a report (with A. Lyons and K. McCourt) on a proposed program to insure home value in Chicago neighborhoods as a way of preventing middle-class flight from the city. He has also co-authored reports on fair housing in Chicago's suburbs, and on community perception of neighborhood change in Evanston, Illinois. Articles by Nyden have appeared in the *American Journal of Sociology, The Nation,* and the *Insurgent Sociologist.*

RICHARD E. RATCLIFF is Associate Professor of Sociology at
Syracuse University. His research has focused on community
struggles over urban development, bank lending practices, right-
wing politics, upper class investment practices and the Chilean
upper class structure. He has also served as a research coordinator
for the Association of Community Organizations for Reform Now
(ACORN). His publications include articles in the *American
Sociological Review, American Journal of Sociology, Social Problems,
Latin American Historical Review* and *Latin American Perspectives.*
His book *Landlords and Capitalists: The Dominant Class in Chile*
(with M. Zeitlin) is forthcoming in 1987.

MARK S. ROSENTRAUB is Professor of Public and Environmental
Affairs and Director of the School of Public and Environmental
Affairs at Indiana University, Fort Wayne. His research has been
published in *Urban Affairs Quarterly,* the *Journal of Urban Affairs,*
and numerous other journals and collections. His recent research
has focused on changes in governmental spending at all levels during the Reagan Administration, the delivery of services to people
with mental retardation, and the impact of changes in Medicare
and Medicaid funding on elders.

EDMOND SNIDER served as a code enforcement officer for several
years, and has worked as a private developer in three major cities
in the Southwest. He received an M.A. in Urban Affairs from the
University of Texas at Arlington and is currently serving as a
public administrator in a major metropolitan area.

GREGORY D. SQUIRES is Associate Professor of Sociology and
Chair of the Department of Sociology at the University of Wis-
consin-Milwaukee. Prior to joining the faculty at UWM in 1984 he
served seven years as a research analyst with the U.S. Commission
on Civil Rights. His research has focused on the racial effects of
uneven urban development. Recent publications include: *Chicago:
Race, Class, and the Response to Urban Decline* with L. Bennett, K.
McCourt, and P. Nyden (Temple University Press, 1987), "Insurance Redlining and the Transformation of an Urban Metropolis," with William Velez, *Urban Affairs Quarterly,* Fall 1987, and
"Inequality in Metropolitan Industrial Revenue Bond Programs,"
Review of Black Political Economy, Spring 1986.

TODD SWANSTROM is an Assistant Professor in the Rockefeller College of Public Affairs and Policy at the State University of New York at Albany. He is the author of *The Crisis of Growth Politics: Cleveland, Kucinich, and the Challenge of Urban Populism* (1985). Along with John Logan, he is the co-editor of a series for Temple University Press titled "Conflicts in Urban and Regional Development".

J. ALLEN WHITT, Associate Professor of Sociology and Urban Affairs at the University of Louisville, is author of *Urban Elites and Mass Transportation* (Princeton University Press, 1982) and (with Joyce Rothschild) *The Cooperative Workplace* (Cambridge University Press, 1986). His major areas of research are the politics of urban growth, networks among corporate elites, and the political-economic role of the performing arts.

Introduction

Chapter 1

PRIVATE ENTERPRISE AND PUBLIC POLICY: Business Hegemony in the Metropolis

Scott Cummings

The election of Ronald Reagan to the U.S. Presidency in 1980 was a statement by the American people that their government has become too large, too expensive, and too intrusive. It is now time to translate that mandate into pragmatic, sensible actions to bring about responsible change in the boundaries that separate the sovereignty of the individual and private institutions from the sovereignty of the government.

Martin Anderson
Assistant to the President for Policy Development
The White House, 1982

After assuming power in 1980, Ronald Reagan began to carry out his campaign promise to privatize public sector institutions and programs. Advised and inspired by supply-side economists, and supported by conservative legislators advocating a return to free market capitalism, Reagan sought to transform tax laws, reduce or eliminate government programs, and maximize private control over investment capital. While primarily intended to curb inflation and stimulate industrial recovery, his economic program directly altered urban development policy and the way in which social scientists think about cities and their inhabitants. Urban policy under Reagan relies heavily upon economic growth shaped by private investment decisions, and a tax reform package requiring that state and local governments raise more of their own revenues.

Under Reagan, the private entrepreneur has become the urban planner of the 1980s. While business elites, speculators, and wealthy financiers have always been involved in downtown development, the Administration has inaugurated a new era of business domination over urban policy. The Reagan Administration has promoted private enterprise, corporate ingenuity, and business leadership as solutions to the problems confronting America's cities. Policy transformations have occurred within the social service arena, as well as in community development programs. The private sector has assumed responsibility for the creation of urban social policy.

"Privatizing" generally refers to the widespread movement to halt or reverse the growth of governmental institutions producing and distributing public goods and services.[1] Proponents of privatizing typically advocate four strategic measures to decrease government involvement in the delivery of city services: (1) existing services should be transferred to private businesses and supplied in response to market dynamics or through voluntary arrangements; (2) public services should be confined to those areas in which the government has historically played a necessary but minor role; (3) services should be financed primarily through user charges rather than by tax dollars; and (4) competition within the private marketplace should regulate the institutional arrangements which produce and deliver municipal services.[2]

The movement to privatize urban services, and the budget cuts accompanying it, reflect widespread dissatisfaction with welfare state liberalism. Reagan's realignment of urban priorities also signifies a fundamental alteration of power relations in the federal policy arena. The urban development agenda of private investors is no longer restricted by liberal hegemony in state and federal legislative bodies. Ideological sentiment endorsing government provision of urban services, or state subsidies to stimulate private investment in housing or urban redevelopment have been removed from the policy agenda of the federal government. In fact, some levels of government are beginning to divest themselves of many service delivery arrangements traditionally located within the public sector. Downtown development projects are being designed and implemented by private investors and business-dominated growth coalitions.

Some non-profit and university hospitals are being sold to private businesses or administered by for-profit, managerial firms.[3] Correctional facilities owned and operated by private corporations are gaining more attention among those in a position to influence criminal justice policy.[4] In the name of efficiency, individual initiative, and market competition, more and more basic urban services are being absorbed by private businesses: sanitation, waste disposal, police protection, medical care, public housing, and assistance to small businesses and minority entrepreneurs.[5] Established social welfare programs are falling victim to tax policies and fiscal schemes designed to return capital to the hands of financiers, speculators, and developers. Presumably, private investors will create jobs, thereby eliminating the widespread need for social welfare payments and related forms of income transfers.[6] Through gentrification and high-rise condominium construction, many of the nation's cities are gradually being prepared for the return of the middle and upper classes.

Most policy analysts agree that Reagan has assigned very low priority to federally sponsored urban programs, and is retreating from previous commitments to spend tax dollars in large cities:

> Most of these programs have been condemned as failures by the Reagan administration, with varying degrees of accuracy. But even programs that produced little useful real output transferred incomes to hundreds of thousands of low-skilled, low-income urban citizens who were having difficulty finding employment in the private economy. Insofar as the Reagan budget recognizes the problems caused by concentrated urban poverty, it proposes mainly to rely on private-sector economic growth and locally raised public-sector revenues.[7]

Reagan's critical attitude toward the welfare state and subsidized urban development projects has also drawn support from the intellectual and university communities. Expressing disenchantment and disillusionment with the liberal policy record, some academicians have recently argued in favor of totally dismantling the wide array of social welfare and urban development programs established during the 1960s and 1970s. According to these individuals, past programs have accomplished so little that the costs fail to justify the benefits produced. Charles Murray recommends a complete rethinking of poverty and community development policy, and suggests scrapping most federal social welfare programs.[8] In a critical appraisal of urban and community development policy, Donald Strickland and Dennis Judd observed that:

These programs seem destined to do little more than house a
particular, relatively small minority of the population. The popular fictions concerning their role in regenerating the lost urban
community are indeed fictions.[9]

A review of the Reagan record shows a systematic reduction of
dollars spent on urban-related social programs. Between 1981 and
1983, expenditures allocated to non-defense programs steadily dropped
as both a percentage of the gross national product and in absolute
dollar figures.[10] The major targets for budget reductions included social
security, Medicare and Medicaid, higher education and student loans,
aid to disadvantaged school districts, unemployment insurance, housing assistance and grants for urban development, grants for job training and creation, financial aid to the poor and the elderly, grants for
urban social services, and legal assistance to the poor. Since the
beneficiaries of these programs are disproportionately located in the
nation's cities, urban areas have been most severely affected by the President's transformation of public policy.

The federal budgets for 1984 and 1985 also reveal significant cuts
in social program expenditures. And the President's budget for 1986
again targeted The Department of Housing and Urban Development,
the Small Business Administration, the community development block
grant program, the Urban Development Action Grant program, AFDC
and other social welfare services and benefits, Medicare and Medicaid,
education, training, and employment assistance programs, and urban
transportation for additional cuts in federal assistance.[11] The Reagan
Administration has coupled the gutting of social programs with a
transfer to state government of administrative and fiscal responsibilities for their remainders. Primary among the programs being
turned over to state government for administration are food stamp and
AFDC benefits.[12] These administrative changes have been implemented in pursuit of greater efficiency and to reduce the amount of federal
tax dollars invested in the provision of services to the poor.

Contemporary Urban Policy and The Crisis of Capital Accumulation

Despite widespread disenchantment with welfare state liberalism
and the glowing characterizations of private entrepreneurs as the new

architects of urban policy, there is no reason to conclude that the nation's cities or their inhabitants will prosper under the development agenda being fostered by Reagan and his corporate supporters. Many of the contributors to this volume present evidence and argument suggesting that the urban crises of the 1960s and 1970s will reemerge in response to the policies being promulgated in the 1980s. The ascendancy of business hegemony in the metropolis and the associated dismantling of the welfare state can be partially understood as a crisis of capital accumulation.[13]

James O'Connor contends that major shifts in federal expenditures mirror class conflicts over domestic priorities and competing interpretations of what constitutes appropriate state fiscal policy.[14] In a free-market capitalist economy, the state constantly labors to create conditions under which profitability and capital accumulation are possible. At the same time, state expenditures must also facilitate conditions which promote class harmony and prevent the emergence of civil disorder. Since competitive capitalism generates inequality and creates a large class of economically marginal people living in cities, the threat of dissent and urban political violence always faces public officials. As a result, those in power are under constant pressure to evaluate their spending priorities. The calculus shaping the evaluation of priorities involves a trade-off between policies capable of managing potential discord and those ensuring adequate profit margins for the capitalist class.[15] O'Connor observes, however, that the state simply does not have enough money to meet "legitimation" and "accumulation" needs to the satisfaction of competing class interests.

As explained by O'Connor:

The capitalist state must try to fulfill two basic and often contradictory functions—*accumulation* and *legitimation*. This means that the state must try to maintain or create the conditions in which profitable capital accumulation is possible. However, the state must also try to maintain or create the conditions for social harmony. A capitalist state that openly uses its coercive forces to help one class accumulate capital at the expense of other classes loses legitimacy and hence undermines the basis of its loyalty and support. But a state that ignores the necessity of assisting the process of capital accumulation risks drying up the sources of its own power, the economy's production power and the taxes drawn from this surplus.[16]

In O'Connor's discussion, various *social investments* and *consumption expenditures* underwrite public policies contributing to continued profitability in the capital accumulation process. Reagan's economic and tax reform programs clearly represent capital accumulation priorities. They are designed to enhance profits, stimulate private investments, and generate economic growth. His policies clearly favor one class over another. The Administration has relentlessly reduced social welfare and urban development expenditures, and sponsored legislation designed to divest the state of its service delivery functions. O'Connor warns, however, that certain social expenditures are required to maintain the legitimacy of the economic order. The myriad of social programs currently being privatized illustrate legitimation expenditures from an earlier era, primarily the social welfare policies and programs adopted during the New Deal and Great Society periods. When political events shift expenditures from legitimation to accumulation, it is safe to assume that a policy calculus has assigned a low probability to the emergence of civil disorder among the urban underclass.

During a legitimation crisis, such as that which surfaced during the 1960s and 70s, the state must make strategic decisions about the allocation of scarce public resources. In the face of civil discord and political movements threatening serious disruption in the social order, the state is often compelled to exercise repressive measures to curb dissent. Rather than exercise coercive power, however, most enlightened public officials act to stabilize competing class interests, and attempt to implement social programs capable of restoring faith in established institutions.[17] The kinds of public expenditures usually required during a legitimation crisis are clearly different from those policies needed when profits and capital accumulation are threatened. Paul Diesing explains the political choices faced by the state when legitimation and accumulation problems emerge simultaneously:

> While the state struggles with the accumulation problem, the legitimation problem also grows more serious as welfare clients and unemployed protest and taxpayers revolt. Consequently, the state is forced to shift expenditures from accumulation to legitimation as soon as the most immediate profitability problems are temporarily managed.[18]

Because the state always hovers close to bankruptcy in its efforts to manage legitimation and accumulation responsibilities, those in power must carefully choose which groups will be potentially alienated by shifts in expenditures from one category to another. Since widespread revolts and civil disorders have not erupted in response to substantial decreases in urban social programs, it appears that the Reagan Administration has temporarily escaped the sharpest edges of a legitimation crisis. At the same time, his response to unstable profits and declining economic conditions has driven the state deeper into serious fiscal instability.

In 1983, an Urban Institute report examining the American economy predicted that the annual federal deficit was on a course which would ultimately exceed $200 billion by 1984, and $300 billion by the end of the decade.[19] While their 1990 prognosis may prove somewhat inaccurate because of movement toward partial economic recovery, more recent congressional estimates indicate that the federal deficit will hover close to $200 billion annually through 1989.[20] Large deficits not only erode the quality of life experienced by the urban underclass and those receiving some form of federal assistance, but also affect the capitalist class as well. As explained by Joseph Pechman, investment activity is directly influenced by spiraling deficits in the federal budget, a fact most disconcerting to finance capitalists:

> The capital markets are concerned about the impact of the deficits on interest rates and on the rate of capital formation, which in turn will have significant effects on the growth and stability of the economy.[21]

More recently, some of Reagan's closest advisors have questioned the wisdom of the Administration's fiscal policies. Former Budget Director David Stockman identified the relationship between Reagan's tax reforms and the budget deficit as the critical flaw in supply-side economic theory.[22] Acknowledging that while the deficit was moving in the right direction and inflation appeared under control, Stockman also warned that massive government borrowing could initiate another spiral of "hyperinflation." Large deficits and a revolutionary transformation of the tax structure contain the potential to push the economy to the brink of another major downturn. The reemergence of political conflict within the nation's cities could escalate the speed with which a deficit crisis might disrupt the precarious balance between legitimation and accumulation expenditures.

Fiscal insolvency also limits the state's ability to manage and divert a capital accumulation crisis. If the federal budget is cut too severely, or the government's borrowing power is curtailed, the state will not have enough money to subsidize infrastructure improvements essential to the maintenance of adequate profit margins. Infrastructure investments in transportation systems, utilities and basic urban services, education and work force preparation augment private profits. By transferring to the state the costs of maintenance and construction, research and development, job training and the acquisition of technical skills, private accumulation is facilitated through public investments.

In the absence of fiscal stability, the state may also be unable to assist industries experiencing accumulation crises, such as automobile production, mining and extraction, steel, petrochemicals, construction and building materials. Without a healthy state treasury, defense expenditures become more problematic, as do the costs of maintaining state workers and military personnel. But if taxes are raised to finance these kinds of social expenditures, corporate profits will decline or a tax revolt might ensue. In addition, most businesses will pass on tax increases to consumers in the form of higher costs for goods and services, or decrease their investment and expansion activities to socially unproductive levels.

O'Connor predicts that when state budgets are chronically in deficit, increases in the costs of goods and services and in the interest rate will inevitably follow, especially if the corporate tax burden moves beyond acceptable levels. Thus far, the Reagan Administration has managed to reduce taxes, bring inflation under control, and stabilize interest rates. Nonetheless, a serious deficit situation has developed and persists; and within the political arena, conflict over the selection of programs to be sacrificed in pursuit of a balanced budget continues to escalate. Class interests align closely with the various options being weighed as potential solutions to the deficit problem: (1) a reduction in the defense budget, (2) a reduction in various entitlement and benefit programs, (3) a reduction in social welfare expenditures, (4) increased corporate and individual taxes, (5) reduced federal borrowing, (6) reduced wages for state employees, and (7) an increase in the deficit.[23]

In the face of persistent class conflict over possible remedies to the state's fiscal crisis, social problems in many cities appear to be getting worse. Current trends signal the inevitable reappearance of a serious legitimation crisis. A Special House Subcommittee on Public Assistance and Unemployment Compensation reported in 1984 that the number of families in the United States living in poverty has steadily increased since 1980.[24] The 39 million people living in poverty in 1983 was the highest number since 1964, and the highest rate of poverty since 1965. The Committee further reports that approximately 868,000 people joined the ranks of the poor in 1983. Most significant is the Committee's observation that "cuts in Federal Welfare spending are largely responsible" for increasing rates of poverty.[25]

Without an expanded base of tangible employment opportunities to compensate for drastic reductions in social welfare expenditures, it is highly probable that the ranks of the poor and underemployed will continue to expand. Because of this, it is likely that the seeds of political dissent are being cultivated by policies favoring accumulation over legitimation expenditures. Should such disorders arise, it will obviously be necessary to reactivate many of the social programs now being sacrificed to capital accumulation priorities.

But even policies which favor capital accumulation and the interests of one class over another do not necessarily guarantee that private investors and speculators, developers and financiers will be drawn to profit opportunities within the urban environment. Barry Bluestone and Bennett Harrison argue that private investment decisions often contradict the public good, and reveal serious conflicts of interest between "capital" and "community."[26] In pursuit of higher profits and lower investments in the cost of labor, many corporations have abandoned cities altogether and relocated in rural regions, or in some cases in other parts of the world. Plant closings and shutdowns devastate the employment base of a city, weaken its ability to provide services, and undermine the structure of neighborhood life and culture.

The mobility of capital and the willingness of industry to offer itself to the highest municipal bidders unleashes destructive competition among cities to attract runaway American businesses or international investment dollars. Irrational and unrestrained competition has led some municipal jurisdictions to compromise seriously their revenue base with lucrative tax abatement incentives, or to make rash commitments to finance infrastructure improvements or initiate land use changes through high-risk public indebtedness or fiscally questionable bonding programs.[27] And those boomtowns which have been successful in attracting industry appear to be creating the same kinds of urban problems located in cities that corporations abandoned only a few years earlier.

When private investors are drawn to profit opportunities in the central cities, revitalization and redevelopment plans typically reflect an attempt to change the use of land from one class of users to another.

Gentrification is a systematic attempt to reverse upper- and middle-class migration to the suburbs. The loss of middle- and upper-income consumers to suburban developers and merchants doing business in large shopping malls represents a tremendous drop in profits and revenues for capitalists with fixed investments in the central city. In order to compete with their suburban counterparts, downtown business elites often require significant state investments in infrastructure improvements, or in related policies ensuring the removal of the urban working class and the poor from areas targeted for renewal. The initiatives often compel local government to support the interests of business elites over those pursued by members of the middle and working class.

Case Studies in Urban Political Economy

This book evolved in response to the growing ascendancy of the private sector in the initiation, formation, and implementation of urban development policy. Freedom of enterprise, business leadership, and the reduction of government spending are the watchwords of contemporary urban policy. Contributors to this volume illustrate the importance of studying business elites and understanding their role in shaping urban development policy. Through the application of critical urban theory, contributors explain the conditions under which private initiative enhances or erodes downtown redevelopment, and elaborate the contention that business elites must be given a preeminent place in urban theory and policy analysis.

Through a case study approach, the development policies of several cities are critically explored and evaluated. The case studies show that the private sector's efforts to revitalize America's central cities have not been uniformly successful. In many cities, business elites have created serious problems which, ironically, will eventually require government remediation. Unrestrained free enterprise is reproducing the same patterns of urban blight that ravaged American cities during the 1960s. In some cities, fragmentation among corporate leaders has seriously undermined renewal efforts and ensured the continued decline of the central business district. In other communities, however, private enterprise has produced a stunning revitalization of the central city. Not all classes and neighborhoods, however, benefit from even successful renewal programs.

Contributions to this volume are organized around four general themes, all drawn from critical urban theory. In the first section of the book, numerous strategies of urban growth are examined. Urban business elites typically establish development coalitions in order to design and implement a growth agenda for their city. Larry Sawers maintains that "owners as a class must seek to organize society and more specifically urban space in order to enhance profit maximization."[28] He also argues, however, that the owning class should not be viewed as a unified elite acting in concert to pursue their collective interests. There is often considerable disagreement among various factions of the local elite. In fact, contends Sawers, "Much of the unsatisfactory nature of the modern metropolis (both from the point of view of the working class and that of the capitalist class) results not from planning by a small cabal of capitalists, but from no planning at all."[29] Local business elites are sometimes unable to implement a growth agenda, or must formulate a growth strategy in the face of cutthroat competition for industry with elites in other cities.

Harvey Molotch has argued that the local development agenda of most cities is shaped by a parochial business elite attempting to use public institutions and personal influence to enhance its own prosperity.[30] He maintains that cities can be viewed as "growth machines" dominated by local business elites seeking to engineer development policy in a manner consistent with their economic interests. In this volume, Molotch clarifies his earlier formulation of "growth-machine politics" by identifying the numerous constraints faced by local elites as they struggle to implement a growth agenda. Growth policies at the local level are seriously compromised by larger economic events, by internal fragmentation and conflict within the business elite itself, and by local activists who block or undermine a development agenda.

The chapter by Allen Whitt elaborates many of Molotch's caveats about the economic and market limits confronting a local business elite. Local developers must mobilize around a flexible growth strategy, one capable of exploiting whatever opportunities appear most expedient. According to Whitt, the local growth coalition in Louisville, Kentucky, has responded to downtown stagnation and decay through creation of a revitalization strategy based on promotion of the performing arts. While reliance upon the arts to stimulate urban growth and revitalization is not new, Louisville's use of this approach illustrates how a business elite in one city unified to pioneer what they view as a downtown "urban renaissance."

In a similar manner, Mark Rosentraub explains how business

elites in numerous cities compete with one another to attract professional sports franchises. Cities in pursuit of franchises typically agree to invest public dollars in the creation of huge arenas and multiple-use facilities capable of housing professional sports. In addition to the costs of stadium construction, cities are usually persuaded to take on significant burdens related to the provision of infrastructure services, such as parking, sewage and drainage, lighting, police protection, transportation design and road construction. These massive public investments are often fiscally questionable, and raise political controversy about state subsidies allocated to highly profitable private enterprises. Rosentraub's case study shows how local elites in Arlington and Irving, Texas, were able to convince local officials to invest tax dollars in a growth strategy tailored to professional sports.

Thomas Moore and Gregory Squires critically examine the costs and benefits of industrial revenue bonds. Drawing from the experiences of Chicago and Milwaukee, they find little or no evidence suggesting that industrial revenue bonds attract new industry or generate new jobs in the urban economy. While many cities rely upon revenue bonds as part of a growth or recovery strategy, there appear to be very few tangible benefits derived from such a policy. Their case study identifies numerous points of conflict between private benefits and the public good.

In the second section of the book, the ability of local business elites to mobilize resources from the local state is examined. Manuel Castells observed that the "urban question" is a crisis in capitalist production and distribution, and reflects the state's attempt to alleviate that crisis through management of collective consumption.[31] By "collective consumption" he means state expenditures on social programs (education, housing, transportation, and health care). Similar to the interpretation developed by O'Connor, Castells argues that because of crises in capital accumulation, state policies must socialize the costs of production and reproduction through expansion of social welfare programs. Simultaneously, however, the state must leave profits in private hands. Because the state is perpetually caught between the persistent needs of the urban working class and the profit margin requirements of the capitalist class, urban policy is a matter of political debate and class conflict. According to many neo-Marxist urbanists, state policy in a capitalist society "sets the course for expanding city budgets, fiscal crises, retrenchment, and urban social protest movements."[32]

The chapters in the second section of the book illustrate how local business elites manage to use their personal influence and private power to extract special concessions from local government. These special concessions subsidize private profit, and promote the class interests of the business elite over those pursued by the working and lower class. The relationship between those in control of the local state and the local business elite, however, is not always as cozy as some neo-Marxists contend. Sawers maintains that progressive mayors and public officials can make modest reforms when elected to office:

> The working class is not powerless in the political arena. The ballot box does offer a degree of leverage over the government.[33]

The "degree of leverage" exercised by the urban working class varies considerably between cities. The chapters in the second section explore the circumstances under which the development agenda of a local business elite can be successfully countered by working-class organizations, community and neighborhood groups, and progressive public officials.

Todd Swanstrom compares the political styles and accomplishments of two progressive mayors: Dennis Kucinich of Cleveland and Raymond Flynn of Boston. He reports that the local elite in Cleveland, especially banking interests, were able to block the reforms proposed and pursued by Kucinich, and ultimately to remove him from office. Flynn, however, has been more successful in dealing with competing class interests in the city of Boston. Swanstom observes that progressive city mayors can implement a reform agenda only with extreme caution and adroit diplomacy. While progressive mayors have considerable latitude in expressing the rhetoric of reform, business elites in Cleveland and Boston still establish the contours of local development policy.

Scott Cummings and Edmond Snider reveal how local development and real estate interests, in cooperation with city officials, orchestrated a revitalization and redevelopment plan for the city of Dallas, Texas. The redevelopment plan transferred land use in the city from one class to another. In this particular case, community and neighborhood groups were powerless in the face of institutional forces over which they had little or no control. An alliance between selected factions of the local business elite and City Hall itself created a potent political force that crushed any opposition to the developmental plan. The Dallas case illustrates a situation in which the interests of the local state and those of the local business elite were identical.

Through analysis of the North Loop development project in Chicago, Larry Bennett and his colleagues find evidence suggesting that the local business elite in that city is often totally unable to organize itself to exploit profit and growth opportunities. Disagreement and competition sometimes create paralysis within the local growth coalition and render it less able to dominate the city's developmental agenda. An additional obstacle frustrating Chicago's business elite is its inability to extract policy concessions from City Hall. With the demise of the Daley machine, Chicago's elite finds itself unable to control local candidates and their political agenda.

The third section of the book presents evidence showing that the activities of some business elites are severely constrained or enhanced by extra-local events and investment trends. Larger economic processes render some local elites totally dependent upon outside capital, and as a result they are willing to generate significant social costs for their city in order to attract new industry and profit opportunities. The activities of local business elites, therefore, must be understood in a national and international economic context. Recent neo-Marxist urban research has revealed the importance of national and international economic events for local land-use decisions. Much of this research has four interrelated themes: (1) a focus on the relationship between local development strategies and national and international sources of capital; (2) a concern over how global capitalism shapes the urban landscape and affects local class structure, class politics, and class culture; (3) an emphasis on how deindustrialization and recapitalization influence local land use and the delivery of urban social services; and (4) an examination of how changes in national and international production shapes the culture and everyday lives of the urban working class.[34]

Joe Feagin's case study of Houston shows how unrestrained free enterprise has produced developmental chaos, and seriously compromised the quality of life in one of America's premier growth cities. The beneficiary of runaway industries from the North and Midwest, Houston, according to Feagin, can be viewed as a free-market disaster area. Incapable of financing the delivery of social services, Houston finds itself unable to dispose of its garbage, control the disposal of toxic waste, or manage the delivery of basic services to its population. Houston's business elite appears to have unrestrained ability to formulate development policy for the city. Freedom of enterprise, however, has produced tremendous social costs for the Houston metropolitan area.

Richard Hill and Michael Indergaard's analysis of Detroit's Downriver communities reveals how the fabric of community life and culture has been decimated by international crises in the steel industry. Powerless to control their own destiny, Downriver communities have fallen victim to global economic forces over which they have little or no influence. Hill and Indergaard explain how community institutions have been transformed by deindustrialization, and describe the relationship between global economic forces and local development decisions.

Thomas Keil presents a historical analysis of competing class interests over local development policy in the Wilkes-Barre–Scranton region of eastern Pennsylvania. Because of its dependence upon outside capital and the collapse of the coal mining industry, the business elite has lost influence over local investment decisions. In addition, a strong trade union movement has managed to gain enough power to prevail against the interests of the local development coalition. At the same time, the local business elite has proven to be remarkably resilient and creative in its ability to pursue profit opportunities, to attract new investment dollars, and to cultivate growth strategies outside the official avenues of power. In the face of capital flight and deindustrialization, however, neither working-class organizations nor the local business elite have been able to consolidate or maintain a consistent level of prosperity.

Drawing from the classic writing of Marx and Engels, especially the latter's description of land-use patterns in Liverpool,[35] radical urbanists have reformulated established theories of urban space. They contend that technological changes in the workplace and population movements within cities are simple reflections of the basic requirements of the capitalist mode of production.[36] Traditional urban theorists, they contend, were incorrect when they argued that ghetto formation was an inevitable response to the complex division of labor, population growth in cities, and the cultural predispositions of inhabitants.

In contrast, the new urban theorists argue that cities are geographically fragmented by the dictates of corporate capitalism. They maintain that competition and conflict between classes and the creation of racial and ethnic enclaves are inevitable by-products of the quest for private profit. Charles Jaret summarizes a major theme appearing in recent neo-Marxist urban analysis by observing that:

The urban complex is understood as the field in which inherent conflicts between classes and class factions are played out. Capitalists attempt to construct an urban environment that allows for efficient production and distribution of goods and services, profitable investments, and for continuous reproduction of a disunited but reliable work force.[37]

Neo-Marxist urban theorists contend that class conflict and struggle have been displaced from the shop floor to city streets and neighborhoods. The organization of urban space is viewed as the manifestation of capital accumulation, and a reflection of the labor market needs of the local business elite. The chapters included in the last section of the book examine the growing polarization of class interests within many cities.

While some cities have managed to revitalize the central business district, renewal has been accomplished through the systematic removal of minority populations and the urban working class from the downtown areas. The mobilization of investment capital to revitalize the commercial core of the city is usually accomplished by land-use changes designed to remove the poor from the inner city and relocate them in other regions of the metropolitan area. As a result, some cities no longer contain an inner city populated by the urban poor, but instead reveal a prosperous downtown juxtaposed alongside impoverished neighborhoods and bankrupt minority suburbs.

Kenneth Neubeck and Richard Ratcliff document the increasing class polarization that has accompanied the transformation of Hartford into a corporate city. At the forefront of the new hi-tech service economy, Hartford's downtown wealth exists against a backdrop of bleak urban poverty. The city is the fourth poorest in the nation, and class polarization is pushing the city to the brink of increasingly serious fiscal and political problems. The authors examine how Hartford's business elite engineered downtown redevelopment, and systematically tried to push the urban poor to the periphery of the city or export them to the surrounding suburbs.

John Logan analyzes the trend toward black suburbanization in Philadelphia. He finds that black suburbanization is characterized by fiscal crises, escalating racial strife, and a local economic base ravaged by deindustrialization and capital flight. Downtown Philadelphia, however, is experiencing a surge of commercial and residential prosperity. Logan contends the shift of blacks from city to suburb is largely shaped by national patterns of deindustrialization and investment decisions which inflate the cost of land in the central city and erode property values in the suburbs. In Philadelphia, black suburbanization is a dream gone sour.

David Daykin examines the limits of progressive reform pursued through community control and neighborhood movements. Using Santa Monica, California, as a case study, he identifies several important limitations confronting a reform agenda implemented through a grassroots political strategy. The Santa Monica case points to numerous flaws in a reform strategy based solely upon the support of neighborhood progressives and community activists. Competition between neighborhoods and the inability of community leaders to transcend parochial interests have made it difficult for Santa Monica's progressives to redistribute downtown wealth to the city's less prosperous neighborhoods.

All contributors to this volume question the ability of private interests to remediate serious problems of urban inequality, and identify numerous dilemmas of contemporary urban development policy. While many students of urban policy concede that the federal programs and strategies initiated during the War on Poverty era had few lasting effects on the nation's cities, they are also pessimistic about exclusively private solutions to urban redevelopment. The authors whose work appears in this volume agree, however, that those studying American cities need to focus more of their analytical efforts on the increasingly important role of business elites in shaping the future of the nation's urban areas.

Notes

1. E.S. Savas, *Privatizing the Public Sector.* Chatham, NJ: Chatham House Publishing, 1982.

2. Ibid.

3. Richard Koenig, "A University Hospital in Louisville Thrives in Its For-Profit Status." *Wall Street Journal,* January 21, 1986, pp. 1 and 20.

4. Lawrence F. Travis III, Edward J. Latessa, and Gennaro F. Vito, "Private Enterprise and Institutional Corrections: A Call for Caution." *Federal Probation,* December 1985, pp. 11–16.

5. Savas.

6. John L. Palmer and Isabel V. Sawhill (eds.), *The Reagan Record.* Cambridge, MA: Ballinger Publishing Company, 1984.

7. Henry J. Aaron and associates, "Non-Defense Programs," in Joseph A. Pechman (ed.), *Setting National Priorities*. Washington, DC: The Brookings Institute, 1982, p. 120.

8. Charles Murray, *Losing Ground*. New York: Basic Books, 1984.

9. Donald Strickland and Dennis Judd, "Capital Investment in Neighborhoods." *Population Research and Policy Review,* 1982, p. 74.

10. Aaron and associates.

11. "Where the Budget Ax Will Fall." *U.S. News and World Report,* February 17, 1986, pp. 20–30; "Summary of Fiscal 1986 Budget Resolution." *Congressional Quarterly,* August 31, 1985, pp. 1702–1705.

12. Edward M. Gramlich and Deborah S. Laren, "The New Federalism," in Pechman, pp. 151–186.

13. William Tabb and Larry Sawers (eds.), *Marxism and the Metropolis*. New York: Oxford University Press, 1978.

14. James O'Connor, *The Fiscal Crisis of the State*. New York: St. Martin's Press, 1973.

15. Ibid.

16. Ibid., p. 6.

17. Frances Fox Piven and Richard A. Cloward, *Regulating the Poor: The Functions of Public Welfare*. New York: Random House, 1971.

18. Paul Diesing, *Science and Ideology*. New York: Aldine Publishing, 1982, p. 254.

19. Gregory Mills and John Palmer, *The Deficit Dilemma*. Washington, DC: The Urban Institute Press, 1983.

20. "$149.2 Billion Deficit-Cutting Plan Approved." *Congressional Quarterly Almanac,* 1984, pp. 143–155.

21. Joseph Pechman, "Introduction and Summary," in Pechman, p. 2.

22. David Stockman, *The Triumph of Politics*. New York: Random House, 1986.

23. *Congressional Quarterly Almanac*.

24. Subcommittee on Public Assistance and Unemployment Compensation, Committee on Ways and Means, U. S. House of Representatives, *Families in Poverty: Changes in the "Safety Net."* Washington, DC: U. S. Government Printing Office, 1984.

25. Ibid., p. 4.

26. Barry Bluestone and Bennett Harrison, *The Deindustrialization of America*. New York: Basic Books, 1982.

27. Ibid.

28. Larry Sawers, "New Perspectives on the Urban Political Economy," in Tabb and Sawers, p. 6.

29. Ibid., p. 14.

30. Harvey Molotch, "The City as a Growth Machine: Toward a Political Economy of Place." *American Journal of Sociology,* September 1976, pp. 309–332.

31. Manuel Castells, *The Urban Question: A Marxist Approach*. Cambridge, MA: MIT Press, 1977.

32. Charles Jaret, "Recent Neo-Marxist Urban Analysis," in Ralph Turner and James Short (eds.), *Annual Review of Sociology,* 9. Palo Alto, CA: Annual Reviews, Inc., 1983, p. 503.

33. Sawers, pp. 7–8.

34. Jaret.

35. Frederick Engels, *The Condition of the Working Class in England in 1844*. London: Swan Sonneschein & Co., 1892.

36. Tabb and Sawers.

37. Jaret, p. 500.

PART ONE
Business Elites and the Growth Agenda

Chapter 2

Strategies and Constraints of Growth Elites

Harvey Molotch

I have argued that virtually all U.S. cities are dominated by a small, parochial elite whose members have business or professional interests that are linked to local development and growth. These elites use public authority and private power as a means to stimulate economic development and thus enhance their own local business interests. They turn their cities, as active, dynamic units, into instruments for accomplishing the growth goals that will enhance their fortunes. The city becomes, for all intents and purposes, a "growth machine."[1] The operation of cities as growth machines has an impact on the quality and distribution of growth within and among urban areas.

After spelling out this growth machine perspective in more detail, I will identify five alternative analytic approaches to understanding the development of U.S. cities. I will argue that rather than being in necessary opposition to the growth machine perspective or to one another, each approach can help explain how urban growth machines operate and how they come to differ from one another. My overall aim is to use the growth machine analysis to arrive at a comprehensive view of the urban system and thus provide a framework for explaining differences among urban areas.

The Growth Machine Argument

In capitalist societies, particularly those such as the U.S., in which land and buildings can be bought and sold as though they were simple

commodities, urban areas become the arena in which property entrepreneurs use government and other civic institutions to maximize
returns on their investments. The best way to make money from such
places is to increase the intensity of economic activity occurring within
one's turf. It is better to have a thousand apartment units on a given
acre of residential land than a single-family house. It is better to have a
bank's world headquarters located on one's commercial parcel than
Joe's Hot Dog Stand. High levels of economic activity provide high
"rents"—whether in the form of monthly payments by tenants to landlords or, what is essentially rent in a different form, higher sales prices
paid by the buyer of property to the previous owner.

     While property entrepreneurs within a locality compete with one
another to push development in the direction of their own property instead of someone else's, all such actors stand to gain in common if activity levels increase in the locality as a whole. Areawide intensification,
ordinarily in the form of increments to the basic economy which, in
turn, generate labor in-migration and other economic growth (e.g.,
wholesale and retail trade), benefits the investments of all local property entrepreneurs. Local real estate investors thus make up a reliable
core for the growth machine elite. Their common urban program is to
attract more jobs, people, and thus rents. Furthermore, just as entrepreneurs within an urban area try to affect the local distribution of
growth, unified city elites compete against their counterparts throughout the country, and even the world, for a maximum share of the spoils
of development for their town, city, or region. There is a sort of "nested"
hierarchy of growth machines in which elites at each geographical
system-level compete for growth among themselves, but then unify
when competing with the larger-scale units that they have a common
interest in overtaking.

     The people who make up growth machines are not just the owners
of land and buildings, but include others who have their fortunes tied
to a specific area's growth. Local financial institutions, because they
often extend loans to property purchasers and businesses within a
given geographic region, develop such a vested interest in local turf. To
the degree that area activity intensifies, their borrowers will be better
able to pay back the loans extended to them. Growth will also provide
more depositors and customers to pay interest on future loans. Similarly, the local newspaper can prosper only to the degree that there are
additional subscribers who in turn will attract more advertising.
Various people whose livelihood involves serving the needs of any of
these entrepreneurs—real estate lawyers, accountants, property man-

agement firms, advertising agencies, construction supply houses, title companies, and so forth—have a similar vested interest in the success of the local growth machine. Even museums, universities, and social service organizations may come to support the growth goal, either to increase patronage or to curry favor from the elites who give money and serve on their boards of directors.

Often playing only a subsidiary role in growth machine maneuvers are corporations that, while perhaps operating locally, can generate their investment return anywhere. McDonald's can franchise its burger shops wherever people end up locating, and General Motors has no principled interest in increasing the number of people who may come to live in the city in which it has built a branch plant. To be sure, elements of cosmopolitan capital that happen to be on the local scene are always sympathetic to the agenda of the local growth machine. The domination of localities by growth interests is completely harmonious with corporate executives' "free enterprise" ideology and helps provide local governments that will honor the wishes of nationwide (and multinational) industry. But corporate capital has no interest in local intensification per se.

Because cities take so much of their form from the striving of competing growth elites, they show little evidence of having been planned by experts, or even of resulting from "free market" competition among entrepreneurs competing to provide the best local products.[2] Instead, the commonplace inefficiency of cities stands as evidence that the local development agenda is, in fact, organized by elites who manipulate land and buildings to enhance rents and profits. Because neither a rational bureaucracy nor a rational market organizes what happens, cities can be overdeveloped, deserted, or inconveniently arranged. Cities are "designed" primarily to maximize returns for the organizationally successful entrepreneurs.

Although growth may increase rents for those situated to collect them, many local citizens are left out of the growth benefits, although they do share—disproportionately in some cases—in growth costs. Tenants often end up paying more rent, not less, when their city grows.[3] Job expansion provides the economically marginal little chance of bettering their employment opportunities, because the plums tend to go to migrants with better qualifications.[4] Environmental degradation affects everyone, particularly the poor, who tend to live and work nearest the pollution and congestion. And as the local political system strives to provide infrastructure to meet increased demand for public services, citizens are threatened by a choice of higher taxes or lower-quality services.

City building through growth machine manipulation has a long tradition. Mayor Ogden of Chicago made sure that his city (and the extensive real estate investments he had in it) would benefit from the railroad boom of the mid-nineteenth century. He did this by securing as many rail routes as possible through his turf (he was also president of several railroads). Chicago grew dramatically from the four thousand people it had when Ogden arrived in 1835, helping him turn an $8,000 land investment into a $3 million fortune within a single eight-year period.[5] The city of Houston beat out Galveston to become the great port of Texas after its elites convinced the federal government to allocate one million dollars (not a small sum at the turn of the century) to build a canal connecting it to the Gulf of Mexico. Millions of dollars more, to deepen and improve the canal, followed.[6]

In a more subtle case, the elites of San Francisco, using their power in Congress, made sure that the southern route of the transcontinental railroad would not terminate in San Diego. They feared that this would make San Diego, with its excellent natural port, a threat to the economic dominance of San Francisco and erode their investments in the Bay Area.[7] They successfully pushed for Los Angeles (with no port at all) to be the southern terminus. In an ironic twist, Los Angeles did eventually overtake San Francisco, but only because later federal grants gave it the world's largest artificial harbor.

Local elites continue to mobilize outside government and private investments to secure their areas' futures. Political parties, elected officials at the local, state, and congressional levels, and business trade and development associations are intrinsic components of the growth machine. The elites of each city and region fight for airport and harbor funding, canals and freeways, defense contracts and subsidies for downtown redevelopment projects, convention centers, sport stadia, university campuses, and even arts organizations. By the time the list of participants and strategies has been completed, a very wide array of organizations and institutions are implicated in the growth machine system.

The precise dynamic of how the growth machine operates undergoes continous change. Thus, for example, local media (as with other types of firms) have increasingly been absorbed by national corporations, eroding to some degree the effectiveness of the city newspaper in unifying parochial elites. More profoundly, the transnationalization of production in the form of a new "international division of labor" has altered the types of constraints under which any given growth elite must operate. Real estate itself, the commodity at the heart of the growth machine system, has been increasingly absorbed into the international system as foreign entrepreneurs buy up significant blocks of U.S. land and buildings.[8] These changes, many of which have been described in previous publications,[9] as well as elaborated in other chapters in this volume, inevitably alter how growth elites operate.

Outside Constraints

Borrowing from the recent work of Mintz and Schwartz,[10] I see local growth elites as having a certain degree of *discretion* that can only be exercised within a set of *constraints*. Local elites must either adapt to these limitations or take pains to overcome them. The specific efforts at adaptation and control over unique conditions give each local growth machine its particular texture and are crucial in making cities different from one another. While virtually all localities may be run by growth machine elites, there are differences in the quality and quantity of growth that each urban area can plausibly attract. If this were not the case, we would have to argue that the relative size of cities is simply a result of the energy and cunning of their property entrepreneurs vis-à-vis their counterparts elsewhere. Although such factors are no doubt important, there are other things that matter in the urban world besides the efficiency of growth elites in implementing their development agenda. These other factors are at least partial determinants of the urban system: (1) geographical features, (2) level of unity among civic leaders, (3) patterns of investment by outside corporate capital, (4) skills of local political leaders, and (5) urban social movements. I will indicate how and why growth machines take their specific forms in response to these factors.

Geographical Constraints

Physical determinants have long been recognized in urban social science as a force in determining how humans use space. Using the metaphor of biological ecology, the human ecologists like Park and Hawley emphasized the overwhelming significance of physical factors. In the ecologists' view, all urban actors, including local entrepreneurs, end up making their investments in the same way as other animal species. Individuals and groups engage in an adaptive struggle, the results of which are determined by the nature of the physical habitat. Guided by an essentially free property market, entrepreneurs allocate land and buildings in such a way that each type of land user ends up in the spot to which it is best fitted, and the places that grow the most do so because their physical nature most efficiently maximizes the survival of the largest numbers. The system always tends toward an efficiency equilibrium, and local elites are nothing more, if they are anything at all, than the passive intermediaries through which the system operates. A city grows larger than other places, for example, because it has the advantage of geographic centrality (which minimizes travel costs to peripheral points) or because of special access to natural harbors, which similarly maximizes efficiency.

Physical determinism has an obvious plausibility in explaining why certain kinds of economic development occur in one city but not in another. Cities on the water, like Baltimore, have an advantage over land-locked places in competition for port development; places with warm climates, like Southern Florida, have a better chance of attracting tourists than regions that are cold in winter. The geographic center of the city at any given moment has a special edge compared to outlying points. But attempts to build a location science on the basis of topography, physical resources, or a "spatial geometry"[11] are doomed to fail. They ignore the human factor of social organization in determining land use,[12] and the politics of land-use profiteering in particular.[13] The fact that Baltimore had a natural port may have helped make that place into a significant city, but San Diego's possession of the same "asset" retarded its development as a major metropolis, as we have seen, for political reasons. As Massey says, "geography matters," but only by looking at geography in social terms can we learn the way in which geography matters. It figures in local elites' considerations, but does not determine the outcome of those considerations.

Growth elites have the job of making the most out of the physical turf they control. Las Vegas became a major tourist and convention center without benefit of geographical centrality, access to any natural port, or even very significant advantages of climate or physical beauty. It simply enacted permissive gambling laws, and thereby made the in-hospitable desert bloom with crap tables, high-rise hotels, and strips of bright neon. By embracing an activity beneath the moral contempt of people in other areas, Nevada's growth elites were able to reap their bonanza. It may not be possible to make a silk purse out of a sow's ear, but elites with enough power or cunning can utterly transform the meaning of physical place. The crucial point, once again, is that outcomes derive from the interaction of the physical and the social, and the social is the dynamic driving force in leading from one formation to another.

Leadership Fragmentation

Some urban theorists have stressed variation in the degree that civic leadership can crystallize and thus pursue its "rightful" role in acting on behalf of citizens' goals. Some people, particularly the higher social classes (in Banfield and Wilson's formulation[14]), are more likely than others to be "public regarding," and the trick is to have such types in control of local policy agendas and decision-making structures. A shortage of persons with this civic-duty altruism, their passivity, or a leadership structure that inhibits their cohesion, leads to frustration of their efforts on behalf of city betterment.

One indirect measure of leadership effectiveness is the ability of local governments to produce "policy outputs." In Hawley's influential analysis, a city with a relatively small proportion of its work force with upper-tier occupations (managers, proprietors, and officials) should be able to operate cohesively and thus bring about policies that boost worthy civic programs.[15] Concentration of power in a relatively few economic hands presumably means there is less capacity for competing groups to frustrate leadership action. At least implicitly, the public goal that can benefit from such cohesion is local urban growth.[16] Hawley used a city's participation in urban renewal programs, quite disastrous for a city by most other accounts, to be the measure of effective urban leadership.[17]

This focus upon urban leadership tends to occur in a theoretical vacuum, with little attention to such factors as conflicts within elites for the spoils of growth or the differential impact of growth upon specific social classes. Leaders are presumed to come rightfully from the higher social circles, and their specific personal or group or class interests in fortune building in the locality are left unexamined. In my analysis, the overwhelmingly significant local "leadership" is the growth elite, which is devoted to its own particular good, often at the expense of other local interests. These elites are not, in principle, concerned with the public welfare but are, as an empirical matter, adept at using public institutions on behalf of private goals. So crude a measure as the proportion of a city's population engaged in high-level occupations indicates little about policy dynamics, although the proportion of people involved in growth machine occupations, like land development, might well be of significance.[18]

The grain of truth in the emphasis on these leaders is that elites do vary in their ability to function effectively, and these variations may affect urban outcomes. As with other groups, growth elites can be ridden with internal dissension, weighted down by incompetent leaders, or afflicted with diversionary agendas. Besides these idiosyncratic differences, the "sediment" of past historic conditions[19] can have an impact on the effectiveness of a given growth elite. A long history of economic prosperity can mean that a given area has in place a well-worked-out system of intra-elite communication, including perhaps university-based expertise upon which to draw in shaping growth strategies. There may exist highly developed networks and connections with political leaders at all levels of government. In other instances, a conservative patrician past may hinder development, as old families with social pedigrees suffocate dynamic growth initiatives. This sort of situation, quite unusual in the U.S., seems to have characterized New Orleans up to the 1970s.[20]

For growth activists, backward or incompetent brethren are, in a sense, external constraints on their ability to pursue development. All local people of wealth and status are useful adjuncts to growth machine functioning; significant degrees of passivity or even defection create difficulties. In places where overall elite mobilization is problematic, the growth activists may have to divert resources away from campaigns for specific projects in favor of internal organizational development. This does not, I caution, make the state of the elites synonymous with the state of their cities. But the attitudes and organizational structures of the local wealthy do enter into the lives of growth activists as a real force and make a difference in growth elites' ability to achieve their development goals.

Capital Flight and Capital Investment

Some constraints upon local elites' discretion come from organizational dynamics well beyond the local level. The system through which national firms and financiers allocate investment resources within and among localities influences all growth possibilities. As cosmopolitan capitalists go about their business of accumulating wealth, rents in various places rise and fall as places' utility to capital accumulation undergoes change. When capitalists were investing in heavy manufacture in the U.S., areas with conditions suitable to such enterprise had a potential edge; proximity to raw materials, water transportation, and a blue-collar labor force were assets.

But for the scholars who study capital as a means of understanding the city—the neo-Marxian school of urban political economy—such ecological factors are secondary. Instead of natural forces guiding capitalists' decisions, the changing pattern of development is dictated by capitalists' drive for profits—the "logic of accumulation." And maximizing profits and maximizing efficiency are not necessarily the same thing. Thus, to use a modern illustration, firms may "run away" from cities where workers are unionized not because they will gain cheaper labor costs, but because they will achieve better control over the labor process.[21] Even if the product can be made more cheaply and efficiently in the "old" city, militant labor may threaten the basis of class relations through which the fruits of efficiency are exploited by the capitalist group. This is a difference between what Gordon[22] refers to as "capitalist efficiency" versus "technical efficiency." Places that are capitalist efficient are not necessarily technically efficient.

The Marxian analysis does share one thing in common with geographical determinism: the city unfolds according to a dynamic beyond the realm of human choice or the capacity of social organization to intervene. If anyone matters at all for urban outcomes, it is the capitalists who make the investments, although they too follow the dictates of capitalism's internal logic. Although there is a proletariat that may protest against low wages and poor work conditions,[23] in Marxian analysis there are no significant local actors in the place allocation process. There are no neighborhood associations, environmentalists, nor—most critical for my purposes—no property entrepreneurs or growth machine activists.

But as various Marxian writers modify their earlier formulations,[24] it becomes increasingly clear that they too recognize the salience of human organization in the making and unmaking of places. We need to agree that while transformations in the overall productive sphere set the terms of local adaption, they do not simply determine it.

More specifically, Chicago was not destined to be the location of the meat industry, the U.S. convention business, or a great deal of heavy manufacturing in steel and consumer goods. There were many spots on the U.S. map that were potential Chicagos (e.g., Gary, Indiana, or Toledo, Ohio). Neither were Los Angeles nor Houston necessarily destined to be the specific sites of later growth booms. It was up to each city's growth elites, in complex interaction with their counterparts elsewhere, to make the organizational manipulations that would secure their city's future. Physical geography also played a role, as did capital forces beyond the city's boundaries. But the limits imposed by the capital accumulation process, like those provided by the physical ecology, do not entail the growth of a specific place for a given purpose.

In recent years, dramatic changes in the mode of production (i.e., the new international division of labor) have changed the kinds of local conditions that best serve capital's needs.[25] The sort of manufacturing that used to dominate places like Chicago and other regions of the U.S. "Frost Belt" either no longer exists or has moved to the Third World. The elites of U.S. cities respond by adapting their places for new roles appropriate for this changing geographical organization of capital. Some cities have become headquarters from which these far-flung operations are managed, or innovation centers where new products and procedures are invented and eventually exported elsewhere. Less happily, some are now relegated to routine production—city "modules" that can easily be replaced by substitute cities in the U.S. or abroad.

Growth elites shape their strategies around these changes over which they have little control. Some hire expensive consultants to tell them what economic sectors will be likely to grow and which, among these, the locality has the best chance to keep or attract. It may be necessary to overcome local resistance to effect the changes. Atlantic City, New Jersey, a decaying tourist town of a bygone era, had to counter citizen resistance to gambling in order to usher in a new boom as a Las Vegas–style resort city. In other instances, elites must phase out a given industrial sector to protect one to which they have given higher priority. The New York City garment industry was sacrificed earlier in this century, in part because the space it needed was more important for the expansion of the nascent Manhattan corporate headquarters economy and its upscale retailing component.[26]

The different capacities of localities to attract particular kinds of investment cause growth elites to search a list of options for those with good chances of success. Sometimes this is done ineptly without regard to the real world of ecological impediments and economic transformation. Millions were wasted constructing Detroit's Renaissance Center in a quixotic effort to build a headquarters- and convention-oriented milieu amidst the economic decline of the motor city. Flint, Michigan, lost millions on a city-subsidized redevelopment project that was designed to attract tourists to its declining downtown.

More realistically, Omaha, Nebraska, taking advantage of the neutral diction of its residents and excess capacity of its phone trunk lines, has become the "800" toll-free phone center of the country.[27] Three amenity-poor California towns, Adelanto, Avenal, and Blythe, competed with one another for designation as the site of a new state penitentiary.[28] Hanford, Washington, "the city that loves nukes," makes a specialty of receiving toxic wastes.[29]

Growth elites must squarely face the constraints that nature and the world economy hand them, but then move heaven and earth to maximize the possibilities that are nevertheless possible. Local growth elites help determine just where economic activities are to be situated, and what social and environmental conditions accompany such activities. Their participation, whether successful or not for their own growth goals, is the link between the local community and cosmopolitan capital.

The Talent of Political Entrepreneurs

A longstanding argument has held that, among the forces shaping U.S. urban development, the crucial actors are politicians who have the special skills to mobilize local resources and lead a city into growth and prosperity. From the "city booster" tradition of urban historians and the biographical profiles written by political scientists come images of "great men of vision." In Mollenkopf's more sophisticated terminology, history is now made by local "political entrepreneurs."[30] The elected officials of this new breed have personality and managerial skills that enable them to mobilize various elite groups, popular opinion and—crucially—the complex provisions of urban aid programs to make development occur. Local political actors are seen as more important than geographical constraints, economic elites (local as well as cosmopolitan), or the quality of non-governmental civic leadership. As Mollenkopf says in his studies of urban politics in Boston and San Francisco, "Though private interests clearly shaped the nature of government intervention, the reverse is even more strongly true." In short, Mollenkopf wants to make sure that "in contrast to much of Marxist analysis, the political receives its due."[31] By "the political," Mollenkopf means the role of talented elected officials who use that talent to get elected and to advance urban projects.

Politicians who have grace and cunning, energy and wit, information and training, are likely to have a better chance for success than their less gifted counterparts. This may give them, for example, the capacity to go directly to the people or build powerful bureaucracies to somewhat insulate themselves from the agendas of growth elites. But more commonly, the talent of politicians is discovered, nurtured, and mobilized by growth elites themselves for their own purposes. It thus may matter that New Haven, Connecticut, had its Mayor Lee: its stunning ability to attract urban renewal funds would not have existed without him.[32] The individual qualities of Chicago's Mayor Ogden may have helped in making his city the crossroads of America. But in each case, the primary attribute these people had was their commitment to local growth. Their personal skills would have meant nothing if they had not been able to be mobilized for growth goals.[33]

Those who stress the relative autonomy of elected officials pay very little attention to how politicians get nominated, elected, appointed, or promoted in the electoral, government agency, and business systems. Campaign contributions remain the mother's milk of U.S. politics,[34] and these funds, especially at the local level, come overwhelmingly from growth machine sectors. Politicians do not even begin to mount a campaign until their "soundings" of large-scale contributors indicate that it might be a viable effort. Whether liberal or conservative on other issues, candidates tend to be dependent on growth coalition support. Sometimes all major candidates in local elections receive their largest contributors from property entrepreneurs,[35] and such interests certainly tend to dominate the winning side.

In recent years, in my own California bailiwick, developers provided the largest block of contributors in the 1985 Los Angeles Mayoral election,[36] the Los Angeles County Board of Supervisor contests,[37] and even in the electoral contests in liberal San Francisco.[38] In New York City, in 1985, over half of the recorded campaign contributors to the Mayor, Borough Presidents, and other members of the city's powerful Board of Estimate, were developers—with financiers making up a good portion of the rest.[39] If anything, all such listings understate growth machine participation because contributors with development interests often list their occupations as "lawyer," "accountant," or "retired," and sometimes make the contributions in the name of their wife or other kin. Nevertheless, I have yet to see campaign contribution data for any significant jurisdiction that contradicts this impression of massive growth-interest funding of local officials.

Even the old political machines, presumably powerful enough to exercise a high degree of autonomy, were more intimately involved in the growth machines dynamic than is usually supposed. Serious studies of city-founding and early development, such as those by Boorstin,[40] Fogelson,[41] and Binford,[42] make clear the intimacy of the connection. Commentaries on the classic urban machines by observers like Bell[43] and Royko[44] intimate that at the core of the political machine was the growth coalition's investments in it. Speaking of Daley's political machine in Chicago, Royko estimates contractors to have been the biggest of all financial contributors, particularly those within the "brotherhood" of the local Democratic Party.[45] Perhaps this is why the urban political machines supported federal housing programs and urban construction—not just because of "pressure" from the working class in need of housing and jobs, but through responsiveness to the development interests both within and outside their own ranks. Under the congressional log-rolling system, the southerners got military bases and agricultural subsidies and the ethnic machines received subsidies for city infrastructure.[46] This was an important part of the unity of a national Democratic Party otherwise deeply divided on ideological grounds.

The old urban governments, whether in Boston or Chicago, were even willing to destroy neighborhoods of their ethnic constituencies on behalf of downtown growth goals. Thus the "urban villagers" of Boston's West End were sacrificed,[47] as were the Italian residents of what is now the University of Illinois campus adjacent to the Chicago Loop.[48] Mayor Coleman Young of Detroit, liberal on all social issues, nonetheless helped quell popular opposition to the levelling of the Poletown area to make way for a new General Motors plant. And in the case of contemporary Hawaii, the Democratic Party officials that have dominated local, county, and state government for the past 30 years are so intimately tied to development interests that it is difficult to distinguish between the two groups.[49]

More convincing than Mollenkopf's stress on the politicians' autonomy is Stone's characterization of elected officials as subordinate to "a business community that is well-organized, amply supplied with a number of deployable resources, and inclined to act on behalf of tangible and ambitious plans that are mutually beneficial to its own members."[50] In the Atlanta urban renewal case investigated by Stone, politicians had little autonomous power. Peterson, who unlike Stone finds nothing objectionable in this business dominance, applauds the fact that development policies "are often promulgated through a highly centralized decision-making process involving prestigious businessmen and professionals. Conflict within the city tends to be minimal, decision-making processes tend to be closed."[51] I thus take more seriously (and generalize more broadly) than Mollenkopf does from a quotation he reprints from *Fortune* magazine: "The most effective form of aggressive behavior is the joining together of politicians and businessmen.[52] And I think the businessmen are the more dominant participants.

Given the dynamic of campaign contributions, the participation of elected officials themselves in real estate deals, and the generalized social prestige and political muscle of mobilized business elites, such "joining" of politicians and growth activists becomes a common and formidable force across a wide range of urban issues. Politicians' autonomy is severely constrained by knowledge of where their bread and butter comes from and of the pervasive influence of the growth elite on local culture and ideology. This means, I would argue, that the number one entrepreneurial skill needed by politicians is the capacity to formulate schemes that benefit growth. I can think of no viable U.S. politicians, whether Jerry Brown, Diane Feinstein, or Willie Brown in California, or Mario Cuomo, Geraldine Ferraro, or Edward Koch in New York, who have managed it any differently. Politicians, like geography, do matter. But at least at the local level, it is the growth machine system that determines how they matter.

Popular Resistance

Americans frequently form voluntary associations to advance common goals. Scholars who take special notice of this fact are prone to attribute much power to these organizations, and think they are decisive in shaping the city system and determining the quality of urban life. In a recent formulation of such a populist view, Castells argues that in the United States (and indeed throughout much of the world) "people produce cities as they make history."[53] Particularly as urban services such as recreation, medical care and welfare become an increasingly significant component of a decent life, citizens find themselves all in the same boat vis-à-vis the bureaucracies that serve them. This means that to better themselves, ordinary people's struggles shift away from the workplace and the labor struggle and into the neighborhood where so much of this "collective consumption" takes place. Along with the concrete aim of bettering urban services, neighborhood activists also seek, according to Castells, the more diffuse goals of neighborhood cultural integrity and community self-determination. Not uncommonly, these ingredients are all present together as effective "urban social movements," and the result, argues Castells, is a great force in making the city.

There are indeed instances in which community organizations have discernable impacts on urban development—at least upon the distribution of growth and its quality within cities. Rich people have long been able, at least on some occasions, to protect their neighborhoods (whether central city or suburban) from encroachments of the poor, the minorities, or commerce.[54] Even low-income neighborhoods, particularly at incendiary moments in history, can have an impact on the shape of the city. In a commonly cited case, The Woodlawn Organization of Chicago, representing a poor black residential area, was able to block a plan of the city government and the adjacent University of Chicago to run a freeway through its northern border.[55] In still another version, environmental and civic planning groups have forced their local governments to install amenities (parks, architectural controls, height limits) that, while perhaps not limiting growth, shape it and alter the conditions under which it occurs.

All such evidence notwithstanding, the prevalence of popular success in shaping urban development is often exaggerated. I have explained elsewhere the reasons I think Castells, in particular, has failed to provide reasonable evidence for his highly romantic view of the power of the people, or even of the numbers of individuals who participate in any way in community organizations.[56] Neighborhood leaders almost always exaggerate the size of their active constituencies. Their occupational hazard is to make a great deal out of even trivial accomplishments and take credit for gains which would likely have occurred without their efforts. A long and discouraging history of community organization studies indicates the uphill battle that neighborhood groups have to wage against local elites, and the almost hopeless challenge facing organizations of the poor and of racial minorities.[57] Affluent residents can often secure their turf against ravages of growth machine dynamics, but these exceptions do not signify a general capacity of urban masses to determine development patterns. Even the notorious anti-growth movements among the affluent, so prevalent in the U.S. in recent years, have had at best only sporadic and temporary successes.[58] Laws limiting growth tend to occur *after* the growth has become a fact, rather than as a means of stopping it, and in any event are seldom effective.[59]

But this does not mean that neighborhood organizations can simply be ignored by either growth elites or urban analysts; although not sufficiently important to change the basic course of city growth, they do influence behaviors, including those of important people. When growth elites adjust to the residential needs of their own social class, they are adapting their money-making schemes to pressures from the neighborhood organizations that represent them as consumers. The presence of a few good neighborhoods can itself be valued by the growth elite as attracting additional capital investment by offering executives an attractive place to raise their families. And particularly in areas with privileged populations and with growth trajectories oriented toward innovation and headquarters activities, there must be some concern for the kind of urban amenities important to elite workers. But the environmental needs of mass populations count for little, except perhaps at the rare historic moments when violent insurrections threaten the stability of the entire metropolis.

However much growth elites adapt to neighborhood pressures, in any case they must do nothing that would hinder overall growth strategies. Concessions occur as part of their growth maneuvering, not in opposition to it. Some growth machines are more "liberal" than others,[60] but this is because their particular growth strategy requires a more long-term, enlightened position on matters of land use, planning, or social issues. Thus, members of some elites may realize that unless professional planners are granted a degree of autonomy, traffic congestion may strangle a city to the point where future growth is choked off. On social issues, a growth elite may come to perceive a reactionary public school curriculum as dangerous to an envisioned growth program of high-tech development. But such social liberalism does not imply that growth elites have less fundamental power, only that they exercise it through a different ideological mode and must contrive policies that keep local conditions consistent with overall development aims.

Synthesis

Growth elites strive to maximize development of their own turf, but as with all other humans—including other elites[61]—they do so under conditions not of their own choosing. Keeping in mind the kind of forces that others' research indicates has impact on the urban system, I have tried to specify the nature of those constraints. Growth elites must manipulate these other forces as best they can and ferret out a way to grow that fits the circumstances. This makes the growth elites the most dynamic, active and deliberate force in shaping local land use and the local policy agenda. But the activities of other groups and the conditions of the physical world intrude on the arena of discretion. The way these constraints intermesh with growth elite strategies determines the shape of cities, their distribution across the landscape, and their differences vis-à-vis one another.

These factors are not equal in the degree that they constrain local elites. The Neo-Marxists are correct in singling out large-scale economic changes, driven by the accumulation dynamic, as the force over which local elites have least control. Thus, for example, without intending to alter cities or the fortunes of their competing growth elites, capital investment in electronics has shifted urban growth outside the borders of the traditional U.S. manufacturing zone, creating new types of development in previously undeveloped regions (e.g., California's Silicon Valley). In Mintz and Schwartz's terminology, this is "structural hegemony." The term "hegemony" implies that domination occurs without necessarily involving direct coercion or even a conscious aim on anyone's part to wield influence. But unlike the way most hegemony theorists use the concept, the basis of dominance is not in the manipulation of symbol systems and deference patterns, but in altering the structure within which others (local elites in this instance) must make their decisions.

For reasons I have tried to specify, the physical world also constrains, but probably in a less coercive way. Elites make tourist meccas out of wastelands and ports out of inland agricultural centers. They fashion instant geographical centers out of former peripheries by installing jetports and freeway crossings. Only in some degree does the physical world establish a structural hegemony over the growth elites. The elites, through their social and physical projects, push the earth around, altering its topography, productivity, climate, and even its long-term capacity to support life. Elite-inspired changes in governmental organizational forms, like the creation of the Army Corps of Engineers and urban redevelopment programs, continuously lessen the relative autonomy of nature to block human schemes.

Even less constraining on elite activity, I would argue, are the other factors of local growth. Civic leaders, even old-line patricians, can be brought to see their material interests in development and their creative role within it. Politicians can be nurtured or extinguished as the changing texture of local growth needs dictate. The rise of almost all politicians, whether local or national, is first screened by local growth elites. Urban popular movements, finally, are overwhelmingly subject to manipulation, cooptation, or simple destruction by development forces.

Within the growth machine perspective, the paramount underlying force operating within the city is the drive for rents and profits that come from place-specific development. I have tried to show how various constraints structure the options available to local elites seeking such gains, thereby affecting the way these elites go about their work of generating growth. By way of a tabular summary, I list these constraints, name the school of analysis that emphasizes each, and specify the underlying urban force that each school, at least implicitly, takes to be paramount. I also indicate the degree that, according to my argument, these underlying forces are significant.

From the overall viewpoint that underlies this table, the capitalist productive system is hegemonic over locality, including the growth elites which must adjust to its changing directions. But within the local realm, it is the growth elites who are hegemonic. In both ideological and structural terms, their dominance over the development process is felt across a wide array of political, economic, and cultural institutions. As I have argued elsewhere,[62] this deep and broad permeation of locality allows growth elites to prepare the ground for capital, thus coupling local agendas with national and international systems of production. We have a two-tiered system of hegemony in the U.S., with material interests in locality at the heart of the lower tier. Social scientists cannot study everything and urban social scientists have their own specialized niche. I offer this local system of hegemony as the central topic of urban analysis.

TABLE 2.1. Analysis of Local Elite Drives and Constraints

Type of Constraint	School of Analysis	Underlying Motive	Degree of Actual Significance
Geography	Human ecology	Efficiency	Moderate
Civic leadership	Policy output	Civic duty	Minor
Cosmopolitan capital	Neo-Marxism	Profit accumulation	Major
Officials' talent	Political entrepreneur	Electoral viability	Minor
Urban social movements	Populism	Collective consumption/ Self-determination	Minor

Notes

1. Harvey Molotch, "The City as a Growth Machine." *American Journal of Sociology,* September 1976, pp. 309–332.

2. Such a view of cities as competing to please people by providing an ideal service mix is offered by Charles M. Tiebout, "A Pure Theory of Local Expenditures." *Journal of Political Economy,* October 1956, pp. 416–424. See also Paul E. Peterson, *City Limits.* Chicago: University of Chicago Press, 1981.

3. Richard P. Appelbaum, *Size, Growth, and U.S. Cities.* New York: Praeger, 1978; Richard P. Appelbaum and John Gilderbloom, "Housing Supply and Regulation: A Study of the Rental Housing Market." *Journal of Applied Behavioral Science,* Winter 1983, pp. 1–18.

4. Richard P. Appelbaum, Jennifer Bigelow, Henry Kramer, Harvey Molotch, and Paul Relis, *Santa Barbara: The Impacts of Growth.* Santa Barbara, CA: Office of the City Clerk, 1974; Appelbaum; Stephanie Greenberg, "Rapid Growth in a Southern Area: Consequences for Social Inequality." Unpublished, undated manuscript, Denver Research Institute, University of Denver, Denver, Colorado; Gene F. Summers, *Industrial Invasion of Non-Metropolitan America: A Quarter Century of Experience.* New York: Praeger, 1976.

5. Daniel Boorstin, *The Americans: The National Experience.* New York: Random House, 1965.

6. Barry J. Kaplan, "Houston: The Gold Buckle of the Sunbelt," in Richard M. Bernard and Bradley R. Rice (eds.), *Sunbelt Cities: Politics and Growth Since World War II.* Austin: University of Texas Press, 1983, pp. 196–212.

7. Robert M. Fogelson, *The Fragmented Metropolis: Los Angeles, 1850–1930.* Cambridge, MA: Harvard University Press, 1967.

8. Robert Jackson, "Foreign Investors Love New York." *Real Estate Review,* Fall 1980, pp. 55–61; David Ricks and Ronald Racster, "Restrictions on Foreign Ownership of U.S. Real Estate." *Real Estate Review,* Spring 1980, pp. 111–115.

9. Harvey Molotch and John Logan, "Tensions in the Growth Machine: Overcoming Resistance to Value-Free Development." *Social Problems,* March 1984, pp. 483–499; Harvey Molotch and John Logan, "Urban Dependencies: New Forms of Use and Exchange in U.S. Cities." *Urban Affairs Quarterly,* December 1985, pp. 143–169; John Logan and Harvey Molotch, *Urban Fortunes: The Political Economy of Place.* Berkeley and Los Angeles: University of California Press, 1986.

10. Beth Mintz and Michael Schwartz, *The Power Structure of American Business.* Chicago: University of Chicago Press, 1985.

44 HARVEY MOLOTCH

11. Doreen Massey, *The Spatial Division of Labor.* New York: Methuen, 1984.

12. See Otis Dudley Duncan, "From Social System to Eco-System." *Sociological Inquiry,* Spring 1961, pp. 140–49; and William Form, "The Place of Social Structure in the Determination of Land Use." *Social Forces,* May 1954, pp. 317–323.

13. See Harvey Molotch, "Toward a More Human Human (*sic*) Ecology." *Land Economics,* June 1967, pp. 336–341.

14. Edward Banfield and James Wilson, *City Politics.* Cambridge, MA: Harvard University Press, 1963.

15. Amos Hawley, "Community Power and Urban Renewal Success." *American Journal of Sociology,* January 1963, pp. 422–431. In Hawley's analysis, numbers of proprietors, managers, and officials is used as a proxy for diversity of economic functions in an area. For a critique of this operationalization, see Roger Friedland, *Power and Crisis in the City.* London: Macmillan, 1982, pp. 38–39; for a critique of Hawley's findings, see Bruce Straits, "Community Adoption and Implementation of Urban Renewal." *American Journal of Sociology,* July 1965, pp. 77–82.

16. See Peterson, for a more complete statement of this assumption.

17. For studies that follow a similar logic, see Terry Clark, "Community Structure, Decision-Making, Budget Expenditures, and Urban Renewal in 51 American Cities." *American Sociological Review,* August 1968, pp. 576–593; and James R. Lincoln, "Power and Mobilization in the Urban Community: Reconsidering the Ecological Approach." *American Sociological Review,* February 1976, pp. 1–15.

18. See Logan and Molotch; Larry Lyon, Lawrence G. Felice, M. Ray Perryman, and E. Stephen Parker, "Community Power and Population Increase." *American Journal of Sociology,* May 1981, pp. 1387–1401.

19. See Allan Pred, "Structuration and the Time Geography of Becoming Places." *Annals of the Association of American Geographers,* August 1984, pp. 279–297.

20. Michael Peter Smith and Marlene Keller, "Managed Growth and the Politics of Uneven Development in New Orleans," in Susan Fainstein (ed.), *Restructuring the City.* New York: Longman, 1983, pp. 126–160.

21. Michael Storper and Richard Walker, "The Theory of Labor and the Theory of Location." *International Journal of Urban and Regional Research,* March 1983, pp. 1–43.

22. David Gordon, "Capitalist Efficiency and Socialist Efficiency." *Monthly Review,* November 1976, pp. 19–39.

23. David Harvey, "Labor, Capital, and Class Struggle around the Built Environment in Advanced Capitalist Countries." *Politics and Society* 6, no. 3, 1976, pp. 265–295; Richard A. Walker, "A Theory of Suburbanization: Capitalism and the Construction of Urban Space in the United States," in Michael Dear and Allan J. Scott (eds.), *Urbanization and Urban Planning in Capitalist Society*. New York: Methuen, 1981, pp. 383–429.

24. See, for example, David Harvey, *The Limits to Capital*. Chicago: University of Chicago Press, 1982, p. 374; Richard A. Walker and Matthew J. Williams, "Water from Power: Water Supply and Regional Growth in the Santa Clara Valley." *Economic Geography,* April 1982, pp. 95–119; Manuel Castells, *The City and the Grassroots: A Cross-Cultural Theory of Urban Social Movements*. Berkeley and Los Angeles: University of California Press, 1983; John Molenkopf, *The Contested City*. Princeton: Princeton University Press, 1983.

25. Robert B. Cohen, "The New International Division of Labor: Multinational Corporations and Urban Hierarchy," in Dear and Scott, pp. 287–315; Massey; Richard Child Hill and Joe R. Feagin, "Detroit and Houston: Two Cities in Global Perspective." Paper read at the 79th Annual Meeting of the American Sociological Association, San Antonio, Texas, August 27–31, 1984; Storper and Walker.

26. Stanislaw J. Makielski, *The Politics of Zoning*. New York: Columbia University Press, 1966.

27. Saskia Sassen-Koob, "The New Labor Demand in Global Cities," in Michael Peter Smith (ed.), *Cities in Transformation: Class, Capital, and the State*. Beverly Hills, CA: Sage Publications, 1984, pp. 139–172.

28. John Hurst, "Two Small Towns Believe That Crime Pays, After All." *Los Angeles Times,* July 31, 1983, pt. 1, p. 1.

29. Judy Licht, "The Nuclear Waste Lottery." *Re:Sources,* Summer 1983, pp. 1–7.

30. Mollenkopf. See also Robert Alan Dahl, *Who Governs?* New Haven, CT: Yale University Press, 1961.

31. Mollenkopf, p. 10.

32. Dahl.

33. See also G. William Domhoff, *Who Really Rules: New Haven Community Power Re-examined*. Santa Monica, CA: Goodyear, 1978; Todd Swanstrom, *The Crisis of Growth Politics: Cleveland, Kucinich, and the Challenge of Urban Populism*. Philadelphia: Temple University Press, 1985.

34. See Dan Clawson and Mary Ann Clawson, "The Logic of Business Unity: Corporation Contributions in the 1980 Election." Paper presented at the

80th Annual Meeting of the American Sociological Association, Washington, D.C., August 26–30, 1985; George Cooper and Gavan Daws, *Land and Power in Hawaii: The Democratic Years.* Honolulu: Benchmark Press, 1985; Steven D. Lydenberg, *Bankrolling Ballots Update 1980: The Role of Business in Financing Ballot Question Campaigns.* New York: The Council on Economic Priorities, 1981.

35. Bill Boyarsky and Jerry Gilliam, "Hard Times Don't Stem Flow of Campaign Gifts." *Los Angeles Times,* April 4, 1982, pt. 1, pp. 1, 3, 22, 23; Cooper and Daws.

36. Frank Clifford, "Contributors to Mayoral Race Seek a Friendly Ear." *Los Angeles Times,* March 25, 1985, pt. 2, pp. 1, 3, 14.

37. Ron Curran and Lewis MacAdams, "The Selling of L.A. County." *L.A. Weekly,* November 22–28, 1985, pp. 24–49.

38. Evelyn Hsu, "S.F. Political Gifts—Developers Lead." *San Francisco Chronicle,* October 25, 1984, p. 1.

39. Josh Barbanel, "Abundant Political Gifts by Developers Faulted." *New York Times,* November 27, 1985, p. 16.

40. Daniel Boorstin.

41. Fogelson.

42. Henry Binford, *The First Suburbs: Residential Communities on the Boston Periphery 1815–1860.* Chicago: University of Chicago Press, 1985.

43. Daniel Bell, "Crime as an American Way of Life," in *The End of Ideology: On the Exhaustion of Political Ideas in the Fifties.* New York: Collier Books, 1961, pp. 127–150.

44. Mike Royko, *Boss: Richard J. Daley of Chicago.* New York: Dutton, 1971.

45. Ibid., p. 75.

46. This North-South symbiosis was suggested to me by G. William Domhoff in a personal communication, January 2, 1986; see his *Fat Cats And Democrats,* Englewood Cliffs, N.J.: Prentice Hall, 1972, pp. 97–103.

47. Herbert Gans, *The Urban Villagers.* New York: Free Press, 1962.

48. Edward C. Banfield, *Political Influence.* New York: Macmillan, 1961.

49. Cooper and Daws.

50. Clarence Stone, "City Politics and Economic Development: Political Economy Perspectives." *The Journal of Politics,* February 1984, p. 292.

51. Peterson, p. 132.

52. Mollenkopf, pp. 242–243.

53. Castells, p. 72.

54. Walter Firey, "Sentiment and Symbolism as Ecological Variables." *American Sociological Review,* April 1945, pp. 140–148; Thomas K. Rudel, Managing Growth: Local Governments and the Social Control of Land Use. New Brunswick, NJ: Department of Human Ecology, Rutgers University, 1983.

55. John Fish, Gordon Nelson, Walter Stuhr, and Lawrence Witmer, *The Edge of the Ghetto: A Study of Church Involvement in Community Organization.* Chicago: Church Federation of Greater Chicago, 1966.

56. Harvey Molotch, "Romantic Marxism: Love is (Still) Not Enough." *Contemporary Sociology,* March 1984, pp. 141–143.

57. See, for example, Harry Brill, *Why Organizers Fail.* Berkeley and Los Angeles: University of California Press, 1971; Steven Katz and Margit Mayer, "Gimme Shelter: Self-Help Housing Struggles Within and Against the State in New York City and West Berlin." *International Journal of Urban and Regional Research,* forthcoming.

58. See Logan and Molotch.

59. Mark Baldasarre and William Protash, "Growth Controls, Population Growth, and Community Satisfaction." *American Sociological Review,* June 1982, pp. 339–346; Logan and Molotch.

60. Swanstrom.

61. Mintz and Schwartz, p. 284.

62. Harvey Molotch, "Capital and Neighborhood in the United States." *Urban Affairs Quarterly,* March 1979, pp. 289–312.

Chapter 3

The Role of the Performing Arts in Urban Competition and Growth

J. Allen Whitt

For local civic boosters in Louisville, Kentucky, the night of October 7, 1984, was a memorable one, a public relations dream come true. All that day television production crews had been stringing cables, setting up transmission equipment, and getting ready for the big event. Much of the area on Main Street in front of the new Kentucky Center for the Arts had been taken over by trucks housing electronic equipment. By early evening the broad front steps leading up to the Center were as bright as a soundstage under the illumination of thousands of watts. At two minutes before 9, the more than two thousand people in Whitney Hall heard the practiced voices of the TV network anchors begin addressing the national audience, setting the stage for what was to come. Then, precisely on the hour, a red light on one of the television cameras switched on. The president of the League of Women Voters welcomed the audience to the Kentucky Center for the Arts, introduced moderator Barbara Walters, and the first presidential debate between candidates Walter Mondale and Ronald Reagan got under way.

Louisville, and the recently opened $33.5 million Center, were in the national spotlight. That pleased a lot of important people in the city. Local movers and shakers and city officials had launched an old-fashioned "booster" campaign. In their efforts to promote the city, they had spent more than $250,000 of public and private money—about half of it from Project 2000, a development-oriented group of top-level corporate and bank executives in the city. Their strategy was to use the presidential debate as an occasion to generate favorable national publicity for the city and the new Center. A few days before, city officials and prominent corporate leaders had tried to woo the visiting news reporters with a pre-debate party, the event being funded by the city as well as such locally based companies as Philip Morris and Ford Motor. The local boosters distributed promotional buttons ("Louisville's Great—Beyond Debate") and glossy information packets about Louisville, and offered free tours to bright spots in town. At famed Churchill Downs, home of the Kentucky Derby, there was even a two-horse "Presidential Derby," featuring "Where's the Beef?" and "There He Goes Again." The Mayor of Louisville vowed that when he met the television news personalities, he would let them know that Louisville was "a city on the move; there are a lot of vital things going on."

There was ultimately some disappointment that the public relations efforts did not bear more fruit. Not as many reporters showed up at the party as had been expected, and none came for the free tours. A few newspapers, such as the *New York Times* and *USA Today* did stories specifically on Louisville or the Center, but most limited their coverage to the debate. In fact, the debate itself appeared to do relatively little to focus attention on the city. Louisville was mentioned only once during the event: by Mondale as he thanked the city at the end of the debate. Nevertheless, many of the local boosters declared themselves satisfied and proclaimed the campaign a success. One of the directors of Project 2000, a banker, said: "We got our money's worth. . . . It helps round out the image that we want Louisville to have." An editorial in the local newspaper also set forth a positive interpretation, and directly connected the boosterism campaign to the desire for urban growth:

> Who knows who was watching shows like "Good Morning America" as the backdrop of the Kentucky Center for the Arts came on screen. Convention organizers, tourists, people who are considering relocating their companies here—you never know how an event like this may make a difference.[1]

The Presidential debate was not the first time that the Kentucky Center had been in the national spotlight. Some 11 months earlier, on November 19, 1983, the official opening of the Center had been marked by a nationally televised gala, lavishly staged by Hollywood producer George Stevens, Jr., who had been imported for the event. For $750 each, attendees saw visiting celebrities (e.g., Charlton Heston, Art Buchwald, Florence Henderson, Douglas Fairbanks, Jr., Marsha Norman, Lillian Gish, Diane Sawyer, Lilly Tomlin), dined on such delicacies as 3,000 fresh strawberries flown in from New Zealand, and were ministered to by 120 white-gloved champagne servers.

Praise was heaped on the Center. Producer Stevens said that it was the newest jewel in the small necklace of cultural centers in America. The president of Humana, Inc.—a hospital management firm headquartered in Louisville, a firm that was bringing publicity to the city by sponsoring mechanical heart operations, and one of the most heavily involved and ardent supporters in the construction of the Center— declared that the city had "built something for the next century." In spite of gaffs such as master of ceremonies Heston almost introducing Mayor Harvey Sloane as the mayor of Nashville, by the time the audience rose to sing "my Old Kentucky Home" at the close of the program, civic pride and tears of happiness were flowing.

One thing closest to the hearts of civic boosters is favorable publicity for their city. Cities often go to great lengths to generate such notice. Not only do they believe that publicity inspires pride and devotion in the local population, as in the case of a professional baseball team that wins a pennant, but it is also thought to be good for business. The city is identified as an up-and-coming place where exciting things are happening. In the minds of local boosters, a positive image may attract new businesses, outside investors, or other desirable land users. The competitive position of the city vis-à-vis others will be enhanced through strategic publicity and systematic image building.

As Molotch has pointed out, the desire to create local conditions and images favorable to urban growth is a central element in the "urban growth machine." The focus of this chapter is not on the Presidential debate nor on the Center festivities. Rather, it is upon the operation of the urban growth machine in Louisville, and how that machine has been attempting to use the Kentucky Center for the Arts as an engine of urban redevelopment and growth, and for local and national image making.

Of course, the performing arts (dance, opera, orchestra, ballet, theater) must not been seen as simply tools to be used by civic boosters to feed the urban growth machine. There are people who have a deep interest in the arts for their own sake. Throughout most of history, the arts have been present and particularly influential in the culture of cities. The link is not new. However, I argue that—due to relatively recent changes in the character and economic base of American cities, the rise of increased public and private support for the arts, and the coming together of a new urban political coalition of arts and urban development supporters—the arts have assumed a central position in the development plans of many cities in the United States. In this, Louisville is far from a lone example.

The first part of this chapter will focus on Louisville as an instructive case of how business elites use the arts to promote urban growth and development. Most clearly indicative of this is the history of the Kentucky Center for the Arts, which will be briefly sketched. Next, I will show that in spite of what local boosters like to project and believe about the unique character of events in Louisville, national trends have greatly shaped the development dynamics of all cities. Many other municipalities are employing the same arts-centered growth strategy. I will outline those national events and give a brief overview of how business elites have organized at the national and the local level in order to promote urban economic development through the arts.

History of the Kentucky Center for the Arts

Earlier than in many cities, Louisville business elites adopted an arts-based growth strategy. In 1963, Louisville Central Area, a private downtown development group consisting of large downtown businesses, developers, real estate brokers, and banks, put forth an initial plan for a Louisville arts center (later, the proposed name of the center was to be changed to include "Kentucky" in a bid to attract state financing). From the beginning, the center was seen as providing an impetus for economic development. A few years later, the former head of Louisville Central Area, now a newspaper columnist, noted that there was sentiment for locating the arts center in the north end of the downtown since the area desperately needed a "shot in the arm"; the community needed the center if it was going to "achieve its stated goal of becoming a regional center."[2]

The history of the proposed center was not without conflict among business elites and between business elites and political leaders. There were debates over exactly where in the downtown area the center should be located, whether it should be in a new structure or a renovated one, what its relationship to nearby structures should be, the kinds of facilities it should contain, how it should be financed, to what extent there should be overall downtown planning, and whether it should be private or public planning. There were conflicts between city and county officials over their roles in the plan, and even a few arguments over whether it should be built at all.

In spite of the wrangling, a more unified coalition of business elites and government officials began to take shape with the election of Governor Julian Carroll in 1975. Reportedly, Carroll asked the Louisville "power structure" to send him a "wish list" of top-priority projects that they would like to see receive state funding. One participant, a well-connected attorney in Louisville who was to become a key figure in the planning of the arts center, Gordon Davidson, recalls that the list had "12 or 15 things," but the Governor picked the arts center as his favorite.[3] The Governor viewed the center as a "potent catalyst" for the revitalization of downtown Louisville[4] and as a way of countering Kentucky's "Li'l Abner" image.[5]

It looked as if plans for the center would move swiftly ahead, but continuing political conflicts and disagreements prevented much progress. By 1977, the Louisville Development Committee (LDC), a Chamber of Commerce organization that had been involved in trying to encourage corporations to relocate to Louisville, had also turned its attention to the issue of an arts center. According to a Chamber publication, Governor Carroll had become impatient with the political infighting in Louisville:

> Through Terry McBrayer, Carroll's commerce secretary, LDC learned the ground rules [for obtaining the promised state money]: consensus by the political leaders and arts groups; or, more bluntly: "Get your act together."[6]

Apparently, the act was shaped up. A broad and cohesive network of the top business elites in the Louisville area began to form around the goal of creating an arts center. Later that year, the LDC produced a report for the Governor outlining the specifics of a proposal which concluded by noting the redevelopment and economic benefits to be expected: "What the Riverfront Stadium has done for Cincinnati, the arts complex can, in a lesser but equivalently important way, do for Louisville." The report appeared to unify and solidify business and political support for the arts center. Carroll appointed a seventeen-member Kentucky Cultural Complex Committee, a group "that glittered with important local names" and was headed by Gordon Davidson. The following year, Carroll got the state legislature to approve a $22.4-million bond issue for the construction of what was then called the Kentucky Cultural Complex.[7]

In late 1979, Carroll left office and a new governor, John Y. Brown, took over. Brown, a man who had himself made a fortune in business and who had powerful ties to important business people, took steps that brought big business leaders even more heavily into the project. Not happy with the magnitude of the state fiscal commitment to the project, he held up the sale of the bonds and appointed a five-member committee to review alternative ways of financing the project. The committee was made up of Davidson as well as a leading Louisville banker, an executive of Humana, the chairman of Royal Crown Companies (who had worked with Brown on the board at Kentucky Fried Chicken), and Brown's state Secretary of Finance. The committee and Brown agreed that state support should end with the already passed bond issue, advocated a larger role for corporate giving, and proposed a private nonprofit corporation to own and run the facility—not the state nor the University of Louisville, as previously envisioned.

Brown next turned to his long-time friend, Wendell Cherry, the president of Humana—a firm destined to open a lavish new corporate headquarters directly across the street from the site of the Kentucky Center. Cherry, who was to later say that he had discussed the economic development role of the proposed Center with Brown,[8] took over the management of the arts center project by becoming chairman of the new non-profit corporation, Kentucky Center for the Arts, Inc., which would build and operate the center. Cherry—and Humana—took an aggressive role in the project, including supervising construction of the facility, and donated large amounts of corporate—and Cherry's own—money.[9] A local corporate fund drive was launched that was said to "include every important name in Louisville business."[10] The earlier fragmentation among business elites had apparently been overcome.

It was clear all along, but especially after the financing package was changed by Brown, that the downtown businesses and banks were very much involved in the promotion of the Center, and that a prime motivation was the boost that the Center was expected to give to redevelopment and urban growth. An elite network of business leaders was activated. Other large-scale development and renovation projects nearby were being planned and built at about the same time, and they were all seen to be mutually supportive. An editorial in the newspaper, a paper owned by a socially elite family whose senior member had been a leading advocate of the Center, said that it would be "one of the best prospects for reviving downtown as a magnet for people after sundown."[11] Under a headline of "Arts Centers Helped Other Cities

Flourish," the paper ran a story quoting the manager of the new center in Nashville—a city often mentioned in Louisville as a point of comparison—as saying that there had been a "great revitalization effort in downtown Nashville," and that the arts center management had been working with local business leaders in efforts to get outside firms to relocate in Nashville.[12] In the early stages of planning, Gordon Davidson had said that the center should be "designed and located so as to get the maximum economic benefit from it."[13]

The building of the Kentucky Center was not an isolated urban development strategy, unique to Louisville. At the national level, a new relationship had been evolving among business, the arts, and the federal government. These changes provided both the motivation and the opportunity for many cities besides Louisville to attempt to use the arts as a spur to urban development.

The National Arts Movement

Creation of the National Endowment for the Arts

The so-called "high" arts traditionally have gathered much attention and support from social elites and wealthy individual patrons. During the 1950s and 1960s, however, important new sources of funding were being created, laying the groundwork for the current urban arts movement. One of the first moves in this direction was taken by President Dwight Eisenhower, who in the mid-1950s suggested that Congress create a national advisory council on the arts. Although his suggestion was not picked up by Congress, an even more important federal role in the arts was put in place during the administration of President Lyndon Johnson a decade later. In the interim, the state of New York created in 1960, under Governor Nelson Rockefeller, the New York State Council on the Arts (NYSCA). During the 1960s, at about the same time as the first stirrings of plans for the Kentucky Center were being felt in Louisville, President John Kennedy demonstrated his interest in the arts; he was influenced by the New York model. Kennedy commissioned a special report on the arts in America in which the philosophy of NYSCA was set forth by Rockefeller associate August Heckscher.[14] President Johnson guided through Congress federal legislation that created the National Endowment for the Arts in

1965. For the first time, a dependable source of funding for the arts was assured. This initiative, however, was not directly tied to an economic development agenda.

The Rise of Large-Scale Corporate Funding

During the 1950s and 1960s, events in the private sector also were moving toward more money for the arts. In this initiative, a Rockefeller also played an important part. The Ford Foundation in the late 1950s began in a significant way to fund projects and programs in the arts.[15] Rockefeller family influence was felt here as well: the Rockefeller Brothers Fund assessed the state of the performing arts and called, in the late 1960s, for private corporations to give more money to the arts. Similarly, the powerful organization of large corporations known as the National Industrial Conference Board[16] became active in the arts field. David Rockefeller gave a speech before that organization in 1966 in which he urged greatly expanded corporate giving. He asserted that the needs of the arts were outstripping the budget of the newly created National Endowment for the Arts and the capacity of wealthy individuals and foundations to give, and suggested that a private organization be set up by the business community for the purpose of encouraging support of the arts by business firms. The following year, in 1967, money from the Rockefeller family, the Rockefeller Foundation, and the Ford Foundation established the Business Committee for the Arts, a group devoted to active promotion of corporate giving for the arts.[17]

By the middle to late 1960s, therefore, the arts had gained increased legitimacy in the minds of business elites, and institutions were in place within both the national business community and within the federal government to channel increased private and public financial support to the arts. The result was a greatly increased amount of money flowing into the arts. By 1978, the budget for the National Endowment for the Arts was almost $150 million;[18] according to the Business Committee for the Arts, private corporations gave over $500 million in 1982.

The increased flow of money into the arts resulted in a great expansion of artistic production companies and performances. The Director of the Design Arts Program of the National Endowment for the Arts has noted that, from the early 1960s to the early 1980s, the number of

American dance companies increased by ten times, small theater groups increased by twenty times, and there were "countless new museums, galleries, studios, and other spaces in which our artists can produce and exhibit work."[19] This growth in arts organizations and performances triggered what one writer has called a "housing crisis" in the arts.[20]

The point to be emphasized here is that the pressure to build physical structures to house the federally and privately sponsored arts expansion created an opportunity for local advocates in cities across the country to attempt to make the arts boom a part of the urban growth and redevelopment process in declining downtown areas. Most of the new facilities were to be built in downtown areas in order to take advantage of the accessibility afforded to arts audiences by central location.

In Louisville and elsewhere, local political coalitions consisting of downtown-oriented corporations, developers, banks, urban planners, government officials, arts supporters and patrons, and often historical preservation groups—old theaters and other historical structures were often used to house the arts—began to take shape, as did the vision of using the arts to renew the central city and change its character. As in many similar cases, the hope of local economic growth and urban development was a potent stimulus to coalition-building and political unity.[21] The arts became a major element (in some cases the sole element) in the urban development effort, not only in New York City as it had long been, but also in the growth and development strategies of many other U.S. cities, including Boston, Baltimore, Winston-Salem, Columbus, Cleveland, Eugene, Alexandria, Tulsa, San Diego, Costa Mesa, Los Angeles, San Francisco, Dallas, Pittsburgh, Denver, Charleston, Madison, Reno, Seattle, as well as Louisville, among others on the growing list.[22]

As an example, in Alexandria, Virginia, a World-War-II torpedo factory has been converted into a combined arts/commercial facility that is now reported to be the "most valuable piece of commercial real estate in Alexandria."[23] In Dallas, Texas, a large section of downtown has been set aside as a "cultural district" to contain a symphony hall, an arts museum, galleries, studios for artists, office buildings, hotels, and other businesses.[24] In one of the best-known cases, a decaying waterfront area in Baltimore is being redeveloped into the extensive Inner Harbor project, a 240-acre area of cultural and arts facilities, parks, a convention center, condominiums, hotels, shops, restaurants, and other commercial developments.[25] In the words of a Baltimore city official: "We have tried to combine animation, public events, image, and economic development into a package ... " resulting in "real dollars and cents" for businesses and the city.[26] In these and other cities, the arts have been incorporated into the urban growth machine in a significant way.

The Appeal of the Arts as a Local Development Strategy

There are several reasons for the special appeal of the arts as a basis for downtown growth and redevelopment.

In the first place, the arts draw people, an attractive proposition to downtown restaurants, shops, hotels, and other businesses. More specifically, the people who come into town to see a play or a ballet usually do so in the evening or on weekends, times outside of normal working hours. In addition to bringing in potential business for shops and the like, the arts are thought to bring vitality, or "animation" in the language of cultural planners, and to be supportive of downtown residential development. Each of these activities is seen as feeding off the others, leading to what economists know as "market synergy."[27] An attempt is often made to further intensify this effect through the building of "mixed-use developments"—"MXDs"—single buildings or clusters of buildings (e.g., a symphony hall, hotel, office building, and restaurant in close proximity or physically connected) that combine cultural and commercial activities and mutually support each other by drawing people and generating spending.

People are of course expected to come mainly from the suburbs and surrounding areas of the metropolitan area, but the vision is often too that tourists from outside the area will patronize local businesses while they are visiting the city. Tourism, especially in the form of convention trade, is heavily stressed by growth advocates, since as two social scientists note:

> cities seek tourists because the convention industry seems uniquely beneficial, essentially a 'free' commodity. Presumably, tourists spend money without taking anything out of the local economy. The convention industry has frequently been described as 'the industry without a smokestack'.[28]

A majority of the people attracted to the street fairs and festivals held in downtown Baltimore are said to come from out of town, and they spend over one hundred million dollars during the season.[29]

In addition to the money that arts audiences spend on dinners, tax-icabs, shopping, and so on, an arts strategy fits in well with the kinds of changes that have been going on in central cities for quite a while. Sub-urbanization of the population and the outmigration of traditional in-dustries and other economic activities have often left the central city with a tenuous social and economic base. With the growing phenome-non of "deindustrialization"[30] and the decline of older central cities, some municipalities are trying to become administrative and service centers as a way of surviving and growing. The vision is to give central cities new economic roles in corporate and governmental administra-tion and in social and professional services, and to bring suburbanites back downtown to shop, find leisure activities, and—more specula-tively—live in apartments and condominiums. The American Council for the Arts began a report by noting: "In the future, central cities will increasingly be dependent on service activities for jobs and income, since manufacturing and even wholesale and retail trade is relocating to the suburbs and beyond."[31] The report concludes that the "arts, while not the most rapidly growing part of the service sector, may be one of the most strategic and pivotal contributors to the economic life of the central city."[32]

The arts growth coalition is also aware that, by and large, a special audience of people is attracted by the arts, an audience not representa-tive of the U. S. population as a whole. The audience tends to be more affluent, more educated, and largely white. For example, while only about 15 percent of the work force is in professional occupations, more than one-half of arts audiences are in professional families. Blue-collar workers make up only about 4 percent of such audiences, while they are about one-third of the U.S. population, and blacks, 12 percent of the population, are only 3 percent of arts attendees.[33] Cultural events such as street fairs and community arts may be more representative of urban populations, but overall the arts audience still comes largely from the higher socioeconomic groups.

The arts appeal to the people who run corporate headquarters-oriented central cities. Arts advocates argue that the arts raise the local "quality of life" and make the city more attractive to businesses that might move into the area. For example, the head of Philip Morris Cor-poration has noted that the arts of a city are important in aiding firms in retaining "key personnel."[34]

The desire to foster downtown growth and redevelopment is not the sole reason corporations give money to the arts.[35] In spite of these other motivations, however, it appears that the role of the arts in stimulating downtown growth and development is increasingly perceived by corporations—and other groups—as a reason for supporting the arts. Business interests have always been at the heart of American urban development alliances.[36] In the arts strategy now taking shape in American cities, businesses, developers, and banks are being joined by arts organizations, historic preservation groups, cultural planners, and others in a new urban growth alliance in which the arts are central.

Often, the interests of all of these groups will be represented in the construction of mixed-use developments that include arts components. Development-oriented organizations at the national level, such as the Urban Land Institute, have pointed out some of the advantages to all parties of cultural MXDs.[37] In addition, MXDs are appealing because they can be used to promote development that is in part federally and partly privately subsidized—by federal grants for the arts, by tax advantages, and by corporate giving. For example, a 1927-vintage movie theater in downtown Indianapolis was renovated and turned into the home of the Indiana Repertory Theater by a combination of business and foundation money, contributions from individuals, funds from the National Endowment for the Arts and the Indiana Arts Commission, and part of an urban development action grant received by the city.[38] In the case of Louisville, the Kentucky Center was built mostly by state of Kentucky money, with additional amounts from corporations, the county, and the city, and has also gained performance support from the National Endowment for the Arts. Additional revenue for the Center comes from its restaurant, concessions, and gift shop.

A number of special financial and legal mechanisms have been used by these coalitions to promote MXDs and other arts-related urban development. These include tax increment financing, the creation of special taxes, urban enterprise zones, revenue bonds, special assessment districts, private/public ownership, special leasing arrangements, and density trade-off zoning.[39]

The latter technique, generally not well-known to the public at large, has one particularly intriguing variant, "air rights transfers." City zoning laws permit buildings to be built to a certain maximum height, say, 30 stories. If a building—such as an art museum—is only three stories high, the city may allow the museum to sell the air rights for the "unused" 27 stories of permitted space to a landowner in another part of the city who wishes to put up, for example, a 32-story building in an area currently allowing only 5-story buildings. Thus, presumably, the museum is happy because it can get money for its unneeded air space; the developer is happy because a taller building can now be built, and the city is happy since it receives more tax revenues—and also may have made a deal with the developer (such as requiring the construction of an arts facility of some kind in the new building) in order to approve the air rights transfer.[40] Air rights transfers have been used, for example, in the South Street Seaport project[41] and by the Museum of Modern Art,[42] both in New York City. The MOMA air rights were used in the construction of a nearby 52-story residential tower, a project that has generated controversy and unhappiness among some residents of the area.[43]

Another such technique for bringing together the interests of developers, arts organizations, and local government is a more traditional real estate transfer scheme. The city has or acquires a piece of historic property, such as a theater. It is sold to a developer, who in turn syndicates it to private investors. The investors are now able to take advantage of the historic property tax provisions on their other income. The newly renovated theater is now leased back by the city from the developer, and the city creates a private non-profit corporation to run the facility. The local performing arts groups now have a new home, and the city has stimulated arts and renovation activity, and possibly given a boost to additional arts-related downtown development.[44]

The non-profit legal status of performing arts groups permits them to more easily receive foundation and government grants and private contributions.[45] For the same reason, non-profit corporations are often created to construct arts facilities, to coordinate adjacent arts-related development activities, and to operate arts centers.[46]

Controversy over the Commercial Role of the Arts

Of course, there have long been commercial aspects to the arts, and ties between the arts and business are not new. However, the evolving role of the arts in urban growth and redevelopment has spawned new and sometimes complex relationships between the making of art and the making of money.

It is relatively easy to see why commercial interests, and developers in particular, might see in the arts the potential for the enhancement of their own profits. As one developer—involved in converting some of the New York 42nd Street pornography district into legitimate theaters—put it: "We are in the development business, not the arts business. We find that actors walking around the streets, theater activities in general, give off good vibrations; they make an area more renewable. If cement factories did that, we would be putting them in."[47]

It is also easy to see why arts organizations—traditionally having to scramble for funds and public support—would find attractive the prospect of new or renovated facilities and increased sources of financial support. Citing the example of the New York Museum of Modern Art's tower project, which has resulted in financial gains for MOMA, arts consultant Weinstein[48] urges arts organizations to become even more attuned to commercially oriented values and practices: "If you absorb as a cultural institution a defined portion of the risk [of a commercial development venture] that the private sector ordinarily accepts, the rewards can be tremendous." He sees the fusion of art and commercialism as good, arguing that a sharp separation between art and commerce is undesirable since it frees the commercial sector from moral and ethical constraints, and permits the arts to retain their "purity" and elitist nature. "If I were building a cultural facility," he says, "I'd build it in a mall."[49]

On the other hand, there are those who are concerned about commercialism in the arts and the new "partnership" among the arts, business, and government. For some arts organizations and arts advocates, there is renewed intensity in the historic debates about the possible corrupting influences of commercial involvement, and among some arts groups, philosophical resistance to increased commercialism.

The new forms of development taking place sometimes pose problems for non-profit arts organizations, such as the tax-related and other legal restrictions placed upon the nature and extent of the direct commercial ties they are allowed to have.[50] As mentioned earlier, there also have been public controversies over the commercial implications and neighborhood-transforming aspects of such things as the Museum of Modern Art's role in developing a 52-story residential tower.

Then too, as in the case of Louisville, the creation of a single performing arts structure has been a rather common feature of arts development. The need to design such facilities to fit the requirements of arts groups as diverse as theater companies, symphonies, opera companies, ballet troupes, road shows from out of town, and other performing companies may pose problems. Resident groups commonly feel that they must put up with physical conditions that are less than ideal for their own needs (e.g., poor acoustics for the orchestra in a theater that is fine for stage plays), that centralized administration (operation and maintenance of the hall, printing of programs, and so forth) is inflexible and inefficient, that they have reduced autonomy, and that they are placed in greater competition with the other arts groups for funds and audiences.[51] Such problems continue to crop up at the Kentucky Center for the Arts.[52]

The Non-controversial Nature of the Arts

The arts are also useful for development purposes because they are not as likely as many other kinds of development—particularly industrial—to generate public opposition, at least at present. Even so-called "hi-tech" industries such as computers and electronics, although eagerly sought by many communities, are not without undesirable features (e.g., recently discovered problems with chemical pollution). The arts, on the other hand, appear to be clean, non-polluting, and largely non-controversial. In the words of the head of the Design Arts Program of the National Endowment for the Arts:

Urban development projects are so complex that, inevitably it seems, constituencies organize against them for various reasons. . . . The arts, however, are like Mom and apple pie; they're consensus-makers, common ground. People can easily focus on the arts activities in a new project, instead of dwelling on the complicated costs and benefits public support for private development activity usually entails.[53]

An arts project as part of a development plan may sweeten the pot and help to prevent possible opposition against further redevelopment or urban growth. Thus, an arts strategy might in certain cases be tried as a kind of Trojan horse for local rentiers and developers in a bid to overcome resistance (particularly in large and controversial displacement projects such as Yerba Buena in San Francisco) to the urban growth machine.[54]

The presumed non-controversial nature of the arts carries over into conceptions of the impact of an arts presence on social relations in a community. Many of the corporate and other supporters of the arts appear to believe that the arts promote social unity and integration. Zukin, a critic of arts-based development,[55] argues that the arts strategy is seen by many to emphasize social harmony, "inner-meaning," anti-

materialism, and limited expectations. Indeed, the promoters of street
fairs and other events say that such things "will bring people together
and not pull them apart . . . "[56] and that they permit citizens "to claim
the open spaces of their cities," to learn to trust each other, and help "to
heal the paranoia of urban life."[57] Some corporate executives, such as
the chairman of Time, Inc., feel that the arts "bring us together, united
in our appreciation and awe."[58]

Molotch has argued that one of the major effects of professional
sports, such as football teams, is to create within an urban area a "we-
feeling" among the populace, a useful prop to civic boosterism and the
operation of the local growth machine.[59] In the same way, the arts are
often perceived—whatever the reality—to inspire social harmony and
devotion to the greater glory and growth of the city.

Conclusion

It is not yet clear whether an arts strategy will ultimately be "successful" in the sense of generating significant profits to the members of
the urban growth machine by making possible large-scale downtown
redevelopment and enhanced urban competitiveness and growth.
There is no doubt that many of the members of the arts-based urban
growth machine—the bankers, corporate executives, developers, rentiers, local government officials, and cultural elites—expect this outcome, and plans have been made accordingly in many cities.

An arts strategy may well be useful in spurring urban redevelopment, bringing people from the upper socioeconomic groups downtown outside of normal working hours, and in supporting the transformation of inner cities into service centers. However, given the historic
limited appeal of the arts to mass audiences—especially the traditional
performing arts—such a strategy, if used as the sole focus for urban
growth, is likely to prove incapable of drastically improving the overall
economic fate of a city. This is particularly true in that arts performances by themselves are unlikely to bring the volume of outside money
into town that may be brought in, for example, by a basic or export industry such as steel or automobile manufacture.

In addition, cities of course are greatly affected by regional,
national, and international economic forces beyond their control. Thus
the success of local urban development efforts—no matter how mut-

ually supporting or skillfully conceived—is by no means assured. In the case of Louisville, for instance, although quite a bit of downtown redevelopment, renovation, and construction has taken place in recent years, and more is in the planning or construction stages, the economy and overall growth potential of the city as a whole have been greatly affected by the national and international decline in traditional industries.[60] Skilled blue-collar workers—a large percentage of the local work force—have suffered high levels of unemployment, layoffs, and plant shutdowns. Not only do the arts generally lack audience appeal to such groups, but the arts are also unlikely to generate much in the way of direct economic benefits or job possibilities for these workers.

The same is true for minority and inner-city residents. As Judd and Collins[61] observe, the most recent form of urban renewal (based on such things as tourism and conventions) "is usually directed exclusively toward the affluent." This is probably even more the case with an arts strategy. Moreover, given that new arts facilities and the associated processes of gentrification may displace inner city residents, an arts strategy may even become—at the extreme—a policy aimed at recapturing the city from them. The possible displacement of less affluent residents from central cities and the use of public subsidies to further arts and other development may eventually spark social protest. For now, however, an arts growth strategy of substantial proportions seems to have taken root at the national level—without much public or scholarly notice.

Notes

1. *Louisville Times,* October 9, 1984.

2. *Courier Journal,* September 3, 1967.

3. George Yater, "Kentucky Center for the Arts: A 17-Year Production," *Louisville Magazine,* November 1983, pp. 17–26.

4. *Courier Journal,* March 3, 1978.

5. Yater.

6. Ibid.

7. Ibid.

8. Ibid.

9. Ibid.

10. Ibid.

11. *Courier Journal,* October 7, 1977.

12. *Courier Journal,* November 25, 1979.

13. *Courier Journal,* October 16, 1977.

14. Sharon Zukin, *Loft Living: Culture and Capital in Urban Change,* Baltimore: Johns Hopkins University Press, 1982, pp. 100–101.

15. Ibid., p. 101.

16. See, for example, G. William Domhoff, "Social Clubs, Policy-Planning Groups, and Corporations: A Network Study of Ruling-Class Cohesiveness," *Insurgent Sociologist,* Spring 1975, pp. 173–84.

17. From several pamphlets from the Business Committee for the Arts (BCA).

18. Paul DiMaggio and Michael Useem, "Cultural Democracy in a Period of Cultural Expansion: The Social Composition of Arts Audiences in the United States," *Social Problems,* December 1978, p. 180.

19. Michael Pittas, "Forward," in Kevin Green (ed.), *The City as a Stage: Strategies for the Arts in Urban Economics,* Washington, DC: Partners for Livable Places, 1983, p. 6.

20. Phyllis Lehmann, "Where Will All the Dancers Dance?" in Green, p. 16.

21. See, for example: Harvey Molotch, "The City as a Growth Machine," *American Journal of Sociology,* September 1976, pp. 309–332; Clarence Stone, *Economic Growth and Neighborhood Discontent,* Chapel Hill, NC: University of North Carolina Press, 1976; J. Allen Whitt, *Urban Elites and Mass Transportation,* Princeton, NJ: Princeton University Press, 1982.

22. Luke Bandle, "Great Expectations in Eugene," in Green, p. 71; Robert Goetsch and Mary Haderlein, "Art for Downtown's Sake," *Planning,* July/August 1983, pp. 10–11; Harvard Business School, "Cultural Revitalization in Six Cities," in Green, pp. 26–27; Harold Snedcof, *Cultural Facilities in Mixed-Use Development,* Washington, DC: Urban Land Institute, 1985.

23. Marian Van Landingham, "The Torpedo Factory," in Green, pp. 72–75.

24. Goetsch and Haderlein, pp. 11–13.

25. Snedcof, pp. 236–237.

26. Sandra Hillman, "Leveraging Prosperity in Baltimore," in Green, pp. 98–99.

27. Snedcof, p. 14.

28. Dennis Judd and Margaret Collins, "The Case of Tourism: Political Coalitions and Redevelopment in the Central Cities," in Gary Tobin (ed.), *The Changing Structure of the City: What Happened to the Urban Crisis,* Beverly Hills, CA: Sage Publications, 1979, p. 185.

29. Hillman, pp. 98–99.

30. Barry Bluestone and Bennett Harrison, *The Deindustrialization of America,* New York: Basic Books, 1982; Zukin.

31. *The Arts and City Planning,* New York: American Council for the Arts, 1980, p. 1.

32. *The Arts in the Economic Life of the City,* New York: American Council for the Arts, 1979, p. 67.

33. DiMaggio and Useem, pp. 187–191.

34. "Philip Morris and the Arts," BCA pamphlet, undated.

35. In addition to tax breaks for philanthropic contributions—the firm is allowed a deduction of up to 10 percent of its taxable income—giving to the arts is seen as good for the corporate image and public relations. In fact, the money that a firm gives to the arts often comes from the public relations or advertising budget (Cultural Assistance Center, "Business Partners for the Arts," in Green, p. 63). Top corporate executives sometimes take a personal interest in the arts, especially given the tradition of support for the arts as an expression of elite social status. See, for example: Paul DiMaggio, "Nonprofit Organizations in the Production and Distribution of Culture," in Walter W. Powell (ed.) *Handbook of Research on Nonprofit Organizations,* New Haven, CT: Yale University Press, forthcoming; DiMaggio and Useem; Joseph Galaskiewicz, *Social Organization of an Urban Grants Economy,* New York: Academic Press, 1985. Giving to the arts can also reflect ideological attachments. The private enterprise system is seen by business leaders as being based on "freedom" and minimal governmental regulation. Parallels are perceived in the world of art. The former Postmaster General and past president of the U.S. Chamber of Commerce, Winton Blount—now chairman of Blount, Inc., an officer of the Business Committee for the Arts, and a member of the Business Council and of the Conference Board—has said: "Art is the innocent carrier of the germ of freedom" (BCA pamphlet, "Business Support to the Arts is Just Good Sense," undated).

36. See, for example: Anne Shlay and Robert Giloth, "The Social Organization of a Land-Based Elite: Promoters of the 1992 World's Fair," paper pre-

sented at the Annual Meeting of the American Sociological Association, Washington, D.C., 1985; Molotch; Clarence Stone; Whitt.

37. In the language of an ULI report (Snedcof, p. 10):

Private developers, seeking ways to create a strong and distinctive market image, include arts and amenities to draw the desired consumers to these complexes and to extend the activity cycle to evenings and weekends.

Public agencies, whose goals are to strengthen downtown areas with development programs that attract residents, workers, and visitors, are willing to share the financial risks of including amenities and cultural uses in mixed-use projects.

For arts organizations, faced with operating costs rising higher than traditional funding sources can support, the use of real estate development rights or the opportunity to participate in major urban development projects can provide a way to gain new facilities and to supplement their funds.

38. Benjamin Mordecai, "A Movie Palace Goes Legitimate," in Green, p. 52.

39. Samuel Stone, "Fourteen Points," in Green, pp. 54–6.

40. Ibid., p. 56.

41. Richard Weinstein, "Creative Financing," in Green, p. 43.

42. Snedcof, pp. 50–51.

43. Weinstein, p. 45; Robert Peck, "Living Over the Museum," in Green, p. 47; Snedcof, p. 50.

44. George Clack, "Footlight Districts," in Green, p. 15.

45. DiMaggio, p. 36.

46. Harvard Business School, in Green, p. 26.

47. Clack, p. 13.

48. Weinstein, p. 45.

49. Quoted in Jane Kay, "Coins and Culture," in Green, p. 32. In fact, San Diego developer Ernest Hahn has put up money for the construction of two arts facilities in his shopping mall (Goetsch and Haderlein, pp. 12–13).

50. *The Arts in the Economic Life of the City,* 1979, p. 109; Peck.

51. Marc Freedman, "The Elusive Promise of Management Cooperation in the Performing Arts," in Paul DiMaggio (ed.) *Nonprofit Organizations in the Arts,* New York: Oxford University Press, forthcoming.

52. Personal interview with Marlow Burt, Director of the Kentucky Center for the Arts, February 6, 1986, Louisville, KY.

53. Quoted in Clack, p. 13.

54. See Harvey Molotch and John Logan, "Tensions in the Growth Machine," *Social Problems,* June 1984, pp. 483-499.

55. Zukin, p. 105.

56. Hillman, p. 98.

57. Karin Bacon, "The Rhythm of City Life," in Green, p. 105.

58. "Improving the Business Climate—Business and the Arts," BCA pamphlet, undated.

59. Molotch, pp. 314-315.

60. Bluestone and Harrison.

61. Judd and Collins, p. 197.

Chapter 4

Public Investment in Private Businesses: The Professional Sports Mania

Mark S. Rosentraub

Introduction

Few things dominate American life to the same extent as sports. What was once a form of entertainment, perhaps designed as a distraction from everyday life, has emerged as an important political, social, and economic force. The range of political actions in sports has varied from the protests of black athletes from the United States at the 1968 Olympic games in Mexico City to the international boycotts of the Moscow and Los Angeles Olympic games in 1980 and 1984.[1] The involvement of politics in sports has not been limited to the Olympic games. Riots among soccer fans from competing countries' games have ravaged South American sports for decades and plagued European meets in the last three years. In the United States, presidents and vice-presidents have rarely missed an opportunity to be seen at important games or to telephone the victors. The obligatory call from the President and the subsequent Rose Garden pictures at the White House are today as common as peanuts and crackerjacks at baseball games.

The social importance of sports is probably best illustrated by what people are willing to do to create a winning team. Nowhere is this more evident than in college sports. While critics and cynics in the 1960s and 1970s had warned that no major college team was without its share of recruiting and amateur sport violations,[2] few thought the problem would be so severe that the University of Georgia would admit in a

1986 lawsuit that members of its national championship football team not only were academically deficient, but had had the posting of failing grades postponed to permit their participation in a post-season bowl game.[3] Not to be outdone, several universities in Texas' Southwest Conference were jolted in 1984, 1985, and 1986 with reports of illegal payments to student athletes that led to their being placed on probation.[4] Indeed, by 1986, few followers of sports were surprised by any of the activities alumni, coaches, and athletes were engaged in in an effort to win games.

With people willing to risk sanctions to win and nations as well as powerful interest groups using sports as a medium for political messages and confrontations, it certainly comes as no surprise that most cities cherish the sport franchises that call their community home. While the Brooklyn Dodgers were romanticized in Ebbets Field and mourned when they moved to Los Angeles, today a virtual state of economic warfare exists between cities to capture and keep sports franchises. Indeed, in the last 35 years, so many teams have moved from one city to another that it would be a cumbersome task to assemble a complete record of these relocations. Following the movements of some teams is like a high school course in American geography.

There are some moves that are easy to follow. The Brooklyn Dodgers moved to Los Angeles and the New York (baseball) Giants moved to San Francisco. Others are a little more complicated. The Cleveland Rams (football) moved to Los Angeles in the early 1950s only to move to Anaheim, California (Disneyland) in the 1980s. The Atlanta Braves moved to Georgia from Milwaukee after spending less than 20 years in Wisconsin; the Braves had come to Milwaukee from Boston. One city in America has had the distinction of losing a team twice. The first version of the Washington Senators moved from the nation's capital to Minnesota; the second edition of the Senators moved to Arlington, Texas to become the Texas Rangers in the 1970s. More recently, sports fans have seen both of New York City's football teams move to New Jersey; the Baltimore Colts abandoned Maryland for Indianapolis; and, the Oakland Raiders are now the Los Angeles Raiders. The Miami Dolphins are currently in the process of building their new home stadium several miles north of the city of Miami and should leave the Miami Orange Bowl by 1987.

The movements of franchises in the United States Football League and the National Basketball Association have not been included in this discussion because there have been so many moves that the picture becomes very confusing. Perhaps the best examples of this confusion comes from two different basketball teams. First, one team moved from New Orleans to Utah. To give the team an "upbeat" image, the team's name in New Orleans was the Jazz. To save on uniform and printing expenses, when the team moved to the more subdued social climate of Salt Lake City, the team did not change its name. Somehow, though, one does not associate Jazz with Utah. The Minnesota basketball team adopted the name "Lakers" to reflect the geography of that state. When the Lakers moved to Los Angeles, the name of the team remained the Lakers. It is hard to imagine how someone would associate the Lakers with the geography of Los Angeles.

Professional teams are not the only sports organizations which move from city to city. In the last five years, two universities have actually moved the site of their home games from central city facilities to suburban locations. Southern Methodist University now plays its home games in Texas Stadium, located in suburban Irving, instead of in the Cotton Bowl, located in one of the lowest income communities in Dallas. The Bruins of the University of California at Los Angeles now play their home football games at Pasadena's Rose Bowl instead of the downtown Los Angeles Coliseum. Of course, it is hard to have much sympathy for Los Angeles, since it convinced the Dodgers to move from Brooklyn, the Raiders from Oakland, and the Lakers from Minnesota.

The driving force behind each of the moves of these teams was the desire by team owners and administrators to make more money and ensure the economic success of their organizations. By themselves, actions of this sort would hardly be of interest; business firms frequently relocate when there is an opportunity to make more money. However, what makes the movement of sports franchises of particular importance are the financial incentives that the owners of professional teams extract from cities before they agree to move. The professional sports franchise movements indicate that team owners do move to make more money, but only after they receive an impressive list of financial guarantees from their new home. Indeed, the old refrain may need to be changed from

> "Root, root, root for the home team" to
> "Spend, spend, spend to get a home team."

The purpose of this chapter is to examine the wisdom of the investments that local governments must make to attract sports franchises. At one time, when teams moved, all that was expected or hoped was stronger financial backing from fans in the new city. However, after the city of Los Angeles agreed to subsidize the Dodgers and their move to the West Coast, a new era was initiated—the era of direct municipal subsidies to the owners of professional sports teams. As the depth of the investment of local governments in sports has increased, it is time to pose a series of questions concerning the wisdom of these investments.

First, do cities make money when they invest in professional sports teams? As other articles in this volume clearly establish, cities have frequently provided fiscal incentives to attract business through tax abatements and revenue bonds. These and other instruments have also been used to lure professional teams from one city to another. Can a city that subsidizes a team expect to find its taxes or other revenues enhanced sufficiently to make the investment profitable? This is the first issue that this chapter will address.

The second issue to be studied involves the social implications of the city's investments. Are these subsidies actually a benefit to all the citizens in a community or are they a method by which higher-income individuals reduce their own risks and investments?

To consider both of these questions, this chapter is organized into four sections. Following this introduction, the second section of the chapter considers the emergence of municipal subsidies as a requirement for a team to move, and provides a case history of the movement of two different teams, the Texas Rangers and the Dallas Cowboys. In the third section, the investments of two cities are contrasted with their economic returns. Based on these data, the final section of this chapter focuses on the two basic questions raised: can cities make money when they invest in professional sports, and are these municipal investments nothing more than subsidies to local business elites to help minimize their risks?

The Return of the Carpetbaggers: Owners and the Movement of Sports Franchises

All of the memorabilia of the old Colts is gone, all taken out of the building that night and dumped into a van ... Buddy Young's shoes ... Unitas' jersey ... all those things that mean nothing to any other city but us.

William D. Schaefer, Mayor of Baltimore, on the midnight
move of the Colts to Indianapolis (Howard Cosell, 1985)

The Beginning of Subsidies

Social scientists are fond of identifying watershed events, those
particular occurrences which change social systems for better or worse.
Because it established the expectation that cities would provide subsidies for the owners of sports teams, the movement of the Brooklyn
Dodgers to Los Angeles and of the New York Giants to San Francisco
changed sports in American life perhaps more than any other event. To
be sure, franchises had moved before the Dodgers and Giants headed
to the West Coast. In the earliest years of professional sports, movements were common, as teams sought markets that would enable them
to maximize profits. In most instances, when movements did occur,
support for a team was declining in one city, usually because there were
two teams in the same area.

In this respect, the movement of the Dodgers and the Giants was
an important exception. There was, of course, another team in the area.
The New York Yankees were in the midst of one of their heralded
streaks of consecutive pennants and championships. Yet, despite the
success of the Yankees, New York had little trouble supporting all three
of its baseball teams. Each of the teams played in different boroughs of
the city. And, at the time of the Dodgers' move to Los Angeles, Brooklyn
as a city would have held the title of the fourth largest in the country,
with a population of more than 1.75 million people. Both the Giants
and the Dodgers had substantial followings among their fans. The
Dodgers, or "Dem Bums" as they were commonly called, were probably
the most loved sports team of any time. With all this love and adulation,
why did Walter O'Malley leave the friendly confines of Brooklyn?
Money was the answer: the potential to earn more money than the
Dodgers could ever earn in Brooklyn.

The ability to earn all this money was a result of professional
sports' receiving special exemption from the anti-trust laws that pro-
hibit businesses from limiting new entrants into the market.[5] In 1956,
there were no major league baseball teams in the state of California; in
fact, there were no teams west of Kansas City in the American League
and of St. Louis in the National League. Exempt from anti-trust legislation, major league baseball, in the 1950s, was really a cartel of sixteen
members who regulated where and when baseball would be played. As

a cartel, the sixteen owners controlled the supply of baseball, since no team could join the leagues without their approval. In any situation where demand for a commodity—in this case a professional baseball team—outstrips supply, cities that desired baseball teams had to offer owners of existing franchises inducements to move.

Los Angeles, on the verge of its tremendous population explosion, wanted a major league baseball team to match its recently acquired football team, the Rams (from Cleveland). To lure the Dodgers to Los Angeles, the city of Los Angeles made a most impressive offer. First, until a new stadium could be built, the Los Angeles Coliseum would be home for the Dodgers. The Coliseum at that time had a seating capacity exceeding one hundred thousand, more than three times that of Ebbets Field. The first baseball game played in the Coliseum, an exhibition game between the Los Angeles Dodgers and the New York Yankees, attracted more than ninety thousand fans. Second, the city of Los Angeles also gave to the Dodgers all the land they would need to build their own stadium, the Chavez Ravine. It is somehow ironic that this land was originally identified as a site for low-income housing, but was given by the city to the O'Malley family for their beloved Dodgers. Finally, all of the promises made by the city fathers in Los Angeles about fan support in their baseball-starved city were ultimately found to be true. The Dodgers regularly attract more than two million fans a year and in some years have attracted more than three million.

While not concerned about the travel costs associated with a West Coast team playing teams mostly located in the East, the Dodgers did desire the creation of a natural rivalry in the West. Perhaps to avoid the hostile reaction of fans if they returned to New York to play the Giants, the Dodgers convinced the city of San Francisco to attract the New York Giants to the West Coast. In one winter, then, the city of New York lost two of its baseball teams to the state of California; more than half a century of fan loyalty was traded for increased profits.

The watershed dimensions of the move of the Dodgers and the Giants were, essentially fourfold. First, the ability of team owners to move their franchises from cities where fan loyalty and support were strong was established. Second, cities were virtually unable to block any move. Third, fan loyalty in the previous location was shown to be of little or no consequence to an owner in deciding to move to a new home, if there were eager fans in the new city. Lastly, and of paramount importance, the precedent of public subsidies for the relocation of professional sports franchises was clearly established. In effect, there was now a basic expectation of substantial inducement involving either a stadium for which the team paid little or no rent, the transfer to the team of a substantial amount of land for the building of a stadium, or some other fiscal inducement to increase the owner's profits if his team was to be moved.

What the Dodgers and Giants did for professional sports was to place them on an equal footing with other businesses with regard to plant relocation. The relocation of other businesses was commonly associated with industrial bonds and tax abatements to reduce a firm's costs and increase owners' profits. The Dodgers and Giants simply wanted this same set of local policies applied to professional sports. Cities, it seems, have always competed for the favor of corporate location decisions. Professional sports differ from automobile plants only in the sense that they represent part of the recreation industry and not the heavy industry for which industrial bonds and tax abatements have been commonly used to attract businesses. If these subsidies were available to owners of other businesses, why should they not be available to owners of professional sports teams? The answer seemed obvious to team owners. In fact, it would actually be easier for professional sports teams to secure subsidies since through their leagues they limited the number of franchises. While fans would remember baseball and football in the 1960s and 1970s as the eras of Maris, Mantle, Robinson, Gibson, Jackson, Namath, Staubach, and the Super Bowl, America's cities would begin to understand how the game of corporate relocation and subsidies was really played. Baseball and football were about to join the corporate ranks and have communities bid for their recreational services.

How the Game is Really Played

In terms of understanding the scope of public sector investment in professional sports, the numbers sometimes become a bit numbing. Within the last decade, for example, it has been reported that the city of New York spent $100 million to keep the New York Yankees from following the New York Jets (football) and the New York Giants (football) to the Meadowlands sports complex in New Jersey. The city of Philadelphia will spend $20 million over 20 years to keep the Philadelphia Eagles from moving to Phoenix; the city of Baltimore spent $24 million to keep the Colts in Baltimore, only to lose the football team to Indianapolis' Hoosier Dome; finally, in 1982, the citizens in Minneapolis–St. Paul voted to support a $55 million bond package to build the Hubert Humphrey Dome to keep the Minnesota Vikings from moving to Jacksonville, Phoenix, or some other city.[6]

While it is certainly possible to consider the policy and societal consequence of public investments of this nature, the real dimensions of the power relationship between sports franchises and local governments are only evident through case study analyses. Only in this way is it possible to understand the subtle and the not-so-subtle pressures used to secure subsidies for sports franchise moves.

The movement of two franchises—one to Texas and the other within Texas—provides a rich background for understanding the tactics used by the professional sports cartel to ensure their financial position. These case studies also vividly illustrate that citizens are frequently ill-informed and ill-advised on the ramifications of the subsidies provided. Lastly, the case studies demonstrate that the economic return to cities from their investments is, at best, dubious, and, at worst, a real loss in terms of earnings and economic growth.

Arlington, Texas, and the Texas Rangers

While trips to the ballpark had usually meant fans going "downtown," by the mid 1960s, there was a movement of professional sports franchises to suburban cities. In part, this movement was a reaction to the greater perceived safety of suburban locations and the observation that wealthier fans, likely to spend more money at games, often lived in the suburbs. In other instances, race was a more obvious factor, as owners sought locations in predominately white areas.

Whatever the reason for the desire to locate in suburban areas, in 1971, the Washington Senators—the second team of that name—began negotiations with several cities, as the majority owner, Robert Short, sought to leave the nation's capital. In 1972, the Senators announced they were leaving Washington for Arlington, Texas. Arlington, a large suburban city midway between Dallas and Fort Worth has, today, a population of more than two hundred and twenty-five thousand in a metropolitan area of more than three million residents. In 1972, with approximately ninety-five thousand residents, it had a stadium for a minor league team which could hold only 12,500 people. The fiscal subsidies that brought the Senators from the nation's capital to a minor league stadium is probably the best example of the use of incentives to benefit a team's owner.

One of the requirements for a city in competing for a professional baseball team is demonstration of popular support for the economic incentives necessary to attract a franchise. Without this tangible evidence, owners might be reluctant to move a team for fear of a possible political backlash against municipal officials who commit public funds for a sports franchise.

The citizens of Arlington (and Tarrant County) declared their interest in starting to attract a major league franchise by passing a $10 million bond issue in May 1970, earmarked, in part, for the development and construction of a stadium with a seating capacity of 12,500. Officials knew that such a stadium would not be sufficient for a major league team; however, it was hoped the passage of the bond and the development of plans to increase the seating capacity of the stadium to major league standards, approximately fifty thousand seats, would illustrate the interest and commitment of Arlington.

All of the improvements to Arlington Stadium were done with public funds. No private money was involved. In terms of convincing voters to support the stadium improvements, Arlington's leaders "sold" professional baseball as the centerpiece of the city's emerging recreation industry. Years earlier, the city had convinced the forerunner of the Six Flags corporation to build one of its largest theme parks in Arlington. Professional baseball would continue the development of the recreational complex that would give the city a base of "clean" industry. After all, baseball and amusement parks do not pollute the air like the smoke from stacks and the other discharge from heavy industries. Arlington's hope was to build a secure tax base on the backbone of clean industry. In this way, the public's investment in the stadium seemed like a very sensible growth strategy. Virtually everyone expected restaurants and hotels to generate jobs and sales tax revenues.

Arlington's leaders were attempting to develop an entertainment "growth pole," and articulated their intentions through a highly organized coalition of prominent local entrepreneurs. A growth pole of economic activity can be considered a collection of related businesses each designed to attract other activities because of the presence of existing facilities. In terms of a city's finances, the local government commits the seed money to start the growth pole; with the existence of several activities, others follow in an attempt to locate in areas thought to be fertile centers for additional business development. In effect, a growth pole can be considered nothing more, but nothing less, than the old adage, "nothing attracts success more than success." Public dollars provide the first rush of success, and then the private dollars follow; at least that is the expectation.

With the Six Flags amusement park and the Texas Rangers baseball team, Arlington's growth strategy entailed using public funds to create an entertainment growth pole which would attract private-sector investments in hotels, restaurants, night clubs, and related activities destined to make Arlington the entertainment capital of Texas. Indeed, in the years that followed, two water theme parks did open in Arlington. A publicly financed effort failed in the mid-1970s; a privately financed park opened in the early 1980s, and still operates.

Arlington was not alone in its desire to create a growth pole of clean industry. In a similar way, the city of Louisville's investment in an arts district; an effort to create a growth pole around a cultural base of activities that not only attract other cultural activities, but industries whose leaders want to live in the emerging cultural center of the Midwest. What Arlington was attempting to do with family entertainment, Louisville was attempting to do with culture. If each strategy was successful, not only would entertainment companies come to the city, but it was hoped numerous other corporations would also, as the recreational opportunities in the area became an excellent element in recruiting employees. In both cities, then, what emerged was a growth coalition comprised of civic leaders, bankers, labor leaders, real estate developers, and other entrepreneurs eager to benefit from the new business.

Such a growth coalition has the potential to become an important political force. As a political force, it not only can articulate its position and demands against opposing viewpoints (anti-growth groups or sentiments), but it can also become a self-reinforcing forum. The value of such a forum should not be underestimated. It is this function of the growth coalition which serves to keep the momentum for economic development moving forward when doubts or criticism arise. In a sense, all members of the coalition can use each other to reinforce the view that growth is good and what is being done is in the best interests of the city and all members of the local business elite. While this self-reinforcement is underway, public funds are being invested, with the members of the growth coalition likely to gain the most from the decision of any sports franchise to relocate in their city.

With the passage of the bond issue and the construction of the sports facility and supporting road network, Arlington's municipal officials opened negotiations with several franchises concerning the possibility of their relocation. With expansion—the addition of new clubs by the major leagues—eliminated as an option for Arlington by the existing owners, attracting an established team became the only route for Arlington if it wanted to be a "major league city."

During the time city officials from Arlington were talking with owners about a possible relocation, two teams did move, but neither selected Arlington. The Seattle Pilots moved to Milwaukee to become the Brewers after the Milwaukee Braves moved to Atlanta. In part, the movement of the Seattle franchise was designed to prevent a legal action by the city of Milwaukee against major league baseball and the Braves. With these two teams having been reassigned, the city of Arlington turned its attention to one of the existing franchises known to be in financial distress—the Washington Senators.

The Washington Senators' franchise has had one of baseball's most interesting histories. The Washington Senators, in 1971, were the second version of the team. The first, perennial losers and the heroes of the Broadway show "Damn Yankees," were taken by their owner, Calvin Griffith, to the Minneapolis–St. Paul area. In an effort to thwart possible federal reprisals against baseball for that move, the American League expanded shortly after and created a second Washington Senators team. This team, owned by Robert Short, was no more successful than its predecessors; by the end of 1971, Mr. Short had accumulated more than $10 million in past-due bills.

While the Senators were clearly a "second division" baseball team, two factors in addition to their fiscal plight made them an attractive commodity. First, since the major leagues had recently expanded, it was unlikely that there would be another expansion soon. Second, when there were relocations of existing teams, the loudest complaints usually came from the state's elected representatives and senators in Congress who could always threaten legislative action against baseball. This threat was obviously less with the city of Washington, D.C. With no senators in Congress, the city was weak compared to the congressional delegation of any state that might be the future home of the Washington Senators.[7]

With these two factors in mind, the American League told cities interested in attracting the Senators that all debts involved had to be settled before any franchise relocation was approved.[8] If any city wanted the Senators, approximately $10 million would have to be given to owner Short. Giving money to the owner of a professional sports team to secure relocation is tricky business for a city, if not plainly illegal. In short, if the city of Arlington was to secure the movement of the Washington Senators to Texas, a way had to be found to transfer money to Short.

To get the money, something had to be sold to the city. In terms of the team's liquid assets, aside from players, teams can sell their concession rights (food, beverages, and souvenirs sold at the stadium) or the broadcast rights to their games not part of the agreements between major league baseball and the major television networks. Under substantial pressure from other cities willing to buy these broadcast rights if the Senators would relocate to their area (the city of Denver had agreed to buy the rights if the Senators would play their home games in Denver's Mile High Stadium), the city of Arlington agreed to give the Washington Senators $7.5 million for the local broadcast rights of team games for a period of 10 years. After the 10 years elapsed, the team would retain ownership of the broadcast rights. With the $7.5 million paid to the Washington Senators, and the execution of a series of additional agreements to expand the existing stadium to a seating capacity of 50,000, the city of Arlington became the home of the Texas Rangers and major league baseball.

Few cities, Arlington included, would actually want to manage the media rights to a baseball team's games. Those are tasks best left to television and radio stations. Prior to the actual purchase of the media rights and immediately after, the city did attempt to find a buyer for the package; none could be found. The costs of establishing and maintaining a local network, the private sector seemed to be saying, could not be amortized over a 10-year lease. The city of Arlington, after buying the rights, found itself in the media business.

The city of Arlington also had other financial investments to make. Not only was the stadium to be improved, but the existing minor league team playing in the stadium had to have its lease cancelled. The total cost of the media rights and the payment of damages to the minor league team came to $8.4 million for the city of Arlington. To expand the stadium to a seating capacity of 50,000 and provide the necessary road and parking improvements, the city planned to spend another $20,360,000. The direct investments by the city, then, totaled $28,760,000. If interest charges are added to this figure, Arlington's total investment amounted to $44,368,451.[9] Under the original agreements with the team, the maximum revenue the city would have received from this investment was to be approximately $22 million. The projected loss, then, would have been the remaining $22 million, which the city hoped to recapture in extra tax revenues, jobs, etc. This projection will be evaluated after reviewing the history of the Dallas Cowboys and the city of Irving, Arlington's neighbor to the east.

As a postscript to Arlington's history with the Texas Rangers, the city could never afford to meet all of its expansion commitments. Revenues at the stadium never reached anticipated levels, as the team posted losing records in several consecutive seasons. After facing an ultimatum that would have resulted in the city's losing the team if the stadium was not expanded, Arlington built an upper deck, expanding seating capacity to approximately 42,500. To do this, the city pledged the parking revenues from the stadium to another bond issue. This had the effect of further reducing the city's income. Faced with continuous maintenance problems, the city agreed in 1983 to end its history in the sports business by "selling" the facility to the Rangers in exchange for a small payment from the team, and the team's agreement to assume all of the bond payments remaining on the stadium, the upper deck, and the parking and road improvements. Each of these bonds, of course, carried interest rates that were lower than those the team could have secured in the bond market if they had borrowed the money, since the income from all municipal bonds are exempt from federal taxes. It would be difficult not to consider this very favorable loan rate as another substantial financial subsidy for the team.

Irving, Texas and America's Team

In American sports, there are a handful of teams that evoke emotional response from all fans. Sports fans either love or hate the New York Yankees, the Boston Celtics, and the Dallas Cowboys. In Texas, you lose your Texas citizenship if you do not love the Dallas Cowboys. The city of Irving, located next to the city of Dallas, loved the Cowboys and was ultimately selected by them as the site of their home field, Texas Stadium.

Beginning with their admission to the National Football League, the Dallas Cowboys played their home games in the Cotton Bowl located in the southern part of the city of Dallas. South Dallas, as it is known locally, is one of Dallas' lowest-income communities, and virtually all its residents are black. The location of the Cotton Bowl in this sort of a community was always a problem for the Cowboys and their season ticket holders. As the team became more and more popular, dissatisfaction with a facility located in a minority community became a larger and larger problem. Fans, the Cowboys argued, did not feel safe at the Cotton Bowl, especially at night.[10] Cowboys' officials developed four separate plans for a new facility. None of these plans were accepted by the city of Dallas. As frustrations grew between the team and the city's business leaders, meetings were held with the city of Irving to discuss the location of a new stadium on the Irving side of the Irving-Dallas border.

What actually developed in Dallas was a dispute between two competing groups of elite economic actors. The established older elite wanted to keep the Cowboys at the Cotton Bowl. They planned to rebuild that part of the city and create an economic growth pole around the success and image of the Dallas Cowboys. The ownership of the Cowboys wanted to create their own economic center in an area where they would control development. A stand-off ensued that sent the Cowboys into the suburbs to find a city willing to permit the team to control the development of a stadium.

After several months of negotiations, the Dallas Cowboys and the city of Irving reached an agreement for the building of Texas Stadium. It was agreed that the city of Irving would build the new home for the team and give the Cowboys a lease for the use of the facility. Included in this lease was a provision granting the Cowboys the right to approve of all other uses of the stadium during the NFL season and to refuse use of the facility to any other football team at any other time of the year, whether a college team or a team from another football league.

To finance the construction of the stadium, it was agreed the city of Irving would sell to each season ticket holder a municipal bond worth $250. No season ticket was to be available without this bond. The sale of the bonds raised $15 million of the needed $25 million for the construction of the stadium. The additional $10 million was secured through the purchase of a senior lien note from the city of Irving by the owner of the Cowboys. The city of Irving, then got into the sports business for no money down, but was ultimately responsible for retiring the $25 million in bonds. It was anticipated that the rent from the stadium, as well as the increased tax revenues as a result of the stadium, would generate the income needed to offset this risk.

The movement of the Dallas Cowboys to Irving provides an illustration of the ability of a team basically to set its own terms for the development of a facility. Elite forces in the city of Dallas were probably guilty of being inflexible in terms of pursuing their own economic agenda; they were not willing to compromise with the Cowboys on a specific location that would have permitted the development of the kind of facility the Cowboys wanted. The team's decision to leave Dallas was a clear lesson of which local elite held the upper hand. The team, through its ability to move, was able to secure the exact kind of facility it wanted.

The Dallas elite that would not compromise with the Cowboys did not, in a total sense, lose by the movement of the Cowboys. A great deal of the economic spinoff from the team still benefits Dallas. When teams come to play the Cowboys, they stay in Dallas' elegant hotels and visit its restaurants. Irving has never developed the total infrastructure necessary to support the ancillary consumption that revolves around football teams. In this sense, then, the Dallas economic elite did not lose by refusing to meet the team's demands.

The city of Irving, while appearing to risk very little, also learned an important lesson. While the ability to have a stadium for little or no money and to become the home of the beloved Dallas Cowboys were obviously important inducements for the city, they also assumed responsibility for the long-term maintenance of the facility. Suppose, before the bonds were paid, the facility needed repairs. All of the bonds negotiated by the city were for 30 years. However, facilities do suffer abuse from normal use and the activities of more than sixty thousand people at most events. If repairs were needed, the city would have to find the necessary revenues. As the city soon realized, the expected financial returns were less than anticipated, as much of the economic activity surrounding the team remained in Dallas. This left the city without a sufficient reserve to repair the stadium and eventually forced the use of public money for the maintenance of normal items associated with the use of the stadium.

Do Cities Subsidize Professional Sports? Arlington and Irving's Economic Returns

The bottom line, so to speak, when a municipality commits funds to a private business project, is the extent to which the investment really increases the city's wealth. Assessing the economic impact of a professional sports team involves at least two important issues. First, at the same time that a city erects a stadium, it is affected by other factors that may influence economic conditions and taxes. These other forces, such as the construction of a new airport, the development of an office center, the extension of tax abatements to attract new industries, etc. could each have a major impact on a city's economy. Second, to actually evaluate the impact of a sports franchise on a city's economy, the emphasis must be on the extra income diverted to local businesses by the presence of a team. Attendance at a game represents one of many recreational pursuits that can be enjoyed in a community. In the absence of a professional sports team, people do spend money on other recreational activities. The key issue is whether or not the existence of the team brings new recreational dollars into a city or keeps the dollars from other communities. Put another way, analysts must be sure the sports investment does not simply reallocate a finite amount of dollars from one sector of the local economy to another.

To assess the impact of the Texas Rangers on Arlington and the Dallas Cowboys on Irving, I compared the tax revenues of these two cities with the two central cities—Dallas and Fort Worth—and five other cities in the Dallas/Fort Worth area similar to Irving and Arlington. Since cities earn money through their sales taxes and property tax revenues, it could be expected that the cities which invested in sports facilities would earn additional tax revenues. It is also possible the cities may have been able to reduce property taxes and increase services, if the sales tax revenues from the sports operations were quite large.

To assess the outcomes from the investments in professional sports, the tax revenues, service levels, and municipal debt in the four years preceding the investments by Arlington and Irving were compared with the same data for the four years after the investments. The data are reported not only for the investor cities, but the two central cities of Dallas and Fort Worth, and the five other cities similar to Arlington and Irving.

The key issue assessed was the rate of change in these revenues and obligations. Being located close together and in competition with one another for residential and business locations, each of the cities were affected similarly by regional phenomenon and engaged in similar developmental policies.

In terms of sales tax revenues, large percentage increases were reported for both Arlington and Irving. Comparing the post-investment period with the pre-investment period, Arlington's annual growth rate increased 45.3% and Irving's increased 42.4%. These increases surpassed the rates for all comparison cities except one, Richardson, which enjoyed a 203.7% increase. Three of the comparison cities actually saw their annual growth rates decline. Both the central cities experienced an increase in sales tax growth with Fort Worth enjoying an increase of 194.3% while Dallas experienced an increase of 18.2% in its annual growth rate.

Arlington and Irving also enjoyed substantial increases in property tax revenues with annual growth rate increases for Irving surpassing all comparison cities and Arlington's increase surpassed by one only comparison city. The increase in Fort Worth's annual growth rate for property taxes in the post-investment period was larger than Arlington's, but not Irving's; Dallas' growth rate was less than either of the investor cities.

In terms of income flow, then, the data in Tables 4-1 and 4-2 indicate that the investor cities did realize an increase greater than most other cities. However, increased revenues by themselves do not mean citizens are enjoying more services for less tax dollars. All municipal investments require support services; it is possible the additional revenues received by Arlington and Irving simply *offset* the costs of traffic, public safety, street maintenance, etc. associated with their investments in sports.

To consider this possibility, Table 4–3 was created, which relates spending for all municipal services to tax collections. A positive number indicates spending for all services increased more than property tax revenues increased; a negative number would mean taxes increased faster than spending for services.

In the pre-investment period, Arlington's spending for services increased 6.4%; in the post-investment period, there was a decline of 1.6%. This meant taxes increased faster than expenditures for services. Spending for services in Irving in the pre-investment period declined by .5% relative to tax increases, but increased in the post-investment period by 2.2%.

In each of the comparison cities except Richardson, spending for services increased in the post-investment period faster than taxes and, in one city, Grand Prairie, the increase in spending for services over tax increases was less in the post-investment period than in the pre-investment period. For both of the central cities there was a substantial decline in the growth of spending for services. Dallas, which had a 10% growth rate during the pre-investment period had a −.8% decline in the post-investment period. Fort Worth, which had a 12.7% increase in the pre-investment period, had a 1.2% increase in the post-investment period.

The last table, which describes the fiscal position of all cities, is a tabulation of bonded indebtedness (Table 4-4) and compares annual growth rates in the pre-investment and post-investment periods. The annual average increase in bonded indebtedness increased 47.1% in Arlington when the pre- and post-investment periods are compared; the increase in Irving was 62.9%. Only one city, Mesquite, had an increase greater than this, and several cities had substantial *declines* in the

TABLE 4.1. Per Capita Sales Tax Revenues, By City: Pre- and Post-Investment Period Revenue (in millions) Period

Cities	Pre-Investment Year				Annual Growth Rate	Post-Investment Year				Annual Growth Rate
	1968	1969	1970	1971		1972	1973	1974	1975	
INVESTOR										
Arlington	NA	$20.84	$22.52	$25.00	9.5%	$27.83	$35.00	$35.24	$31.68	13.8%
Irving	$15.03	15.26	16.42	18.20	6.6	20.26	23.28	28.61	26.53	9.4
COMPARISON										
Garland	NA	15.49	16.45	18.09	8.1	21.32	20.03	22.72	22.39	1.6
Grand Prairie	11.87	12.08	12.63	13.85	5.3	15.22	21.09	22.15	18.88	7.4
Hurst	NA	17.29	20.91	26.69	24.2	29.17	30.13	33.82	40.40	11.5
Mesquite	12.52	13.82	15.87	21.04	18.9	23.86	25.86	29.44	30.12	8.1
Richardson	14.96	15.21	14.71	16.20	2.7	19.92	19.58	23.58	25.21	8.2
CENTRAL										
Dallas	24.94	26.99	27.46	29.26	5.5	32.60	44.44	49.21	39.39	6.5
Fort Worth	19.85	20.45	20.54	21.99	3.5	23.22	29.63	32.17	31.20	10.3

NA: not applicable

Source: Sales Tax Reports, Office of the Comptroller, Austin, Texas, 1968–1975.

TABLE 4.2. Total Property Tax Collections, By City: Pre- and Post-Investment Period Tax Collection (in thousands) Period

Cities	Pre-Investment Year					Annual Growth Rate	Post-Investment Year				Annual Growth Rate
	1967	1968	1969	1970	1971		1972	1973	1974	1975	
INVESTOR											
Arlington	$2,189	$2,390	$2,762	$3,074	$3,532	12.7	$3,956	$5,019	$5,561	$6,175	16.0%
Irving	2,350	2,537	2,603	2,913	3,045	6.7	4,602	5,759	7,241	8,693	23.6
COMPARISON											
Garland	843	1,301	1,346	1,746	2,218	27.4	2,873	3,538	2,950	3,366	5.4
Grand Prairie	1,078	1,346	1,621	1,801	2,391	22.0	2,699	3,031	3,368	3,836	12.4
Hurst	612	798	909	1,044	1,197	18.3	1,475	1,519	1,615	1,567	2.0
Mesquite	1,516	1,609	1,742	1,914	2,254	10.4	2,653	3,455	3,686	3,944	14.1
Richardson	2,041	2,398	2,721	2,985	3,469	14.2	3,742	4,358	4,780	5,350	12.7
CENTRAL											
Dallas	55,822	59,103	61,173	68,561	80,939	9.7	89,735	94,170	99,084	104,918	5.3
Fort Worth	18,067	16,829	17,974	19,733	21,886	4.9	23,118	24,208	25,687	31,664	11.1

Source: Moody's Investors Services (1967–1977), Municipal and Government Manual. New York: Moody Investment Service

TABLE 4.3. Relative Growth Rates in Property Taxes and Spending for Services, by City: Pre- and Post-Investment Period

City	Period Pre-Investment (1967-1971)	Period Post-Investment (1972-1975)
INVESTOR		
Arlington	6.4%	− 1.6%
Irving	−0.5	2.2
COMPARISON		
Garland	−1.0	1.9
Grand Prairie	9.2	7.0
Hurst	−3.8	11.5
Mesquite	−4.3	4.9
Richardson	4.7	−0.5
CENTRAL		
Dallas	10.0	−0.8
Fort Worth	12.7	1.2

Note: If coefficient positive, growth rate in spending greater than growth rate of property taxes; if negative, growth rate of taxes greater.
Calculation: [Annual Growth Rate in Spending]−[Annual Growth Rate of Property Taxes]
Sources: City Budget Reports, 1968–1975.

rate at which debt was increased when pre- and post-investment periods are compared.

In summary, the two investor cities, Arlington and Irving, did see their revenues increase more than most of the comparison cities. For residents of Arlington, however, this increase in revenues *did not* translate into more public services for less dollars. Indeed, Arlington's expenditures for services did not increase as rapidly as did property taxes. Residents, then, were paying more taxes and receiving the same or fewer services. Residents of Irving were in a somewhat better position after their city's investment. They saw their services increase with their tax payments, but the rate of increase was larger in several of the comparison cities. These other cities, then, were able to improve services for fewer tax dollars without investing in professional sports. Finally, both Arlington and Irving increased their debt substantially and at a rate that surpassed all cities in the study except one. During the period studied, several cities actually reduced the rate at which they ac-

TABLE 4.4. **Average Annual Percentage Changes in Bonded Indebtedness By City**

Cities	Pre-Investment Period	Post-Investment Period	Percent Change
INVESTOR			
Arlington	20.4%	30.0%	47.1%
Irving	12.4	20.2	62.9
COMPARISON			
Garland	11.0	11.7	6.4
Grand Prairie	14.1	12.0	−14.9
Hurst	6.2	7.3	17.7
Mesquite	2.7	4.8	77.8
Richardson	8.9	6.6	−25.8
Central Cities			
Dallas	10.0	5.0	−50.0
Fort Worth	7.7	−0.6	−107.8

SOURCES: Annual budgets of all cities, 1967 through 1975.

cumulated debt. Arlington and Irving's residents have a legacy of debt which will continue for at least two decades.

Elites and the Use of Public Resources

The experience of Arlington and Irving in the 1970s with professional sports is not unlike the trials and tribulations other cities are facing today. Within the last few years, the city of Los Angeles, a legend in the history of convincing franchises to come West, witnessed the move of the Rams out to Anaheim, only to recover by luring the Oakland Raiders to Los Angeles. Both moves involved the pledging of millions of dollars of public money for the enhancement of facilities to permit greater profits for the owners of the Rams and the Raiders. Now, as this chapter is prepared for publication, the New Jersey Meadowlands Sports Complex has presented New York Yankee owner George Steinbrenner with a proposal to build a new facility for the Yankees, guarantee the Yankees an annual paid attendance of 2.2 million people, and pay the Yankees' rent at their old home in the Bronx through the end of their lease in 1999. These rental payments would amount to approximately $17,000,000. The Meadowlands Complex of New Jersey is preparing an offer in excess of $125 million to lure the Yankees across the Hudson River.[11] By comparison, the cities of Arlington and Irving in Texas may have performed minor miracles to land professional teams as cheaply as they did. Still, the nagging question remains, "Is the spending of public money and the issuing of municipal bonds for professional sports franchises an appropriate use of public resources?"

We live in an era when "economic development" and "revitalization" are key policy phrases for cities.[12] In such instances, it is hard and often politically inadvisable to speak against any form of economic development. Yet the evidence available on economic returns from professional sports franchise raises serious questions about the wisdom of investment of public funds in these projects. For smaller cities like Arlington and Irving, it seems difficult and, in the long run, unlikely that they can ever recoup the benefits generated by a professional sports franchises. There are, indeed, economic returns, but these are probably enjoyed by an entire region, and not just the host city unless it is very large and can encompass all the ancillary spending that occurs as a result of fans' attendance at games (e.g., sales tax revenues from restaurants, hotels, and so forth).

Can a large central city like New York or Dallas capture the economic benefits of professional sports? Put another way, should the City of New York spend an additional $100 million to keep the Yankees there? The City spent $100 million 10 years ago to keep the Yankees home,[13] yet the Yankees are restless again.

If the results from Dallas offer any indication, New York will be likely to reap substantial benefits from the Yankees even if the Yankees move to New Jersey. Virtually all of the teams that play in Texas Stadium, including the Cowboys themselves, stay in hotels in Dallas, not in Irving or Arlington, the night before each game. Through 1981, only one American League team that came to Texas to play the Rangers stayed in an Arlington hotel. Visitors to the area still seem to prefer Dallas to Irving, unless they stay at the airport, which is actually closer to Irving than Dallas. The best illustration of Dallas' ability to capture the economic benefits of Irving's investment is the fact that the Dallas Chamber of Commerce has always paid the costs of proposing to the NFL that Texas Stadium be a site for the Super Bowl. The Dallas Chamber is well aware that an Irving Super Bowl would be served by

Dallas' hotels and restaurants, not those in Irving. Central cities have the support structure of hotels and restaurants that offer the ancillary services that professional teams and their fans require. Central cities are the large attraction, and people will stay in New York when they want to go to the game in the Meadowlands, or in Dallas when they come to see the Cowboys.

If the economic returns from professional sports franchises are so speculative for smaller cities and tend to accrue to a region or a large central city, then why do smaller cities still consider spending so much for teams? The answer to this question lies in the assessment of who, within these cities, benefits and how they manage to form a growth pole political force that manages to convince local officials of the prudence of investing public resources in professional sports.

There are elites in each area that bids for a franchise who will reap considerable gain if the team does select their city. Land prices will rise dramatically, and there are franchise agreements (souvenirs, food, support services, legal fees, etc.) that are also very profitable. These gains are even more profitable if the elite does not risk its own resources but commits public funds to a team. Beyond its time investment, which is likely to be substantial, a local elite need risk none or little of its own money while negotiating on behalf of a city to seek relocation of a team there. If the relocation is arranged there will be substantial profit for the elites. And, since the local government is usually responsible for the money committed, even if the venture fails in the long run, the short-term profits for the elites can be substantial. For example, suppose after fifteen years a stadium needs repairs, or a team decides to move to another city. The profits made by certain members of the elite will already have been reaped, and the financial responsibility for maintaining the stadium, even if vacant, and its roads will be borne by the public sector.

With these kind of incentives, a basis for the formation of a local growth coalition is established. It simply remains for the coalition to convince well-intentioned public officials, and the electorate if public support is needed, of the potential economic and tax benefits of clean industries similar to professional sports.

This analysis is not meant to suggest that all of the individuals involved with the relocation of franchises are corrupt or seek to use the public's resources to better themselves economically. To the contrary, there are many people who do get involved in the professional sports mania for the spirit and honor of their communities. In New York City, William Shea did everything in his power to bring National League baseball back to the city, and he did get the Mets to Queens, if not to Brooklyn or Manhattan. In Arlington, Texas, Tom Vandergriff, the city's former mayor and representative in Congress, also stands as a leader who thought professional sports would benefit all of Arlington. These are examples of individuals caught up by the whirlwind of support generated by a growth coalition which convinced itself that all elements in the city would "win" with professional sports.

While the case is clear in terms of the economic position of smaller cities and their investment in professional sports, a related issue which must be addressed is whether or not central cities should try to attract teams because of the economic growth they will bring. The answer to this question lies in the overall economics of professional sports. Because of the economic structure of professional sports, teams have been able to pay athletes astronomical salaries. The list of player millionaires grows yearly. In recent years, for example, Kareem Abdul Jabbar, Don Mattingly, Dwight Gooden, Dave Winfield, Steve Garvey, and a host of other athletes have been paid annual salaries in excess of one million dollars. At the same time, the market value of most franchises, if not all, continues to increase. In 1985, the Dallas Cowboys were sold for more than $50 million. Clearly, there are large profits for both owners and laborers in this industry. With these profits and salaries (not even counting earnings from the product endorsements frequently made by star players), there would seem to be no justification for the involvement of local funds in sports projects. If public funds are used, it is a perverse form of subsidy: in essence, when governments commit their ability to borrow funds at favorable rates or their tax dollars to a professional sports team, they are subsidizing the incomes of individuals who regularly earn hundreds of thousands of dollars and corporations whose worth is clearly substantial. It almost appears that the middle and lower classes are being asked, through their elected officials and governments, to reduce the risks of investment for individuals and corporations whose income and wealth are but dreams for the millions who pay their local property taxes.

If these issues were not sufficiently sobering, there is still the question of what cities do with the sports facilities abandoned by teams that move. Both Oakland and Baltimore have facilities that are now used only half the year. If the Cowboys leave Irving or the Rangers leave Arlington, both of these cities will have to deal with abandoned properties just as other cities have had to deal with abandoned plants and factories. In this manner, cities not only have to commit public funds to secure a team, but they also must commit funds to "clean up" after the teams move to another city. It seems cities, once having invested in professional sports, cannot win, whether the team stays or leaves.

If professional teams can afford to pay athletes more than one million dollars for a single season and retain an extremely high value in the marketplace, these same teams should be able to afford their own facilities for practice and for games. That would leave cities free to deal with the pressing issues of housing and health care for people who long ago could not afford the costs of a ticket to the "Old Ball Game," much less the peanuts, popcorn, and crackerjacks. With returns on investments in professional sports as substantial as they are, it is time the elites involved in these businesses took the capitalistic risks they are so fond of recommending for others and stopped using the collective fiscal strength of cities to minimize their risks.

Notes

1. Harry Edwards, *The Sociology of Sport*. Glenbrook, IL: Dorsey Press, 1973.

2. Ibid.

3. Ezra Bowen, "Blowing the Whistle on Georgia." *Time,* February 24, 1986, p. 65.

4. David McNabb, "TCU Football Program Faces Loss of 25 Scholarships over Two Years." *Dallas Morning News,* sec. B, April 24, 1986, p. 1.

5. Steven R. Rivkin, "Sports Leagues and the Federal Anti-Trust Laws," in Roger G. Noll (ed.), *Government and the Sports Business*. Washington, DC: The Brookings Institution, 1974, pp: 387–410.

6. Howard Cosell, *I Never Played The Game*. New York: William Morrow and Company, 1985, p. 118.

7. Mark S. Rosentraub, "Financial Incentives, Locational Decision-Making, and Professional Sports: The Case of the Texas Rangers Baseball Network and the City of Arlington, Texas," in M.S. Rosentraub (ed.), *Financing Local Government: New Approaches to Old Problems*. Fort Collins, CO: The Western Social Science Association, 1977, pp. 51–68.

8. Ibid.

9. Ibid.

10. Mark S. Rosentraub and Samuel R. Nunn, "Suburban City Investment in Professional Sports: Estimating the Fiscal Returns of the Dallas Cowboys and the Texas Rangers." *American Behavioral Scientist,* January/February 1978, pp. 393–414.

11. John C. Dearie, "The New Jersey Yankees?" *The New York Times,* April 8, 1986. p. 27.

12. Terry Clark, Gerd M. Hellstern and Guido Martinotti, "Local Financial Crisis and Urban Innovation," in Terry Clark, Gerd M. Hellstern, and Guido Martinotti (eds.), *Urban Innovations as Response to Urban Fiscal Strain.* West Berlin: Verlag Europaische Perspektiven, 1985, pp. iii–viii.

13. Cosell; Dearie.

Chapter 5
Public Policy and Private Benefits: The Case of Industrial Revenue Bonds

Thomas S. Moore and Gregory D. Squires

Economic development has become the watchword among public officials at all levels of government. Urged on by their counterparts in the private sector and confronted with very real fiscal crises, public officials increasingly believe they cannot begin to respond to the variety of problems and responsibilities they face without first addressing the issue of economic development. In view of the deindustrialization of America, and particularly of the nation's "Rust Belt," economic development has dominated the policy agenda among public and private elites in the urban metropolis. With a few notable exceptions, the concept of economic development has been defined quite narrowly, and quite consistently, with the conservative ideology shaping recent urban policy.

This chapter examines the impact of one of the most popular economic development tools—industrial revenue bonds (IRBs). After describing the ideological perspective that has driven economic development policy, we will show how the rationale for industrial revenue bonds flows logically from that "definition of the situation." We review the available evidence on the impact of IRBs, including an empirical analysis of job generation in one statewide and two municipal IRB programs. Critical flaws are identified both in the rationale for and the implementation of IRBs and in the larger perspective in which they are rooted. We conclude with a discussion of potentially more productive avenues to economic development in general and utilization of IRBs in particular.

Growth Ideology as Economic Development

The prevailing perspective on economic development can be simply stated: by reducing taxes and government regulations, cutting social spending in order to reduce the federal deficit, and creating a good "business climate" (i.e., one conducive to private capital accumulation), entrepreneurship will flourish once again and more wealth will be generated, with enough trickling down to benefit all income groups. A host of financial incentive programs for business have consequently been created or expanded at all levels of government as cities and states across the nation compete with each other to attract businesses that, hopefully, will create jobs and generate economic development in their communities.[1] Industrial revenue bonds (IRBs) are currently among the most popular incentives.

Although long the stuff of conservative political philosophy,[2] these principles were explicitly stated by George Gilder[3] in a book labelled as "an inspiration and guide for the new administration" by one of President Reagan's closest advisors.[4] The administration subsequently offered an economic recovery program predicated on these principles.[5]

Perhaps the most controversial dimension of this approach lies in the call for government to reverse course and come to the aid of the wealthy, even at the expense (although presumably only in the short run) of the poor.[6] Business Week argued in 1980 that the "aspirations of the poor, the minorities, and the environmentalists," and other "special interest groups must recognize that their own unique goals cannot be satisfied if the U.S. cannot compete in world markets."[7] At all levels of public and private life, leaders listened and conceded that social problems would have to wait for economic growth, narrowly defined in terms of private capital accumulation.

If the Reagan Administration crystallized and catalyzed the implementation of this philosophy, it was in fact building on a growth strategy that originated at least 40 years ago. Over the past four decades the United States has looked to economic growth to resolve its social problems[8] and cities have served as "growth machines" facilitating the accumulation of capital by the private sector.[9] According to one tabulation, the number of state and local financial incentive programs offered in efforts to lure new industries or help existing firms to expand increased from 184 to 426 between 1966 and 1975[10] and the count is rising.[11] According to another, public subsidies to business grew from

$77.1 billion (9.2% of GNP) to $303.7 billion (13.9% GNP) between 1950 and 1980.[12]

The almost universally accepted approach to economic development, among public officials, is illustrated by marketing tactics employed by communities in presumably diverse states like South Carolina and Wisconsin. For example, the South Carolina Development Board advertises, "We know that healthy business is the goose that lays the golden egg. So we've developed special tax incentives to keep the goose alive."[13] The Greenville Chamber of Commerce boasts that the state has the "smallest organized work force" and several other advantages, including a pro-business climate, conservative political support, and low taxes[14] (and the push is on to develop more of these incentives). A Governor's Task Force on the Economy recently noted that, "Government must help provide the incentives to entice new industry to locate here and existing industry to expand here." In that report, the task force called for a "tax structure and investment incentive program ... in line with neighboring states" and in response to the state's perceived "massive regulatory costs," a matching of "regulatory reform at the federal level with similar reform at the state level."[15]

Similarly, Wisconsin boosters have published a poster and run advertisements in several neighboring state newspapers under the caption, "How to find a warm business climate without migrating south." The poster continues, "If attractive business taxes and responsive government sound like something worth chirping about, talk to Forward Wisconsin. We'll show you a tax comparison that will help you warm up to Wisconsin in a hurry. We'll demonstrate how our new Permit Information Center and Business Hotline can make short work of rules and regulations."[16] So-called conservative and progressive communities are sounding more and more alike. In most states, the "boosters" are composed of local business elites aligned with public officials and other community leaders.

Chinks in the Pro-Growth Armor

Despite the widespread acceptance among public officials of the pro-growth/pro-business approach to economic development—particularly in the declining centers of the Northeast and Midwest—it has not gone unchallenged, even within the business community itself. A concomitant development of the proliferation of financial incentive and industrial attraction programs across the country has been the emergence of (fragmented) research efforts to determine their effectiveness. The general picture that emerges is that tax breaks and other financial incentives are not significant factors in creating new jobs or generating economic growth. This conclusion is reached in a wide range of academic research,[17] government and university monographs,[18] neighborhood and community group reports,[19] and journalistic accounts.[20]

Several reasons are given for the ineffectiveness of incentives. Arguing that government regulations and taxes do not explain productivity problems in the U.S. economy, some analysts point to the narrow, short-term orientation of American management compared to their overseas counterparts, particularly the Japanese, as a more critical problem.[21] A related consideration is the wave of conglomerate mergers that has drained capital from potentially productive uses to finance "paper entrepreneurship."[22] The fact that most of the financial assistance has gone to large firms, while small firms are the largest job generators, is another factor.[23] Perhaps the most critical finding is that because such financial incentives are designed to appeal to market forces and the profit interests of private corporations, they are predicated on precisely those forces that accounted for economic decline in the first place. That is, because of the virtually unrestricted mobility of capital, investment dollars will flow where the market offers the highest returns, with many cities and entire regions of the country confronting serious social costs due to the flight of capital. The dynamics of private investment decision making that caused economic decline are looked to as the source of reinvestment and economic growth.[24] One significant consequence of these developments is that minority communities have suffered the most from disinvestment, and benefited least from the array of incentives.[25]

In addition to the available research on the pro-growth strategy, the performance of the economy itself raises challenges to the financial incentive/industrial attraction approach. The recession of 1982–1983 that followed enactment of most of President Reagan's economic proposals the previous year resulted in Congress's being far less pliant than in the President's first year. And with unemployment rates over 7 percent (and more than twice that rate among blacks) at the height of the "recovery,"[24] the economy remains the central domestic issue among public officials.

Industrial Revenue Bonds: The Escalating Costs of a Capital Subsidy

Industrial revenue bonds (IRBs) have become one of the most popular, expensive, and controversial programs in the urban economic development arena. What is perhaps most remarkaable is how widespread they have become when there is so little research on their effectiveness. What research has been done, in fact, generally fails to provide evidence that they have met the intended purpose, and strongly suggests IRB programs have generated a number of economic dislocations and social costs that appear to be working at cross-purposes with the stated objectives.

Industrial revenue bonds are tax-exempt bonds issued by state and local governments to provide financing for private-sector investment in industrial plants and equipment. The intended recipients of the financing are small industrial enterprises. Because the earnings on the bonds are exempt from federal taxes, the bond purchasers, generally banks or other financial institutions, accept lower rates of return on their investments. As a result, jurisdictions issuing the bonds are able to use the proceeds of bond sales to make below-market-rate loans available to those small businesses that apply and qualify for such financing. Although issued by state and local governments, these loans are, in effect, subsidized by the federal government. Repayment of the loans is the responsibility of the firms receiving them, not the unit of government issuing the bonds. Therefore, if the firm defaults, the loss is borne by the bondholder. Since the direct costs of IRBs are paid by the federal treasury while the costs to states and municipalities are generally hidden from public purview (as discussed below) and because issuing authorities assume minimal risks, the use of IRBs as a tool for economic development has increased substantially in recent years.

IRBs were initially used in Mississippi in the 1930s to promote rural development. Cities and states in the Northeast and Midwest began using IRBs in the 1960s to finance capital expansion for large corporations. Today, they are offered in all fifty states.[27] Issuance of IRBs grew from $100 million in 1960 to $12.7 billion in 1982.[28] The critical issue raised by the proliferation of such subsidies was posed by the Congressional Budget Office: "Under what circumstances do federal subsidies to lower the borrowing costs of private industry serve a public purpose?"[29]

The primary purpose of IRBs is to create jobs by encouraging the expansion of small businesses. A second major objective is to stabilize the tax base of urban communities experiencing severe fiscal problems resulting from deindustrialization and declining economic activity generally. IRBs are viewed by their proponents as valuable tools for depressed urban communities in general and minority neighborhoods in particular.[30]

These sentiments are reflected in most state and local enabling legislation that has authorized the issuance of IRBs.[31] For example, Wisconsin's enabling ordinance noted

> that industries in this state have been induced to move, . . . that economic insecurity due to unemployment is a serious menace to the general welfare of the people of the entire state, . . . which has resulted in a reduction of the tax base of counties, cities and other local governmental jurisdictions impairing their financial ability to support education and other local governmental services, . . . that there is a need to stimulate a larger flow of private investment, . . . it is declared to be the policy of this state to promote the right to gainful employment, business opportunities and general welfare of the inhabitants thereof and to preserve and enhance the tax base by authorizing municipalities to issue revenue bonds . . . in the public interest.

The statute concludes: "the revitalization of the central business districts of the municipalities of this state is necessary to retain existing industry in, and attract new industry to, this state."[32]

The principal federal statute governing the issuance of IRBs is the Revenue and Expenditure Control Act of 1968 (Pub. L. 90-364), which provided the federal tax exemption for bonds issued to finance quasi-public facilities (e.g., airports, wharves) and services (e.g., pollution control, health care) and selected small industrial and commercial developments. The Act limited the exemption to $1 million. By 1978 Congress had raised the cap to $10 million, except for those projects in distressed areas receiving Urban Development Action Grant (UDAG) funds under Section 119 of the Housing and Community Development Act of 1974, for which the limit was set at $20 million. In addition, where the amount exceeds $1 million, total capital expenditures on all of a single firm's facilities in the city or county cannot exceed $10 million for the six-year period extending from three years prior to the bond issue to three years after the issue.[33] With the Deficit Reduction Act of 1984, Congress cut back on the use of IRBs by tying the limit to statewide population, although certain public projects were exempted from the cap.

Congress mandated that IRB financing be directed to particular purposes, but these were defined broadly enough to permit a wide variety of uses as states and localities exercised broad discretion in their issuance of bonds. More than half the states issuing bonds place no further restrictions on their use than those provided by the federal legislation.[34] Though billed as a job-creation and -retention program, rarely do the rules require such results. The typical approach was expressed by Richard C. Kotenbeutel, a research analyst with the Wisconsin Department of Development, who wrote, in regard to that state's enabling ordinance, "There are no job creation or retention obligations specified in the statute. It is believed that the capital investment financed with bond proceeds will provide the business with the plant capacity which will require additional employees."[35]

Despite the public purposes to which IRBs are supposed to be directed, they have been used to finance private tennis clubs, ice cream parlors, ski lodges, and other luxury recreational facilities.[36] As a result of such abuses, Congress eliminated the federal tax exemption for bonds financing such recreational facilities in the Tax Equity and Fiscal Responsibility Act of 1982.

Although individual abuses of IRB programs often received widespread media coverage, issuance of IRBs mushroomed until recently, when Congress set new limits with the 1984 tax act. As indicated above in terms of both the number of states issuing bonds and the dollar volume of IRBs, they have become an increasingly prominent component of state and local economic development efforts.

As the use of IRBs grew, so did the controversies. Although intended for small industrial enterprises, particularly those experiencing difficulty in obtaining credit through conventional financial markets, IRB projects have provided financing to large, well-financed commercial ventures such as K-Mart, McDonalds, and Marshall Fields.[37] A preliminary survey of Wisconsin's IRB program found that over half of the firms that received such financing employed over 100 people, and 31 percent employed more than 250. One consequence is that IRBs are not going to the small business sector of the economy that is the most effective generator of new jobs.

A related problem is that IRB projects are not effectively targeted to those districts with the greatest need for jobs and economic development. Because the revenue loss is concentrated at the federal level, and because the technical nature of the program makes it unlikely that its local costs will be understood or opposed by the electorate, local officials have little or no incentive to limit or target its uses. Any benefits appear to be realized without diverting resources from other groups. Targeting the subsidy, on the other hand, would require costly decision-making procedures and leave local officials vulnerable both to charges of favoritism and to blame in cases where rejected applicants subsequently relocate or fail.[38] Consequently, most localities award the subsidy indiscriminately with the rationale that it will attract new businesses while retaining local firms and helping them expand. Research in Ohio and Massachusetts found that those areas receiving the highest concentration of IRB-financed projects were in fact not the communities experiencing the highest unemployment rates.[39] And despite such provisions as Wisconsin's non-discrimination requirements, racial minorities and women are underutilized in the work force of firms receiving IRB financing.[40] A study of Chicago's IRB program found that in addition to being underrepresented among the employees of IRB firms, minorities and women were also underutilized in the work force of the vast majority of financial institutions that purchased the bonds; furthermore, less than 1 percent of IRB projects had financed minority-owned businesses.[41]

A number of market dislocations are created by IRBs which adversely affect the efficiency and competitiveness of the U.S. economy generally. According to neoclassical economic theory, public subsidies to private businesses effectively shift production from lower-cost to higher-cost operations, thus rendering the economy less competitive in international trade. And unlike a general tax cut, which does not affect the relative price of inputs, IRBs lower the price of capital, thus altering the capital/labor ratio and, contrary to the stated objective, encouraging the replacement of workers with machines. Several municipal finance officers note that the growth of IRBs has created competition in the bond market, raising interest rates generally and increasing the borrowing costs of government for more critical public purposes like schools, road repairs, and other infrastructure investments.[42] In addition, they provide what may be an unfair, if not illegal, competitive advantage for selected private businesses. In sum, IRBs constitute a windfall for the businesses benefiting from subsidized, below-market-rate loans, and for the investors who profit from this addition to their portfolios, at substantial costs to other segments of the community.

IRBs have also accounted for an increasingly regressive shift in the tax burden as the expanding volume of tax-exempt bonds has enabled high-income taxpayers to shield a greater proportion of their income.

The exact dollar value of this income shelter is not known, but it has been estimated that for every $2 of interest-cost savings to firms receiving IRB financing, the federal government loses $3 in tax revenues.[43] In other words, one-third of the benefit of tax-exempt financing is captured by the bondholders. If the annual federal tax loss from IRBs is conservatively estimated at $3 billion, this amounts to a regressive shift of $1 billion each year.

The one criticism of IRBs that finally caused Congress to act is the drain on the federal treasury. The revenue loss increased from $1 billion in 1981 to $3.7 billion in 1984. Fearing annual tax revenue losses reaching more than $5 billion by 1987, Congress placed limits on the issuance of IRBs in the 1984 tax act.[44]

Job Creation and the IRB Program: An Empirical Assessment

The lack of publicly available information on the administration and effectiveness of IRB programs is a problem frequently cited by a variety of researchers.[45] To date, little progress has been made in determining how employment levels change among subsidized firms or how these changes compare with those among firms that do not receive such assistance. In an effort to shed some light on these issues, this section summarizes recent findings on the job creation associated both statewide with Wisconsin's IRB program and locally with the programs administered by the cities of Chicago and Milwaukee.

A Wisconsin Department of Development (DOD) study of that state's IRB program reported in 1980 that more than $1 billion of the bonds had been sold between 1971 and 1977 on behalf of 443 companies that registered a net employment growth of 14,140 jobs. Acknowledging that this employment growth was not directly attributable to the subsidy, the report nonetheless concludes that the social benefits, primarily job creation, offer "strong testimony to the program's success."[46]

This conclusion may be ill-founded. Aside from the possibly spurious association between the receipt of the subsidy and the subsequent employment gains, the report based its assessment solely upon data on these particular establishments. It did not examine the employment histories of the parent firms, many of which encompass numerous establishments. In order to determine more precisely how many net jobs were associated statewide with Wisconsin's IRB program, listings of the establishments receiving the bonds between 1976 and 1978 were obtained from the DOD. The net job changes of these establishments and, in the case of Wisconsin companies, their parent firms were then calculated over the period 1976 to 1981 from the Unemployment Compensation Contributions Reports (UCCR) of Wisconsin businesses. (These time points were chosen in an effort to minimize the effects of the business cycle while remaining within the time-frame of the capital expenditure limit governing the use of the subsidy.) Summing the net gains among the subsidized establishments yielded a total of 3,085 new jobs, or 11.8 percent of the 1976 employment base of 26,084. By comparison, the net gain of 3,038 new jobs among the parent firms was only 7.3 percent of their considerably larger 1976 base of 41,427 employees. (See Table 5.1.) Since the locus of investment decisions is usually the parent firm, assessment of the job growth associated with a subsidy program should include data at the level of the firm. Evaluations based solely upon data per establishment are likely to confuse intrafirm employment shifts with net new jobs. In this case, the focus on subsidized establishments rather than parent firms results in overestimation of the impact of the subsidy.

The bias that results from confusing employment shifts with net job creation is only one of the problems frequently associated with

TABLE 5.1. Components of Employment Change Among Firms and Their Subsidized Establishments, Wisconsin, 1976–1981

Business Change	Subsidized Establishments			Parent Firms		
	Number	Percentage	Jobs Added	Number	Percentage	Jobs Added
New Firms	12	8%	2,346	10	7%	1,940
Expansion	78	55	5,211	79	56	7,301
No Change	3	2	—	3	2	—
Contraction	31	22	−1,996	33	23	−2,956
Closings	18	13	−2,476	17	12	−3,247
TOTAL	142	100%	3,085	142	100%	3,038

Source: Calculated from Unemployment Compensation Contributions Reports, Wisconsin, 1976-1981.

evaluations of subsidy programs. Another is the misleading use of averages. Net job gains are often presented as though they were evenly distributed among the subsidized establishments or firms, thus conveying an impression of stable job growth. The components of change analysis presented in Table 5.1 reveals just how misleading this impression can be. By dividing the total net employment gain of Wisconsin's IRB recipients into the components of job gains (due to the "birth" of new businesses and the expansion of those already existing) and job losses (due to the "death" or contraction of existing businesses), this analysis conveys the actual dynamics of employment change. One-quarter of the IRB-user firms (and a comparable proportion of their subsidized establishments) show either no employment growth or a job loss over the period, while an additional 12 percent ceased operations altogether. Although this net job loss was more than offset by the job gains of those firms initiating or expanding operations, the fact that more than a third of the subsidized firms show declining employment underscores the danger of assuming that subsidies directly and uniformly stimulate job growth.

The employment totals reported in Table 5.1 indicate that Wisconsin's IRB program is associated with aggregate job growth. These statewide data fail to address the issue of which workers are likely to benefit from the job gains, however. One well-known summary of the research on this issue concluded that capital is more easily substituted for unskilled than for skilled labor.[47] In other words, for a given capital subsidy we expect to see smaller job gains (or larger job losses) among unskilled than among skilled workers. This expectation was borne out in an Ohio study of the job growth among firms receiving IRBs. Only 31 percent of the jobs associated with receiving an IRB were in categories for which there was a labor surplus, leading the authors to conclude that IRBs are not an effective means of generating employment for those most in need of a job.[48]

This greater substitutability of capital for unskilled labor may partially explain the relatively poor job creation performance of the IRB business recipients in two major metropolitan areas. The city of Chicago recently examined the 101 projects funded since the inception of its IRB program in 1977 through June of 1984 and found that the total employment of recipient businesses had dropped from 17,670 to 15,356, a 14 percent decline.[49] Almost 45 percent of the businesses had experienced job losses and 82 percent failed to meet their initial projected employment goals. Collectively, these businesses had projected an increase of 6,847 jobs. Instead, they suffered a loss of 2,314 jobs, leav-

ing their total employment in 1984 at 38 percent below the anticipated level.

A similar picture emerges for Milwaukee. Data obtained from the
city of Milwaukee on 41 business recipients of IRB financing between
1973 and 1980 showed a 15 percent decline, as total employment
dropped from 7,966 to 6,764. (This employment decline was calculated
from the receipt of the subsidy—for individual businesses this could be
any year between 1973 and 1980—up to 1984 in order to highlight the
employment performance of businesses after being subsidized.) Over
46 percent of these businesses experienced job losses, and 64 percent
failed to meet their projected goals. Initially projecting 897 new jobs,
the 1984 employment level of these Milwaukee businesses was almost
24 percent below the anticipated level. In the two metropolitan areas
IRB-funded projects thus appear to be associated with employment declines. The job losses in the subsidized businesses in Chicago were
found to be comparable to those of manufacturing businesses that did
not receive the loans. However, the fact that their employment performance was no better than that of comparable metropolitan businesses
suggests that IRBs are an inefficient form of capital subsidy and that
capital subsidies are an inefficient means of generating new jobs.

Policy Implications

A new social contract appears to be emerging, one which calls for
additional financial rewards for the wealthy but punitive sanctions for
the poor. The terms of this contract are being challenged, however. In at
least a few communities public officials are beginning to adopt a community collective-bargaining approach to urban economic development.

Industrial revenue bonds constitute one clause in the new social
contract, but not all the terms are being met. The incentives are being
delivered to businesses, but the presumed public benefits are not being
realized. Simply put, IRBs are not an effective job-generating mechanism. They do offer "free" money for many state and local economic
development programs. They provide cheap loans for businesses. And
they enhance the portfolios of bondholders. But they do not effectively
accomplish their stated purposes, and they generate several social
costs. The benefits to businesses and bondholders reduce federal tax

revenues. To the extent that the shortfall is replaced, it is lower-income taxpayers who foot the bill. IRBs increase the cost of many public services, or contribute to the cutback in those services. They create distortions in the market which reduce the overall efficiency and productivity of the economy, and encourage the replacement of labor with capital-intensive machinery. These costs might be justifiable if bond projects were directed toward economically distressed communities and populations, but they are not so targeted at the present time. Perhaps the fundamental flaw in IRB programs is that, like financial incentive/ industrial attraction strategies generally, solutions to prevailing economic problems are premised precisely on the dynamics of private capital accumulation that caused the problem in the first place.

Congress has initiated some efforts to reform the IRB program, but it is clear that those efforts were not motivated by the failure of the program to deliver the expected public benefits. That the IRB program was never made contingent upon such benefits is evidenced by the repeated decision to delegate administration to state and local officials who have little incentive to target or otherwise restrict the use of the subsidy. If IRBs serve a public purpose, it is that of stimulating a somewhat larger flow of investment than would occur in their absence. However, with one-third of the federal tax loss captured by investors, IRBs are a particularly inefficient means of stimulating investment. And with any employment gains that might result from the higher levels of investment being offset at least in part by the substitution of capital for labor, they are to that degree an even less efficient means of generating new jobs.

To the extent that firms receiving IRB financing do generate jobs, the direction of causation remains unclear. Any firm planning to expand has an obvious incentive to apply for this subsidy. Job differentials between IRB firms and those not receiving such assistance may be more a function of the IRB group's ability to secure financing in the market, or simply their decision to expand, than of the ability of the subsidy to stimulate new investment.

Due to the advantages IRBs offer significant sectors of the economy and the desire of public officials at least to try to do something about the very real problems they face, IRBs are likely to be around for a while. The question becomes, Can they be utilized to more effectively meet the intended objectives? If this question is to be answered affirmatively, then public officials must develop a far different vision of the role of government than is currently in vogue. They must view their role more as positive actors in shaping the development of their communities than as passive providers of incentives in hopes that someone else will do the job for them.

In doing so, the first step is to reconsider the role of the market. For most people, in both the public and private sector, market processes are accepted as unalterable givens, to which public policy must acquiesce. If the market signals the death knell for some communities, that is simply part of the "creative destruction of capitalism" from which presumably most will benefit eventually. According to this perspective, the city, in the words of Thomas Bender, "has no legitimate existence prior to or superior to the claims of the market. In contemporary discussion of urban economies, of urban growth and decline, we are repeatedly counseled to accept passively the decision of the market, however tragic its local consequences."[50] For cities experiencing fiscal crises and their associated social costs, this means packaging and marketing incentives that will, in the words of American Enterprise Institute economist Richard B. McKenzie, "meet the competition"[51] and attract private capital.

Such a posture obscures the political forces shaping market processes. It denies the significance of place, culture, and community, and reduces people to movable quantities in an international capital market. It results in an abdication of public concerns in favor of the private interests of a privileged few. Morality and democracy become defined in terms of what serves the preferences of private capital. As Bender concluded:

> We have excluded the means of life from the realm of political discourse. As a result, the political activism we see in our cities is too often merely defensive and negative, obstructing the antisocial acts of the government or business, but not signficantly shaping the pattern of capital investment in our cities. Local activism too often produces instead divisive conflict over municipal services rather than larger movements to recapture political control of the urban economy under conditions of democratic participation.[52]

The question becomes, then, how can the public act to democratically shape investment and exercise control over those decisions that affect local communities in general and their economies in particular. Democracy requires that public officials, workers, residents, and other members of the community have a voice in those decisions—including capital investment and other financial decisions—that determine their future. This does not preclude capital mobility or structural transformations from one industry to another. But it does require explicit attention to social costs as well as private benefits so that both are equitably distributed. This also does not deny a role for the market as an arbiter for distribution, again as long as public and private costs and benefits are explicitly entered in the equation. The public's posture on economic development cannot be just a reactive one. Rather the public sector must play a positive role in shaping future development through more democratic processes and structures.

In some communities public officials and other community leaders are beginning to take a community collective-bargain approach. For example, the city of Chicago recently issued an economic development plan calling for balanced growth among the different neighborhoods throughout the city, and broader public participation in economic development planning. One part of the program is a linked development effort whereby downtown developers would provide concrete resources and lend their expertise to neighborhood groups on projects in communities outside the central business district.[53] In Santa Monica, California, the city has negotiated agreements with real estate developers in which they have agreed to construct low- and moderate-income housing, public parks, day-care facilities, and other public amenities in return for permits to build commercial office towers and luxury hotels.[54] The construction of a nuclear power plant in Midland, Michigan, was fought by local citizens, leading to the development of alternative energy sources in that community.[55]

Judicious use of industrial revenue bonds could be included as part of a democratic approach to the strategic development of urban communities. In order for IRBs to be effective, they would have to be more explicitly targeted to economically depressed areas. And there would have to be explicit commitments on the part of those receiving the assistance to work to effect its purposes. The target could be geographic areas where unemployment is particularly severe, assuming the jobs to be created match the skills of the available but unemployed work force. Another target might be an industry for whose products there is an effective demand and social need. Or perhaps there might be a critical linkage among productive or potentially productive firms in diverse sectors that could be developed through IRB financing. A stagnant but potentially productive facility might be assisted by an IRB, turning a vacant property that may currently serve no other purpose than to attract vandals into a taxpaying enterprise that provides jobs and a useful product for the community. In administering IRB programs, public officials need not spell out in advance all the types of projects which would be eligible. What is critical is that the program not be operated on simply a take-all-(creditworthy)-comers approach, as is currently the case. Projects must be targeted to meet democratically determined and explicitly negotiated public goals.

In most cases, the goals would be stated in terms of job creation. If public dollars are to be used to create jobs, then there should be provisions that require subsidized firms to state in advance, and then meet, employment goals. Issuing authorities must collect far more information on the projects they consider and finance. Applicants should state how many jobs they propose to create, what kinds of jobs that will be created and the salaries or wages of the positions, and how affirmative action policies and current contractual agreements with unions will be followed in all hiring and promotion. Public officials must assure that such job creation projections represent new jobs and not simply transfers among establishments within firms. Annual progress reports should then be required of successful applicants and monitored by the appropriate administrative authority. Public reports should be issued on an annual basis indicating how the performance of each IRB recipient compares with the initial goals. Job creation, not just projections, should be required and effectively enforced. Provisions can be incorporated to allow for certain unanticipated circumstances that would result in the failure to meet goals despite good faith efforts to achieve them. Such occurrences, however, should be the exception rather than the rule. It is not sufficient to simply "believe" that job generation will result from the issuance of an IRB.

If the regulations are to have any meaning, of course, there must be sanctions for those who do not comply, including repayment of the subsidy, immediate repayment of the loan, debarment from future IRB projects, and other steps appropriate to assure compliance.

The city of Chicago is currently considering a requirement that firms repay the balance of their loan and a portion or all of the subsidy they have received if they fail to meet their goals.[56] This action follows controversy surrounding an IRB that Playskool, a subsidiary of Milton-Bradley, obtained in 1980, under which the company said it would add 500 employees to a work force of 1,100. By 1984 Playskool had experienced a reduction of 400 employees, although it continued to be a profitable operation. Milton-Bradley then acknowledged that the initial goals were unrealistic. Playskool was then sold to Hasbro, who announced its intention to close Playskool and merge the facilities with operations on the East Coast.[57] Following a consumer boycott and a lawsuit filed by the city of Chicago, Hasbro repaid the full balance of the loan, agreed to retain approximately 100 employees temporarily, and funded a job search program for the displaced workers.[58] In one sense, the Hasbro incident illustrates Bender's assertion regarding the defensive nature of current political initiatives in the economic development arena. Yet it also illustrates one community's efforts to affirmatively challenge the capital investment decisions of one company rather than passively accept what some observers would dismiss as a business's perhaps unfortunate but necessary response to market forces.

Such reforms would be most effective, of course, if they were made at the national level. Because state and local officials are basically tapping federal dollars to provide this subsidy, many have argued that they would put their own communities at a competitive disadvantage if they enforced any stringent regulations while their neighbors did not. In addition, as noted earlier, potential political costs provide disincentives to targeting IRB projects. But in the absence of these kinds of reforms IRBs will continue to represent another ineffective incentive that will exacerbate the social costs of deindustrialization and uneven development. And as the Hasbro incident illustrates, there are tangible benefits to be realized by communities that do act, even without the desired federal action, to protect their legitimate interests.

If IRBs are to become a vehicle of reinvestment rather than disinvestment, they must be utilized within the context of a broader effort at strategic planning for economic development. Such efforts must be predicated on the democratic participation of public officials, and all segments of the community they represent, in identifying objectives and implementing strategic plans for meeting them, rather than on wishes they hope will come true by way of passive appeals and acquiescence to market forces.

Notes

1. See Robert Goodman, *The Last Entrepreneurs: America's Regional Wars for Jobs and Dollars.* New York: Simon and Schuster, 1979; James C. Cobb, *The Selling of the South: The Southern Crusade for Industrial Development, 1936–80.* Baton Rouge: Louisiana State University Press, 1982.

2. Milton Friedman, *Capitalism and Freedom.* Chicago: University of Chicago Press, 1962.

3. George Gilder, *Wealth and Poverty*. New York: Basic Books, 1981.

4. William Casey, Comment on book cover, Gilder.

5. Ronald Reagan, "Address by the President to a Joint Session of Congress on a Program for Economic Recovery," February 18, 1981.

6. Thomas Byrne Edsall, *The New Politics of Inequality*. New York: W.W. Norton, 1984.

7. "The Reindustrialization of America." *Business Week,* June 30, 1980.

8. Alan Wolfe, *America's Impasse: The Rise and Fall of the Politics of Growth.* Boston: South End Press, 1981.

9. Harvey Molotch, "The City as a Growth Machine: Toward a Political Economy of Place." *American Journal of Sociology,* September 1976, pp. 309–332.

10. Barry Bluestone and Bennett Harrison, *Capital and Communities: The Causes and Consequences of Private Disinvestment*. Washington, DC: The Progressive Alliance, 1980.

11. Mel Dubnick, "American States and the Industrial Policy Debate." *Policy Studies Review,* January 1984, pp. 22–27.

12. Ira C. Magaziner and Robert B. Reich, *Minding America's Business: The Decline and Rise of the American Economy*. New York: Vintage Books, 1982.

13. "Taxes in South Carolina." South Carolina State Development Board brochure, 1980.

14. Greeneville Chamber of Commerce, *Do These High Technology Companies Know Something You Don't?* Greeneville, South Carolina Chamber of Commerce, undated.

15. Report of the South Carolina Governor's Task Force on the Economy. Undated.

16. "Move Forward in Wisconsin." Poster published by Forward Wisconsin, Milwaukee, Wisconsin, 1984.

17. See Michael Wasylenko, "The Location of Firms: The Role of Taxes and Fiscal Incentives," in R. Bahl (ed.), *Urban Government Finance*. Beverly Hills, CA: Sage Publications, 1981; Michael I. Lugar, "Some Micro-Consequences of Macro-Policies: The Case of Business Tax Incentives (BTIs)." Proceedings of the National Tax Association, 1981; Barry Bluestone and Bennett Harrison, *The Deindustrialization of America*. New York: Basic Books, 1982; Robert Lekachman, *Greed is Not Enough: Reaganomics*. New York: Pantheon Books, 1982.

18. See Roger Schmenner, "The Manufacturing Location Decision: Evi-

dence from Cincinnati and New England." Cambridge, MA: Harvard-MIT Joint Center for Urban Studies, 1978; Michael Kieschnick, *Taxes and Growth: Business Incentives and Economic Development.* Washington, DC: Council of State Planning Agencies, 1981; David M. Gordon, *The Working Poor: Towards a State Agenda.* Washington, DC: Council of State Planning Agencies, 1979.

19. "Tax Dollars in Chicago." Chicago: Chicago Jobs Coalition, 1982.

20. Arthur Schlesinger, Jr., "Neo-Conservatism and the Class Struggle." *The Wall Street Journal,* June 2, 1981; John Kenneth Galbraith, "And Let's Not Weep for the Rich." *Chicago Tribune,* June 28, 1981; "Enterprise Zone: Latest Way to Fight Urban Blight." *Chicago Tribune,* September 10, 1981; "Unfairness in Reagan Plan." *Chicago Sun-Times,* February 24, 1981.

21. Robert H. Hayes and William J. Abernathy, "Managing our Way to Economic Decline." *Harvard Business Review,* July-August 1980, pp. 67–77.

22. See Robert B. Reich, *The Next American Frontier.* New York: Times Books, 1983; Robert Sherrill, "Mergermania Reigns: The Decline and Fall of Antitrust." *The Nation,* March 19, 1983, pp. 338–339.

23. David Birch, "The Job Generation Process." Cambridge, MA: MIT Program on Neighborhood and Regional Change, 1979; Ralph Nader and Jerry Jacobs, "Battle to Lure Industry Costly." *Chicago Tribune,* November 12, 1979.

24. Bluestone and Harrison; Joshua Cohen and Joel Rogers, *On Democracy: Toward a Transformation of American Society.* New York: Penguin Books, 1983.

25. John Carl Scholz, "The Racial Implications of the 1981 Tax Act." Paper presented at symposium of the Leadership Conference on Civil Rights, May 4, 1982; Illinois Advisory Committee to the U.S. Commission on Civil Rights, *Shutdown: Economic Dislocation and Equal Opportunity.* Washington, DC: U.S. Government Printing Office, 1981.

26. "The Employment Situation: March 1985." *Bureau of Labor Statistics* (Washington, D.C., U.S. Department of Labor), 1985.

27. Alice M. Rivlin, "Statement by Alice M. Rivlin, Director, Congressional Budget Office, before the Committee on Ways and Means, U.S. House of Representatives," Congressional Quarterly, June 15, 1983.

28. Congressional Budget Office, *Small Issue Industrial Revenue Bonds.* Washington, DC: U.S. Government Printing Office, 1983; Committee on Ways and Means, U.S. House of Representatives, "Trends in the Use of Tax-Exempt Bonds to Finance Private Activities, Including a Description of H.R. 1176 and H.R. 1635." Washington, DC: U.S. Government Printing Office, 1983.

116   THOMAS S. MOORE AND GREGORY D. SQUIRES

29. Congressional Budget Office, *Small Issue Industrial Revenue Bonds.* Washington, DC: U.S. Printing Office, 1983.

30. Subcommittee on Oversight, Committee on Ways and Means, U.S. House of Representatives, *Small Issue Industrial Revenue Bonds.* Washington, DC: U.S. Government Printing Office, 1981.

31. Jacquelyn Harder, *Industrial Revenue Bonds: Regional and National Issues for Economic Development and Public Policy.* Chicago: Illinois-Indiana BiState Commission, 1983; David R. Allardice, *Small Issue Industrial Revenue Bond Financing in the Seventh Federal District.* Chicago: Federal Reserve Bank of Chicago, 1982.

32. Wisconsin Stat. Sec. 66.521(1)(a)(c).

33. Congressional Budget Office, 1981, pp. 3, 11, 12; Subcommittee on Oversight, 1981, pp. 25, 26.

34. Subcommittee on Oversight, p. 5.

35. Richard C. Kotenbeutel, letter to Thomas S. Moore, January 8, 1985.

36. Congressional Budget Office, pp. 18, 19.

37. Subcommittee on Oversight, pp. 363–371.

38. Sandra Kanter, "Theory of the Little State: Business-Government Relations on Formation of State Economic Policy," in Steven Redburn and Terry Buss (eds.), *Public Policies for Distressed Communities.* Lexington, MA: D.C. Heath, 1982; Michael J. Wolkoff, "The Nature of Property Tax Abatement Awards." *Journal of the American Planning Association,* Winter 1983, pp. 77–84.

39. Thomas A. Pascarella and Richard D. Raymond, "Buying Bonds for Business: An Evaluation of the Industrial Revenue Bond Program." *Urban Affairs Quarterly,* September 1982, pp. 73–89; Margaret Dewar, "The Usefulness of Industrial Revenue Bond Programs for State Economic Development: Some Evidence from Massachusetts." *New England Journal of Business and Economics,* Spring 1981, pp. 23–24.

40. Wisconsin Advisory Committee to the U.S. Commission on Civil Rights, *Business Incentives and Minority Employment.* Washington, DC: U.S. Government Printing Office, 1982.

41. Illinois Advisory Committee to the U.S. Commission on Civil Rights, "Industrial Revenue Bonds: Equal Opportunity in Chicago's IRB Program?" Draft report, 1983.

42. Subcommittee on Oversight, pp. 211–217.

43. John E. Chapoton, "Statement before the House Committee on Ways

and Means." *Treasury News* (Washington, DC: U.S. Department of the Treasury), 1983.

44. Committee on Ways and Means.

45. Congressional Budget Office, 1981, p. 12; Allardice, p. 55; Chicago Jobs Coalition, pp. 1–4; Wisconsin Legislative Audit Bureau, *Industrial Revenue Bonds*. Madison: Legislative Audit Bureau, 1981.

46. Richard Kotenbeutal, "Economic Impact of Industrial Revenue Bond Usage in Wisconsin," Madison: Wisconsin Department of Development, 1980.

47. Daniel Hamermesh and James Grant, "Econometric Studies of Labor-Labor Substitutions and Their Implications for Policy." *Journal of Human Resources,* Fall 1979, pp. 518–542.

48. Pascarella and Raymond.

49. "1984 Chicago Industrial Revenue Bond Monitoring Study." Chicago: Chicago Department of Economic Development, 1985.

50. Thomas Bender, "The End of the City." *Democracy* 1983, pp. 8, 10.

51. Richard B. McKenzie, "The Case for Plant Closures." *Policy Review,* Winter 1981, pp. 119–133.

52. Bender, p. 20.

53. Development Plan, *City of Chicago* May, 1984.

54. Derek Shearer, "Citizen Participation in Local Government: The Case of Santa Monica, California." *International Journal of Urban and Regional Research,* 1984, pp. 573–586.

55. Harvey Molotch and John Logan, "Tensions in the Growth Machine: Overcoming Resistance to Value-Free Development." *Social Problems,* June 1984, pp. 483–499.

56. Personal interview with Ray Gibson, *Chicago Tribune* reporter, Chicago, January 23, 1985.

57. "Toy Firm Rapped on Move East." *Chicago Sun-Times,* October 18, 1984; Susan Rosenblum, Midwest Center for Labor Research and West Side Jobs Network, letter to Gregory D. Squires, October 17, 1984.

58. R.C. Longworth, "Toymaker Cuts Deal with City on Closing." *Chicago Tribune,* January 19, 1985.

PART TWO
Business Elites and Local Government

Chapter 6

Urban Populism, Uneven Development, and the Space for Reform

Todd Swanstrom

In the early 1970s, the debate about the future of central cities in America was captured in the title of an article by Alexander Ganz and Thomas O'Brien: "The City: Sandbox, Reservation, or Dynamo?"[1] The question is still not settled. Some argue that cities are becoming dumping grounds for the economically obsolescent[2] or are themselves becoming obsolete.[3] Others argue that cities are taking on new life as nerve centers of the new information-based economy.[4] While the issue is by no means settled, it is becoming increasingly clear that the best answer to the question is "All of the above."

To paraphrase Charles Dickens' *A Tale of Two Cities,* for central cities, "This is the best of times, this is the worst of times." A drive through almost any older central city will reveal what are, for all practical purposes, two cities: one rich, the other poor; one growing, the other declining; one full of hope, the other full of despair.

The dynamic city is centered around downtown. Even the poorest central cities are enjoying growth in downtown white-collar professional employment. Gleaming towers of glass symbolize this economic dynamism. While, overall, central cities are still losing population, as a spin-off of their rapidly expanding downtown service sectors, almost every city is experiencing gentrification—the influx of young professionals into previously deteriorated neighborhoods around the

I would like to acknowledge the help of Peter Dreier, Dennis Keating, Robert Kerstein, and Bruce Miroff.

core. In most cities, however, gentrification has hit only a few neighborhoods—islands of wealth in a sea of residential deterioration.

In contrast to booming downtowns, the older ethnic and minority
neighborhoods are suffering from disinvestment. Neighborhood decline is the result of longstanding poverty, as well as the inability of the
urban working class to make the transition from manufacturing to service jobs. The old manufacturing economy provided relatively well-
paid jobs that required little education or advanced training. As these
jobs are eliminated by automation or flee the city in search of lower
wages, the blue-collar working class is forced to fend for itself in the
new service economy. For the most part, its members lack the education and skills to qualify for the white-collar professional jobs that are
locating downtown. If they do get jobs in the service sector, chances are
they will be low-paid and less secure. Evidence is mounting that jobs in
the emerging service economy cluster at the top and bottom of the earnings scale, generating what is called a "missing middle."[5]

Mayors have long been aware of the problems of what is now
called the "bipolar city" and styles of leadership have evolved to address these issues.[6] In the 1960s and 1970s, the dominant style of big city
mayors was "liberal." Liberal mayors, such as Carl Stokes of Cleveland
and New York's John Lindsay, did not attempt to stir up class resent-
ments but worked to co-opt dissent by funding programs for the poor.
The essence of the liberal style of leadership was an effort to foster both
economic growth and redistribution. Redistributive policies, however,
relied for the most part not on local taxes and initiatives but on the
largesse of federal grants and poverty programs.

The withdrawal of the federal government from such programs,
together with the increased vulnerability of local economies to external
economic forces such as deindustrialization, contributed to the demise
of the liberal style of mayoral leadership and its replacement by what
can only be called a "neo-conservative" style. The essence of neo-
conservative mayoral leadership, perhaps best exemplified by New
York Mayor Ed Koch, is a concentration on economic growth, even at
the expense of redistribution. Neo-conservatives place emphasis on
policies that will enhance the attractiveness of the city for mobile investors and high-income residents. Even though growth policies may
result in greater inequality, it is argued that in the long run they will
stimulate economic expansion that will benefit everyone. Since minorities are heavily represented among the poor, neo-conservative mayors
often rely on veiled, or not-so-veiled, racial appeals to mobilize voters
in their favor.

Recently, however, a new style of mayoral leadership has arisen that is neither liberal nor neo-conservative, but what I call "urban populist." E. E. Schattschneider once argued that whoever controls the political agenda controls politics.[7] Urban populist mayors seek to redefine the agenda of city politics. First, they seek to displace ethnic and racial divisions with economic division: the haves versus the have nots. Second, once the terrain is shifted to economics, populist politicians seek to shift the issue from one of growth to one of distribution. In the absence of federal initiatives, populist politicians attempt to devise local solutions to the problems of uneven development. In the words of Huey Long, how can cities "share the wealth"? For cities today, this largely is a matter of spreading the wealth of downtown to the neighborhoods.

Historically, urban populism is best understood as an extension of the neighborhood organizing movement into the local electoral arena. Diffuse urban populist movements have arisen in many cities and in many cases have even taken control of city governments, including Hartford under Nicholas Carbone, the Berkeley Citizen Action (BCA) movement, the tenant-oriented insurgency in Santa Monica, Harold Washington in Chicago, and three recently elected mayors in New Jersey (Jersey City, Hoboken, and East Orange).[8] The two cases I will examine here are Dennis Kucinich, Mayor of Cleveland from 1977 to 1979, and Raymond Flynn, elected to a four-year term as mayor of Boston in 1983.

My goal here is to assess the prospects, both economic and political, of urban populism. Given the withdrawal of the federal government from urban policy, the question of how much local governments can address problems of poverty is especially pressing. The argument here is directed against those who assert that cities have little or no room for redistribution given external market pressures. Perhaps the most compelling version of this argument is Paul Peterson's *City Limits*.[9] Redistributive issues, Peterson argues, are forced off the local agenda because, everyone recognizes, they will harm the interests of the city as a whole in attracting wealth. Variations of the argument that market forces severely limit what cities can do about inequality can be found on the left[10] and on the right.[11] While it is true that market imperatives constrain what city governments can do, the constraints are not as tight, I will argue, as they are generally portrayed. The centralization of high-level service sector functions in the downtowns of central cities presents an economic "opening" for local populist movements to address problems of uneven development.

While economic trends create openings, it takes skillful political leaders to exploit these openings. Kucinich and Flynn are both skillful politicians, and an analysis of their administrations reveals the political strengths and weaknesses of urban populism. In the final analysis, I will argue, the limits of urban populism are more political than economic.

Cleveland and Boston: The Pain of Economic Transition

Media stereotypes would have us believe that Cleveland and Boston are two dramatically different cities. Cleveland is the epitome of a dying industrial city, the "Mistake on the Lake," with little future except as the butt of Johnny Carson jokes. Boston, on the other hand, represents everything that is chic and trendy, with Faneuil Hall and Quincy Market standing as visible symbols of its success. In fact, Cleveland is not as poor as its image implies and Boston is not an unalloyed success. Both are essentially industrial cities undergoing the painful transition to a service-based economy. Indeed, both cities have experienced the classic symptoms of urban decline.[12]

The most obvious indicator of their decline is loss of population (See Figure 6.1.) Cleveland is continuing to lose population. Boston, on the other hand, according to a recent census estimate, gained 7,725 residents between 1980 and 1984. This is a testament to Boston's booming service economy, but it must be put in the context of the loss of 238,450 residents between 1950 and 1980.

The dominant source of the huge population losses in both cities has been moves out of the central city to the suburbs. With only 20 percent of the regional population located in the central city in 1980, Boston ranked near the bottom of all metropolitan areas; at 30 percent, Cleveland was not far behind. Significantly, it was the middle class that was moving out to the suburbs, not the poor. In 1979 the median family income of Boston residents was only 70.3 percent of median income in the region; in Cleveland, it was only a hair better, 70.4 percent. In both cities, the ratio of central city to suburban income has been declining rapidly since 1949.

Both cities lost significant employment in wholesale and retail trade, which largely followed the exodus of population to the suburbs. Both cities also suffered tremendously from the loss of manufacturing

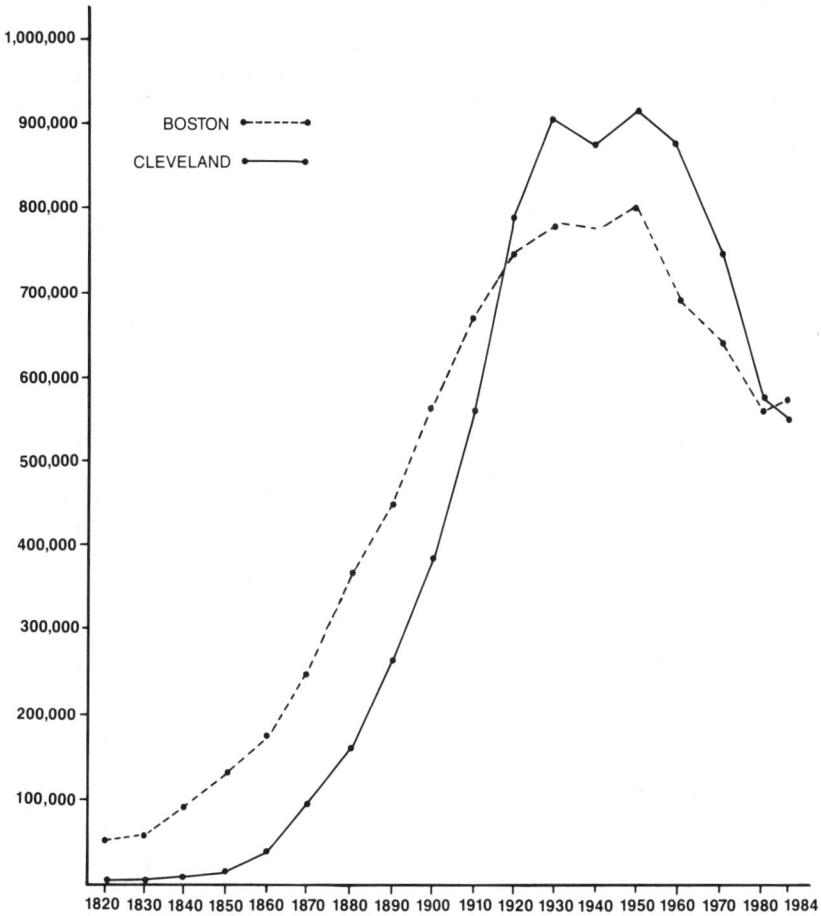

Figure 6.1. Population Trends: City of Cleveland and City of Boston, 1920–1984.

jobs, which were the backbone of their economies up until the 1950s. While the percentage loss was about the same, Cleveland has been hurt more by deindustrialization because its economy was originally more dependent on manufacturing. Between 1947 and 1982, the city of Cleveland lost a phenomenal 131,100 manufacturing jobs; Boston lost 54,300 manufacturing jobs during the same period. (See Figure 6.2.)

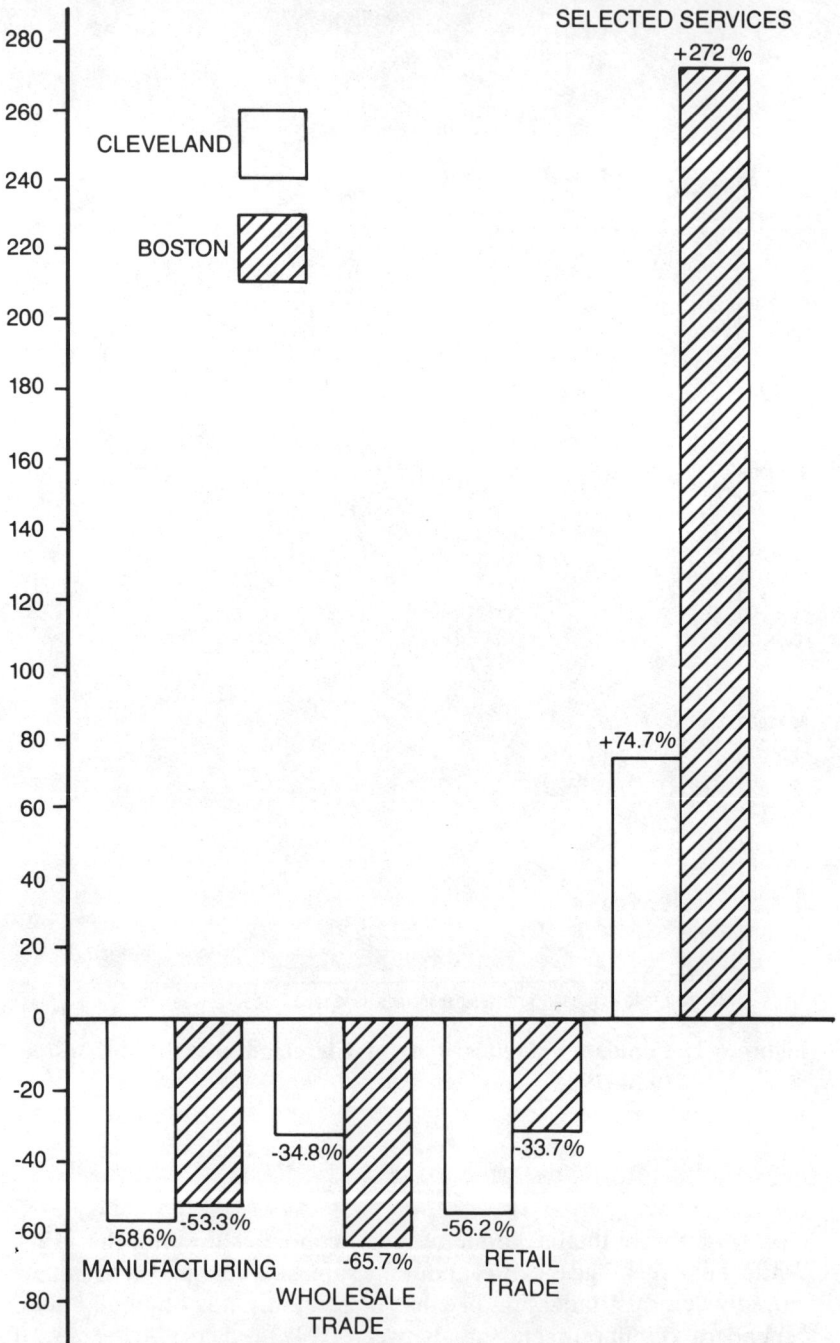

Figure 6.2. Percentage Change in Employment by Sector, City of Cleveland and City of Boston, 1948–1982.

Largely as a result of this economic dislocation, both cities suffer from low average incomes and high poverty rates. Out of the twenty largest cities in the United States in 1979, Boston and Cleveland ranked 17th and 18th, respectively, in median family income. In both cities, more than 20 percent of the population lives below the poverty level. Even though Boston is in the midst of a job boom, there are still frightening pockets of joblessness. As Robert Kuttner wrote in the *Boston Globe:* "Inner city Boston has the same dreadful youth unemployment rates as Cleveland or Detroit—40 and even 50 percent."[13]

In the midst of these negative trends is one overwhelming positive trend: the growth of white-collar service employment. While the growth has been much more spectacular in Boston, both cities have enjoyed a downtown office building boom in recent years. Cleveland is a corporate headquarters city, ranking fifth in the nation in 1979, with 24 of the top 1,000 industrial corporations headquartered there. Boston has fewer corporate headquarters, but Boston firms tend to be internationally oriented, whereas Cleveland's are more regional.[14] In both cities, the jobs that tend to locate in the city are in what are called "advanced corporate services"—high-level corporate control and planning functions.[15] They are centered in downtown areas mainly because of the "agglomeration economies" associated with the concentration of business services.[16] While employment in selected services went up 75 percent in Cleveland from 1948 to 1982, employment in business services increased 285 percent. In Boston, employment in business services increased 444 percent.

While many high-paying service-sector jobs are being located in Cleveland and Boston, most of them are not going to city residents. In both cities, most in the work force are commuters. In fact, out of the twenty largest U.S. cities in 1980, Boston and Cleveland rank second and third, respectively (after Washington, D.C.), in a low ratio of employment to residence. Studies have shown that not only do most jobs go to suburbanities, but the higher-paying the job is, the more likely it is to be filled by somebody who does not live in the city.[17] One of the principal differences between Boston and Cleveland is that Boston is experiencing significant gentrification as a spin-off from its service employment; Cleveland has had almost no gentrification.

In sum, Boston and Cleveland are both industrial cities making the transition to a service economy. In Cleveland, the transition has been more painful because it was more dependent on industry—but the process is essentially the same. In both cities, there is a mismatch between the types of jobs that are being located in the city and the job qualifications of city residents. The result is uneven development, between classes and between geographical areas. This uneven development has left its mark, in turn, on the political systems of both cities.

Kucinich: The Politics of Confrontation

The rapid rise and fall of Dennis Kucinich (pronounced Koo-SIN-itch) has been interpreted as an expression of the crisis of growth politics in Cleveland.[18] Growing up in the ethnic ghettos bordering the steel mills in Cleveland's "flats," Kucinich knew what the growth crisis meant for inner-city residents. His political base was the blue-collar ethnics, stuck in a dying industrial economy and largely excluded from the benefits of suburbanization and growing white-collar employment. Kucinich built his political career by playing upon the fears of inner-city ethnics left behind by the economic transition using a confrontational political style resembling (in words used by one historian to describe Huey Long) "a political buzzsaw," ripping into everyone and everything in his path.[19]

One effect of Cleveland's growth crisis was increased efforts by the public sector to attract wealthy investors and residents. These economic development efforts, however, did little to help those who needed it the most. Urban renewal, for example, built corporate headquarters, educational complexes, and luxury housing, but did little for low-income housing and neighborhoods. In fact, urban renewal destroyed more housing than it built, and is credited with being a major cause of Cleveland's Hough and Glenville riots in the 1960s.[20]

In the 1960s, Cleveland politicians began to run in opposition to growth politics and the corrupt collaboration alleged between the public and private sectors. In 1971, Ralph Perk, aided by a young Councilman named Dennis Kucinich, was elected mayor on a populist platform that included opposition to tax abatements for business and a pledge to retain and rehabilitate the municipally owned utility, known as Muny Light. Citing fiscal and economic pressures, Perk eventually reneged on both of these commitments. Before the 1977 election, anti-abatement activists distributed 50,000 information sheets in key wards. Kucinich rode the anti-abatement sentiment, as well as his vocal support for Muny Light, into the mayor's office in 1977.

Kucinich's urban populist program turned growth politics inside out: instead of spending public money on attracting wealthy investors and residents, government would concentrate on basic benefits and services for the neighborhoods. Constituencies that might be divided on social, ethnic, or racial issues could be united, Kucinich argued, on economic reforms. Kucinich's political style was confrontational—a form of Alinsky-style community organizing carried into the electoral arena. Like the grassroots neighborhood organizations in Cleveland, Kucinich used protest as a political resource, constantly attacking those inside the political system who, he alleged, were corruptly beholden to special interests. (See Figure 6.3.)

Kucinich was the archetypal political outsider; he developed his political organization almost completely outside the established political parties. Kucinich attacked his run-off opponent in the 1977 mayoral election, for example, in classically populist fashion: "Feighan is not his own man. He belongs to the party bosses, lock, stock and barrel. If the bosses elect the mayor who's going to be the mayor's boss? The people? No way."[21] As an independent political entrepreneur, Kucinich came into office with few of the ties and obligations that bind most politicians. Free to pursue his populist program, at the same time,

Figure 6.3. St. Dennis and the Dragon

Kucinich lacked clout with the powerful interests in Cleveland politics—with business, with political elites, and with city employees.

Kucinich needed all the political clout he could muster in order to
deal with Cleveland's deepening economic and fiscal crisis. The city's
middle class, and along with them its tax base, was moving rapidly to
the suburbs. After reaching a peak in about 1960, Cleveland's property
tax base shrunk rapidly in inflation-adjusted dollars.[22] Kucinich in-
herited a large city debt, both short-term and long-term. In addition, he
found himself in a life-and-death struggle with the area's private
utility, Cleveland Electric Illuminating Company (CEI), to save the
municipally owned utility, Muny Light. Nine days after Kucinich
assumed office, CEI filed a certificate of judgment of lien on lands and
property of the city to recover disputed debts owned CEI by Muny. A
federal judge ordered the city to pay the debt or face dismissal of a $10
million antitrust suit it had filed against CEI. Kucinich was able to
squeeze money out of operating expenses to pay the disputed debt, but
this only exacerbated the fiscal crisis in other areas.

The corporate elite in Cleveland was hostile to Kucinich from the
beginning. Numerous times during his first year in office, for example,
local bankers refused to refinance short-term city notes, a practice that
had been routine during previous administrations. As a result, the city
was forced to finance them out of its meager cash reserves. This captured the attention of the national bond rating agencies, which downgraded the city's bond rating, eventually shutting Cleveland out of the
national bond market. A short time later, an Ernst and Ernst audit
revealed that $52 million in bond money for capital projects had been
misspent for operating expenses, most of it during the Perk Administration. Cleveland was in perilous financial condition.

Meanwhile, Kucinich was engaged in a hard-fought recall election, which he survived by a mere 236 votes. A short time later, area
banks again refused to refinance some notes. This time Kucinich went
on the offensive with the kind of anti-capitalist rhetoric rarely heard in
American politics:

> Unless the banks begin to respond to the needs of Cleveland
> residents, a tremendous uprising of anger and bitterness will be
> directed against them. . . . This administration will be in the
> forefront of a movement to severely hamper normal business
> operations of area banks if they do not begin to respond to the
> needs of the city government and city residents. The banks leave
> us no choice but to fight back to save our city.[23]

The fiscal crisis came to a head in Cleveland's December 1978 default. It began when six local banks refused to refinance $14 million in short-term notes due December 15. Knowing that city government lacked the funds to pay the notes, the banks deliberately put Kucinich on the horns of a dilemma: the banks would refinance the notes only if the city agreed to sell Muny Light to CEI; otherwise, the city would go into default. Either way, Kucinich's political career would suffer irreparable damage. Kucinich refused to sell Muny Light and Cleveland became the first major city since the Depression to go into default.

The most thorough examination of Cleveland's default, a staff study for a subcommittee of the U.S. House of Representatives Committee on Banking, Finance and Urban Affairs, came to the conclusion that "factors other than hardnosed credit judgments entered into the picture."[24] The report suggested that the political animosity of the bankers toward Kucinich precipitated Cleveland's default. After all of the evidence is examined, there is little doubt that Cleveland's default was indeed political.[25] The banks used their control over credit to discredit a populist mayor with whom they had become locked in confrontation. As Brock Weir, Chairman and Chief Executive Officer of Cleveland Trust, the largest bank, said after default: "We had been kicked in the teeth for six months. On December 15 we decided to kick back."[26] Voters subsequently approved Kucinich's decision to retain Muny Light, as well as an increase in the local income tax to pay back the defaulted notes. Cleveland remained in default throughout Kucinich's two years in office, however, and the onus of default contributed significantly to his defeat in the next election.

Kucinich was blamed for Cleveland's fiscal problems even though he had done little to cause them. (See Figure 6.4.) In fact, a case could be made that Cleveland's fiscal situation improved during the Kucinich Administration: the city incurred almost no new debt during his term in office; city government paid off considerable debt accumulated during earlier administrations; serious audits were finally performed on the city's chaotic financial accounts; and the city's payroll was reduced almost 20 percent. Nevertheless, the banks were able to smear Kucinich with the onus of default, creating the impression in the minds of voters that investment should not return to the city until Kucinich was removed as mayor.

To the extent that banks can use their control over credit to destabilize a populist administration, it would appear there is little room

Figure 6.4. Mayor Gets a D for Default

for local economic reforms. However, I argue elsewhere that the opportunity for banks to exert that kind of power is rare,[27] occurring above all
when the city is shut out of the national bond market. For the most part,
the restraints on populist reform are political in nature, not economic,
as is demonstrated by looking at Kucinich's treatment of tax abatement.

Kucinich: Taxes and the Business Climate Factor

    Before Kucinich became mayor, the Cleveland City Council, with
the support of Mayor Perk, passed a series of multi-million dollar
abatements for downtown building projects. As we saw, Kucinich campaigned successfully for the mayor's office in 1977 promising to oppose
future abatements. Once in office, Kucinich kept his promise. Not only
did he veto all abatement legislation that came out of the City Council,
but all enabling legislation as well. The Council consistently overrode

his vetoes by lopsided margins. Kucinich, using his powers as chief executive, effectively killed the projects, anyway, by freezing federal funds, halting construction of water and sewer lines, and, in general, promising to make life miserable for the projects by foot dragging on demolition, police protection, and other services. Using these questionable methods, Kucinich succeeded in preventing any more abatements from being put into effect during his administration.

Research studies overwhelmingly support the conclusion that local property taxes have little effect on investment location decisions.[28] Local property taxes are such a small portion of the cost of doing business (on the order of 1 or 2 percent) that they are rarely decisive in investment decisions. Moreover, their cost is reduced by the fact that they can be written off as an expense for federal tax purposes. As we saw, specific sectors of white-collar employment are strongly attracted to downtown. Downtowns do not have to compete directly with suburban locations for many forms of white-collar employment; many firms must locate downtown for the prestige, business contacts, and specialized business services that are located only there. Studies of local tax abatement programs to attract white-collar employment have been generally critical.[29]

The experience in Cleveland shows that Kucinich's throttling of tax abatement had little effect on downtown investment. In fact, after Kucinich killed tax abatement, Cleveland enjoyed a downtown building boom that lasted for about five years. During the two years of the Kucinich Administration, over $240 million in downtown construction was planned or in progress, three-fourths of it without tax abatement. Surprisingly, Kucinich's successful opponent in 1979, Republican George Voinovich, came out against tax abatement, stating in a campaign leaflet, "I'm convinced downtown can flourish without tax abatement...." Voinovich kept his promise, and downtown Cleveland flourished.[30] Sohio built a $200-million headquarters without abatement. The National City Bank building, built in 1980 for $59 million with the aid of a substantial tax abatement, was sold in 1983 for a $30 million profit—with the tax abatement transferred to the new owners! Given such rapid inflation in downtown real estate, clearly, tax abatements are unnecessary.

While Kucinich may have won the economic battle on tax abatement, he lost the political war on economic development. Economic trends continued pretty much as before, with growth in the downtown service sector and decline in industry. Even though Kucinich had little impact on investment trends, he was charged with having poisoned the business climate. "As soon as you start talking against tax abatement, they say you are anti-business," lamented Kucinich. "My administration is not anti-business."[31] Unfortunately, Kucinich's confrontational rhetoric played into the hands of business elites who attempted to smear Kucinich with the charge of having poisoned the business climate.

With the exception of default, business leaders did not manipulate investment in order to influence political decision making. Business did manipulate something, however, that was just as valuable politically: how the public *perceived* ongoing investment trends. For example, when Diamond Shamrock, the nation's 178th largest industrial corporation, with headquarters in Cleveland, announced that it was moving to Texas, newspapers gave front-page treatment to the claim of its president and chief executive officer that the reason was "the political, economic and educational climate in Cleveland and particularly the anti-business attitude on the part of the city administration."[32] Overwhelming evidence points to the conclusion that Diamond Shamrock's move was dictated by economic considerations internal to the corporation, not by city politics.[33] This did not allay the impression created in the minds of voters, though.

In the 1979 re-election campaign, Kucinich tried to mobilize his populist constituency with attacks on his opponent, George Voinovich, as a tool of corrupt economic elites. Jumping on a Voinovich quote that appeared in the *New York Times,* "I like fat cats," Kucinich distributed a detailed leaflet, titled "Who Owns Voinovich?" listing over four hundred contributors to Voinovich campaigns. Midway through the campaign, however, a tragic accident occurred that forced Kucinich to abandon his confrontational strategy: Voinovich's young daughter, Molly, was killed by a hit-and-run driver. Personal attacks would now only create sympathy votes. Kucinich was forced to defend his record.

It was very difficult for Kucinich to switch gears and defend his record. For one thing, this was not his style. In addition, his administration had never projected much of a positive program. Kucinich's achievements were mostly negative—stopping tax abatement and saving Muny Light. Conditioned by months of crisis headlines, the voters were not about to believe that Kucinich had improved city services or developed a sophisticated alternative to business subsidy schemes. Ironically, Kucinich, who had promised to unite the city with economic reforms, turned to racial manipulation in a desperate last-ditch effort to win the election. On the white West Side, Kucinich smeared his opponent as the "black" candidate; on the predominantly black East Side, he portrayed himself as the "black" candidate and criticized Voinovich as "an anti-black Republican."

The constant confrontations not just with business, but with the City Council, neighborhood associations, and the media, created a siege atmosphere. The voters were exhausted. Moreover, although many respected Kucinich's courageous stands against big banks and corporations, they did not want to risk the chance that these stands were damaging the city's economic climate. Kucinich's opponent, Voinovich, played effectively upon these fears with a low-key campaign that emphasized cooperation instead of conflict. Using the campaign slogan, "Together we can do it," Voinovich, aided by half a million dollars in his campaign chest (almost three times what Kucinich raised), won the election easily, with 56 percent of the vote. Cleveland's short experiment in urban populism was over.

Boston: Populist Growth Politics

Like Kucinich, Raymond Flynn grew up in an inner-city ethnic neighborhood, South Boston. According to the 1980 census, South Boston is 99 percent white and 58 percent Irish, with over one-fifth of the residents living below the poverty line. Flynn's father was an immigrant longshoreman; his mother worked as a cleaning lady in downtown office buildings. A star basketball player in high school and college, "Plain Ray" Flynn, as his supporters call him, served eight years in the state legislature, where he reflected well the views of his constituents. A prominent opponent of busing, Flynn generally voted conservative on social issues and liberal on economic issues.

Elected to a citywide city council seat in 1978, Flynn's views evolved to fit his broader constituency. He reversed his earlier conservative stands, for example, on the Equal Rights Amendment, the death penalty, and fair housing. Over the years, however, Flynn was consistent in his support for the underprivileged, including tenants' rights, rent control, and welfare assistance. In 1983, Flynn used his populist blend of liberal and conservative positions to mount a surprisingly successful campaign for mayor.

The 1983 race for mayor cannot be understood, however, without first examining the career of Kevin White, who dominated Boston politics as mayor from 1967 to 1983.[34] Interestingly, White ran for mayor in 1967 on a pro-neighborhood and anti-downtown platform, vowing to respond to the needs of the neighborhoods against insensitive urban renewal projects. He also enjoyed the support of the business community, which saw him as the moderate alternative to Louise Day Hicks, whose racially polarizing rhetoric frightened many liberals. White beat Hicks in a close race.

Once in office, White worked both sides of the street, promoting downtown development with substantial tax breaks and initiating a series of progressive policies to help those left behind by "The New Boston." In 1968, for example, he established the Little City Hall program to decentralize governmental functions to the neighborhoods.[35] He took public stands opposing airport expansion and construction of the interstate highway network.[36] An advocate of rent control, White campaigned for mayor in 1975 on the slogan, "When Landlords Raise Rent, Kevin White Raises Hell."[37]

Under constant fiscal pressure that forced massive layoffs of city employees, however, White gradually withdrew his support for redistributive policies and concentrated instead on expanding the tax base through downtown development. Shortly after the 1975 election, he supported "vacancy decontrol," a phase-out of rent control. In 1978, the Boston Redevelopment Authority scrapped its neighborhood planning program and, in 1981, White abolished the Little City Halls. Wounded by the busing crisis of 1974–75, White increasingly withdrew from taking strong stands on racial issues and ignored low-income housing to the point that the Boston Housing Authority fell into receivership. White's earlier populist style gradually faded. In the early years, White refused to ride in the massive city limousine and bought a Ford station wagon instead. "But by the mid-seventies, he was back in a limo."[38] Showing insensitivity to rising housing costs, White praised gentrification, calling it "a good thing that richer, professional people are moving in, buying condos."[39] As real estate developers became key contributors to his campaigns, White seemed increasingly mesmerized by downtown development. In fact, a scandal over campaign contributions from developers was partially responsible for White's decision not to run for re-election in 1983.

In 1983, the Boston City Council passed a linkage law that would have required downtown developers to contribute to low-income housing before receiving zoning approval. White vetoed linkage, saying it would drive developers away. Eight of the nine candidates for mayor supported linkage. The two top vote-getters in the primary were Flynn and Black neighborhood activist, Mel King, both of whom relied on grassroots neighborhood support. David Finnegan, who opposed linkage, raised $1 million, more than twice as much as Flynn and King combined, but finished well behind them in the vote.

Flynn emerged from the pack using a time-honored technique in Boston politics: stirring up the poor ethnics, largely Irish Catholic, against the Yankee bluebloods and downtown Republicans. "Every mayor of Boston in this century has run against downtown and for the neighborhood."[40] Flynn's candidacy was given crucial popular legitimacy by early support from tenants' groups and neighborhood organizations. Using classic populist rhetoric, Flynn charged that Finnegan was trying to "buy" City Hall and called for a redistribution of the wealth of downtown to the neighborhoods. In the final election run-off Flynn and King proclaimed startlingly similar pro-neighborhood and pro-tenant positions on most of the major issues. While the campaign was remarkably free of racial rancor, nevertheless, with the city only 22 percent Black, King had an uphill battle. Flynn won with 65.6 percent of the vote.

Up to the point he was elected mayor, Flynn's career resembled Kucinich's in important ways. Like Kucinich, Flynn made a name for himself, and collected a string of press clippings, by attacking the establishment and defending the underdog. Like Kucinich, Flynn downplayed social and racial divisions, emphasizing that inner-city residents could be united on basic economic issues. Like Kucinich, Flynn's populist rhetoric during the campaign, "raised expectations in tenements and anxiety levels in some downtown office suites."[41]

Since becoming mayor, however, Flynn has exchanged the populist rhetoric of confrontation for the liberal rhetoric of compassion and cooperation. His inaugural speech, which reverently referred to neighborhoods thirteen times in nineteen minutes, did not threaten the business community, but instead called for business growth *and* neighborhood renewal.

> The tall and beautiful buildings which grace our city's skyline are monuments to a broad vision which every great city must possess. But these towers of granite and glass must not come at the expense of displacement or neighborhood neglect. We are committed to the progress of downtown revitalization. But we are equally committed to ensuring that no neighborhood in Boston is left behind.[42]

His 1986 State of the City Address continued these themes, calling for "the fusing of economic growth and economic justice." Midway through his first term, Flynn disavowed the populist politics that had, to a significant degree, catapulted him into the mayor's office: "The era of insecurity and confrontation has given way to the politics of caring and compassion."[43]

Flynn's actions in office have been consistent with his promise to pursue both growth and redistribution. In 1985, Flynn signed an executive order that expanded Boston's jobs policy from publicly funded to privately funded projects. For major new construction or rehabilitation projects to get building permits, they must have 50 percent of their work force composed of Boston residents, 25 percent minorities, and 10 percent women. The requirements are for each trade, so that the quotas cannot be satisfied by concentrating the needy in the lowest-paid occupations. Flynn supported rent control but failed to get it passed by City Council. In December 1985, however, Flynn succeeded in passing one of the country's strongest condominium conversion ordinances: "Our priority must be *shelter for people, not for taxes,*" Flynn said.[44] Under pressure from neighborhood and tenant groups, Flynn proposed speeding up the linkage payments for housing, and adding a new building construction fee for job training. In addition, the Flynn Administration inaugurated a parcel-to-parcel linkage program where developers are allowed to develop lucrative downtown plots only if they agree to develop and provide jobs for residents in depressed neighborhoods like Roxbury.

Together with these redistributive reforms, Flynn has pursued growth policies designed to make Boston more attractive to investors and lenders. While the Flynn Administration has attempted to guide development in a rational orderly process, it has not stood in the way of growth. Unlike Kucinich, there have been no rhetorical attacks on the business community; businessmen have been reassured that they are needed and wanted. Perhaps Flynn's most significant achievement so far was his ability to join with business leaders and convince the Massachusetts legislature to approve two new revenue sources for Boston: excise taxes on jet fuels and on hotel rooms. Flynn has taken a number of other steps to put the city's financial house in order, including establishing a capital planning process, improving revenue and expenditure projections, and cutting city personnel. Moody's Investors Service upgraded the city's bond rating from a noninvestment grade, BA, to BAA, an investment grade, and Flynn's actions were praised by the business community.[45]

Linkage and the Politics of the Property Tax

More than any other policy, linkage symbolizes the populist shift in Boston politics. An attempt to "spread the wealth" by tying the growth of downtown to the growth of neighborhoods, linkage is the mirror image of tax abatement. Under tax abatement, cities cut taxes on downtown development in order to attract new investment that will, it is hoped, trickle down to benefit residents of inner-city neighborhoods. Linkage essentially puts an additional tax on downtown development in order to *guarantee* that some of the benefits of growth will be spread out to the rest of the city. These relatively small exactions, proponents of linkage argue, will not harm investment.

The idea of taxing downtown in order to benefit neighborhood residents is not new in Boston politics. Throughout this century, Boston politics has been characterized by a conflict between working-class ethnics in the neighborhoods and the Yankee Brahmins downtown. One manifestation of this conflict has been a longstanding, and largely successful, effort to tax downtown businesses at a higher rate than neighborhood housing and small businesses. For years, Boston politicians have played games with tax assessments. Using differential assessment practices, the tax rate on downtown commercial property was kept higher than the tax rate on housing. In addition, a system of spot assessments was used to keep commercial assessments higher and pry campaign contributions out of recalcitrant businessmen.[46] James Michael Curley, Boston's legendary four-term mayor (1914–17, 1922–25, 1930–33, and 1946–49), was perhaps the most successful practitioner of tax politics. "Old Boston pols tell stories of Curley walking through downtown with aides, suddenly pointing to a building and announcing to one of them, 'I want $10,000 more out of *those* bastards next year.' "[47] Boston's high property taxes were used to fund public works that employed Curley's working-class constituency.[48]

Between 1929 and 1960, however, only one new office building was built in Boston, and the drought was blamed on high taxes. Indeed, because the state legislature is controlled by suburban interests, Boston has not been allowed to develop new alternative sources of revenue. As a result, Boston had (and still has) the highest property tax burden of any major city in the country, nearly twice that of second-place Chicago.[49] Beginning with the Prudential Center in 1961, Boston's mayors attempted to boost downtown development with a series of formal and informal tax abatements. Since 1960 there have been 108 for-

mal tax abatements (called "121A agreements").[50] These abatements
were used to forestall legal challenges to the higher effective tax rates on
downtown commercial property.[51] In 1978, Mayor White united with
citizens' groups and labor unions to pass, over business opposition, the
Property Tax Classification Act, which legalized taxing business at a
higher rate than residential property.

A short while later, this fiscal structure began to collapse. In 1978, a
commercial landlord successfully sued the city for overpayment of
taxes prior to the Classification Act. Boston was forced to refund between $45 and $75 million in taxes.[52] In 1979, Massachusetts voters
passed Proposition 2½, which limited property taxation to 2.5 percent
of the total taxable fair cash value of all property in the community.
Boston's was more than twice this. To come into conformity with
Proposition 2½, Boston was forced to cut $144 million from its property
tax revenues in 1982 and 1983. Almost one-fifth of the municipal work
force was eliminated.[53]

The fiscal crisis had a number of important effects. First, it
weakened Mayor White and contributed to his decision not to run in
1983. Second, the lawsuit and Proposition 2½, whose primary beneficiaries were business, contributed to a kind of backlash against
downtown. At a time when downtown was booming, municipal government was being put through the ringer. Moreover, gentrification was
putting tremendous pressure on low- and moderate-income housing in
Boston. The sense of relative deprivation created by Boston's uneven
development, along with tax cuts for business, created a conducive atmosphere for Flynn's populist rhetoric and the policy of linkage.

Linkage was a response to Boston's housing-affordability crisis.
According to the National Association of Realtors, Boston had the hot-
test real estate market in the nation: from the second quarter of 1984 to
the second quarter of 1985, the median sale price of homes increased a
phenomenal 37 percent.[54] In the city of Boston, as in many other cities,
the link between downtown office development and rapidly inflating
housing prices is evident.[55] Neighborhoods around the downtown area,
such as the South End and Back Bay, experienced gentrification and
displacement beginning in the mid-1970s. Since then, gentrification
has spread to virtually every area of the city.

In March 1983, the Boston City Council passed a linkage policy
modelled on San Francisco's.[56] Mayor White vetoed the law but a short
time later appointed an advisory committee to make a recommendation on linkage. A 1983 study by the Boston Redevelopment Authority
documented the link between downtown development and housing in-

flation.[57] Between 1982 and 1992, the report estimated, downtown development alone would bring 18,445 "new" resident workers into Boston, creating demand for an additional 12,298 housing units. Mayor White's advisory committee issued its report in favor of linkage in October 1983;[58] linkage became law shortly before Flynn took office.

Boston's linkage ordinance requires that any commercial project exceeding 100,000 square feet must either pay a fee of $5 per square foot to a neighborhood housing trust fund or produce equivalent low- and moderate-income housing units. Most developers have opted for the fee, which is due in twelve annual installments beginning at the completion of the project. Linkage will raise an estimated $37 to $52 million over a ten-year period.[59] Payments will not begin, however, until April 1987. Under pressure from housing activists, in November 1985, Flynn proposed speeding up and increasing the linkage exactions. Payments would start upon issuance of a building permit and would be spread over seven years instead of twelve. In addition, Flynn called for an additional $1 per square foot for job training. Overall, Flynn's proposed changes would almost double the "present value" of the linkage payments.

The burning issue in linkage is whether it will discourage investment, the so-called "Golden Goose Question."[60] As we saw in the case of tax abatement, local property taxes are not a significant factor in investment location decisions. Property taxes are simply too small a portion of the cost of doing business. The same could be said of linkage exactions. The existing formula in Boston will cost developers $0.42 per square foot per year for twelve years.[61] Office rents in Boston are approximately $34 per square foot for class A office space. Linkage exactions, then, will increase office rents by a little more than one percent (assuming that the entire burden is borne by the tenant and not the developer). Since the fee can be deducted as a business expense on federal taxes, the burden is even less. A less than one percent increase in office costs will not have a significant impact on Boston's booming office market. In 1984–85, Boston had an estimated $3.1 billion in development—more office construction per capita than any of the nation's other nineteen largest cities.[62] Experience in San Francisco, which has a higher linkage fee than Boston, indicates that it has not deterred investment.[63] "We've checked with economists and real estate people," says Dean Macris, Director of San Francisco's Planning Department, "and we can't find any evidence that it's been harmful."[64]

The relatively small size of linkage costs suggests that they will not have much impact on private-sector investment. The small size of the linkage exactions also suggests, however, that the funds will not be adequate to meet the needs the program is designed to address. In fact, the needs far exceed the resources. A Boston Redevelopment Authority study, for example, estimated that between 1982 and 1992, just the demand created by expanding downtown office employment would create the need for 12,298 new housing units.[65] At a low estimate cost of $70,000 per unit, meeting the need would cost $861 million. Yet linkage will only bring in $37–$52 million under the original formula.

Linkage is basically a local method to address problems that Boston city government is using in the face of federal cutbacks in urban programs and continued hamstringing of Boston's revenue sources by State government. Linkage does not make up for the loss of federal funds, however. Boston's federal job-training funds fell from $66 million in 1979 to $5.5 million in 1985. The $1 per square foot for job training proposed by Flynn will produce some $7–$10 million in funds over a seven-year period—hardly enough to make up for the annual $60.5 million shortfall. By using its control over land use to tie zoning approval to linkage fees, Boston has been able to raise revenue without getting the approval of state government, but the new revenue source is limited.[66]

Conclusion: Political Leadership in a Shifting Urban Arena

The centralization of advanced corporate services functions in the downtowns of central cities has created an opening for the redistributive demands of urban populists. What actually happens, however, is not economically determined but depends on political will, on skillful intervention. In *The Contested City,* John Mollenkopf highlights the role of the political entrepreneur—"one who gathers and risks political capital or support in order to reshape politics and create new sources of power by establishing new programs (or 'products')."[67] Both Kucinich and Flynn fit the definition of populist political entrepreneurs. Kucinich, however, barely survived a recall and was soundly defeated for re-election after only two years.[68] The lesson of Kucinich seems negative: that populist policies generate economic and political instability, a sure path to voter rejection. Flynn, on the other hand, is enormously popular. According to a recent poll, 80 percent of the citizens approve of the way he has managed the city.[69] Flynn appears to be a shoo-in for re-election. What explains the contrasting political fortunes of Kucinich and Flynn and what can we learn from these two experiences about the promise of urban populism?

Certainly one of the most important differences is the greater economic prosperity of Boston compared to Cleveland, which puts Boston city government in a stronger negotiating position. "The economy of Boston is the driving force," observed Flynn, "that allows us to go to the negotiating table from a position of strength."[70] City government is able to use its powers over land use to capture some of the unearned increment, as Henry George would call it, of rising downtown real estate values and recycle it to ameliorate problems of uneven development.

for killing an ineffective abatement program, while Flynn, who has gone much further by demanding compulsory payments from developers, has enjoyed considerable corporate support and little business opposition. Once again, part of the explanation is economics: in Boston developers are so anxious to get part of the downtown action that they are not about to complain about a miniscule linkage fee; they just include it as part of the cost of doing business in Boston. It is a classic non-zero-sum game: an expanding pie enables everyone to have a bigger piece, and no one is forced to take a loss. Cleveland, on the other hand, is desperate for development and voters are more susceptible to charges that populist policies will kill off investment. Even in Cleveland, I would argue, additional taxes could be placed on the growing downtown sector without affecting investment trends. However, it would be difficult to justify such additional taxes on Cleveland downtown development on the basis of a link between office development and loss of inner-city housing. In Cleveland, there is almost no gentrification by downtown office workers. Indeed, suburbanization has left an oversupply of housing in the inner city, leading to depressed prices and extensive abandonment in many neighborhoods.

While economics makes a difference, the contrasting political fortunes of Kucinich and Flynn can be explained more by the differences in their political styles than by the differences in the economies of their cities.[71] In a recent book on mayoral leadership, Barbara Ferman argues that there is an important difference between coalitions for getting elected and coalitions for governing. "Conflict, for example, is a viable strategy for mobilizing support within the electoral arena but often is too divisive to use as a governing strategy."[72] Ignoring this lesson, Kucinich carried the confrontational politics of his campaign into the mayor's office. To a great extent, Kucinich was a victim of his own rhetoric. His lack of a positive program made it easy for the media to paint his celebrated confrontations with the powers-that-be as part of the problem—not the solution. The withdrawal of investment for political reasons in the city's default helped legitimize the charge that Kucinich was responsible for disinvestment in other areas—even though this was not true. Since Kucinich left office, Cleveland's economy, contrary to popular media perceptions, has not turned around.[73] Nevertheless, Kucinich's successor, George Voinovich, has skillfully employed an inclusive non-confrontational style to become one of the most popular mayors in Cleveland's history, decisively winning three straight mayoral elections.

The title of a recent book on the struggles of blacks to achieve equality in urban politics, *Protest is Not Enough,* could serve as an epitaph for Kucinich's experiment in urban populism.[74] The theme of the book is that political responsiveness to black demands was greatest where demand-protest efforts reinforced electoral mobilization. Political incorporation succeeded when autonomous black electoral organizations became part of a governing coalition through alliances with white liberals. Moreover, I would argue, to govern a city effectively, the governing coalition must represent more than a bare majority. Weak and divided political parties, the penetration of local government by narrow interest groups, and the ability of state and federal, as well as private, actors to frustrate city initiatives all accentuate the need for broad political support. As the implementation literature shows, even after passage of a policy, there are many veto points; in order to implement a program effectively, governments must negotiate a series of simultaneous bargains with diverse actors, private as well as public.[75]

Flynn seems to have incorporated these lessons well into his governing strategy. In his 1986 State of the City Address, Flynn continued to down play the populist rhetoric of his campaign and called instead for "building bridges across the gaps of income and opportunity."[76] Recognizing that city government alone cannot solve the underlying problems of poverty and neighborhood decay Flynn has attempted to pull together a broad coalition, including big business, around a program of social amelioration. Much of the glue that holds this coalition together is Flynn's personal popularity as a man of decency. Taking a page from the book of Ronald Reagan, Flynn projects a positive vision of the future and in his speeches stresses his commitment to fundamental values, like family and neighborhood.

In many ways, Flynn's political style could now more accurately be termed liberal than populist. Alan Wolfe describes the essence of post-war American liberalism as a compromise between growth and reform: New Deal commitments to social reform were diluted by the devotion of liberals to economic growth. According to Wolfe, liberalism "sought its goals without threatening the prerogatives of the wealthy and the powerful. It offered social justice without pain, a better life without mobilizing the energy to achieve it."[77] Like post-war liberalism, Flynn's inclusive political strategy relies heavily on economic growth to cover over redistributive conflicts. While effective in the short run, the politics of decency and inclusiveness will not mobilize the neighborhood forces that could pressure for advancing the redistributive agenda in the long run.

Without an organized left, Flynn's redistributive agenda will be in political trouble when Boston's economic boom cools off. Eventually, rapid development or recession will create an office glut. Business interests will use this opportunity to roll back redistributive policies by blaming linkage for the drying up of investment. The business climate issue may play well with voters in Roxbury or Charlestown, who are hurting from unemployment and who are not mobilized into any populist organizations. Also, experience has shown, local fiscal crises are often used to justify the jettisoning of redistributive policies.[78] Both Kucinich's and Flynn's predecessors (Perk and White) moved from populist positions to conservative ones under the pressure of "fiscal responsibility." Without movements to empower populist constituencies, populist programs will be possible at the local level, ironically enough, only at the sufferance of business elites.

Notes

1. Alexander Ganz and Thomas O'Brien, "The City: Sandbox, Reservation, or Dynamo? " *Public Policy,* Winter 1973, pp. 107–123.

2. George Sternlieb,"The City as Sandbox." *The Public Interest,* Fall 1971, pp. 14–21; Norton E. Long, "The City as Reservation," *The Public Interest,* Fall 1971, pp. 22–38; Ira Lowry, "The Dismal Future of Central Cities," in Arthur P. Solomon (ed.). *The Prospective City.* Cambridge: MIT Press, 1980, pp. 161–203.

3. Elaine Morgan, *Falling Apart: The Rise and Decline of Urban Civilization.* London: Souvenir Press, 1976; Richard Louv, *America II.* New York: Penguin, 1985.

146 TODD SWANSTROM

4. Jean Gottman, *The Coming of the Transactional City.* College Park, Maryland: University of Maryland, Institute for Urban Studies, 1983; Alexander Ganz, "Where Has the Urban Crisis Gone?" *Urban Affairs Quarterly,* June 1985, pp. 449–468.

5. Thomas M. Stanback, *Services: The New Economy.* Totowa, N.J.: Allanheld, Osmun, 1981; Barry Bluestone and Bennett Harrison, *The Deindustrialization of America.* New York: Basic Books, 1982; "The False Paradise of a Service Economy," *Business Week,* March 3, 1986, pp. 78–81; Barry Bluestone and Bennett Harrison, *The Great American Job Machine.* Washington, DC: Joint Economic Committee, 1986.

6. The term "bipolar city" is from George Sternlieb and George W. Hughes, "The Uncertain Future of the Central City." *Urban Affairs Quarterly,* June 1983, pp. 455–472.

7. E.E. Schattschneider, *The Semisovereign People.* New York: Holt, Rinehart and Winston, 1960.

8. John Atlas, "Tenant Uprising." *The Nation,* January 11, 1986, pp. 12–14. For an insightful discussion of urban populism in Hartford, Cleveland, Berkeley, Santa Monica, and Burlington, see Pierre Clavel, *The Progressive City.* New Brunswick, NJ: Rutgers University Press, 1986.

9. Paul Peterson, *City Limits.* Chicago: University of Chicago Press, 1981.

10. Harvey Molotch, "The City as a Growth Machine: Toward a Political Economy of Place." *American Journal of Sociology,* September 1976, pp. 309–332; Fred Block, "The Ruling Class Does Not Rule," *Socialist Revolution,* May-June, 1977, pp. 6–28; Robert Goodman, *The Last Entrepreneurs,* New York: Simon and Schuster, 1979; Bluestone and Harrison; Francis Fox Piven and Richard Cloward, *The New Class War.* New York: Pantheon, 1982, pp. 90–91; Roger Friedland, *Power and Crisis in the City.* New York: Schocken, 1983; Michael D. Kennedy, "The Fiscal Crisis of the City," in Michael Peter Smith (ed.), *Cities in Transformation.* Beverly Hills, CA: Sage, 1984, pp. 91–110.

11. Gurney Breckenfeld, "Refilling the Metropolitan Doughnut," in David C. Perry and Arthur J. Watkins (eds.), *The Rise of the Sunbelt Cities.* Beverly Hills, CA: Sage, 1977, pp. 231–258; William E. Simon, *A Time For Truth.* New York: Berkley, 1979, ch. 5; President's Commission for a National Agenda for the Eighties, *Urban America in the Eighties: Perspectives and Prospects.* Washington, DC: U.S. Government Printing Office, 1980; *President's National Urban Policy Report.* Washington, DC: U.S. Government Printing Office, 1982; Donald A. Hicks, "Urban and Economic Adjustment to the Post-Industrial Era," *Hearings Before the Joint Economic Committee, 97th Congress of the United States,* Part 2. Washington, DC: U.S. Government Printing Office, 1982.

12. A Brookings Institute study of urban decline ranked Cleveland and

Boston 2 of 9 cities experiencing the "worst decline" among the 153 cities examined. Katherine L. Bradbury, Anthony Downs, and Kenneth A. Small, *Urban Decline and the Future of American Cities.* Washington, DC: Brookings Institute, 1982, p. 51.

13. Robert Kuttner, "Unemployment mid the Jobs Boom." *Boston Globe,* December 14, 1984.

14. R. B. Cohen, "The New International Division of Labor, Multinational Corporations and Urban Hierarchy," in Michael Dear and Allen J. Scott (eds.), *Urbanization and Urban Planning in Capitalist Society.* London: Methuen, 1981, p. 302.

15. The term "advanced corporate services" was coined by Robert Cohen, *The Corporation and the City.* New York: Conservation of Human Services Project, 1979.

16. Gerald Manners, "The Office in Metropolis: An Opportunity for Shaping Metropolitan America," *Economic Geography,* April 1974, pp. 93–110; Stanback; Peter Daniels, *Service Industries: Growth and Location.* Cambridge: Cambridge University Press, 1982; Gottman.

17. *Downtown Projects: Opportunities for Boston.* Boston: Boston Redevelopment Authority, 1984, p. 24; Todd Swanstrom, *The Crisis of Growth Politics: Cleveland, Kucinich, and the Challenge of Urban Populism.* Philadelphia: Temple University Press, 1985, pp. 77–78.

18. The following section on Cleveland is based on my book, *The Crisis of Growth Politics,* cited above. The term "growth politics" was originated by Molotch; see especially his article cited in note 10, above.

19. T. Harry Williams, *Huey Long.* New York: Alfred A. Knopf, 1969, p. 681.

20. Earl Selby and Robert S. Strother, "Cleveland in Crisis: An Urban Renewal Tragedy." *Reader's Digest,* May 1968, pp. 237–244; Philip W. Porter, *Cleveland: Confused City on a Seesaw.* Columbus: Ohio State University Press, 1976, p. 186; David A. Snow and Peter J. Leahy. "The Making of a Black Slum Ghetto: A Case Study of Neighborhood Transition." *Journal of Applied Behavioral Science,* November 1980, pp. 469–471.

21. Quoted in Joseph Wagner, "Jesting Kucinich Jabs for Next Round." *Cleveland Plain Dealer,* October 6, 1977.

22. Swanstrom, p. 91.

23. Kucinich press release, quoted in "Role of Commercial Banks in Financing the Debt of the City of Cleveland." Committee on Banking, Finance and Urban Affairs, Hearing before the Subcommittee on Financial In-

stitutions. House of Representatives, Washington, DC: U.S. Government Printing Office, 1980, pp. 317–320.

24. Subcommittee on Financial Institutions, Committee on Banking, Finance and Urban Affairs, U.S. House of Representatives, *The Role Commercial Banks in the Finances of the City of Cleveland.* Washington, DC: U.S. Government Printing Office, 1979, p. 240.

25. For full documentation on this point, see Swanstrom, 1985, and Swanstrom, "Urban Populism, Fiscal Crisis, and the New Political Economy," in Mark Gottdiener (ed.), *Cities in Stress: A New Look at the Urban Crisis.* Beverly Hills, CA: Sage Publications, 1986.

26. Quoted in Julie Wiernik and Thomas Geidel, "Weir Warm to Rhodes' Plan for City." *Cleveland Plain Dealer,* January 12, 1979.

27. Swanstrom, *The Crisis of Growth Politics,* pp. 229–232.

28. For a sampling of the vast literature on the ineffectiveness of state and local tax incentives, see John F. Due, "Studies of State-Local Tax Influences in Location of Industry." *National Tax Journal,* June 1961, pp. 541–563; Advisory Commission on Intergovernmental Relations, *State-Local Taxation and Industrial Location.* Washington, DC: U.S. Government Printing Office, 1967; Benjamin Bridges, "State and Local Inducements for Industry: Part 3," in Gerald S. Karaska and David Bramhill (eds.), *Locational Analysis For Manufacturing.* Cambridge, MA: MIT Press, 1969; Bennett Harrison and Sandra Kanter, "The Great State Robbery." *Working Papers,* Spring 1976, pp. 57–66; Jerry Jacobs, *Bidding for Business.* Washington, DC: Public Interest Research Group, 1979; Roger Vaughan, *State Taxation and Economic Development.* Washington, DC: Council of State Planning Agencies, 1979; Michael Kieschnick, *Taxes and Growth.* Washington, DC: Council of State Planning Agencies, 1981; Michael Wasylenko, "The Location of Firms: The Role of Taxes and Fiscal Incentives," in Roy Bahl (ed.), *Urban Government Finance.* Beverly Hills, CA: Sage, 1981, pp. 155–190; Roger Schmenner, *Making Business Location Decisions.* Englewood Cliffs, NJ: Prentice-Hall, 1982.

29. Bureau of Performance Analysis, *Performance Audit of the Industrial and Commercial Incentives Board.* New York: Office of the Comptroller, March 12, 1979; Todd Swanstrom, "Tax Abatement in Cleveland." *Social Policy,* Winter 1982; R. Andrew Parker, "Local Tax Subsidies as a Stimulus for Development: Are They Cost-Effective? Are They Equitable?" *City Almanac,* June 1983, pp. 8–15. One of the few positive evaluations of local property tax abatement programs is found in Daniel R. Mandleker, Gary Feder, and Margaret P. Collins, *Receiving Cities with Tax Abatement.* New Brunswick, NJ: Center for Urban Policy Research, 1980. However, the evidence there on the crucial question of the effect of tax abatements on investment location decisions (pp. 30–41) is sparse, contradictory, and inconclusive.

30. In 1986, however, Voinovich reversed his anti-abatement stand by supporting a $42.9 million abatement for a housing project in University Circle.

31. Quoted in "Tax Abatement Draws Ire of Embattled Kucinich." *Columbus Citizen-Journal,* June 28, 1978.

32. Diamond Shamrock's ranking comes from *Fortune,* May-June 1979; the quotation is from Michael Kelly, "Diamond Shamrock to Leave Area." *Cleveland Plain Dealer,* May 30, 1979.

33. Daniel J. Marschall, "Why Did Diamond Shamrock Go?" *Cleveland Plain Dealer,* June 16, 1979; "Media Distorts Reason, Purely Economic." *Northern Ohio Business Journal,* June 11, 1979.

34. For a fuller account of White's career, see Martha Wagner Weinberg, "Boston's Kevin White: A Mayor Who Survives." *Political Science Quarterly,* Spring 1981, pp. 87–106; Barbara Ferman, *Governing the Ungovernable City.* Philadelphia: Temple University Press, 1985.

35. Eric A. Nordlinger, *Decentralizing the City: A Study of Boston's Little City Halls.* Cambridge, MA: MIT Press, 1972.

36. Alan Lupo, Frank Colcord and Edmund P. Fowler, *Rites of Way.* Boston: Little, Brown & Company, 1971.

37. Boston Urban Study Group, *Who Rules Boston?* Boston: Institute for Democratic Socialism, 1984, p. 49.

38. J. Anthony Lucas, *Common Ground.* New York: Vintage, 1986, p. 619.

39. "A Tale of Two Cities." *Time,* August 30, 1982, p. 23.

40. Martin F. Nolan, "Glorious Traditions, Political Realities." *Boston Globe,* November 11, 1984.

41. Walter V. Robinson, "Headaches for the Next Mayor." *Boston Globe,* October 23, 1983.

42. "Flynn's Inaugural Address." *Boston Globe,* January 3, 1984.

43. Raymond L. Flynn, "State of the City Address," *Boston Globe,* January 8, 1986.

44. Raymond L. Flynn, "Letter to City Councillors," *Boston Globe,* December 12, 1985. (emphasis in original).

45. "Boston Called a Model City." *Boston Business Journal,* November 18, 1985.

46. E. J. Kahn III, "The Day the Banks Saved Boston." *Boston Magazine,* November 1981; Dudley Clendinen, "Contractors, City Workers Are White's Biggest Fans." *New York Times,* January 9, 1983.

47. Michael Kinsley quoted in Diane B. Paul, *The Politics of the Property Tax.* Lexington, MA: Lexington Books, 1975, p. 79.

48. Boston Urban Study Group, p. 10.

49. Douglas Muzzio and Robert Bailey, "Economic Development, Housing, and Zoning: A Tale of Two Cities." Paper delivered at the annual Meeting of the Urban Affairs Association, Norfolk, Virginia, April 17–20, 1985, p. 13.

50. Boston Urban Study Group, p. 22.

51. Paul, p. 85.

52. Boston Urban Study Group, p. 38.

53. *Ibid.,* p. 24.

54. Fox Butterfield, "Soaring Price of Boston Homes Laid to Strong Local Economy." *New York Times,* September 22, 1985.

55. Office development may not only generate additional demand for housing, it may also absorb much-needed housing investment. Anthony Downs argues that changes in the financing of real estate, such as the deregulation of lending institutions, led to overcapitalization in commercial and office development and undercapitalization of residential real estate. *The Revolution in Real Estate Finance.* Washington, DC: Brookings Institute, 1985. Downs' argument fits the pattern in many cities. See Robert Guenther, "Construction Boom Persists Despite Record Rate for Vacancies." *Wall Street Journal,* November 15, 1984.

56. Although San Francisco was the first city to enact a linkage policy, a number of other cities have since followed suit. The best overviews of linkage policies are Douglas Porter (ed.), *Downtown Linkages.* Washington, DC: Urban Land Institute, 1985; and Dennis Keating, "Linking Downtown Development to Broader Community Goals: An Analysis of Linkage Policy in Three Cities." *Journal of the American Planning Association,* Spring 1986, pp. 133–141.

57. *Boston's Prospective Development and the Linkage to Housing Needs.* Boston: Boston Redevelopment Authority, October 1983.

58. Advisory Group, *Report to the Mayor on the Linkage between Downtown Development and Neighborhood Housing.* Boston: City of Boston, 1983.

59. *Ibid.*

60. Keating, p. 133.

61. Advisory Group.

62. *The Flynn Administration at Mid-Term.* Boston: City of Boston, January 8, 1986.

63. Keating, p. 138.

64. Quoted in John Powers, " 'Linkage' Revision Provokes Friction." *Bos ton Globe,* July 28, 1985.

65. Boston Redevelopment Authority.

66. Boston's linkage ordinance was struck down by a State Superior Court in April 1986, *Bonan et al. v. the General Hospital Corporation et al.,* Superior Court Civil Action No. 76438. A few months later the Supreme Judicial Court of Massachusetts reversed the decision of the lower court on procedural grounds and upheld linkage.

67. Mollenkopf, p. 6.

68. While Kucinich was defeated for the mayor's office, he still has considerable populist appeal. In 1982, Kucinich ran for Secretary of State in Ohio on a shoestring budget and garnered a surprising quarter of a million votes. In 1983, Kucinich was elected to Cleveland's City Council again. Kucinich declined to stand for re-election in 1985 in order to run for the Democratic nomination for governor. He later withdrew from that race.

69. Brook Larmer, "Boston's Flynn at Midterm: Turning His Rhetoric into Substance." *Christian Science Monitor,* January 13, 1986.

70. Quoted in Irene Sege, "Flynn Wants Change in Linkage Donations from Development." *Boston Globe,* May 18, 1985.

71. Economic factors cannot account for major policy patterns. New York City, for example, which has probably had more office building and housing inflation than Boston, nevertheless, has enacted generous tax abatements for office and luxury residential construction, mostly in Manhattan. As of 1983, past and future commitments of property tax subsidies totalled $2.7 billion. Koch has opposed linkage, and in 1984 a Koch-appointed study commission refused to endorse any linkage policies. See Frank Domurad and Ruth Messinger, *Citizen Program to Eliminate the Gap.* New York: The City Project, 1983, pp. 23–27; Parker, p. 8; Keating, p. 137.

72. Ferman, 1985, pp. 10 and 13.

73. See Swanstrom, *The Crisis of Growth Politics,* Appendix.

74. Rufus P. Browning, Dale Rogers Marshall, and David H. Tabb, *Protest Is Not Enough.* Berkeley and Los Angeles: University of California Press, 1984.

75. Jeffrey L. Pressman and Aaron Wildavsky, *Implementation.* 3rd ed. Berkeley and Los Angeles: University of California Press, 1984; Martin A. Levin and Barbara Ferman, *The Political Hand.* New York: Pergamon Press, 1985.

76. Flynn, "State of the City."

77. Alan Wolfe, *America's Impasse.* New York: Pantheon, 1981.

78. Martin Shefter argues that fiscal crises are not aberrations but integral mechanisms of urban politics for reconciling conflicting pressures-in-particular, tensions between the need to please voters and control social conflict and the need to please creditors and promote the local economy. During periods of fiscal crisis, redistributive state spending is usually curbed. *Political Crisis/Fiscal Crisis.* New York: Basic Books, 1985.

Chapter 7

Municipal Code Enforcement And Urban Development: Private Decisions and Public Policy In An American City

Scott Cummings and Edmond Snider

Introduction

Over the past several decades, public policies to redevelop central cities in the United States have focused largely on attempting to mobilize, through various tax and profit incentives, the initiative of the business community.[1] Liberal sociologists and political scientists usually refer to business involvement in the formulation and implementation of urban redevelopment policy as reflecting the tradition of *privatism*.[2] Historically, local officials have promoted urban redevelopment schemes implemented through the establishment of "working partnerships" between the public and private sectors. Through these working partnerships, the public good is presumably pursued and enhanced.

The neo-Marxist literature dealing with urban redevelopment shows that public-private renewal schemes are often used to enhance the interests of local business elites. Most neo-Marxist scholars are highly critical of the existing literature describing how traditional urban renewal policies are formulated and implemented. Most studies of urban redevelopment decisions typically fail to identify patterns of collusion between local government policies and the redevelopment plans of private businessmen, or the extent to which urban development policies are championed by charismatic political figures in behalf of wealthy investors and private developers.[3]

While some case studies of business-dominated urban development committees are available,[4] the authors usually fail to explain the extent to which local elites dominate a city's redevelopment agenda. Despite the criticism of existing literature, however, very few neo-Marxist scholars have examined how local government actually implements the redevelopment plans of private businessmen.[5] With the exception of Domhoff's recent reanalysis of Dahl's classic study of New Haven, Connecticut,[6] and related work by Zukin, Ewen, and Hartman, there exist very few case studies illuminating local business domination over urban renewal policy.[7]

This chapter reports the results of an extensive case study of how one American city participated in a plan to redevelop a large residential section of its downtown area. The case study partially illuminates how this city allowed selected branches of its formal municipal structure to be used for purposes of implementing the redevelopment plan itself. Unlike traditional renewal policies implemented through eminent domain and write-down of land value, the case study examines how the process of code enforcement and a financial scheme that removed market risks for investors were used to transform land-use patterns in the city of Dallas, Texas, from one class of users to another. The case is developed to show that local business elites have available numerous redevelopment tools, many of them less interventionist and controversial than outright land and real estate condemnation.

Strategic Code Enforcement as an Instrument of Urban Redevelopment

Differential enforcement of municipal building and housing codes is one of the most powerful levers available to city governments attempting to transform residential and land-use patterns in an urban area. Through code enforcement, municipal officials can seriously alter both the supply and quality of a city's housing stock, especially in poor neighborhoods slated for renewal.[8] And depending on how codes are enforced, the quality of life for the urban poor can be improved or eroded.[9] Hartman, Kessler, and LeGates identify several strategies of code enforcement available to city governments interested in transforming land use and residential patterns within an urban area.[10] These strategies often produce rent increases, displacement, and abandonment.

When landlords are forced by municipal authorities to make investments that will bring their property into conformity with existing housing codes, they typically pass along the cost of improvements in the form of rent increases. This practice further strains the precarious fiscal stability of many low-income urban tenants. If an individual landlord calculates that the costs of improvements are too high, the property itself might be removed from the rental market altogether. Abandonment is a possible by-product of housing codes which are rigidly enforced by city government.[11] In fact, the lobbying activities of many urban apartment associations stress the idea that the supply of low-income housing will contract if housing codes are enforced too vigorously. On the other hand, large investments in improving the housing stock found in some low-income areas can also lead to displacement. Rent increases produced through code enforcement can drive out existing tenants, or create fiscal incentives leading to the conversion of existing apartment units into condominiums, and, if the housing stock is suitable, widespread patterns of gentrification. Strategically enforced codes can be used by city government to upgrade existing housing stock or to spur a change from one class of residents to another.

Another potential effect of strategic code enforcement within American cities is physical clearance and demolition. Constant and sustained pressure to upgrade existing housing can result not only in abandonment, but also in the actual demolition of the property itself. Most American cities are legally empowered to raze buildings that, after repeated warning to owners, fail to meet city codes. Owners are typically held liable for the costs incurred by the city should real property have to be demolished. It is obvious that demolition produces a direct and severe strain on the supply of existing low-income housing. It inevitably leads to overcrowding, and initiates a spiraling demand for the even fewer units that are within the financial reach of poor and working-class families. While a considerable literature exists dealing with how the Urban Renewal and Model Cities programs resulted in the demolition of the housing stock in poor urban neighborhoods, and subsequently transformed the lives of America's urban poor,[12] relatively little is known about the relationship between local code enforcement and urban redevelopment.

The case study reported here illuminates the conditions under which municipal government in American cities can use the code enforcement process in a rational and deliberate manner. More specifically, the case study reveals the degree to which a specific city strategically used municipal codes and enforcement personnel to produce changes in both urban land use and residential patterns within a designated geographic area. While code enforcement activities can be viewed as random events shaped by natural patterns of physical deterioration within specific urban neighborhoods, the evidence in our case study shows that city government strategically targeted an area for concentrated and sustained code enforcement activities. If an area of the city has been selected by private investors for renovation and renewal, it is obvious that some degree of contact must be established between the developers and those branches of city government responsible for building codes and permits, code enforcement, and the administration of city housing and service delivery policies. This case study clarifies the actual interface between City Hall and private developers, and as such, reveals in more detail the neo-Marxist contention that municipal government is often highly responsive to the needs of local business elites, and can be viewed as a mechanism of class domination and control.

The central argument of this chapter is that strategic code enforcement activities in American cities are best understood as a manifestation of class conflict over land use within an urban area. More specifically, we view municipal government as an institution which articulates the needs and interests of urban business elites. Municipal government not only articulates the needs and viewpoints of a dominant business class within the city, but legitimates the power of that group over other class interests. City government does this by implementing policies and programs that advance or protect the economic and financial concerns of the city's business classes. We treat code enforcement as a strategic weapon of class conflict and domination. In order to illustrate this observation more fully, we will elaborate briefly the relationship between suburban development and downtown deterioration. We will also show how code enforcement reflects competition between urban and suburban investors and speculators.

In recent years, traditional and orthodox theories of urban land use in American cities have been subjected to serious criticisms.[13] Sharply departing from social ecology theory, as well as more pluralistic models of municipal interest-group processes and free-market equilibrium, radical economists and sociologists have developed explicitly Marxist conceptions of how urban space is allocated and developed.[14] Wilhelm has criticized traditional ecological theory for failing to recognize the importance of rational self-interest and profit maximization as primary determinants of major land-use and zoning decisions.[15] Developing a more explicit class conflict approach, Powell argued that decisions over urban land use are made by powerful property holders and developers in pursuit of maximized profit.[16] Conflicts over how urban land might be used are usually lost by the groups without access to investment capital and political influence.

Geographer David Harvey has developed more detailed criticisms of classical land-use theory by identifying the various groups involved in making important land-development decisions: occupiers, realtors, landlords, developers, financial institutions, and governmental agencies.[17] He argues that those groups and institutions with greatest access to investment capital shape the urban landscape. Similar interpretations have been forwarded by Castells; he maintains that urban growth and development is "dominated by capitalist industrialization" and "entirely governed by the logic of profit."[18] Lamarche, as well, views the use of urban space as determined by the speculative investment interests of a propertied class.[19] This class is motivated primarily by the search for maximized profits and high investment yields. The observations of Harvey, Castells, and Lamarche are applicable to the American urban scene, and more specifically to this case study.

The radical approach to urban land use can be used to explain the contradictory and strained relations that often develop between the central city and its surrounding suburbs.[20] As a result of unplanned urban development, real estate speculators and developers seeking profits in suburban areas have helped to erode the commercial and business vitality of the central city. The erosion of the central city's economy represents a fragmentation of interests within the propertied classes. As explained by Ashton, local business elites have massive investments in the decaying urban centers which they cannot easily abandon.[21]

The corrosive aspects of American suburban development on the vitality of the central city's business and fiscal stability illustrates the irrational and contradictory nature of unplanned, capitalist urban development.[22] It also explains the fragmentation and competition characteristic of metropolitan government. Molotch and Mollenkopf argue that powerful developers and propertied interests dominate metropolitan political bodies in a manner that serves to stimulate urban growth as well as urban renewal.[23] What is of particular interest to this study, however, is the competition and associated conflicts of interest which are often initiated within the propertied classes as a result of suburban development. Competition may occur between various factions of the local business elite, or between the local elite and national investors and speculators.

As explained by Markussen, suburban governments in the United States typically attempt to attract both industry and those residents of the city who can contribute to the business vitality of the suburbs.[24] Middle- and upper-class movement to the suburbs represents a tremendous drop of purchasing power within the central city. As a result, American suburban development often produces conflict and competition within the propertied classes, especially between those with fixed investments in the central city and their local or national counterparts pursuing business investments in the surrounding suburbs. While there may be conflict and competition within the propertied classes, there is not a corresponding increase in the power or bargaining position of the urban working and lower classes. According to Markussen, the autonomy of suburban jurisdictions enables them to escape the fiscal burdens of the central cities but continue to enjoy many of the benefits.

It is within the larger framework of urban redevelopment, suburban development, and intra- and inter-class conflict that this case study should be understood. It is our thesis that municipal code enforcement in American cities is both a weapon of class conflict, and a manifestation of intra-class competition among urban and suburban land developers and speculators. Consistent with neo-Marxist interpretations, we view municipal government as an institution capable of legitimating the policies and development plans of local business elites, and as an instrument of class domination and control. We also see it as a potential weapon in a struggle between urban and suburban business elites. Our actual case study is drawn from a plan to revitalize a large section of the central city of Dallas, Texas. In order to explain the redevelopment plan, and illustrate how the case of Dallas corresponds to the radical formulation just elaborated, we will present some descriptive information.

Suburban Development and Urban Renewal in the American Sunbelt: The Dialectics of Metropolitan Growth

By most objective standards, Dallas has been a prosperous American city. It is a center of financial and commercial vitality in the southwestern United States, and has been considered by many observers as a centerpiece in the economic emergence of the "sunbelt" as a major power in the American economy. Its unemployment rate has been low by national standards, and the potential quality of life is considered to be among the best in the nation. Dallas' population growth from 434,462 in 1950 to nearly one million residents in 1980 reflects its emergence as a center of American capitalism. The emergence of Dallas as a regional center of Southwestern financial capital, however, must be seen in light of the suburban development that has accompanied it.

The city itself was growing, but so was the entire Dallas–Fort Worth metropolitan region. Associated with this metropolitan growth and expansion was a concomitant shift in the racial and class composition of both Dallas and Fort Worth, its sister city thirty miles away. In 1950, blacks comprised about 13 percent of Dallas' population. By 1980, the proportion of black Americans residing in Dallas approached 30 percent. The proportion of Spanish-speaking people living in both Dallas and Fort Worth has increased sharply over the past decade. The degree of racial polarization and residential segregation in both cities is extremely high.[25] Further, the ghettos and barrios of Fort Worth and Dallas reveal all the symptoms of neglect and decay which are found in central cities all over the United States.

While these population tranformations were taking place, the suburbs between Dallas and Fort Worth were experiencing equally rapid growth and change. At present, the Dallas–Fort Worth metropolitan area is one of the fastest growing regions in the United States. Suburban growth, however, has been qualitatively different. The major suburbs between and surrounding the two cities—Arlington, Irving, Richardson, Hurst, Euless, Bedford, Garland, and Lancaster—are predominantly white, professional and managerial and high income. The homogeneous class and racial composition of the suburbs has been encouraged by court-ordered busing in Dallas,[26] and by a refusal on the part of many suburban jurisdictions to participate in federally sponsored housing and community development programs.[27] Simply stated, suburban political autonomy, white flight, and the suburbanization of industry, while contributing to the prosperity of the metropolitan region as a whole, have eroded the business and commercial vitality of the two central cities.

Arlington, Richardson, and Irving, three of the largest suburbs in the area, have huge industrial parks. A large General Motors assembly plant is located between Arlington and Grand Prairie. Without adequate metropolitan public transportation available, central city residents do not have easy access to the places where business, industry, and jobs are being located. In addition, the construction of massive suburban shopping malls throughout the suburban regions has further undermined the business vitality of downtown Dallas and Fort Worth. Even the Dallas Cowboys football franchise has left the legendary Cotton Bowl for Texas Stadium, a facility located in suburban Irving. The Cotton Bowl, part of the state's fairgrounds, is surrounded by South Dallas, one of the nation's worst black ghettos.

As Ashton argues, the suburban governments within the Dallas–Fort Worth metropolitan region have attempted to insulate themselves from the low-income and minority residents found in central cities.[28] They have also pursued investment and development strategies that compete with the Dallas–Fort Worth business interests. As the neo-Marxist perspective contends, when business interests in the central city are threatened by suburban growth and development, urban elites must turn to the state (in this case local government) to find ways to guarantee profitability and to restore or protect a competitive advantage. Central city business interests often try to use municipal government in a manner that underwrites their own investments, usually at the direct expense of working- and lower-class groups. This may be done by requiring or compelling the diversion of tax dollars to subsidize business relocation schemes or renewal programs, rather than using public funds to provide social services to the urban working class. Local business elites may also get the city to implement policies and plans allowing them to compete more effectively with suburban business elites. A plan to revitalize a large section of downtown Dallas illustrates how code enforcement can be used as a mechanism to provide a competitive edge to urban rather than suburban business interests.

The Local Business Elite and City Government

We gathered data for the case study from city council minutes, newspaper accounts, and interviews with public officials, city administrators, and code enforcement personnel. Additional information was gathered from documents and records within the city of Dallas Department of Housing and Urban Rehabilitation; this branch of city government is responsible for code enforcement, as well as implementing the city's housing policy. We also gathered information from various public records dealing with real estate transactions, code enforcement and city service delivery. We also used informants in the study. Various individuals within city government provided us with interdepartmental communications, their own observations on the degree of articulation between departments, and the degree of contact between various city departments and those private agencies designing and implementing the redevelopment plan. Since many of the decisions examined in this study were made in quarters not subject to social science scrutiny, we do not have complete data capable of illuminating all aspects of the research question. Where data are deficient, our conclusions are more narrow; in addition, we have been careful to indicate to the reader where the data and findings are less than fully supported. Although some of our data sets are not complete, the total pattern of evidence is consistent with the larger argument developed in the preceding pages.

We present the findings in two sections. The first deals with a description of the origins of the redevelopment plan. The second details how the city used the code enforcement process to help implement the redevelopment strategy. The last section of the chapter examines the findings within the framework of the neo-Marxist model of urban land use and discusses the policy implications of the data.

Findings I: The Plan and the Subsidy

In the face of the larger patterns of metropolitan growth and development just described, Dallas announced plans to initiate a major effort to revitalize decaying neighborhoods in the city, in hopes of reversing the outward migration of middle- and high-income residents to the suburbs. The plan was publicly announced in 1975, but it was obvious that negotiations between the city and private developers had taken place well before then. What follows is a reconstruction of events prior to 1975 and up to 1978.

In March 1975, the city manager of Dallas publicly delivered a unique proposal to the City Council: an innovative plan calling for the redevelopment and revitalization of a large inner-city residential area. This plan had the city of Dallas guaranteeing all property acquisitions in the area made by private developers by initiating a "buy-back" land policy. This unique provision meant that the city would be responsible for buying back land at $2.25 a square foot from a private developer if the redevelopment project turned out to be unmarketable. The stated purpose of this proposal was to encourage the redevelopment of areas within the Dallas core that had deteriorated over the years. In principle, the logic behind the plan was similar to slum clearance under the Urban Renewal program. The city manager reasoned that there appeared to be a growing interest in the housing market within inner-city neighborhoods, as demonstrated by major revitalization and gentrification efforts taking place in the historic East Dallas area. A major goal of the city manager's plan was to attract the middle and professional classes back to the inner city. The city manager at that time publicly proffered his "buy-back proposal" as the Area Redevelopment Plan (ARP). The program was adopted by Council resolution on March 31, 1975.

The transcripts of the City Council meeting at which this proposal was broached and approved reveal several significant features of the plan. First, the ARP could ultimately commit the city to a total buy-back guarantee of ten million dollars, depending on how much land was involved. Local tax dollars would be used to guarantee the redevelopment scheme. Second, this financial commitment on the city's part would be for the land only, and not applicable to any improvements built upon the land by the developer. The financial risk associated with all real improvements would be the sole liability of the developer. The total arrangement would be formalized by contract between the city and the developer after the developer's acquisition of the land, and would be binding only for the land itself. We shall show strong if circumstantial evidence of direct involvement of private business elements in the Council decision-making process itself. Our case study reveals that public institutions and processes were used in a manner that promoted the interests of private developers. Public-sector resources were used to both legitimate and subsidize the plan. As announced, the buy-back guarantee of $2.25 per square foot would ostensibly be the city's chief responsibility in the plan. However, the Council transcripts reveal that in the contract with each developer, the city would also agree to make such improvements as street revisions, installation of utilities, reorganization of open spaces, and the updating of public facilities such as fire stations within the area. Thus, the city of Dallas also committed itself to extensive economic obligations for infrastructure improvements and social service delivery.

The minutes also revealed that developers had first to secure their own financing for acquiring the property, without municipal support. Second, any contract between the city of Dallas and the developer would leave the private investors liable for all improvements on the land; the city would accept no liability for any houses built in the redevelopment area. Third, the contract would have a sunset provision, cancelling the city's buy-back obligation within a specified period of time. The development had to follow a timetable once under contract; however, this agreement would have several stages at which the developer could step out of the contract. If the contract dates passed before completion of the project, then the private developer would forfeit the buy-back option. This appeared to be the biggest risk in the plan for the private developers. Otherwise, it is clear that the plan, at base, was attempting to remove the market risks for private investors. There were two other stipulations in the plan which affected potential risks for the developer; however, the degree of investment uncertainty appeared minimal. First, the developer was required to purchase a minimum of 80,000 square feet, approximately two city blocks. This provision, hypothetically, was bound to be met by any developer, because such tract size was necessary to ensure the architectural homogeneity of the project. The other stipulation was that the land in the project had to be within a two-mile radius of the geographic center of the city. Without this stipulation, the plan would be of little value for revitalizing areas within the inner city.

By virtue of the mechanics in the proposed plan, the city of Dallas was taking on some significant financial responsibilities. Consistent with free-market rhetoric, the official justification of this obligation was that private developers needed adequate financial incentives to redevelop deteriorated areas within the central city. The city manager's office suggested it was making a very positive move toward "saving the inner city" by passage of the plan. In July 1975, the Council took another step toward providing additional incentives for developers by agreeing to include interest charges in the revolving guarantee account. Thus, the city now agreed to pay for the land and for interest charges on the developer's expenditures if the plan failed to materialize. However, this was not to be the final financial commitment on the part of the city. In January 1978, the City Council agreed to increase the maximum land guarantee by $1.00 per square foot, thus raising the total guarantee for the buy-back policy to $3.25 per square foot.

Although the plan was made public in 1975, the details of land-use planning had taken place long before the city manager approached the Council. While there is inadequate data describing the specifics of the private negotiations between City Hall and the developers, we subjected several events to analysis. Although March 23, 1975, marked the actual date that the Dallas city manager formally proposed the Area Redevelopment Plan to the Council, and on March 31, the City Council approved the idea by endorsing the ARP, other parties within City

Hall and in the target neighborhoods knew of the plan and its implications for Dallas at a much earlier date. In April 1974, a major real estate firm in the city had started acquiring properties within an inner-city area just east of downtown Dallas. In fact, on the day of the plan's presentation to the City Council, the local papers reported that this firm had already purchased some fifty parcels of land within the area discussed by the city. Inasmuch as the broker had bought the land under the auspices of a trusteeship, it was apparent that he was purchasing the land for other interested, yet unnamed parties. The identity of the real buyer did not surface publicly until 1976.

It was evident to city staff and affected citizens within the area that something major was in progress. The real estate broker was purchasing property within the selected area at a rapid rate, and was rather obtrusive in doing so. Speculation as to the identity of the real buyer ran from out-of-state corporations to the city of Dallas itself. The broker remained silent on the subject, saying only that he was purchasing the property as a trustee for parties who preferred to remain anonymous. In the spring of 1976, the public was greeted with an announcement—the covert buyer of all the land for the ARP was the Fox and Jacobs Company, a major home builder in the southwestern United States, and one of the largest in the nation.[29]

The company's plan as announced was to redevelop the area by clearing all old and deteriorated structures and building new single-family residences aimed at middle- and upper-middle-income buyers. The developers were planning to acquire between 60 and 80 acres of land prior to the start of new construction. On this land, they planned to construct up to 60 new homes, initially priced between $40,000 and $80,000. This cost figure was increased in August 1978, and an average price tag per dwelling of $70,000 was publicized. At present, the houses sell for about $140,000. The entire redevelopment project was given a projected total cost in the vicinity of $80 million. The president of the firm was quoted as saying, "We're not doing this as a favor to anyone. This is a business proposition and we plan to make money from it."[30] If the project failed, the firm's investment in the land was guaranteed by the city's "buy-back" policy.

The developer stated that their company had conducted a market survey and certain respondents had expressed interest in owning homes near their downtown jobs. For this reason, they had begun acquiring property in 1974 through a local real estate firm. In January 1977, the president of the firm announced that the original guarantee of $2.25 per square foot would be insufficient to cover any losses incurred if the project failed. In January 1978, he met with the city manager and requested an increase in the "buy-back" figure to a total of $3.25, or an increase of $1.00 per square foot. He felt this addition was warranted due to inflated land costs and higher-than-anticipated prices for property being held by remaining owners within the target area. This guarantee increase was approved by the City Council the day after the developer's conference with top Dallas administrators. All members of the Council, save one, voted for the increase, based on the mayor's premise, "It is proper for the City to increase its commitment," in order to save the central city.[31]

As of February 1978, the private developers had acquired 55 acres of land, approximately 25 acres short of the total they called a "critical mass" needed to begin the project. These developers also indicated that as of February 28, 1978, they would no longer purchase property within the area. They also stated it would take up to nine months for the corporation to make a decision as to whether the project would proceed to actual construction. However, the developers publicly announced in May of 1978 that they planned to proceed with construction of the project, despite the fact that they had not been able to purchase the desired amount of land: the "critical mass" of about 80 acres.

The president of the firm met with city officials in January 1979 in order to add to the new buy-back guarantee. The City Council altered its policy of 1978 in deference to his request. After announcing his intention to proceed, the developer made known other city policy changes he needed in order to make the project succeed. These included exemptions to zoning and subdivision regulations, and street modifications. He argued that these changes were necessary and important to the success of the plan. The concessions were ultimately granted, and we will discuss them in detail below.

We contend these events reveal the fact that major land-use decisions in Dallas were made primarily by powerful developers and real estate speculators, in conjunction and in collusion with public officials. Although we do not know how the business transactions between the public and private sectors were negotiated, it is obvious that serious discussions over land-use planning had taken place well before the ARP became public. Our observations were confirmed by informants within City Hall. Unfortunately, we do not know how the "deal" was actually brokered, negotiated, and legitimized prior to its public approval by the Council.

Nonetheless, we did secure an inter-office memo, dated October 1978, from informants within city hall, which described the events taking place between the developer, the city manager's office, and the Department of Housing and Urban Rehabilitation (DHUR). The memo, circulated among key administrative personnel within DHUR, explained that the city manager had been "making a very strong pitch for us to be as receptive as possible to all requests from Fox and Jacobs for deviations from standard practices [zoning, city ordinances, and so forth]—because of the extreme importance the city places on the project." The memo further explained that various ordinances would have to be applied flexibly in order to ensure the success of the project.

It is certain that private investors would not purchase substantial amounts of property in a low-income neighborhood without strong commitments and pledges from city hall. In addition, since the council had to ultimately approve the plan itself, it is likely that their endorsement of the scheme was obtained well before the actual vote took place. Little public opposition to the plan was voiced by the City Council. This was due to the fact that Council members were elected primarily on an at-large basis, many being themselves representatives of business and real estate interests. Minorities and low-income groups, especially those residing in the area, had little official opportunity to influence this major land use decision because they were politically disenfranchised by the electoral procedure. While selected aspects of the "working partnership" between private developers and city hall must remain ambiguous, we have a considerable amount of data showing how various branches of city government were used to legitimate and implement the developers' plan. City codes were applied in a strategic and deliberate manner.

Findings II: Code Enforcement

To illustrate the specific manner in which code enforcement was used to implement the redevelopment scheme, we compared the ARP target community with a similar geographic area of the city.[32] We were interested in determining the magnitude of the city's intervention in the housing market of the target community. We estimated intervention by examining whether the city strategically and differentially applied code enforcement activities in one area of the community but not in another.[33]

The communities selected for redevelopment consisted of the area within two census tracts near downtown Dallas: about half of Tract 16 in all of Tract 22.01. On the basis of demographic data (see Table 7.1),

TABLE 7.1. Selected Areas by Population and Housing Characteristics, Dallas, 1970

Characteristic	A.R.P. Area		Comparison Area	
	Census Tract			
	16.00[a]	22.01	25.00	26.00
I. Proportion of Population	(N = 1,625)	(N = 1,629)	(N = 4,737)	(N = 1,798)
Black	92.0%	25.0%	89.7%	6.6%
Anglo	6.6	54.7	7.4	79.8
Mex-Am	1.2	19.2	2.3	12.8
Other	0.2	1.1	0.6	0.8
II. Age Distribution	(N = 1,625)	(N = 1,629)	(N = 4,737)	(N = 1,798)
0-15 Years	31.9%	19.4%	36.3%	29.7%
16-34 Years	25.6	29.4	28.8	21.3
35-45 Years	11.1	12.5	10.3	8.1
46-60 Years	12.6	13.9	11.4	17.1
Over 60 Years	18.8	24.8	13.2	28.8
III. Family Income Levels (Annual)	(N = 272)	(N = 297)	(N = 1,121)	(N = 504)
Less than $5,000	63.7%	38.4%	47.5%	19.4%
$5,000-$9,999	29.8	45.8	40.6	42.3
$10,000-$25,000	6.5	13.8	11.3	36.3
Over $25,000	—	2.0	0.6	2.0
IV. Housing Occupancy	(N = 629)	(N = 662)	(N = 1,482)	(N = 653)
Owner-Occupied	9.7%	5.9%	25.9%	61.8%
Renter-Occupied	90.3	94.1	74.1	38.2
V. Age of Housing	(N = 737)	(N = 730)	(N = 1,645)	(N = 686)
Built Prior to 1949	76.1%	82.9%	66.3%	87.8%
1950-1965	21.6	14.5	29.5	12.2
1966-1970	2.3	2.6	4.2	—
Post-1970	—	—	—	—
VI. Housing Condition	(N = 737)	(N = 730)	(N = 1,645)	(N = 686)
Substandard (lacking some or all plumbing facilities)	5.3%	5.3%	2.5%	2.0%

Source: Calculated from 1970 Census.
[a]Only Census Blocks within C.T. 16.00 that are within Study Area.

two similar non-redeveloped areas were selected for comparison: Tracts 25 and 26. These two tracts were in proximity to the central business district, and each had characteristics similar to one of the ARP target neighborhoods. The ages and racial compositions of the four tracts were very similar. Among both the ARP and the comparison tracts, there was a predominantly black and an integrated community. All four areas were of low or moderate income, although Tract 26 revealed a higher proportion of households with incomes in the $10,000 to $25,000 category. The ARP area was overwhelmingly populated by tenants; a higher proportion of owner-occupied households was found in the comparison neighborhoods. Vacancy levels in all areas were similar. The ages of the units were very close in all four areas, as was the total proportion of units considered substandard. Overall, the four areas were reasonably similar.

To illustrate how city codes were used to assist the private developer's plan, we examined appropriate records at the city of Dallas Department of Housing and Urban Rehabilitation from 1973 to 1978. This corresponds roughly to the period in which the major buying activity of the developers and their real estate associates were at their peak. Analytically, the time series analysis within the two areas corresponds to a pre- and post-test. We were interested in determining if code enforcement activities were used in a manner that assisted the private developers in their attempt to purchase real estate in the target community. Like the buy-back subsidy plan itself, it seemed reasonable to suspect that the city also might provide assistance to the developer by increasing its code enforcement activities in the redevelopment area. As previously explained, by increasing code enforcement activities a city can create incentives for landlords or other property owners to sell out to private speculators and investors.

The city of Dallas housing policy is codified in the *Housing and Urban Rehabilitation Standards Ordinance.*[34] This ordinance sets forth specific requirements for minimum standards that must be met in all housing units within the city. Any housing unit or structure found in violation of these minimum housing codes is subject to referral to Municipal Court or other bodies seeking to bring the unit into compliance. Property owners of substandard housing units may be subject to court fines of up to two hundred dollars, or tax liens may be assessed on their property for corrective actions, such as the demolition of substandard units. In the latter case, the owner may be liable for all costs associated with demolition.

Citizen complaints are the chief mechanisms by which city personnel began code enforcement proceedings against an owner and his property. Citizens register complaints with the city Department of Housing and Urban Rehabilitation (DHUR) about suspected substandard housing conditions. Field inspectors are responsible for investigating these complaints. If violations of the housing regulations are found on the property, the owner is notified and the code enforcement process begins. Often, property owners are required by city officials to make substantial and costly repairs to the substandard property.

Another means of identifying substandard units by city inspectors is through "open and vacant" inspections. Any structure or unit found vacant and open so as to allow unauthorized entry is deemed to be a definite fire hazard by the city ordinances. All code enforcement officers are legally empowered to require that such units be secured and that any other code violations be remedied by the owner. The final mechanism for code enforcement is initiated by inspectors themselves. An unwritten policy for DHUR inspectors is to investigate housing units in violation of ordinance provisions in the following order: (1) citizen complaints; (2) "open and vacant" property; (3) inspector initiated investigation on a "worst-first" basis. Thus, an inspector within the city of Dallas can start the code enforcement process on his or her own accord simply by notifying an owner of obvious or major code violations.

Strategically enforced codes might motivate an owner to consider selling a substandard property rather than repairing it. By doing so, the landlord might make an immediate profit over his original purchase price because of the inflated real estate market. Moreover, by selling the property, the owner will no longer be burdened with the worries of taxes, poor tenants, repair bills, or city ordinances. Thus, vigorous code enforcement by city officials could indirectly encourage the sale of properties by owners, and, thereby, indirectly assist an individual in purchasing property from owners who normally might not be ready to sell. In other words, active code enforcement and a rigidly enforced housing policy could easily create a buyer's market for substandard housing.

Since citizen complaints are the chief cause for housing code enforcement, it follows that an increase in citizen complaints, giving rise to code enforcement activity in the ARP area, could stimulate owners to sell out to those spearheading the redevelopment plan. Only limited complaint data were available for 1973 and 1974. The Department of Housing and Urban Rehabilitation kept incomplete records of citizen complaints until January 1975, at which time complete files were es-

tablished. The absence of hard data for 1973 and 1974 was partly rec-
tified through interviews. Code enforcement personnel were of the
opinion that activities during those years did increase over previous
years.

Housing complaints increased between the years of 1975 and 1976,
a fact which code enforcement personnel claimed was an extension of
1973–1974 patterns. (See Table 7.2.) While this was true for both study
areas, very sharp increases apeared in the ARP census tracts. Moreover, the actual number of complaints registered was significantly
higher in the ARP than in the comparative area, especially given the
much smaller number of units in the ARP areas. In 1975, 111 citizen
complaints were made in the ARP area while only 61 were made in the
comparative area. This is a ratio of nearly two to one. In 1976, the total
number of citizen requests in the ARP area increased to 159, or by 42.3
percent, while in the comparison community, there was an increase of
only 16.4 percent for the same year. Then in 1977, both areas experienced decreases in the total number of complaints registered with
Housing and Urban Rehabilitation. From 159 complaints in 1976, the
figure for the ARP target area declined 84.3 percent, while the comparison community experienced a drop of 25.3 percent, or from 71 complaints to 53. This declining trend continued in 1978.

The redevelopment scheme was made public in 1975; records at
the Dallas County Courthouse reveal that much of the purchase of
property for the ARP was done during 1975 and 1976. It is important to
note that it was during these same years that the largest volume of complaints were registered with the city concerning housing code violations
within the target area. The number of housing complaints closely
parallels the most rapid periods of property acquisition within the project area. (See Table 7.3.)

We do not know who actually registered the citizen complaints. It
is unlikely, however, that tenants themselves initiated calls to city hall.
Tenants in Dallas are not an organized interest group, and are offered
only marginal legal protection as consumers in the state of Texas. Consequently, they are not prone to challenge the maintenance habits of
landlords in a court of law. Furthermore, tenants' rights groups in East
Dallas were actively trying to stall the redevelopment project and were
critical of the city's code enforcement activities in the ARP area. While
it is conceivable that the developer hired people to complain to city
hall, we have no evidence that would corroborate this possibility.

The relationship between the volume of registered complaints and
the acquisition of property by the developer is further mirrored by the

TABLE 7.2. Citizen Complaints for Selected Census Tracts, Dallas, 1973-1978

	A.R.P. Area				Comparison Area			
	Census Tract 16.00[a]		Census Tract 22.01		Census Tract 25.00		Census Tract 26.00	
Year	No.	% Change	No.	% Change	No.	% Change	No.	% Change
1973	3	—	1	—	N/A	—	N/A	—
1974	5	67%	6	500%	N/A	—	N/A	—
1975	42	740	69	1,050	57	—	4	—
1976	70	67	89	29	59	4%	12	200%
1977	15	−79	10	−89	29	−51	24	100
1978[b]	5	−67	2	−80	9	−69	9	−63
Total	140		177		154		49	

[a]Only Census Blocks within C.T. 16.00 that are within Study Area
[b]Data through October 1978.
N/A = not available

TABLE 7.3. Housing and Urban Rehabilitation Code Enforcement Cases and Property Acquisitions in ARP Area, Dallas, 1973–1978

Year	H & UR Complaints No.	Sold To Developer No.	%	H & UR Inspector Initiated No.	Sold To Developer No.	%	Total H & UR Cases	Sold To Developer No.	%
1973	4	3	75.0%	5	4	80.0%	9	7	77.8%
1974	11	11	100.0	0	0	0	11	11	100.0
1975	111	72	64.9	69	59	85.5	180	131	72.8
1976	159	101	63.5	121	62	54.5	280	167	59.6
1977	25	16	64.0	2	2	100.0	27	18	66.7
1978	7	5	71.4	4	3	75.0	11	8	72.7
Total	317	208	65.5%	201	130	64.7%	518	342	66%

decreasing numbers of complaints. More specifically, the purpose behind the acquisitions was announced midway through 1976. The rate of
property acquisitions began to slow in the latter part of that same year.
If anonymous complaints were used as a mechanism for initiating code
enforcement, and thus for stimulating property sales, such use was
greatly curtailed by 1977. While we do not have data that more clearly
illuminate the link between anonymous code enforcement and property acquisition, it is clear that as the total number of properties acquired
by the developer rapidly grew in 1975 and 1976, so did citizen complaints. As purchases declined, due to whatever reasons, so too did the
volume of citizen complaints regarding housing conditions.

There is more evidence that partially clarifies the relationship between complaints, code enforcement policy, and property acquisitions
by the developer, namely, anonymous citizen complaints and inspector-initiated cases. (See Table 7.3.) For each of these types of code
enforcement activities, the number of properties subjected to them and
then acquired by the developer can be shown. It is clear that most of the
units subject to code enforcement were eventually bought by the
developer. The data (see Table 7.3) again point to a strong relationship
between city code enforcement activities and property acquisitions.
Although there is no conclusive evidence that proves that code enforcement was being orchestrated in concert with the developer's need to acquire property, the evidence clearly suggests this latter interpretation is
more plausible than one rooted in fortuitous or random events.
Furthermore, code enforcement personnel within DHUR did admit
privately that they were instructed "from above" to increase code enforcement activities in the ARP area, a fact further illustrated by the
memo cited earlier.

The developer and his agent purchased large amounts of property
that was being investigated, for whatever reason, by the city code enforcement staff. Over 60 percent of all property in code enforcement
cases in the ARP area during the study's time span was eventually
purchased by the developer—during the process of code enforcement.
The purchase–code enforcement linkage was especially strong in 1975–
1976. There appears to be no significant difference in how the city started its action. In other words, the percentage of properties bought by the
developer is relatively similar for some years in both anonymous complaints and inspector-initiated cases.

Another observation that can be drawn from the data is that while
both citizen complaints and inspector-initiated cases increased from
1975 to 1976 in the ARP area, the proportion of units purchased by the

developer after 1975 was lower for two years. This may be explained by the fact that the developer had been trying to acquire only a "critical mass" of property, and could thus be more selective about the structures and lots purchased after 1975. Moreover, as the figures reveal, inspector-initiated cases dropped drastically after 1976, just as did property acquisitions. A plausible explanation for this decrease is that as the developer and his agent acquired title to properties within the ARP area, the structures were quickly demolished. During the span of this study, over 275 structures were demolished, 92 percent by the developer. It is very understandable, then, why complaints about city housing code enforcement were so greatly reduced—the vast number of demolitions in peak years left very few housing structures that needed city attention.

The economics of the relationship between city code enforcement and the rapid acquisition of property in the ARP area are easy to reconstruct. Hypothetically, the developer or his agent could have made a property owner an offer to purchase his or her land. Initially, the landholder may have had very little incentive to sell the property, and if it was rental property, the income was possibly high enough to convince the owner not to sell. An anonymous complaint could have been made about suspected housing code violations at the property in question, and code enforcement activity could then have been initiated. Rather than go to the expense of making repairs at the behest of city inspectors, the property owner was offered a way out—sell the property to an already waiting and willing buyer. Further, if units are being razed, it is obvious that the value of one's investment is in jeopardy, and that the neighborhood itself is about to be transformed. The demolition of buildings soon after they had been purchased undoubtedly convinced many owners that the time to sell was close at hand. Lastly, many owners were probably anxious to sell, irrespective of external sanctions or incentives. Therefore, another plausible interpretation is that the simple designation (or rumored designation) of an area for redevelopment by the local media may have encouraged some landlords to undermaintain their buildings. Since their structures are likely to be purchased anyway, there are very few incentives for landlords to invest money in costly repairs. The decision to keep maintenance costs low may increase the likelihood of code violations, and thus reinforce the plans of both the city and the private developers.

Except for the observations on the part of inspectors and the interoffice memo, we have no direct evidence leading us to assert conclusively that the city's housing personnel were formally instructed by the manager's office to more vigorously enforce codes in the ARP area. Nor do we have data proving that the developers hired people or directed members of their staff to initiate anonymous complaints. At the same time, we are comfortable in suggesting that inflated rates of complaints, private decisions by landlords to undermaintain their property, and administratively induced investigations are the most plausible explanations of the linkage between code enforcement and the buying patterns revealed in the data. In addition to this explanation, we do have additional data showing that, by contrast, other city building and ordinance codes were eventually modified or disregarded in order to facilitate implementation of the redevelopment plan. These data represent an overall pattern of evidence revealing the interface between private actions and public policy.

The developer was eventually granted permission to build new units on smaller lots than is required by Dallas city ordinances. Shorter and wider lots allowed the builder to construct townhouses upward rather than outward, thus more efficiently using the land purchased. Further, he was allowed to cover 80 percent of the land with improvements, rather than 60 percent, as is called for by city ordinance. These two modifications allow the developer to increase the density of new construction, thus maximizing return on investment. In addition, the developer requested that the streets within the target area be smaller than normal, and that provisions for sidewalks be eliminated. These two modifications also made it possible to maximize the density of land use within the redevelopment area.

Present city codes call for at least six-inch water mains for all fire hydrants; eight-inch mains are required when more than one hydrant will be served by a single water line. This code is required in order to maintain adequate water pressure in case of large fires. The developer has been allowed to install six-inch mains for the entire project, even though several hydrants will be serviced by a single line. Modifications were also made in the city ordinance that stipulates both the number of and distance between fire plugs in new development projects, so that they could be fewer and farther apart. Lastly, the developer was allowed to bury water and utility lines under the narrow paved streets themselves; these lines are typically buried under the sidewalk or the shoulder of city streets, thus providing less traffic disruption if they have to be repaired. All these modifications will permit the developer to minimize the costs associated with the project and maximize return on investment.

Present Dallas ordinances for water service codes also require that a 3/4-inch line be provided for each residential lot in new development projects. A line of this size provides about .44 total water volume capacity, a figure based upon pipe size and water pressure that the city considers minimal for adequate water services. The developer has been allowed to use a one-inch line to service two residential units. Although this will reduce the water pressure to both units (especially during peak consumption hours), it will also permit the builder to reduce investment costs. The city also presently requires that each residential lot be serviced by a six-inch sewage line connected with the larger main lateral facility on the street. The developer has been allowed to connect two units to the six-inch line by a "double-Y" device. In effect, this means that a sewage blockage in one house will potentially affect the adjoining unit. Nonetheless, this modification, too, will reduce the developer's costs.

Class Conflict, City Government, and Urban Redevelopment

Our case study probably raises as many questions as it answers. We could not penetrate the political and social barriers preventing us from learning exactly how public and private actors negotiated the terms of the ARP redevelopment scheme prior to its public approval in 1975. We do not know the full story behind the city's decision to increase code enforcement activities in the target area. We do not know how city staff and the city manager's office negotiated with members of the City Council to obtain approval of the plan in 1975, and to win further concessions in subsequent years. All in all, however, the case represents a slickly articulated example of public and private interests working in concert: an illustration of the kind of "political muscle," "clout," and "cooperation" that local business elites expect from local government.

Despite limitations in our data, it is quite clear that public and private interests acted with a single purpose to initiate a redevelopment plan in Dallas. It is clear, furthermore, that a major motive underlying the redevelopment scheme itself was a desire to reverse or stem the tide of middle- and upper-class migration from the central city to the suburbs. The welfare of Dallas, as perceived by its local business elite and city officials, was viewed as dependent upon the prosperity and vitality of private initiative. Private enterprise was equated with the public good and promoted by City Hall as the savior of the "inner city." Since

1978, the ARP project has been well under way. Bryan Place (as the project is now called) is apparently doing well, and was recently the subject of a feature story in Dallas' *Scene Magazine*. According to the story, the clientele is primarily professional and upper-income, and marketing efforts are largely directed toward this type of consumer. The housing units are tastefully decorated and appropriately stylish for their bourgeois and urbane clientele.[35] As mentioned previously, the price of each unit is about $140,000 or above.

Critics of the role of the business community in the implementation of American urban policy have questioned the equation of private interests with the public good.[36] Radical scholars, in particular, contend that renewal projects promote displacement and overcrowding of the disadvantaged, further worsening the lives of the urban poor.[37] Harvey and Lamarche contend that American urban development and redevelopment are governed entirely by the logic of profit, and as such only serve the interests of the propertied classes.[38] In discussing renovation and slum clearance projects in American cities, Hartman, Kessler, and LeGates reasoned: "Public intervention of the type represented by urban-renewal programs can be seen simplistically as a measure to 'improve' the usage of land; it forcibly acts to change use from one class of users and beneficiaries to another."[39]

In the Dallas case, it seems apparent that the interests and needs of working-class citizens living in the ARP area prior to renovation were largely disregarded by the city and the local business elite. Obviously, displacement resulted from the demolition of units in the ARP area, thereby initiating further strains on the limited housing supply available to low- and moderate-income families in the city. Residents of the ARP area, largely poor and working-class tenants, were clearly at the mercy of institutional forces over which they had little or no control. The private decisions of landlords, in response to offers to buy their property, could not be strongly influenced by tenants. Interviews with tenants' rights activists in the city established that residents were typically informed after the fact that the house in which they were living had been sold. In the face of wealthy developers and builders, private financial institutions and speculators, absentee landlords and city hall itself, the political influence available to low- and moderate-income tenants was paltry, if not non-existent. The East Dallas Tenants' Alliance attempted to provide political and social support for many of the displaced residents. Their influence, however, was also meager in comparison to the institutional forces behind the renovation effort.

We also have no evidence leading us to agree with city officials that the project will help "save the city," especially in light of the abundant literature documenting the harmful effects of renewal on the lives of the urban working class. Nonetheless, our case study made it clear to us that powerful developers and those in high administrative positions within City Hall saw their efforts as legitimate attempts to rescue the central city from further decay. What is critical in their formulation of American urban policy, however, is the fact that a partnership between public officials and the local business elite is an alliance from which the urban working and lower classes are largely excluded. And as long as municipal government articulates the needs and interests of a dominant business class, and legitimates the interests of that class over other class interests, the equation of private initiative with the public good remains ambiguous.[40] Also critical is that competition between suburban and urban business elites over the purchasing power and residential choices of middle- and high-income families is a game in which the American urban working and lower classes do not participate. In this game, the poor and working classes are simply moved or displaced to another geographic area of the city, like pawns on a rich man's chess board.

Notes

1. Another version of this chapter appears in *Review of Radical Political Economics,* Winter 1984, pp. 129–150.

2. Timothy Barnekov, Daniel Rich, and Robert Warren, "The New Privatism, Federalism, and the Future of Urban Governance: National Urban Policy in the 1980s." *Journal of Urban Affairs,* Fall 1981, pp. 1–14; Timothy K. Barnekov and Daniel Rich, "Privatism and Urban Development: An Analysis of the Organized Influence of Local Business Elites," *Urban Affairs Quarterly,* June 1977, pp. 431–460.

3. Roscoe Martin and Frank Munger, *Decisions in Syracuse.* Bloomington: University of Indiana Press, 1961; Amos Hawley, "Community Power and Urban Renewal Success." *American Journal of Sociology,* January 1963, pp. 422–431; James Q. Wilson (ed.), *Urban Renewal: The Record and the Controversy.* Cambridge, MA: MIT Press, 1966; Edward Banfield, *Political Influence.* New York: Free Press, 1968; see also Robert Dahl, *Who Governs?* New Haven: Yale University Press, 1961; Mike Royko, *Boss.* New York: New American Library,

1971; Robert Caro, *The Power Broker.* New York: Random House, 1974; Dennis Clark, "The Expansion of the Public Sector and Irish Economic Development." in Scott Cummings (ed.), *Self-Help in Urban America.* Port Washington, NY: Kennikat Press, 1980.

4. J.R. Lowe, *Cities in a Race with Time.* New York: Random House, 1967; R. Lubove, *Twentieth-Century Pittsburgh.* New York: John Wiley, 1969; R. E. Edgar, *Urban Power and Social Welfare: Corporate Power in an American City.* Beverly Hills, CA: Sage Publishers, 1970; A. R. Talbot, *The Mayor's Game: Richard Lee of New Haven and the Politics of Change.* New York: Praeger, 1970; K. R. Peteshek, *The Challenge of Urban Reform: Policies and Programs in Philadelphia.* Philadelphia: Temple University Press, 1973; Raymond Wolfinger, *The Politics of Progress.* Englewood Cliffs, NJ: Prentice-Hall, 1974.

5. One exception is Joe Feagin, *The Urban Real Estate Game.* Englewood Cliffs, NJ: Prentice-Hall, 1983.

6. G. William Domhoff, *Who Really Rules?* Santa Monica, CA: Goodyear, 1978.

7. Sharon Zukin, *Loft Living.* Baltimore: Johns Hopkins University Press, 1982; Lynda Ann Ewen, *Corporate Power and Urban Crisis in Detroit.* Princeton, NJ: Princeton University Press, 1977; Chester Hartman, *Yerba Buena: Land Grab and Community Resistance in San Francisco.* San Francisco: Volcano Press, 1978.

8. Schuyler Jackson, "Housing Code Inspection Subjected to Some Critical Comments and Some Suggestions for the Future." *Journal of Housing,* November 1970; Thomas K. Gilhool, "Social Aspects of Housing Code Enforcement." *Urban Lawyer,* Summer 1971.

9. Robert E. Novick, "The Physical and Mental Health Aspects of Code Enforcement." *Urban Lawyer,* Summer 1971.

10. Chester Hartman, Robert Kessler, and Richard LeGates, "Municipal Housing Code Enforcement and Low Income Tenants." *The Journal of American Institute of Planners,* 1974, pp. 90–104.

11. George Sternlieb and Robert Burchell, *Residential Abandonment: The Tenement Landlord Revisited.* New Brunswick, NJ: Rutgers University Press.

12. Herbert Gans, *The Urban Villagers.* Glencoe, IL: Free Press, 1962; James Q. Wilson; Marc Fried, *The World of the Urban Working Class.* Cambridge, MA: Harvard University Press, 1973.

13. D. Claire McAdams, "A Power-Conflict Approach to Urban Land Use: Towards a New Urban Ecology." Paper presented at the Annual Meeting of the Southwest Social Science Association, Dallas, Texas, April 1981.

14. William Tabb and Larry Sawers (eds.), *Marxism and the Metropolis.* New York: Oxford University Press, 1978.

15. Sidney Wilhelm, "The Concept of the 'Ecological Complex' : A Critique." *American Journal of Sociology,* 1964, pp. 241–248.

16. Elwin Powell, *The Design Discord.* New York: Oxford University Press, 1970.

17. David Harvey, *Social Justice and the City.* Baltimore: Johns Hopkins University Press, 1973.

18. Manuel Castells, *The Urban Question: A Marxist Approach.* Cambridge, MA: MIT Press, 1977, p. 116.

19. Francois Lamarche, "Property Development and the Economic Foundations of the Urban Question," in C. G. Pickvance (ed.), *Urban Sociology: Critical Essays.* New York: St. Martin's Press, 1976, pp. 85–118.

20. David Gordon, "Capitalist Development and the History of American Cities," in Tabb and Sawers, pp. 117–152.

21. Patrick Ashton, "The Political Economy of Suburban Development," in Tabb and Sawers, pp. 64–89.

22. Barry Bluestone and Bennett Harrison, *The Deindustrialization of America.* New York: Basic Books, 1982.

23. Harvey Molotch, "The City as a Growth Machine: Toward a Political Economy of Place," *American Journal of Sociology,* September 1976, pp. 309–332; Mollenkopf. "The Post War Politics of Urban Development," Tabb and Sawers, pp. 117–152.

24. Ann R. Markussen, "Class and Urban Expenditures: A Marxist Theory of Metropolitan Government," in Tabb and Sawers, pp. 90–112.

25. Scott Cummings (ed.), *Racial Isolation in the Public Schools: The Impact of Public and Private Housing Policies.* Arlington, TX: Institute of Urban Studies, University of Texas at Arlington, 1981.

26. Mark S. Rosentraub, Scott Cummings, and Rosalind Young, "One-Way Busing and Community Psychology: School Desegregation at Minimal Costs." *Urban Education,* October 1983, pp. 317–335.

27. Cummings.

28. Ashton.

29. Martin Maher, *The Builders.* New York: Simon and Schuster, 1978.

30. *Dallas Morning News,* January 9, 1977.

31. *Dallas Morning News,* January 11, 1977.

32. The logic of the comparison corresponds to an ad hoc quasi-experiment, in which outcome measures are gathered and compared between a treatment and a non-equivalent control group. See Thomas Cook and Donald Campbell, *Quasi-Experimentation: Design and Analysis Issues for Field Setting.* Chicago: Rand McNally, 1979; Scott Cummings and Mark S. Rosentraub, "Evaluation Research: How to Negotiate Scientific Rigor." *Social Work Research and Abstracts,* Fall 1978, pp. 16–24.

33. The ARP corresponds to the treatment group in which the experimental stimulus—the selection and designation of a parcel of land as a redevelopment opportunity—is present. The comparison area serves as the control group where all else is approximately equal between the two communities, save for the absence of the quasi-experimental stimulus.

34. *Urban Rehabilitation Standards Ordinance.* Dallas, TX: City of Dallas, Department of Housing and Urban Rehabilitation, 1978.

35. Si Dunn, "Inside Bryan Place." *Scene Magazine, Dallas Morning News,* 1980, pp. 6–7.

36. Barnekov, Rich, and Warren.

37. Michael Harrington, "Can Private Industry Abolish Slums?" *Dissent,* Winter 1968, pp. 1–8; William Tabb, *The Political Economy of the Black Ghetto.* New York: Norton, 1970; Feagin.

38. Harvey, Lamarch, Castells.

39. Hartman, Kessler, and LeGates. p. 223.

40. Harvey; Molotch; Mollenkopf.

Chapter 8

Chicago's North Loop Redevelopment Project: A Growth Machine on Hold

Larry Bennett, Kathleen McCourt, Philip W. Nyden, and Gregory D. Squires

At a distance, the politics of post–World War II urban redevelopment in Chicago correspond very closely to the "growth machine" characterization that has been applied to many American cities.[1] An aggressive business elite has devoted much time and substantial resources to promoting a new, twenty-first-century Chicago, and members of the business elite have been at the forefront of specific development projects. Local public officials, including elected executives and legislators as well as planning, redevelopment, and housing bureaucrats, have worked closely with the business elite and pursued public policies generally consonant with the latter's redevelopment agenda.

The results of this alliance have been quite predictable. The physical environment of Chicago's downtown—the old Loop, plus adjoining areas to the north, west, and south—has been enhanced and insulated from surrounding portions of the central city. A notable part of this central area enhancement has been the construction and rehabilitation of thousands of units of middle- and upper-income housing. The resultant residential districts are not only close to downtown work places but have easy access to the city's prized lakefront parks and cultural complexes. At the same time the physical reorganization of

A portion of this chapter is drawn from Gregory D. Squires, Larry Bennett, Kathleen McCourt, and Philip W. Nyden, *Chicago: Race, Class, and the Response to Urban Decline.* Philadelphia: Temple University Press, 1987, ch. 6.

central Chicago has exacted its costs. Urban renewal on Chicago's South Side required massive demolition of low-rent, mainly black neighborhoods, and the dislocation of this area's residents sent shock waves throughout the city's South and Southwest Sides.[2] As in other cities, suitable replacement housing never matched the demolition accomplished by urban renewal. Finally, Chicago's downtown redevelopment has been the centerpiece of a one-sided strategy of city planning that has shown little concern for any neighborhood away from the city's core area.

Nonetheless, this general portrayal does not tell the whole story of redevelopment in Chicago. For in fact, particular projects dear to the hearts of the city's business and political leaders have been stalled or substantially reshaped, as demonstrated by the North Loop project discussed later in this chapter. A number of circumstances have distinguished the politics of redevelopment in Chicago from the pure growth machine initially described by Harvey Molotch. First, members of Chicago's Democratic machine and other local politicians are not as a rule drawn from the ranks of the real estate industry. Although machine politicians have certainly cooperated with the redevelopment agenda of the downtown business elite, in particular instances they have shown themselves to be sensitive to other constituencies, such as neighborhood movements.

Second, although Chicago's business leaders share a fundamentally consistent vision of the city, and as a result constitute the single most important force in setting the redevelopment agenda, their interests are not absolutely uniform. For instance, corporate leaders and major real estate developers do not always act in concert. Similarly, businesses and developers whose investments are in different geographic locations often find themselves at odds with one another. Consequently, the business elite is sometimes divided over the merits of particular projects, with competing factions mobilizing influence in behalf of their own plans, or in opposition to their competitors'.

In recent years, as will be forcefully demonstrated by the evolution of the North Loop Project, two new actors have come to play an important, albeit sporadic, role in Chicago's redevelopment politics. Historical preservationists are well organized in Chicago, and they can mount powerful opposition to projects that threaten the city's wealth of architecturally significant structures and districts. Chicago neighborhood organizations number in the hundreds, and many of them are quite conscious of the city's uneven economic development. When they have gained access to specific politicians or the decision-making mechanisms that regulate redevelopment, neighborhood organizations have proved to be aggressive opponents of business-dominated, downtown-fixated redevelopment planning.

Through a detailed examination of the North Loop redevelopment project we shall demonstrate how these various constituencies have shaped and modified the course of growth machine politics in Chicago, and attempted to adapt the local political system to suit their redevelopment agendas. Before turning to this case study, it is necessary to sketch in more detail just how redevelopment has typically been carried out in the city.

Implementing Post-World-War-II Redevelopment in Chicago

In keeping with initial postwar redevelopment planning in other American cities, Chicago's first steps in this direction were fitful and locally divisive. Prominent politicians, important business and civic leaders, and many corporations and financial institutions were unconvinced that drastic action was in order. Consequently, the redevelopment initiative was seized by a few individuals with a commanding vision of a new Chicago and in possession of the institutional resources to promote their dream. In the words of historian Arnold Hirsch: "The key figures coordinating the efforts of these large interests were Milton C. Mumford, an assistant vice-president of Marshall Field and Company, and Holman C. Pettibone, president of the Chicago Title and Trust Company. More than any others, they were the architects of Chicago's postwar plans."[3] Mumford and Pettibone drafted the enabling state legislation authorizing downtown and neighborhood redevelopment in Chicago. They also negotiated the agreement by which the New York Life Insurance Company financed the city's first middle-income residential redevelopment project, Lake Meadows, south of the Loop and adjoining Lake Michigan.

There was some neighborhood-based opposition to Lake Meadows, but it was insufficient to halt execution of the project. Nevertheless, the failure of another ambitious redevelopment plan sponsored by developer Arthur Rubloff, indicated that downtown business interests could not be counted on to uniformly applaud such initiatives. Rubloff's Fort Dearborn project proposed to consolidate local, state, and federal government offices on a site north of the Chicago River (and thus outside the Loop) and to surround this government complex with thousands of units of middle-income housing and commercial space. Unfortunately for Rubloff, his plan generated opposition from Loop real estate owners and retailers, as well as attorneys who would be inconvenienced by the relocation of the government offices. With the mobilization of this opposition, Mayor Richard J. Daley lost interest in the project, which ultimately died when Rubloff failed to attract private investors.[4]

The mid-1950s mark the point in time when a more unified view of Chicago redevelopment emerged. In 1957 Chicago established a new Department of City Planning whose first significant action was the preparation of a "Development Plan for the Central Area of Chicago." The development plan portrayed a tightly concentrated downtown core ringed by parking garages and accessible by a network of expressways. Major proposed physical investments included a new government center, a University of Illinois campus, and a consolidated transportation center. Finally, the document proposed middle-income housing for up to 50,000 families on the near North and South Sides.[5] A number of private groups advised the Department of City Planning in the drafting of the central area plan, notably a new organization called the Chicago Central Area Committee (CCAC).

CCAC dates from this period; its board of directors included representatives of Chicago's leading corporations, banks, utilities, and business service firms. In the ensuing three decades its role in downtown planning became formalized. For instance, in 1973 the concluding report of the city's comprehensive plan, dealing once again with Chicago's downtown core, was published not by the Planning Department but by CCAC.[6] Ten years later CCAC published a new central area plan, which is now under consideration by the city for adoption as its framework for future downtown development.[7]

In the thirty years since its formation, CCAC's vision of Chicago has been quite congruent with the view articulated in the 1958 development plan. The physical upgrading of the downtown is the linchpin of overall city development, and downtown upgrading is equated with private investment in corporate headquarters, speculative office construction, new commercial and recreational space, and public infrastructure improvements. To realize these intentions, members of CCAC—either as individuals or through their firms—have directly participated in major downtown investments. For example, an abandoned railhead to the south of the Loop has been converted into a residential "new town in-town" called Dearborn Park. This complex was first publicly proposed in CCAC's Chicago 21 Plan of 1973, and its implementation was in large part financed by CCAC members.[8] In fact, CCAC had been working on this project for years, as indicated by its executive director in late 1965:

> Ultimately, of course, this development program will be a City of Chicago project, but in the meantime we hope without a fanfare or publicity, which as you know is our way of operating, and with the help of private financing to develop a whole new concept for building a city within a city that would house as many as 100,000 people primarily, but not exclusively, designed for middle-income families with children.[9]

This quote also underlines CCAC's desire to influence Chicago development as inconspicuously as possible. Nonetheless, this group senses that it has achieved more than a modicum of success in realizing its planning goals. Its 1983 annual report recalled that:

> In 1973, the CCAC and the City of Chicago presented a new set of guidelines for development of the central communities area, entitled Chicago 21. . . . Of the 32 (projects) originally proposed, four have been completed, 19 are underway and 12 are currently under study. Only one project suggested in Chicago 21, the Franklin Street subway, has been completely cancelled.[10]

In short, the last three decades have witnessed the mobilization of a powerful Chicago business consensus regarding the overall shape of city development, and particular participants in this consensus have done much to implement its vision. However, CCAC's successes have not resulted from a total domination of the redevelopment process. The city government and the local Democratic Party are not dependent on the business elite, and in effect they have all been autonomous partners in reshaping Chicago. Second, CCAC does not represent one significant segment of the local business elite, the city's several major real estate developers. The latter frequently pursue individual projects that are incongruent with the intentions of CCAC, and in some instances possess the wherewithal to see them through even without CCAC's approval.

The city government's role in planning and redevelopment has involved far more than cooperating with the business community in preparing planning documents. It has committed a substantial share of its infrastructure investments to projects that beautify the Loop, link it with suburban communities and O'Hare Airport, and otherwise sustain the downtown's status as the economic focal point of the metropolitan region. Under the provisions of urban renewal legislation, the city has used the power of eminent domain to take sites and turn them over to private developers. In the last decade Community Development (CDBG) funds and Urban Development Action Grants (UDAG) have been used to induce or augment private investment. The city has consistently implemented local land-use and housing regulations in a fashion consistent with the needs of private developers. During Daley's twenty-one-year tenure as mayor, he was viewed as the chief facilitator of local redevelopment. In essence, developers and redevelopment officials sought the mayor's approval of their plans with the knowledge that Daley's backing cemented the city's commitment to expediting their projects.

As the last of the big-city machine bosses whose organization was built on a network of local ward organizations, Daley's aggressive urban renewal policy of the 1950s and 1960s seems incongruous. Indeed, long-time city planner Ira Bach recalled that Daley was "disabused of there being any slums. How could Chicago have slums?" When confronted with figures to demonstrate their existence, Daley accepted them only "ungracefully."[11] Bach's comments reveal the other important characteristic of the city government's planning and redevelopment apparatus. Daley, the mayor with neighborhood roots as well as a commitment to rebuilding the city, filled his top planning and redevelopment staff positions with men such as Bach, James Downs, Phil Doyle, and Lewis Hill, all firmly committed to the notion that massive renewal and private redevelopment were keys to building a new Chicago.[12]

The overall substance of postwar planning and redevelopment in Chicago resulted from the interaction of these interdependent forces. Dominant downtown businesses arrived at a general consensus in support of an environmentally upgraded central area devoted to corporate headquarters, business services, and cultural, recreational, and tourist uses. City planning and redevelopment officials shared this vision of a new Chicago, and over the course of forty years have taken advantage of a variety of federal programs to implement it. A powerful mayor came to view the rebuilding of Chicago as an important testament to his leadership, supported the redevelopment initiatives proposed to him by business notables and his planning advisors, and used his ubiquitous clout to achieve cooperation in redevelopment by the various relevant city agencies and federal oversight bureaus.

For all its power, this development alliance has had its internal stresses, and on occasion has been unable to push through prized projects. Developer Arthur Rubloff encountered opposition to the Fort Dearborn project from major property holders whose investments would be threatened by his plan. Furthermore, Mayor Daley's political base was such that he did not need to go along with the Fort Dearborn proposal. When Fort Dearborn project proponents sought Daley's firm commitment to move City Hall north of the Chicago River, the mayor refused.[13]

A later development controversy, involving the Crosstown Expressway proposed for the western boundary of the city, exposed other weaknesses in the local growth machine. The city initiated the Crosstown's planning in the 1960s. From the start, however, neighborhood organizations on the city's Southwest and Northwest Sides criticized the highway and aggressively mobilized neighborhood opposition. Several of the affected neighborhoods were loyal constituencies of Democratic Party stalwarts. Although the city persisted with some form of Crosstown plan until the late 1970s, Mayor Jane Byrne at last dropped the project. The decade-and-a-half Crosstown dispute demonstrated that grassroots opposition could block ill-conceived development projects, particularly if this opposition made life difficult for ward-level politicians as well as the mayor.[14]

The Fort Dearborn and Crosstown cases are two instances of a local growth machine's inability to implement particular development proposals. It should be emphasized that these were two exceptions during a quarter century in which the main elements of a business-initiated redevelopment agenda were successfully implemented. Nonetheless, they remain instructive as predictors of several dilemmas faced by the agents of redevelopment in the post-Daley era. In the examination of the North Loop project that follows, we will describe an effort by the city government to carry forward the redevelopment agenda sketched in previous paragraphs. Its difficulties can be attributed to some of the longstanding characteristics of the local political system as well as the diminished capacity of Daley's successors to orchestrate the local government's role in the redevelopment process.

Redeveloping Chicago's North Loop

The origins of the North Loop project were quite typical of redevelopment planning during the Daley era. Its context was the decline of Chicago's traditional retailing and entertainment center, the Loop. On the eastern margin of the Loop runs State Street, whose large department stores (notably Marshall Field and Carson, Pirie, Scott) had once dominated Chicago retailing. By the early 1970s these stores were not only subject to the ubiquitous competition of suburban shopping malls, but along Michigan Avenue north of the Chicago River had emerged a new central area shopping district, whose retailers were further cutting into State Street sales. The Loop continued to be a busy district, but its shopping clientele was increasingly black, a fact emphasized by the fare offered in some of the area's movie theaters along State, Randolph, and Dearborn streets. Infrequent white visitors to Chicago's downtown often comment on this area's concentration of porno houses, although in fact, the majority of the downtown theaters have not booked pornographic films. The films shown there—Kung Fu action melodramas and the like—tend to draw a predominantly young, male, and minority moviegoer. The presence of this fairly intimidating group of customers also appears to have discouraged the established, large-scale real estate holders and commercial interests in the Loop.

As was also characteristic of Daley-era redevelopment planning, the North Loop project's impetus came from Chicago's business elite. By the early 1970s the State Street Council, which has traditionally spoken for the street's big retailers, was discussing the prospect of clearing some of the blocks to the southwest of the retail district. These discussions eventually came to the attention of Arthur Rubloff.[15] At the same time, Rubloff was working with Mayor Daley on the identification of a suitable site for a new central library.[16] Rubloff linked the interests of Daley and the State Street merchants by proposing that the city clear a large area whose margins were the west side of State Street, Wacker Drive overlooking the river, Randolph and Washington Streets on the south, and Clark and LaSalle Streets to the west. (See Figure 8.1.) This tract would be developed primarily for commercial uses, but within it would be the new library. The city's Department of Urban Renewal prepared a preliminary study of the area at the end of 1973; at this time, legislation was introduced in the City Council to establish a Commercial District Development Commission under whose auspices the North Loop project would be carried out.[17] This board was authorized in 1975.

In the mid-1970s Arthur Rubloff initiated negotiations on the North Loop project, proceeding without much public notice. Mayor Daley died in 1976, but Rubloff was intent on pursuing his unofficial mandate, which he interpreted to endorse total demolition and re-

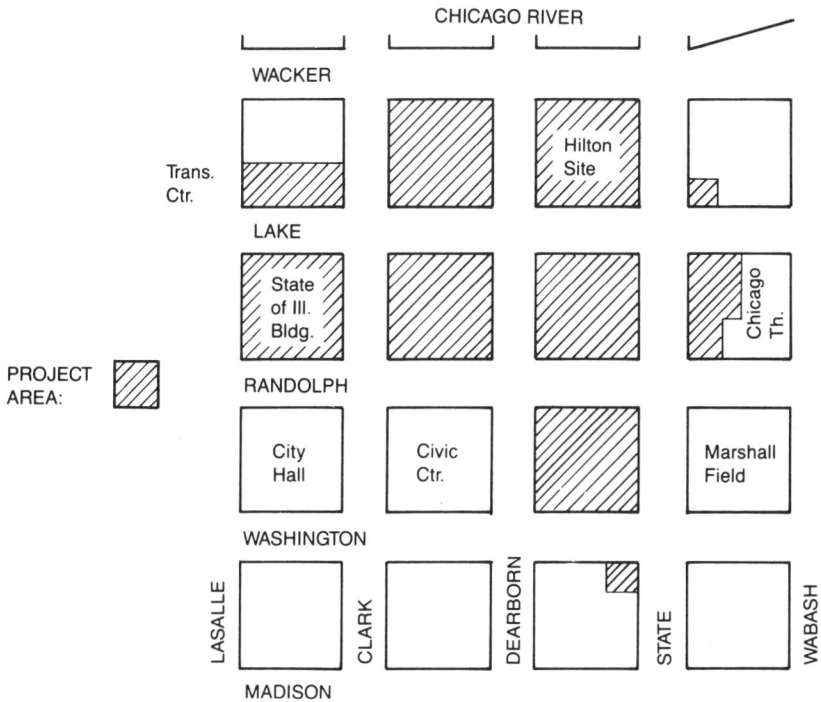

Figure 8.1 The North Loop Redevelopment Area

construction of the North Loop site. In early 1978 the city prepared a UDAG application to support North Loop redevelopment, the details of which would later generate controversy; in the summer of that year the North Loop emerged as a significant public issue. In August, Rubloff released his redevelopment plan, in conjunction with an agreement with Hilton Hotels, Inc., to erect a large convention hotel on the northeast corner of the redevelopment area.[18] During the same month, Rubloff and Governor James Thompson held a press conference to announce the construction of a State of Illinois Building (to consolidate state offices in the city) on the westernmost North Loop block.[19] To punctuate the year's flurry of North Loop activity, the fall of 1978 brought an amended UDAG proposal to the federal Department of Housing and Urban Development, seeking aid only for the block to be sold to Hilton.[20] A month later, the Commercial District Development

Commission approved the North Loop project, thus granting the city authority to exercise eminent domain in the project area.

Although 1978 was a year in which formal progress was substantial, by early 1979 countervailing forces were set in motion that arrested the preceding year's advances. First, Rubloff's total demolition plan did not sit well with the city's preservationist groups. Since the early 1970s, Chicago's preservationists have adopted a markedly more aggressive role in commenting on local planning issues. Their activities are coordinated through organizations such as the Landmarks Preservation Council of Illinois, and many preservationists are socially prominent individuals with ties to the city's business and political leadership. Furthermore, Mayor Michael Bilandic, who was apparently quite willing to acquiesce in the Rubloff plan, was unexpectedly swept from office by Jane Byrne in February 1979. Before the election, Byrne had criticized the North Loop plan; once she was in office, Rubloff's direction of North Loop planning ceased.[21]

The next steps in planning the project indicated its suddenly ambiguous status. In Chicago, redevelopment projects must be approved by the Chicago Plan Commission, an advisory body comprising civic, real estate, and political leaders, and by the City Council. In April 1979, the Chicago Plan Commission held hearings on the North Loop; and although it decided in favor of the project, substantial opposition was voiced. Notably, the Landmarks Preservation Council, an influential civic group, the Metropolitan Housing and Planning Council, and a representative of the National Trust for Historic Preservation spoke against the development plan.[22] Their common complaint was that the city documents did not sufficiently specify general design guidelines or particular buildings to be preserved.

Although both the Chicago Plan Commission and the City Council eventually approved the North Loop project, in the following months concerted opposition to it took shape. Among the structures threatened with demolition were Chicago's oldest and grandest movie house, the Chicago Theater on the east side of State Street, and two former legitimate theaters, the Harris and the Selwyn at the corner of Dearborn and Lake streets. From 1978 on, two local business groups were at work on studies to preserve the Chicago Theater and ensure its economic viability. In addition, the Landmarks Preservation Council and an associated group, the Performing Arts Center of Chicago, commissioned an architect to produce a renovation plan for the Harris and the Selwyn, which these groups envisioned as performance spaces to be shared by several local theater and dance companies.[23]

By the summer of 1979 Mayor Byrne had reversed her previous position and named a new North Loop project coordinator, Charles Shaw, like Rubloff, a private real estate developer. The precise significance of Shaw's substitution for Rubloff is difficult to discern. One view holds that Rubloff was unacceptable to some of Byrne's political advisors. Possibly more important, Shaw's appointment coincided with CCAC's raising of North Loop redevelopment to the top of its list of priorities.[24] Shaw, like Rubloff before him, was to oversee project negotiations and participate in site development.

Financial details of the project also began to emerge. Mayor Byrne sought approximately $50 million (to be raised by notes issued to a consortium of local banks) as the city's direct expenditure, and tax abatement legislation was approved by the Cook County Board to reduce the initial property levy on redevelopment sites in "blighted commercial areas."[25] Then in the spring of 1980 a new set of development guidelines were submitted to the City Council, this document committing the city to the preservation of several of the landmark buildings.[26] In 1980 the city also signed a development contract with Hilton Hotels. In addition to a tax abatement estimated to be worth $70 million, the hotel chain was granted power of approval over redevelopment around its hotel site.[27]

The latter months of 1980, though, brought more trials for the project. By late summer the city's "sweet" deal with Hilton was reported in the press; and by virtue of one of the frequent political squabbles that rocked her administration, Mayor Byrne's ability to deliver on this contract was undermined. The city's proposed thirteen-year $70 million tax reduction for the Hilton site was subject to approval by the Cook County Tax assessor, Thomas Hynes. Hynes is an ally of the late mayor's son, Richard M. Daley, who was expected to challenge Byrne in the 1983 Democratic primary for mayor. In August when Hynes refused to review the city's abatement request without detailed information on each North Loop block, it was widely supposed that his action was an effort to undermine the Mayor. Hynes's ruling, nonetheless, was strictly advisory. He rejected the form of the city's proposal but not necessarily its substance. Nevertheless, over the next year until his formal disapproval of the proposal, a cloud was cast over the entire project.[28]

Furthermore, and probably due to their cognizance of civic opposition to the North Loop plan, federal Department of Housing and Urban Development officials began to signal doubts concerning the UDAG proposal.[29] By reducing its request from $25 million to $7.9

million, the city had also reduced the area for which it sought federal aid. Excluded were those portions of the original North Loop site in which historic structures were located (by this time seven such buildings were on the National Register of Historic Places). UDAG funds cannot be used to raze buildings so designated, and HUD suspected the city of site "segmentation" with the intention of going ahead with demolitions using local funds. If this were so, the reduced UDAG might be withheld.

Finally, in November 1980, Shaw released plans of his vision of the North Loop, which salvaged several historic structures and greatly increased its residential composition. However, Shaw's proposal was greeted with mixed reviews. Some reactions characterized the designs as "Buck Rogers-ish," and Shaw's intention to create a consolidated cultural center was unsatisfactory to the management of existing facilities such as Orchestra Hall and the Civic Opera House, the homes of the Chicago Symphony Orchestra and the Lyric Opera.[30]

Just a few months later Shaw withdrew as project coordinator, thus scotching his recently released development plan. He was replaced by Miles Berger, another local developer, but as chairman of the Chicago Plan Commission, presumably more attuned to city decision-making processes. In the following months, the city's development model shifted considerably. Unlike Shaw and Rubloff, whose coordination of the North Loop was tantamount to personal development rights, Berger only oversaw city planning of the project and negotiations with prospective private developers. He had no direct financial stake in the proceedings; under his direction, competitive bidding for individual blocks was inaugurated—with developers' plans then subject to comprehensive guidelines set by the city.[31]

A new political barrier to the North Loop was also emerging. The details of the Hilton contract were eliciting opposition on two fronts: neighborhood groups that objected to the size of the subsidy and advocated increased municipal attention to neighborhood services and economic development and downtown businesses, presumably envious of so much city largesse directed at a single firm. The former, composed of neighborhood groups such as the Lakeview Citizens Council, the South Shore Commission, and the Northwest Community Organization, represented middle- and working-class neighborhoods well away from the Loop. They called meetings and submitted petitions to County Assessor Hynes under the banner of the Campaign Against the North Loop Tax Break. The financially well-heeled business opposition formed the Property Conservation Council and commissioned Jared Shlaes, a prominent real estate analyst, to prepare a study of the Hilton deal's real cost and prospective benefits for the city. The membership of this group was drawn from among downtown hotel owners as well as other major property holders. The Shlaes report was readied in time for the Assessor's hearings on the tax abatement in November 1981.[32]

County Assessor Hynes scheduled three days of hearings, November 14–16, 1981, to review the Hilton abatement. The Dean of Loyola University's law school presided, and the several hundred pages of testimony by dozens of community groups, real estate experts, civic notables, and city officials were the basis for Hynes's report the next month. Much of the testimony was hostile to the abatement; and given the assessor's political estrangement from the Mayor, it was not unexpected when he turned down the Hilton deal. Nonetheless, Hynes's counterproposal was a judicious blend of political and substantive considerations. In effect, although refusing to approve the contract as negotiated between the city and Hilton, Hynes indicated his willingness to support a contingent tax abatement. Reductions in local property tax obligations would be scaled to the degree of the hotel's profitability—the better it did the less the tax break.[33] Hilton officials, who all along had taken an inflexible posture in the face of criticism of their arrangement with the city, reviewed Hynes' counterplan and rejected it. For a few more weeks they insisted that they would obtain financing even in the absence of the tax abatement, but in March 1982, Hilton Hotels, Inc., formally withdrew from participation in the North Loop project.

In the wake of what city officials characterized as a catastrophic setback for the North Loop project, there was some headway made in 1982. The owners of one of the district's historic structures, the Delaware Building, were confident enough of the city's intention to preserve their building for them to initiate its rehabilitation.[34] The northwest block of the development area was cleared to make way for the Transportation Center, which would consolidate downtown airline ticket offices, concentrate taxi and limousine service, and include parking. The city had used the bulk of its North Loop bond proceeds to acquire two and one-half blocks at the north end of the project area. The larger part of this tract was to be sold to Hilton, but in mid-1981 the city had solicited separate bids on its westernmost portion. Development specifications for the other blocks in the project, in anticipation of developer bidding, were also being prepared; and in what was becoming an annual ritual, new guidelines for overall development were drawn up.[35] Finally, the city advertised for new proposals for the Hilton site. In December 1982, a consortium of local developers and the Americana Hotels offered the sole bid on the parcel. Their plan to build a smaller hotel, with retail space and other amenities on State Street, was quickly accepted by the city.[36]

Thus, when Harold Washington assumed the mayorality in April 1983, he took on the stewardship of a huge redevelopment site whose decade-long history was just beginning to make the step from design to steel and concrete. Furthermore, the city had used most of its North Loop funds in acquiring the two and one-half blocks north of Lake Street. There was speculation that Mayor Washington, who had campaigned against downtown redevelopment at the expense of neighborhood improvements, would terminate the North Loop project. In fact, the Washington Administration did not appear to consider this option, although its approach to planning and executing the project was different from the preceding administration's.

Probably the surest sign that Mayor Washington intended to continue the North Loop project was his appointment of Elizabeth Hollander as city planning commissioner. Hollander had previously served as executive director of the Metropolitan Housing and Planning Council, a group that had criticized the early planning of the North Loop project, but which also supported the notion of an intensely used, multiple-purpose downtown core. Hollander's agency now aggressively pursued a hotel developer for the Hilton site, contending that only a hotel would generate the around-the-clock pedestrian traffic essential to rejuvenate the entertainment area to the south. The search for this developer, however, was frustratingly difficult. The Americana group that bid on the site in late 1982 had been unable to raise the cash necessary to purchase the site from the city, and in the intervening two years two other developers bid but then reneged on their offers for the site.[37]

In 1984 the city also restructured the project's financing. With most of its funds already expended, and most of the project area still to be acquired, it had little choice. In April, the City Council approved a tax increment financing arrangement, by which funds for site acquisition, clearance, and preparation could be raised by selling bonds to be repaid through property tax increases pursuant to development of the North Loop blocks. The April 1984 ordinance forecast that the city's North Loop expenditures would run in excess of $200 million.[38]

Lastly, in contrast to the Byrne administration, Mayor Washington's planners adopted what might be called a "quiet diplomacy" strategy of block-by-block negotiations with prospective developers. In mid-1985 the city received bids on the troublesome Hilton site and the block to its west, which appeared likely to yield development.[39] A mixture of city, federal, and private funds was raised to purchase the Chicago Theater, although in this instance the political and legal complications were such as to make quiet diplomacy impossible.[40] Negotiations on several other parcels within the district were under way. In some cases the city considered reducing its redevelopment role (and fiscal obligations) by substituting "redevelopment agreements" with the private developers in lieu of municipal condemnation and acquisition in advance of redevelopment.[41]

The North Loop and Chicago's Growth Machine

A number of factors account for the unsteady course of the North Loop redevelopment project. One of these is the segmentation of political and economic power within Chicago. Due to the persistence of active ward-level organizations within the Democratic party, politicians can come to prominence in Chicago whose base of support does not include the city's business elite. This is not to suggest that local politicians hold the upper hand in relations with the business elite (nor that they typically perceive their interests at odds with those of the city's business leaders); rather, some politicians are in the position to make decisions without reference to the interests of the business elite. As it happens, Jane Byrne—whose stewardship corresponded with the Hilton tax abatement agreement—was not one of these politicians. A party maverick, lacking the ward organization allegiance commanded by Richard J. Daley, Byrne did not have the kind of autonomous political base that would permit negotiating a tough development agreement with Hilton and other potential investors in the North Loop. In contrast, County Assessor (and 19th Ward Democratic Committeeman) Thomas Hynes is just the sort of Chicago politician who might overrule a deal such as the Hilton abatement. Alienating Hilton corporation executives or other local business leaders caused him no immediate harm, nor is it likely that his opportunities for pursuing higher office were undermined.

In the wake of Daley, this party apparatus, with its capacity for producing political leaders who are not beholden to the business elite, is not always a reliable collaborator with the city's growth coalition. Mayor Daley worked with the business elite, and they jointly promoted a blueprint for Chicago that served the interests of both business and the Mayor. The Mayor, as part of the bargain, directed the government actors whose participation was integral to implementing redevelopment. Neither Michael Bilandic, Daley's initial successor, nor Jane Byrne were able to control governmental redevelopment action in this way. Current Mayor Washington is even more constrained by his break with the Democratic Party, but his redevelopment agenda may not presuppose the kind of action sought by his predecessors.

Thus, the peculiar nature of Chicago's being governed by a strong political party, once so amenable to direction by the formidable Daley, by virtue of its current fragmentation proves to be something of an obstacle to sustaining a growth coalition. Yet party fragmentation alone does not account for the circuitous process of North Loop redevelopment. For example, County Assessor Hynes's veto of the Hilton deal was enabled to some degree by his recognition that important elements of the local business community were not enamored of the tax abatement scheme.

The CCAC vision of Chicago may very well conform, in a substantive sense, to the expectations of most business leaders in the city. But procedurally, several major real estate developers do not feel bound to plan their investments accordingly. Moreover, the size of the city and the diversity of its development opportunities have militated against either CCAC or the city government's claiming that some particular project is essential to the future growth of Chicago. Finally—and once more with particular reference to the Hilton abatement controversy— the ideology of Chicago's business elite has yet to accommodate tax abatements as a commonplace government tool for inducing investment. This may seem remarkable (and it has not prevented the city from using any number of other direct or indirect development incentives), but—unlike New York City—private downtown investment in Chicago has not so far proceeded on the assumption that there will be an accompanying tax abatement. A consequence of these several factors is that in the absence of a smoothly functioning government redevelopment apparatus, divisions within the business community itself helped stall the North Loop project.

Yet the story of the North Loop is not merely one of government/ political fragmentation and divisions within the business elite. Preservationist groups and neighborhood organizations played an important role in criticizing the initial total demolition plan offered by Rubloff and, later, the Hilton tax abatement. More recently, opposition by community groups was combined with skepticism from Mayor Washington's administration to block private-sector plans for a 1992 Chicago World's Fair.[42] There is no question that, compared to those of twenty years ago, the architects of Chicago's development agenda must take into account the views of a much wider array of neighborhood and planning-oriented interests. Neighborhood groups, in particular, are well situated to influence the thinking of the ward-based politicians of Chicago. However, as a counterforce to Chicago's growth coalition, local community groups have yet to unite on a citywide agenda that critiques the growth coalition in general and commands the allegiance of a broad, mobilizable constituency.

Indeed, the various critics of North Loop planning have been most uneasy partners. The arts groups and preservationists did not disagree with the premise of redevelopment, but rather with the scale of demolition and the quality of the environment built in reconstruction. The neighborhood organizations, and ironically the business opponents too, raised the question of the economic costs and benefits to be derived from subsidizing the Hilton corporation. At present, representatives from neither side of the opposition are especially generous in crediting the role played by their "allies" in modifying the North Loop plan.[43]

The North Loop project demonstrates that in the mid-1980s, Chicago growth machine politics are in an evident state of flux. The constant in the mix is the mobilized but somewhat imperfectly coordinated business agenda. The other main agent of urban redevelopment, city government, is presently held by a mayor responding much more than his predecessors to minority and neighborhood constituencies. Yet even if Mayor Washington is succeeded by a politician drawn from the regular Democratic organization, it is unlikely that the new mayor will command city decision-making institutions and resources in the systematic manner of Richard J. Daley. Outside Chicago's halls of corporate and political power, neighborhood organizations and other groups uneasy with orthodox development techniques play a larger role in reacting to specific development measures. At this time, however, they have not coalesced to frame an alternative vision of Chicago backed with political muscle sufficient to place it on the public agenda.

Notes

1. Harvey Molotch, "The City as a Growth Machine: Toward a Political Economy of Place," in Harlan Hahn and Charles Levine (eds.). *Urban Politics Past, Present, and Future.* New York: Longman, 1980, pp. 129–150.

2. Arnold R. Hirsch, *Making the Second Ghetto: Race and Housing in Chicago, 1940–1960,* New York: Cambridge University Press, 1983.

3. Hirsch, p. 101.

4. On the Lake Meadows opposition, see Hirsch, pp. 130–132. The Fort Dearborn project is described by Edward C. Banfield, *Political Influence,* New York: Free Press, 1965, pp. 126–158.

5. *Development Plan for the Central Area of Chicago.* Chicago: Department of City Planning, August 1958.

6. *Chicago 21: A Plan for the Central Area Communities.* Chicago: Chicago Central Area Committee, September 1973.

7. *Chicago Central Area Plan: A Plan for the Heart of the City.* Chicago: Chicago Central Area Committee and City of Chicago, March 1983.

8. David Emmons, *Dearborn Park/South Loop New Town: A Project in the Chicago 21 Plan.* Chicago: Citizens Information Service, January 1977.

9. Randall H. Cooper, "The Near South Side—a Chicago Opportunity." Presentation to the Railroad Terminal Authority Commissioners, December 14, 1965, p. 3.

10. *1983 Annual Report.* Chicago: Chicago Central Area Committee, March 12, 1984, pp. 5–6.

11. Personal interview with Ira J. Bach, City of Chicago Director of Development, December 21 and 23, 1983, Chicago, Ill.

12. In addition to Hirsch, George Rosen's *Decision Making Chicago-Style: The Genesis of a University of Illinois Campus.* Urbana: University of Illinois Press, 1980, leads one to the same conclusion.

13. Banfield, pp. 148–150.

14. Elliot Arthur Pavlos, "Chicago's Crosstown: A Case Study in Urban Expressways," in Stephen Gale and Eric C. Moore (eds), *The Manipulated City.* Chicago: Maaroufa Press, 1975, pp. 255–261; Grant Pick, "The New Improved Crosstown." *The Reader* (Chicago), January 13, 1978. pp. 1, 22–29.

15. Personal interview with Jared Shlaes, president of Shlaes Inc., July 7, 1984, Chicago, Ill.

16. Personal interview with Charles Wolf, vice-president of Rubloff Development Corp., May 9, 1983, Chicago, Ill.

17. "Staff Report: North Loop Study Area." Chicago: Department of Urban Renewal, October 2, 1973.

18. Richard Christiansen, "Chicago at the Crossroads: A Report on the

Redevelopment of the North Loop." *Chicago Tribune,* November 9, 1980, sec. 6, p. 18; Arthur Rubloff, Letter to the *Chicago Tribune,* June 20, 1980, sec. 3, p. 2; *North Loop Redevelopment.* Chicago: Rubloff Development Corporation, N.D.

19. The State of Illinois Building was financed and built independently of the remaining North Loop blocks. From this time on it was no longer considered part of the project.

20. Joe Kolman, "The Trial of the Chicago 21." *The Reader* (Chicago), October 10, 1979, pp 1, 18–29; Paul Gapp, "Failure to Guarantee Preservation of Buildings Perils N. Loop Funds." *Chicago Tribune,* August 3, 1980, p. 5.

21. Wolf, interview.

22. Ed McManus, "Chicago Plan Unit OKs North Loop Renovation." *Chicago Tribune,* April 12, 1979, sec. 3, p. 8.

23. Christiansen; George Papajohn, "The Chicago Theater Tug-of-War." *Chicago Tribune,* March 14, 1982, sec. 5, pp. 3, 5.

24. Evidence of CCAC's reluctance to support the Rubloff plan is provided by its *Annual Reports* and "Newsletter." During the five years that Rubloff retained control of the project, it received little attention in either publication, and Rubloff's role in project planning was not noted. However, as soon as Shaw took over the North Loop, it was prominently featured in both publications.

25. Robert Davis, "Banks to Put up \$50 Million to Aid North Loop." *Chicago Tribune,* July 21, 1979; Lillian Williams, "Co. Panel Approves 'Blighted' Tax Break." *Chicago Sun-Times,* February 26, 1980, p. 58.

26. John McCarron, "Good, Bad News for North Loop Project Backers." *Chicago Tribune,* April 7, 1980, sec. 3, pp. 1, 3.

27. John McCarron and Stanley Ziemba, "Contract Lets Hilton Corp. Control North Loop Plan." *Chicago Tribune,* August 17, 1980, pp. 1, 12.

28. William Juneau, "Assessor Rejects N. Loop Tax Break Bid as 'Incomplete." *Chicago Tribune,* August 20, 1980.

29. Gapp.

30. Richard Christiansen, "Arts, Not Edifices, Come First" and Paul Gapp, "Good Show, But Questions Remain." *Chicago Tribune,* November 14, 1980, sec. 4, p. 1.

31. Stanley Ziemba, "City Gets Its N. Loop Act Together." *Chicago Tribune,* October 21, 1982, sec. 2, p. 12.

32. John McCarron, "Study Charges City Gets Short End of Tax Break for Hilton." *Chicago Tribune,* November 9, 1981, p. 4; Raffaela Y. Nanetti, "Com-

munity Groups as Alternative Political Organizations in Chicago." Photo copy, School of Urban Planning and Policy, University of Illinois at Chicago, April 1983; Shlaes, interview.

33. "Report and Decision of Cook Co. Assessor on the Application of the City of Chicago for Class 7 Certification of the State-Wacker Area." Chicago: Cook County Assessor, December 8, 1981; Stanley Ziemba and David Axelrod, "Hynes' Hilton Decision Avoids Political Fallout." *Chicago Tribune,* December 9, 1981, p. 4.

34. At about this time the owners of the State-Lake Building, an older office and commercial structure that is not a historic building, also committed themselves to rehabilitating their property.

35. Ziemba.

36. Stanley Ziemba, "City Council O.K. Is Expected on Sole North Loop Bid." *Chicago Tribune,* December 16, 1982, sec. 2, p. 8.

37. John McCarron, "3d Developer Drops Hotel Plan for North Loop." *Chicago Tribune,* April 2, 1985, sec. 2, pp. 1, 6.

38. *North Loop Tax Increment Redevelopment Area; Redevelopment Plan and Projects.* Chicago: City of Chicago, April 1984; Personal interviews with Glenn Steinberg, Director of North Loop Planning, June 27, 1984, and July 15, 1985, Chicago, Ill.

39. Rudolph Unger, "Two North Loop Bids Win City's Backing." *Chicago Tribune,* August 7, 1985, sec. 2, p. 3.

40. Until the city was able to arrange the financing to purchase the Chicago Theater, its owners were threatening to demolish it. In the fall of 1984, City Council opponents of Mayor Washington sought to trade one of the other North Loop project blocks for the theater. Stanley Ziemba, "Sale of Chicago Theater Completed." *Chicago Tribune,* October 30, 1985, sec. 2, p. 2.

41. Steinberg, interview, July 15, 1985.

42. Hank De Zutter, "Fair Questions: Citizens Seek Entrance to 'Age of Discovery'." *The Reader* (Chicago), April 4, 1983, pp. 3, 31; R.C. Longworth, "World's Fair of 1992—What It Means for Chicago and You." *Chicago Tribune,* May 8, 1983, pp. 1, 12; John MCarron and Daniel Engler, "Seeds of Fair Demise Were Planted Early." *Chicago Tribune,* June 23, 1985, pp. 1, 11.

43. Chester Hartman, in *The Transformation of San Francisco.* Totowa, NJ: Rowman and Allanheld, 1984, p. 325, notes a somewhat similar split between San Francisco's fair housing advocates and groups committed to controlling the pace of growth.

PART THREE
The Social Costs of Urban Growth and Decline

Chapter 9

Tallying The Social Costs of Urban Growth Under Capitalism: The Case of Houston

Joe R. Feagin

Introduction: Houston's Growth

Many urban problems are the social costs of the private enterprise system predominant in U.S. and Western European cities. Most discussion of urban problems has targeted declining cities such as Detroit and Newark. The social costs of growth in boomtowns have received much less attention. Since the pre-eminent U.S. boomtown from the 1950s to the early 1980s was Houston, Texas, it is instructive to examine the social consequences of urban growth in this "capital of the Sunbelt."

Now the nation's fourth largest city, Houston, is called the "oil capital of the world" because of the oil, gas, and petrochemical companies in the area. Since the 1920s the velocity of investments has accelerated, to the point that thirty-four of the nation's largest oil companies now have major administrative, research, and production facilities in the Houston area, as well as hundreds of other oil and gas companies and thousands of related support firms. In 1980 one-quarter of U.S. oil refining capacity was centered in this Gulf Coast area, together with half of U.S. petrochemical production. The flow of profits to the oil-petrochemical sector over the three decades from 1950 to 1980 provided the capital that ultimately lies behind much of Houston's dramatic growth. The expanding oil-petrochemical economy generated a propulsive dynamism that attracted not only large non-oil companies but also capital from banks and insurance firms for major development projects, including four hundred office towers, numerous industrial parks, dozens of shopping centers, and hundreds of residential subdivisions.

Calculating The Price of Growth In A City: Some Theoretical Ideas

PROFIT AND GROWTH

The capitalist system of investment, production, and marketing is a powerful agency for the transformation of cities. Growth typically hinges on the decisions made by controllers of capital calculating profit at the firm level. In this chaper, I am primarily concerned with the social costs of for-profit decisions made by industrial and commercial development capitalists, decisions which generate dramatic urban growth (and decline). "Social costs" have been defined as the negative consequences of for-profit production—costs not paid for by an individual firm but shifted onto third parties.[1] In capitalistic societies, generally speaking, investment and production decisions are made without a prior accounting of societal consequences. Costs are calculated at the microeconomic level of the individual company in terms of its profits, its future net revenues, or its share of the market. Decision-making by these criteria will seek to reduce internal costs, while ignoring social costs that can be displaced onto third persons. Many urban problems are created because decision-making affecting whole communities is made at the level of the individual firm.

President C.E. Wilson of General Electric once emphasized this view: "Certainly there is nothing antisocial in profit. I think the truth of the matter is that—given access to all as buyers and sellers—the profit earned by the wise businessman is a measure of the service he has rendered to his market, in terms of a value placed on those services by the buyers, individually and collectively."[2] The need for economic growth, according to a Boston Federal Reserve Bank booklet, is a common justification for profit seeking: "In a private enterprise system the hope for profits encourages new production, investment and economic growth."[3] At least since the 1930s growth, both in U.S. society and in U.S. cities, has been viewed and measured in these narrow economic terms.

The Short-Run View and the Market

One review of U.S. business-school literature found that new managers are taught to make decisions based on such factors as short-run profitability, market share, and annual sales growth.[4] Conservatives and liberals alike accept decisions aimed at the market as the primary adjudicator of what is or is not produced. An individual firm's market-oriented decision to produce a given product for sale is judged as positive solely in terms of that firm's short-term profit accounting.[5] But when numerous companies make decisions that create, for example, cancer-causing pollutants or high urban unemployment from corporate relocation, it becomes clear that the market process can be very negative for the larger urban context. Yet these social costs occur not because companies cannot plan for the future. Indeed, large corporations are "the most ardent and successful planners in the United States."[6]

Why are urban-based corporations able to create environmental and other social problems by shifting their social costs off onto other people? Because they have greater economic and political power. In a society with vast inequality in income and in the ability to make decisions about jobs and resources, the production and distribution decisions of companies, particularly large firms, are hard for ordinary citizens to resist or change.[7] Challenging power and resource inequality is made difficult by the fact that many social costs (e.g., high cancer rates in Houston from extensive pollution) may take a long time to show up in individuals or in a community.

Moreover, the situational context of narrow, firm-level cost accounting can multiply the negative effects. Cities are in the first instance physical, geographical environments into which corporate and other human action has intruded. The physical environment has its own regularities and laws—for example, ground and surface water flows, air patterns, rainfall, soil characteristics. If these environmental givens are ignored when profit-centered investment and production decisions are made, then the consequences of such decisions may well be negative.[8] Within a given natural environment, the rate of economic growth is also linked to the velocity of capital in manufacturing, real estate, and construction. Bluestone and Harrison have noted that the impact of city growth is greatly shaped by capital "velocity":

How much expansion can be absorbed, and how quickly, depends on the dynamics of the people and the environment of the community involved. With suitable planning and reasonable forecasts, new schools can be built, teachers hired, roadways, water, and sewage systems constructed, and job training set up. But when the capital influx is totally unrestrained, the absorptive capacity of the social system can be quickly overwhelmed.[9]

Government Assists "Free" Enterprise

DEFENSIVE EXPENDITURES

Local city government in the United States is faced with pressures from its local business elite to subsidize the development costs of companies making capital investments within its boundaries. It is pressured to accelerate economic growth and to recruit corporations in manufacturing and other industries. But local government is also faced with pressures from its citizenry to deal with urban services requirements and the waste problems of growth as well. A local government makes "defensive expenditures" for such items as road, water, sewage, and toxic waste problems. These expenditures accelerate as growth increases. The absorptive capacity of social and governmental systems can be overwhelmed. The scale of defensive expenditures is affected by the general process of urban growth, but that scale has been extended since World War II by the "simultaneous process of spatial centralization and business-size related concentrations of productions in an increasingly urban society.[10]

When local governments operate to facilitate the location or expansion of pollution-causing firms, or when they retreat from the planning and intervention necessary to deal with the broad service problems created by private profit making, they actually cooperate in inflicting social costs on the urban citizenry.

Local and Federal Government Subsidies: "Good Business Climates"

Government tax and other resources have often mobilized business development. Government officials in many cities and states have competed vigorously to entice companies to their areas. The result is a broad array of tax and other subsidies that are in fact unnecessary. Studies have shown that regular tax credits and tax-exempt bonds are available to industrial and development capitalists in most urban areas, so special subsidies have only a mild effect on location and investment decisions. The aggressive bidding by communities for industry only improves profit margins. Subsidies make development less expensive for industrial and development capitalists, wherever they go, and thus more expensive for taxpayers.[11]

Ordinarily, where projects are not too risky and profits are likely to be large, developers prefer to go ahead with little government involvement. If there is a "strong market," the private sector wishes to minimize government involvement. Where risks are greater, however, even conservative executives in major private enterprises may seek out government assistance. For example, one important federal subsidy for private development was provided by the 1977 Housing and Urban Development Act, which authorized Urban Development Action Grants (UDAG) to local governments in areas with specified poverty, housing, and unemployment problems. Instead, UDAGs have often been used for streets, utilities, and other services for various types of private residential, commercial, and industrial projects benefitting affluent suburbanites.[12]

Local governments are pressured by business elites to provide parking facilities, tax abatements, public services, zoning permissions, and administrative assistance in finding federal grants and loans. Hidden government subsidies for the builders of downtown developments include zoning changes to permit development, tax abatements sharply reducing taxes, cheap land provided by clearance programs, and utilities.[13] All across the country government officials have played a role in downtown office development, providing money for services such as new roads and sewers, giving away public land by closing streets and by urban renewal projects, and constructing business-oriented projects such as convention centers and parking garages.[14]

Thus local government is in partnership with entrepreneurs, often furnishing a broad array of subsidies essential to private profitmaking in the cities. This is certainly true of Sunbelt cities like Houston. Of course some defensive expenditures for roads and sewers are necessary; but it is often the case that infrastructure expenditures must be kept at the lowest level possible, particularly for ordinary citizens. The reason for this is that too much action on roads, sewers, water systems, and toxic waste problems can be costly. And that covered cost is paid out of local individual and business taxes. Since the local growth coalition, the business elite, demands a "good business climate" with low taxes, then it follows that public services and defensive expenditures must be kept at the minimal level consistent with firm level profitability.

The Laissez-Faire View of Houston's Leaders

This portrait of a capitalist system creating costs in an urban setting seems to fit Houston like the proverbial glove. Houston is famous as a free-enterprise city where individual firms calculate advantage or disadvantage primarily in terms of present and future profits and market power. Houston is a city whose leaders have propagated the strongest possible ideology of the free market. For example, a 1980 advertisement for Houston placed in *Fortune* magazine accented the good business climate and free-enterprise gospel:

> Houston, by virtue of being in Texas, reaps the benefits of a state that has one of the best business climates in the nation. It is not just lukewarm toward business, it is pro-business. It welcomes new ideas and people. There's little in the way of red tape. Free enterprise is still the gospel.[15]

As a result of this wide-open, free-enterprise approach to economic and urban development, recognition of the seriousness of most of Houston's social costs has come slowly, particularly to Houston's leadership. The free-enterprise dynamism of the city is seen as minimizing social problems such as poverty, a point emphasized by former mayor and Chamber of Commerce head Louie Welch:

> The free market place has functioned in Houston like no other place in America. It has a method of purging itself of slums. No city is without poor people, but the opportunity not to be poor is greater than in most cities. The work ethic, and opportunities, are strong here.[16]

Yet, since the late 1970s, the seriousness of Houston's problems has increased to the point that complaints from the citizenry have become a source of concern for the city's elite. One tack has been to blame the general public either for creating the problems themselves or for an unwillingness to pay for needed services.[17]

Another tack can be seen in a mid-1980s boosterism campaign designed to reduce citizen complaints about social problems. A new business organization called "Pro-Houston" was created—with prominent Houston executives from major oil companies and banks on its board—to play down local social problems, to emphasize what "the city is doing right," and to get the citizens to volunteer to solve what problems there are.[18]

In regard to local governmental intervention for planning or restricting growth, Houston has seen relatively limited governmental intervention, particularly before the late 1970s. A 1980 guidebook on Houston extols the laissez-faire government atmosphere and the close relationship between government and business: "Much of the city's growth can be attributed to the local government's attitude of cooperation with the business community."[19] In his preface to the guidebook, ex-mayor Welch emphasized the importance of local government's assisting in maintaining a free-market city.[20] This emphasis on a partnership between government and business has meant poor city services, a weak regulatory bureaucracy, and business-government cooperation in major development projects of interest to the local business elite. The laissez-faire ideology has led Houston's leadership to reject some federal aid, such as urban renewal, but it has not kept the leadership from going to Washington, D.C. for federal assistance to improve the Port of Houston ship channel, bring order to oilfield competition, build major airports, and construct essential infrastructure projects.

That leadership has also fought to keep taxes low. In order to maintain the city's image of fiscal conservatism (in the 1970s Houston was the only major American city with an AAA bond rating by Wall Street), that elite has kept government operating expenditures relatively low, thus permitting a low tax rate. One result of these relatively low, city budgets has been a limited array of city services and an infrastructure of aging streets, inadequate and aging water and sewer systems, and substandard police and fire facilities, particularly in the central city area.

Toxic Waste Disposal: The Industrial Growth Problem

One major social cost of continuing industrial growth in a city with a laissez-faire leadership ideology can be seen in Houston's major toxic waste problems. Since cheap toxic waste dumping, unrestricted by government, is linked to industrial profitability, it is perhaps not surprising that Houston's eastside residential communities face the looming spectre of a Love Canal disaster. The cost of cleaning up the toxic waste dumps has not been tallied up on chemical firm ledgers. It will be, and is being, paid for by the local citizenry.

The expanding industrial investment in Houston since the 1920s has brought a rapid growth in toxic waste, particularly in the last two decades. Houston Gulf Coast area industries in the early 1980s produced three million tons of toxic waste each year. In addition, billions of gallons of contaminated water are dumped into local wells. A great deal of hazardous waste flows to or through Houston by barge, truck, airplane, railroad car, and pipeline; in 1982 a total of 1.9 billion gallons of hazardous waste was handled.[21]

In 1984 the Republican head of the EPA, William Ruckelshaus, described the greater Houston area as one of the worst hazardous waste disposal areas in the nation because of its nine major toxic waste dumps that are on the Superfund list, as well as its 100 toxic waste sites not on that list. Ruckelshaus said that "the Houston area has bigger problems because it has more of the industries [that produce the waste]."[22] Ruckelshaus was referring to the large number of chemical and petrochemical plants in the area. As a major center of growth in industrial production between 1920 and 1982, Houston has serious toxic waste dump problems that have not yet been cleaned up. Such great quantities of industrial waste would be a problem in any metropolitan area. But the magnitude of the problem in Houston has been exacerbated by weak or nonexistent regulation of disposal by the local government, and the lack of attention to this problem by the private sector. In the early 1980s there were only 14 waste disposal firms for the entire nine-county area around Houston. Some concerned local officials have worried openly that increasing amounts of toxic waste will show up in the city's sewage system from illegal dumping into sewer manholes, but they have not yet taken the action necessary to prevent such a possibility.

In May 1985 a helicopter search of 150 square miles between Houston and Galveston discovered two "hot Spots" where low-level radioactive waste had been dumped. Moreover, a 1985 Houston *Chronicle* front-page story reported that local health officials were investigating the possibility that a Houston company had made barbecue pits out of metal drums that had once contained toxic chemicals such as benzene and toluene.[23]

There are also regular stories in the Houston press on the impact of toxic waste on local residential communities, as well as the occasional citizen protest over this pollution. For example, a waste disposal firm, Nuclear Resources and Services, applied for a permit to expand waste facilities in southeast Houston. Construction equipment was burned at the site, presumably by local residents. An executive of the firm had to be protected from an angry crowd there by the Houston police. In another case the residents of a subdivision in northeast Houston organized protests against a proposed polychlorinated biphenyl (PCB) waste storage site. A disposal company was proposing to store more than fifty thousand gallons of the dangerous substance.[24]

Southern areas of the city have had the greatest number of toxic waste problems. In 1983–1984 local officials in the "South Houston" community were pressing the federal EPA to clean up a 13-acre toxic waste site known to be' contaminating ground water with cancer-causing PCB waste and twelve other toxic waste chemicals. Most city residents live within a mile of the dump. The Texas Department of Water Resources had recommended the dangerous dump to the EPA for federal "Superfund" cleanup, but the EPA was very slow in providing aid. Local residents were fearful that PCBs and other toxic wastes were spreading throughout the underground water system because of the many abandoned oil and gas wells in the area.[25] And in the fall of 1983 the Texas Department of Water Resources began moving to clean up a major 25-acre waste dump near the South Houston community of Friendswood. Contaminated by chemical waste from a nearby plant, the dump was leaking toxic waste into surface water running off the site.[26]

Houston's central commercial artery, the ship channel, is lined with large-scale industrial development, as well as residential communities. Several dozen major landfill areas have been built up in this southeast area of Houston since the petrochemical revolution of the 1940s. One environmental activist said that there are dozens of "Love Canal crises" just waiting to be discovered in the industrial areas of Houston. For example, Deer Park, a community of 25,000 residents in the southeastern sector, faces many toxic waste disposal problems because of numerous dump sites. Commenting on one high-rise landfill there, a local resident noted that:

This is a mountain of Class I [most poisonous] waste. I'm scared to death that a hurricane or tornado will knock the thing over.

Mother Earth can't hold it. This is not a democracy. It is a dictatorship by industry when we have to live like this.[27]

Sewage and Garbage Disposal

SEWAGE PROBLEMS

Rapid population growth has paralleled industrial growth; and industrial and population growth in a weak-services, low-tax governmental framework has meant major problems in routine sewage and garbage disposal. Sewer problems have plagued the Houston area since the early 1900s. As early as 1916, a Houston mayor publicly worried that too much city sewage was being dumped into the Buffalo Bayou, a central watercourse. Since that time Houston's historic Buffalo Bayou has become a major artery for disposing of sewage from rapid development. In the mid-1980s Houston officials were discussing the dumping of millions of gallons of raw sewage daily from Houston's elite central city residential areas called River Oaks into Buffalo Bayou. In the mid-1970s the city government had promised by 1978 to deal with those sewage overflows, but as of 1985 the problem was still not being solved.[28] By the mid-1980s, more than twenty million gallons of sewage wastewater was flowing down the Bayou from city and private-development sewage plants daily. Additional permits have sought to dump millions of gallons more each day. The Bayou has become anaerobic in some places, with little in the way of aquatic life.[29]

By the early 1980s the city had 4,000 miles of sewers and 44 treatment plants. The plants have frequently violated state wastewater effluent standards; in January 1980 half the 44 plants were in noncompliance. In 1974 the Texas Water Quality Board ordered the city to improve its wastewater facilities. The city was forced to take action, limiting sewer hookups. A sewer moratorium covering three-quarters of the city was implemented, in order to cut down on sharp increases in the sewage being processed at many treatment plants. Many developers and homeowners have had to revise building plans as a result.[30] Large tracts of land cannot be sold or developed because of a lack of sewer capacity. Moreover, developers who had already secured sewer permits on parcels of land have traded them to other developers without permits, informal trading in what are locally called "poop futures."

Late in 1983, a 200-million-gallons-per-day sewer processing facility was completed in north Houston, releasing portions of the northern area for development. Yet there was no rush to use the new facility, in part because of the 1983-1984 recession in Houston and in part because there were inadequate pumping stations and sewer lines for many areas to be served by the new treatment plant.[31] Even with the new plant, most development areas in the central city remained under a sewer moratorium in the mid-1980s.

One should note that the sewage crisis is linked to the inadequacy of local planning. The head of the city's wastewater division has said in effect that Houston's growth is unpredictable and unplanned:

> And in many cases a developer would first build a warehouse or other structure that had low-volume sewage needs and then, after the city had built lines to serve it, would change the use of the land to high-rise condominiums or other buildings that need much larger sewer lines.[32]

The absence of zoning laws and the weak character of local government planning are revealed in these comments. The sewage problem has been costly in terms of the city government budget. The city wastewater division's budget increased sharply between 1975 and the early 1980s as did the capital improvement budget for sewage facilities. In addition, Houston's sewer bonds were downgraded in 1983 by bond-rating agencies. Neglect of sewage problems in the past means high costs for local taxpayers in the present and future.

One result of the sewer moratorium has been a significant increase in the number of small sewer plants put up by the developers inside and outside the city limits. In most cases the city of Houston is required to repay a developer for the plant and must eventually replace the temporary facility with regular city service. The developer, in the meantime, is supposed to maintain the plant. Maintenance has been a problem, and older plants often violate the state effluent standards.[33] Development capitalists who build projects in areas outside Houston's city limits have relied heavily on Municipal Utility Districts (MUDs), which they create in order to secure bonds for utility projects. The utilities built are not well regulated because state and local governments in Texas generally do not have the staff and/or the authority to make sure such facilities as sewage plants meet quality standards. As a result, many private sewage plants are in fact a primary source of surface water pollution. A major cost for the city of Houston has been the upgrading of substandard sewage treatment facilities in MUD areas that have been annexed by the city.

Compared to other major metropolitan areas, Houston has few satellite cities. But one of these, Pasadena, has also faced major problems of growth over its life history. Thus in the spring of 1984 the Attorney General of the state of Texas sued the city of Pasadena for polluting local waterways with inadequately treated effluents from its sewage treatment plants.

GARBAGE DISPOSAL

Disposal of the city's garbage is a major problem. Urban growth has meant increasing garbage and thus accelerating demand for landfill in which to bury trash. No community wants such areas to be developed near them. As a result, Houston has seen a number of battles over new landfill areas in which to bury the city's constant flow of garbage. The city government has not developed much in the way of resource recovery facilities; in the early 1980s about 75 percent of the city's refuse went directly to landfill areas well out from the center of Houston. The largest landfill was expected to be exhausted by 1985 because of rapid growth. In 1983 a Chamber of Commerce report highlighted the severity of Houston's waste problems and recommended that the city contract out for all garbage pickup, build new landfill sites in all quadrants of the city, and put $500 million into waste-to-energy facilities.[34]

Location of landfills has been discriminatory. Between 1953 and 1978 a total of 21 solid waste sites were authorized by the Texas Department of Health for the Houston area. Of these, 11 (52 %) have been in black communities, even though Blacks made up only 28 percent of the Houston population and occupy less than 20 percent of the residential space in the city. Six landfill areas with state permits received municipal garbage between 1970 and 1978, five of which were in black neighborhoods at the time they opened. The sixth was becoming a predominantly black area in the early 1980s. Four other landfills used in the past twenty-five years do not have state permits, but have received municipal garbage. All are in black neighborhoods.[35] Moreover, all of Houston's five garbage incinerators, operating from the 1920s to the 1970s, were located in black or hispanic neighborhoods.

Recurrent Water Problems

Sustained rapid growth has also created interrelated water problems, which have been aggravated by the velocity of growth and the low-tax approach of local government.

SUBSIDENCE

Many areas of Houston are sinking as a result of growth. Houston has in recent years drawn about 60 percent of its water supply from primary wells, and the rest from three lake reservoirs. But this dependence on pumping water from wells is changing, because of the soil subsidence it creates. This subsidence has been created by the compacting of clay soils as areas of southeast Houston have sunk 6 to 8 feet since 1943, and central city areas have subsided 3 to 5 feet in the same period. In 1983, one large northwest area sank 2 to 3 inches; the total drop there in the 1975–1983 period was 14 inches. In the southwest quadrant land is sinking even more rapidly, with a 3 to 4 inch drop in 1983 alone. Most of the west side subsided 0.6 to 1.0 feet in the 1978–1983 period. A major reason is that much of the groundwater still being pumped in the greater Houston area is being pumped out from under the rapid development areas on the west side. Such subsidence continues to exact costs from ordinary homeowners. In 1985 just one foundation company reported that it was repairing 200 home foundations annually because of subsidence, at an average cost of $5,000 per foundation.[36]

There are plans to deal with subsidence in the west Houston area by building two major water treatment plants that would allow increased use of surface water. But the cost of this obvious solution is now too high. It would require huge increases in water rates and major capital improvement bonds. The past neglect of this water-related problem by the local growth coalition today means very expensive solutions. Again the costs of past development have been transferred to present and future generations.[37]

REGULAR FLOODING

In the mid-1980s, Joseph Goldman, the chair of disaster services for the Red Cross in Houston, noted that the number and intensity of floods in the Houston area was increasing "faster than you'd expect," and that as a result the number of flood victims was rising. Because of subsidence, high annual rainfall, and flat topography, Houston has had major flooding in at least 20 of the years between 1907 and 1984. Average annual losses now run about $36 million. Houston's officials have dealt with flood problems with a disaster relief approach involving insurance. A government plan restricting development in flood-prone areas has long been considered as too interventionist for the local business elite.[38]

A major cause of flooding in many areas of the city is the subsidence already discussed. When this sinking is coupled with increased water runoff from private-profit development projects upstream, downstream areas along major creeks and bayous can suffer major flooding on a routine basis. Moreover, about one-fifth of Harris County's flood plain area has urban development, along bayous, streams, and other watercourses. There has been massive residential and commercial development in the watershed areas on the west side of Houston. Since natural drainage in the area is generally from west to east, a high level of west-side development has brought a substantial increase in water runoff after rains, flooding west-side areas as well as downtown.[39]

By the mid-1980s the magnitude of the problem was beginning to be discussed even by Houston's business elite. Some modest action was forthcoming from the government. Thus the Harris County Flood Control District has recently required that detention ponds be built by developers putting new large-scale real estate projects in areas where the drainage systems are overloaded. Yet because existing developments are not covered, this requirement will not stem much of the flooding. In 1984 a local Chamber of Commerce Task Force Group on Planning recommended a $922 million capital improvement program over 25 years, to correct the most pressing drainage problems.[40]

WATER SUPPLIES

Much local water is being consumed by local industries, at relatively low rates. Water supplies for the city, drawn increasingly from surface water sources, are projected to be adequate for the growth expected in the Houston area until 1992. But there are periodic problems with water pressure. A 1980 summer heat wave dropped the water level in Lake Houston and forced the city to reduce water pressure substantially. While the amount of water available is considered adequate, the pumping stations and treatment facilities necessary to maintaining adequate pressure during periods of drought have not been constructed. Indeed, in 1984 the Texas Health Department withdrew its special "state approved" designation for Houston's water systems because the city did not have adequate water storage facilities, particularly for a time of crisis such as a major drought or a hurricane. A City Planning Commission report, moreover, has noted that Houston's water system will not be able to handle Houston's expected growth after 1992. Then the costs will have to be paid.[41]

The quality of surface water has deteriorated because of growth. One example is Lake Houston, the source of drinking water for four in ten Houstonians. In the mid-1980s the Houston Health Department reported that water samples taken from Lake Houston had fecal coliform bacteria counts ranging from 5,500 to 17,000 organisms per 100 milliliters of water, well above the safety standard of 400 organisms.[42]

Because of rapid suburban development in the lake area, in the outlying MUDs sewage flows into the lake through small treatment plants, many of which are overloaded and discharge inadequately treated effluent. Private for-profit developers have created the sewage problems, but they themselves do not pay the lion's share of the costs. According to a mid-1980s City Council study, there are more than 200 small sewage treatment plants in the Lake Houston watershed, plants which release 50 million gallons of effluent daily into the lake. Rapid real estate investment and development in the 3,000-square-mile watershed of Lake Houston is the critical generating factor behind the lake's severe pollution problems.[43]

In 1983, the Texas Attorney General filed a lawsuit against a developer and a private utility company for operating a polluting sewage plant. The suit alleged that homeowners served by the plant had been deceived into believing that the plant was approved. A second lawsuit against another utility responsible for an inoperative sewage plant was filed at the same time. Both plants were discharging raw or partially treated effluent into Lake Houston. Five other sewage plants have been considered for similar suits. Other surface water in Houston has also been contaminated by pollution.[44]

Large corporations have played a significant role in Houston's water pollution problems, as we noted previously in discussing the impact of toxic waste on groundwater. Utility companies have contributed to water pollution problems. Rapid growth in electricity demand in the Houston area has meant major utility construction projects, some of which have generated far more coal ash and wastewater than their designers had projected. In the mid-1980s the federal EPA ordered Houston Lighting and Power to cease discharging millions of gallons of untreated wastewater into lakes and streams near its coal-fired plants.

The Impact of Air Pollution

The east side of Houston is the industrialized area of the city. The east side is a band of industrial areas along the ship channel and Galveston Bay; some of these areas are within the city limits. The complexity of chemical-related accident, waste, and pollution problems can be seen in an area like Texas City, to the southeast of Houston. Texas City has ten square miles of chemical plants, oil refineries, and industrial waste incinerators. In 1947 a vessel loaded with ammonium nitrate exploded; the chemical explosion and accompanying fire killed 576 people and injured 4,000. Since then a few workers have been killed every year or two in various explosions, fires, and toxic exposure incidents at industrial plants in the area.[45] Some of the nation's most seriously toxic waste dumps are there as well. Local workers have complained of accidents at the workplace, of deafness, and of cancers. One study at a plant producing 375 million pounds of chemicals and plastics annually found a high rate of brain cancer among the workers there.[46]

Industrial smog developed in Houston in a major way in the period from 1940–1960. Pollution associated with rapid industrialization continues to be a major social cost of manufacturing growth. In 1981 a Houston newspaper article began with the following comments on an area in the industrialized southeast:

> Lifeless bodies of small blackbirds dot the roadside leading to the Battleship Texas (a local monument). And wild rabbits romp along the Battleground Road in the buff, for they have lost their fur. Oak trees behind the San-Jacinto Monument are stripped too—of their tinsel-like Spanish moss.[47]

Both researchers and local residents have attributed these problems to the air pollution of the area. Air pollution problems are not confined to this southeastern area of Houston, nor is the human population exempt. A recent study of cancer death rates by the M.D. Anderson Hospital and Tumor Institute revealed that the Greater Houston Area has had one of the highest lung cancer death rates in the U.S., at 47 deaths annually per 100,000 population—twice the national rate of 22. Air pollution is one of the likely causes.

Weakly restrained industrial pollution has played a role in Houston's air problems. For example, in the southeast community of Deer Park, PCBs can be burned legally. PCBs have been banned from production in the United States, but there are plenty of chemicals in dumping areas like those in Deer Park. Residents complain that their trees are dying and that people there suffer from skin rashes and respiratory problems. Areas near industrial plants have reported disproportionate incidences of vasculitis and similar skin diseases thought to derive from toxic air and water pollution. Local residents have held meetings with hundreds in attendance and have picketed the landfill that has a permit to burn PCBs. An interview with an executive of one disposal company burning PCBs revealed that up to one-half of the PCB burned is brought in from out of state. Millions of pounds of PCBs have been burned at the Deer Park facility, as well as a million pounds of other deadly chemicals.[48]

The city government in Houston has appeared to vacillate on the question of enforcement of pollution standards for industries. In 1983 the City Council voted unanimously to sue a local chemical company because of air pollution resulting from the handling of toxic chemicals. The city's legal department argued that haphazard handling of toxic chemicals such as methyl bromide and malathion had resulted in toxic air pollution in the area. Yet in a more recent case the city's health department seemed to be dragging its feet. In May 1985 the Houston Health Department decided not to process local citizen complaints about air pollution at a USS Chemicals facility, but rather to pass the complaints along to the Texas Air Control Board.[49]

In the mid-1980s the Texas Air Control Board began a research effort to systematically examine air pollution in four counties covering Houston and adjacent Gulf Coast areas. Ten substances, from PCBs to arsenic to formaldehyde and vinyl chloride, were examined. Preliminary surveys revealed that 235 industrial plants in the four counties were emitting hazardous substances into the air.[50] In 1982–1983 the EPA put the Houston area on notice that certain types of construction might be banned and that federal funds might be terminated if air pollution were not reduced. Citing Harris County (Houston) for high levels of ozone and suspended particulates, the EPA proposed a ban on the construction of new oil refineries and petrochemical plants. The head of the Texas Air Control Board noted that pollution in Houston was more related to industrial plants than to cars.[51]

Persisting Traffic Problems

Auto Congestion

Rapid industrial growth and consequent pollution growth has significantly *decreased* geographical mobility in Houston. In the last decade auto and truck travel has become extremely difficult and costly. With nearly 2.5 million registered vehicles in the city, the city's 4,600 miles of roads cannot accommodate everyone without significant congestion. One survey of six major freeways found that in peak traffic periods the average distance one could drive from the downtown area had been reduced by one-third between 1969 and 1979. On several major roads the distance one could travel from downtown in a 30-minute period at peak hours had dropped by 50 percent.[52] The major reasons for this sharp drop in distance travelled are that autos increased at a rate of twice that of population and that freeway use increased at a rate more than four times that of freeway capacity. In 1985 the Texas Department of Highways and Public Transportation commissioned a 21-month study of severe traffic problems on IH-10, Houston's major east-west artery. The norm for "good flow" on a major highway lane is 11,000 vehicles a day, but each day this freeway carries at least 28,000 vehicles per lane on its most congested sections.[53]

The increase in auto traffic has contributed to a high death rate. In the early 1980s Houston was by far the most dangerous of the larger U.S. cities to drive in, with an annual traffic fatality rate of 23 per 100,000, nearly twice that of Detroit (12.7), and more than twice that of cities like New York (9) and Philadelphia (7.5). In addition, there is a high level of conflict between drivers on Houston's streets and freeways. During a ten-month period in 1983, the Houston Police Department received 161 formal complaints of violent conflict on the roads, including some that resulted in fatalities.[54]

A highway-centered transportation system has become costly to maintain, and few cities will ever be able to raise the money to maintain and rebuild their auto-focused transportation infrastructure. A Houston Chamber of Commerce study proposed spending an incredible $16.2 billion for 300 miles of new freeways and for 30 miles of high-capacity transitways. Billions more would be needed for repairs. Texas has benefitted more than any other state from federal intervention; 40 percent of the cost of the state highway program has been federally subsidized. Yet even with this mammoth subsidy, highway-dependent cities like Houston will be unable to afford to maintain their highway systems in the long run.

MASS TRANSIT

In the 1970s, traffic problems got so troublesome that by 1978 Houstonians had approved the creation of a Metropolitan Transit Authority (MTA), to be funded by a one-percent sales tax, with a mandate to improve the bus system and move toward a rail transit system. In the early 1980s Houston's mass transit carried only 54 million passengers annually, compared to the comparable city of Pittsburgh's 103 million riders. A study by the American Public Transit Association revealed Houston to have one of the worst public transit systems in the United States. Low taxes and laissez-faire government have meant poor services. As the head of the MTA board put it, "Nobody paid attention to transit here for 20 years or more. Our bus service was probably the worst in the country. We got so much growth, people did not prepare; people were complacent."[55]

POTHOLES AND ROAD MAINTENANCE

The rapidly increasing truck and auto traffic, coupled with the effects of rainfall and shifting clay soils, have caused a rapid deterioration of many city streets. Houston's one or two million potholes are said to be the nation's worst example of such problems. As a result, there has been a sharp increase in maintenance costs and in capital expenditures for street maintenance, which went from $14.2 million in 1975 to $46 million in 1980. Yet even with these large increases in expenditures, Houston has spent less on roads than comparable cities. One 1978 study of Houston's per capita expenditures for street maintenance compared Houston with eleven other Sunbelt cities. Houston spent less per capita then nine of the other cities.[56]

Another physical dimension that makes Houston's traffic dilemma a long-term issue is the lack of zoning in Houston. The absence of zoning (and much urban planning) has resulted in huge buildings located close to major traffic arteries and in the closing of critical cross-streets to create large mega-blocks for development. In 1982 the formerly laissez-faire City Council adopted an ordinance imposing some modest restrictions on development, the main purpose of which is to improve traffic flow.[57]

Service Neglect: Moving Toward A Crisis

A high velocity of industrial and population growth in Houston's low-tax, weak-government setting has meant serious deficiencies in the services provided by city and county governments. But these are not the only major deficiencies in local services for the citizenry. For example, rapid growth has brought severely overcrowded jail facilities. In 1983 two police officers sued the city over unsafe conditions at the city jail, including crowded jail corriders and cells.[58] The current city jail was built in 1952 for a city of 700,000; now it is seriously overcrowded and a firetrap.

In 1977, a U.S. Interior Department study ranked Houston 140th among cities in parkland per capita. Houston had more than 500 square miles of territory but only 6,200 acres of parkland. By the mid-1980s city government efforts had increased its parkland, but the city still ranked very low. Houston had far less parkland (4.9 acres per 1,000 people) than comparable cities like Phoenix (34 acres per 1,000) and Dallas (27 acres). Houston has been so slow to develop recreational park facilities that the Texas Parks and Wildlife Commission rejected Houston's request for an additional $2 million in state money to build new parks, because of lack of progress in spending earlier grants.[59]

This low-tax city also has serious shortages of critical government personnel. Since the early 1970s Houston has been the construction capital of the U.S. Yet between 1978 and 1983 the city of Houston *decreased* its staff of building inspectors from the already low figure of 128 to 116, most of whom now make dozens of inspections a day, a speed not conducive to thoroughness. And proposed city budgets show no significant increases in inspectors.[60] From 1975 to 1980 Houston's firefighting personnel grew 18 percent, less than population growth in that period. The fire department's operating budget nearly doubled in that period, from $43.9 million to $82.2 million, but these budget increases have not brought the city up to national fire-fighting standards. In 1980 the city had only 1.5 fire-fighters per 1,000 population, below the national standard. A similar problem exists in regard to police protection.[61] Overall, compared with Atlanta, Phoenix, and Denver, Houston has fewer municipal employees per 1,000 population.

Black Residential Areas: Cleared for Growth?

Uneven development is not only characteristic of investment patterns across cities, but also distinctive in patterns of investment within cities. Market-dominated growth has destroyed one major black community in the central city area, and is about to destroy another. In a weak-government city there are no political officials with sufficient clout to protect the elderly, minorities, and poor—those most vulnerable to the abuse of power by the local development industry. The Fifth Ward area in northeast Houston has suffered from the growth plans of the white business elite. The Lyons Avenue area there was once a major center for Houston's Black citizens, with major places of entertainment, Black businesses, and churches. Today the area has long stretches of abandoned houses and boarded-up stores; Lyons Avenue is now called "Pearl Harbor" because of its bombed-out look.[62] Once a racially integrated area, the Lyons area is now predominantly composed of low- and moderate-income black families. Decisions by Houston's growth-oriented elite to build two major highways through the area, starting in the 1940s, have resulted in the destruction of this black community.

Bulldozing The Fourth Ward

Just west of downtown lies one of the oldest black communities in Texas, the Fourth Ward. The area is a cohesive black community, with friendly neighbors, numerous churches, and black-owned businesses. Because of its nearness to downtown areas, development capitalists have eyed the area for redevelopment. In order to legitimate the bulldozing of the area, business leaders have periodically spoken of the area as a "blighted neighborhood" or as a "bleak collection of shacks." This verbal labelling of an area is essential to legitimate the destruction of this community. Yet one Houston resident who knows the area disagrees with their verbal attack:

> The Fourth Ward I know is a beautiful place, where neighbors
> actually know each other, kids play outside in the streets, older
> folks sit on their porches and chat with neighbors . . . and there's
> a warm feeling of community that's found almost nowhere else
> in Houston.[63]

The 7,000 mostly black residents have been anticipating redevelopment for more than a decade; the wooden "shotgun" houses have been allowed to decay by absentee landlords. Portions of the Fourth Ward have already been transformed into parking lots and glassy office towers.

Consultant reports have suggested that the area be redeveloped, but they have offered no real solutions to the housing plight of black tenants. Because of its laissez-faire ideology in regard to government intervention in the economic sphere, Houston has little public housing—about five thousand units; private developers have shown little interest in constructing moderate-income housing. In the early 1980s there were 4,500 families and individuals on the waiting list for public housing.[64]

One of the key features of the Fourth Ward is Allen Parkway Village, a major project containing a significant portion of Houston's public housing. In 1984 the American Civil Liberties Union (ACLU) submitted a brief on behalf of public housing applicants charging the Houston housing authority with deliberately being "overly bleak" in assessing the Allen Parkway Village's physical condition in order to get around federal standards prohibiting the destruction of public housing. The city's housing authority estimated rehabilitation costs for the project at a rather extreme figure of $36,000 per unit. The city has been planning the destruction of the project and leasing the property to private developers. In September 1984 the city housing authority applied to the federal Department of Housing and Urban Development to bulldoze the project and to build 975 new public housing units, plus 525 private apartments available to low-income people, elsewhere in the city. The site itself would be made available to Houston developers on a long-term basis. The ACLU brief charges that the Village is still structurally sound and that city housing officials have intentionally held back on spending $10 million in federal dollars that they received in 1979 to rehabilitate public housing units. The brief also charges the Houston housing authority with excluding blacks from the Village in favor of Indochinese tenants who will be easier to evict once the project is cleared for destruction by the federal government.[65] Local officials scoff at the idea that Houston's poverty is of great consequence. The former mayor and Chamber of Commerce head, Welch, in an interview with the *New York Times,* boasted that Houston is the capital of the free enterprise system, and the city's wealth of opportunities were the permanent cures for slums and poverty.[66]

The Free Enterprise City In Fiscal Crisis: Low Taxes and Red Ink

A March 1983 issue of the *Houston Business Journal* proclaimed: CITY IN THE RED: HOUSTON FEELS THE HEAT OF FISCAL CRISIS. The lead sentence in the front-page article asked, "Is Boomtown going bust? Is the Bayou City sailing into the straits of New York City?" These questions would have been unthinkable just a few months before Houston's newspapers began dramatizing the unprecedented fiscal crisis in the "shining buckle of the Sunbelt." In 1982 Houston's general fund balance was $70 million; in 1982 this dropped to only $16 million. By fiscal year 1983 it slumped to a projected deficit position of $43 million. Like northern "fiscal crisis" cities, Houston has also found itself with expenditures rising much more rapidly than tax revenues. In order to maintain the $16 million surplus for June 1983 that the city had promised to bond rating agencies, the Houston city government juggled funds from its revenue-sharing account to its general account, a strategy tried in such other cities in crisis as New York and Cleveland.[67] The crisis of multi-million-dollar budget deficits continued into the 1984-1987 fiscal years. One intriguing aspect of Houston's financial crisis is that it was not caused by factors alleged to be causes of fiscal trauma in northern cities. Houston's business-oriented government managed to engineer a fiscal crisis without high taxes, "troublesome" unions, or "high-paid" government workers.

Some have attributed the crisis to the oil-gas recession, which hit Houston in 1982-1983. This is part of the story, but only part. The more fundamental reasons are closely tied to the postponed costs of industrial and population growth examined previously. In the mid-1980s Houston's city comptroller noted in a speech that there was a gloomy fiscal picture facing Houston, a retrenchment period with the possibility of service cutbacks. He attributed the problem to necessary increases in spending for local services and to the persisting lack of *planning* by government officials, noting that the "ill-planned days of the past are over in Houston."[68] In the 1970-1982 period Houston saw government revenues grow from $300 million to $1 billion. But after 1976 revenue increases from the two major local taxes, property and sales tax, slowed considerably. In the same period city government expenditures increased much more rapidly, with requisite sewer expenditures alone going up 88 percent and airport expenditures by 160 percent. Sharply rising costs for local services are forcing government budget increases. Costs are rising in large part because of past growth and because of the neglect of infrastructure, the under-built and inadequately maintained facilities across the city. The minimal-government approach of Houston's first 140 years is no longer viable; its long-term costs have finally been recognized in city government reports.[69]

Prior to the mid-1970s the business elite and the city government it dominated were able largely to ignore the needs of inner-city minority communities, but in the 1970s the growing power of minority voters and civil rights litigation led to a more representative mayor and city council—and thus to successful demands from central city residents to expand public services. In order to provide these services, Houston's business elite broke with its long-time anti-federal-government stance and accepted some federal funds for social services. The effective enfranchisement of minority voters has put upward pressure on the city government's budget.

Ironically, the mid-1980s budget cuts of the Reagan administration have serious implications for Houston's city government, because most federal funds have been used for capital construction projects. Gradually, Reagan cuts have reduced the city government's ability to fund infrastructural projects desired by the business coalition and citizens in general, such as sewer facilities, airline terminals, and mass transit systems, and to support programs for its politically active minorities. Tax stabilization has been the major benefit from increasing federal aid to the city of Houston since the mid-1970s. A sharp increase in local taxes would have been required in the late 1970s if the federal aid had not been utilized.[70]

Another aspect of Houston's current fiscal crisis is its low-tax taxation structure. The fiscal conservatism guiding Houston has resulted in a weak tax base for Houston's government. Property taxes, set at a relatively low level, are the major source of revenue, since there are no state or local income taxes. The 1982–1983 recession affected oil and real estate companies and thus reduced tax revenues. In addition, the 400-plus MUDs in the Houston area create major liabilities for the city. When the MUD areas are annexed, the city often faces substantial expenditures to provide adequate utilities to replace the poorly built and poorly maintained facilities built by developers. And even without annexation the MUD utilities create major city costs, as when untreated effluents from MUD facilities flow into Lake Houston, forcing sharp increases in water treatment costs.

Conclusion: Citizens View The City's Problems

Growth in this Sunbelt boomtown has brought many social costs in its wake. Just how this capital of the Sunbelt is doing depends on one's perspective. From a corporate view of profitmaking, Houston's market-oriented economy has been very good. Centered on the oil and gas industry, and assisted by major retail successes, Houston's economy has until recently looked very prosperous to those with the wealth to invest in the area. Periodic recessions may force some belt tightening, but there is still a good business climate; there are still no state or local income taxes, and few unions. And there is a business-oriented city government.

But from the ordinary Houstonian's point of view the shining buckle of the Sunbelt has its tarnished side, with its toxic wastes, air and water pollution, traffic congestion, lack of affordable housing, poor mass transit, and generally inadequate government services. Awareness of the costs of growth is increasing. A recent survey of Houstonians found that when asked about rapid growth and development, 71 percent of the sample said growth was not a good thing or expressed mixed feelings about it. Only 28 percent felt growth was unequivocally a good thing.[71]

Moreover, surveys of Houston residents in the four years between 1982 and 1985 found a growing percentage who felt that private/public control of air and water pollution was poor or fair, rising from 67 percent in 1982 to 70 percent in 1985. In three surveys between 1983 and 1985, the overwhelming majority thought living conditions in the city had not improved over the last three or four years. By the 1980s Houston's residents were supporters of environmental action by government, even if such action meant higher taxes. In a 1985 survey, 46 percent felt government was spending "too little" on protecting the environment, whereas only 7 percent said "too much." Sixty-two percent opposed any relaxation of efforts to control pollution in Houston, even if that would stimulate the local economy. And 61 percent felt that protecting the environment was so important that improvements should be made, whatever the cost.[72]

Taxes seem to be of less concern to the citizens than to the business elites who worry about the "good business climate." In the Houston surveys just noted, on the issue of taxes, more than half of Houstonians interviewed in 1985 said they would, if given a choice between raising taxes or reducing city services, prefer an increase in taxes. It is a good thing too that Houstonians are willing to pay higher taxes. Since the city's ruling business elite has postponed paying for many social costs for so long, a massive increase in taxes will be required. Given that such a massive tax increase is unlikely, the more likely result will be a combination of somewhat higher taxes and a growing problem of deteriorating services and service delivery. Houston clearly demonstrates that, in the long run at least, unrestrained capitalist development and a first-rate quality of life are not compatible in a modern city.

Notes

1. Karl Kapp, *The Social Costs of Private Enterprise.* New York: Schocken Books, 1950, pp. 13–25.

2. Francis X. Sutton, Seymour Harris, Karl Kaysen, and James Tobin, *The American Business Creed.* Cambridge, MA: Harvard University Press, 1945, p. 72.

3. *Introducing Economics.* Boston: Federal Reserve Bank, 1984, p. 27.

4. Dan Luria and Jack Russell, *Rational Reindustrialization.* Detroit: Widgetripper Press, 1981, pp. 30–34.

5. David Smith, *The Public Balance Sheet.* Washington, DC: Conference on Alternative State and Local Policies, 1979, p. 3.

6. Martin Carnoy and Derek Shearer, *Economic Democracy.* Armonk, NY: M.E. Sharpe, 1980, p. 233

7. For an extended discussion of this point, see Carney and Shearer, pp. 233–250.

8. Kapp, pp. xiv–xv.

9. Barry Bluestone and Bennett Harrison, *The Deindustrialization of America.* New York: Basic Books, 1982, p. 106.

10. Christian Leipert, *The Other Economic Summit 1985.* Unpublished paper, Wissenschaftszentraum, Berlin, 1986, p. 13.

11. Smith, pp. 4–5.

12. Christopher Kurz, "Public/Private Leveraging of Urban Real Estate." *Mortgage Banker,* November 1980, p. 13.

13. Chester Hartman, Dennis Keating, and Richard LeGates, *Displacement: How To Fight It.* Berkeley, CA: National Housing Law Project, 1982, pp. 147–148.

14. Sam Bass Warner, *The Urban Wilderness.* New York: Harper and Row, 1972, pp. 34–35.

15. Editors, "Houston: The International City." *Fortune,* July 14, 1980, p. 36.

16. Chandler Davidson, "Houston: The City Where the Business of Government Is Business." Unpublished paper, Rice University, Houston; 1981, n.p.

17. *Houston Initiatives: Phase One Report.* Houston: Rice Center, 1981, p. 55.

18. "Pro-Houston Wants to See Some Spirit Here." *Houston,* January 1984, p. 35.

19. Unibook, Inc., *Houston: City of Destiny.* New York: Macmillan, 1980, pp. 60, 82.

20. Ibid., preface, n.p.

21. Jerry Laws, "Houston Clearinghouse for Hazardous Materials." *Houston Post,* September 23, 1984, p. 1D.

22. Laurel Brubaker, "EPA Head Dumps on City's Waste." *Houston Business Journal,* October 8, 1984, p. 12A.

23. Bill Dawson, "Toxic Drums May Be at Sites Where Barbecue Pits Made." *Houston Chronicle,* March 8, 1985, sec. 1, p. 1.

24. Harold Scarlett, "Residents Organizing to Fight Proposed PCB Storage." *Houston Post,* October 7, 1983, p. 28A.

25. Tom Curtis, "PCBs Threaten Water in South Austin." *Dallas Times Herald Southwest Edition,* July 17, 1983, p. 29A.

26. Harold Scarlett, "State Plotting Cleanup of Waste Site That Now Borders on Subdivision." *Houston Post,* September 21, 1983, p. 6A.

27. Bonnie Britt, "West Houston Is Slowly Sinking, But Solutions Are Expensive." *Houston Chronicle,* May 29, 1983, sec. 7, p. 8.

232   JOE R. FEAGIN

28. Harold Scarlett, "Will River Oaks Sewage Still Go to Bayou?" *Houston Post,* July 5, 1984, p. 6D.

29. Harold Scarlett, "Additional Wastes Could Turn Buffalo Bayou into Giant Sewer." *Houston Post,* July 25, 1982, p. 1J.

30. Patricia Cronkright, "Houston's Sewer Moratorium: Putting the Squeeze on Growth." *Houston Business Journal,* December 8, 1980, sec. 1, p. 1.

31. Dick Bryant, "Inner City Ready to Grow as Sewer Moratorium Ends." *Houston Business Journal,* December 5, 1983, sec. A, p. 1.

32. Ibid., p. 22.

33. Patricia Cronkright, "Developers Use Detention Ponds to Fight Floods." *Houston Business Journal,* January 9, 1984, sec. A, pp. 1, 12.

34. Tom Kennedy, "Chamber Reveals Proposals for Flood Control, Waste Pickup." *Houston Post,* September 21, 1983, sec. A, p. 8.

35. Robert D. Bullard, "Solid Waste Sites and the Black Houston Community." Paper presented at Annual Meeting, Southwestern Sociological Association, San Antonio, March 17-20, 1982.

36. Allan C. Kinball and Leslie Loddeke, "West Side Subsidence Speeds Up." *Houston Post,* March 28, 1985, p. 1A.

37. Bill Boulter, "Subsidence Solution Outlined by Engineer." *Houston Post,* March 23, 1984, p. 5B.

38. *Houston Initiatives,* pp. 27-28.

39. Ibid., pp. 34-35.

40. Cronkright, "Developers Use Detention Ponds," p. 1.

41. Geoffrey Leavenworth, "Houston: Will It Choke on Its Own Success?" *Texas Business,* December 1980, p. 31.

42. Harold Scarlett, "Public Cautioned to Avoid Polluted Sections of Lake Houston." *Houston Post,* October 20, 1983, sec. A, p. 6.

43. *Report of the City Council Committee on Lake Houston.* Houston: Houston City Council, January 16, 1984, p. 6.

44. Harold Scarlett, "Buffalo Bayou: Mechanical Aeration Proposed for Stream." *Houston Post,* October 21, 1983, sec. C, p. 5.

45. Paul Sweeney, "Life—and Death—on the Job in Texas City." *Texas Observer,* November 6, 1981, pp. 1, 10-11.

46. Ibid.

47. Bonnie Britt, "Pollution Far More than an Abstract Term to Frustrated Deer Park Residents." *Houston Chronicle,* November 15, 1981, sec. 7, p. 1.

48. Ibid., p. 4.

49. Bill Dawson, "Haughton Passes Pollution Complaint to Air Control Board." *Houston Chronicle,* May 10, 1985, sec. 1, p. 27.

50. Harold Scarlett, "Air Research Expanded: Experts Briefed on Study of Gulf Coast Pollutants." *Houston Post,* July 28, 1983, sec. A, p. 8.

51. Carlos Byars, "EPA Sanctions Could Ban Construction along Ship Channel unless Moves to Clear Air Taken." *Houston Chronicle,* February 2, 1983, sec. 1, p. 10.

52. *Houston Initiatives,* p. 22.

53. Kim Cobb, "Katy Traffic Expected to Worsen for a While." *Houston Chronicle,* May 3, 1985, sec. 1, p. 27.

54. Wayne King, "Unfriendly Driving Explodes into Violence on Texas Freeway." *New York Times,* December 16, 1983, sec. A, p. 10.

55. Robert Reinhold, "Houston Ponders Public Transit Plan." *New York Times,* September 28, 1982, sec. Y. p. 11.

56. *Houston Initiatives,* p. 50.

57. In the mid-1980s, zoning was again proposed, but remains controversial.

58. "City Jail Report Cites Poor Staffing, Safety." *Houston Chronicle,* January 18, 1983, sec. 1, p. 1.

59. Mark Carreau, "Houston's Park System Could Be at Its Most Critical Juncture Ever." *Houston Post,* November 8, 1982: sec. A, p. 1.

60. Mark Carreau, "Inspection Inadequacy Called Curb to Building." *Houston Post.* July 28, 1983, sec. A, p. 8.

61. Margaret Downing, "Hiring Your Own Cop Pays Off." *Houston Post,* February 6, 1984, sec. A, p. 3.

62. Bill Minutaglio, "Houston's Baddest Street," *Houston Chronicle Magazine,* June 12, 1983, pp.

63. Kathy Collmer, "Fourth Ward," letter to editor. *Houston Chronicle,* November 9, 1984, sec. 2, p. 11.

64. Davidson.

65. Mark Carreau, "ACLU Brief Challenges Assessment of Allen Parkway." *Houston Chronicle,* sec. 1, p. 20.

66. Davidson.

67. Dick Bryant, "City in the Red: Houston Feels the Heat of Fiscal Crisis." *Houston Business Journal,* March 21, 1983, sec. A, p. 1.

68. Mike Snyder, "Labor Says City Facing 'Retrenchment'," *Houston Chronicle,* February 23, 1982, Section 1, p. 10.

69. *Overall Economic Development Program for the Economic Development Target Area.* Houston: City of Houston, May 31, 1978, p. 12.

70. Susan A. MacManus, *Federal Aid to Houston.* Washington, DC: Brookings Institute, 1983, p. 59.

71. Thomas H. Mayor and Richard Murray, *1983 Houston Metropolitan Area Survey.* Houston: Center for Public Policy, University of Houston, 1983, p. 5.

72. Stephen L. Klineberg, "The Houston Area Survey—1985." Unpublished report, Rice University, March 1985.

Chapter 10

Downriver: Deindustrialization in Southwest Detroit

Richard Child Hill and Michael Indergaard

Introduction

"Downriver" is a collection of blue-collar communities nestled against one another along the Detroit River, south and west from the central city of Detroit. Downriver grew with the steel industry. At the turn of the century Downriver became a steel supplier to the auto industry and later a plant location for car builders and parts suppliers in search of large plots of cheap land fronting a waterway. Downriver also became home for immigrants from Europe and the southern United States who came to work in the plants and mills.

Since the 1970s, Downriver's factories have been collapsing like dominoes—the local manifestation of a global economy in crisis and transition. A sense of shared fate tied to heavy industry led these blue-collar communities to organize the Downriver Community Conference, an intergovernmental development organization whose logo is DOWNRIVER spelled out in block letters beneath a picture of industrial smokestacks. But the world's metal-bending industries face a classic crisis of overproduction. There is more capacity than demand. This is true today, and according to industry analysts, it will be true tomorrow. And that suggests fewer companies, fewer jobs, lower wages, and reduced social services in Detroit's Downriver communities in the years ahead.

What follows is a case study of the devastation done to a cluster of communities by the crisis in the world steel industry and by the strategies U.S. steel corporations have adopted to meet that crisis. Our study also suggests that localities face momentous challenges as they try to mount counteroffensives that match the global scope of the forces that threaten their future. But since Downriver's communities aren't alone in facing this challenge, it behooves us to preface our case study with an overview of the general forces at work.

Deindustrialization

From the close of World War II until the late 1960s the United States experienced relatively stable and balanced economic growth. But in the years to follow, the nation's manufacturing industries began to contract, industrial productivity declined, corporate profits plunged, and structural unemployment moved skyward.[1] Fathoming the implications of America's industrial slump has since become a kind of cottage industry in itself, and scholars continue to offer the public one intriguingly titled book after another: *The Zero Sum Society, Economic Democracy, Minding America's Business, The Next American Frontier, Beyond the Wasteland,* and *The Second Industrial Divide,* to mention just a few.[2] But it was Barry Bluestone and Bennett Harrison who tagged the downward economic trajectory in a way that is probably most in tune with public apprehensions; they called it the "Deindustrialization of America."[3]

Bluestone and Harrison introduced the notion of deindustrialization to a U.S. audience, but they didn't originate the concept. They borrowed the idea from some British economists who used it to describe the declining ability of British manufacturers to earn enough foreign currency through exports to pay for the raw materials and capital equipment they must import to keep their industries growing.[4] Bluestone and Harrison's own analytic contribution was to stretch the deindustrialization concept to cover other sources of harm to a nation's industries besides declining international competitiveness. Under the deindustrialization heading they added: (1) various forms of disinvestment in net productive capacity, ranging from milking the company coffers, to running down plant and equipment, to outright plant closure; (2) the transfer of capital from one business activity, economic sector, or region to another; and (3) the reallocation of profits from productive to speculative or merger activity.[5]

Drawing upon a range of secondary data, Bluestone and Harrison reached the conclusion that corporations had, in fact, "deindustrialized" a sizeable fraction of U.S. business capacity during the 1970s. The authors estimated that during the 1970s as many as 32 to 38 million U.S. jobs disappeared through closures or interstate and international relocations of factories, stores, and offices. In a more recent investigation, which covered manufacturing plants with 100 or more employees between 1978 and 1982, Candee Harris discovered that, on average, 900,000 jobs were lost through plant closings each year.[6] The human consequences of deindustrialization often include long-term unemployment, loss of family income, decline in occupational status, loss of health insurance and pension rights, deterioration in physical and mental health, lost tax revenue, and shrinking social services. Because these social costs don't appear on corporate profit-and-loss ledgers, they aren't paid for by business (dis)investors. Workers and their communities must bear the toll.[7]

Findings like these sparked a debate about industrial policy in the United States, a debate that has technical, political, and ideological dimensions. On the technical side, analysts disagree about the direction U.S. manufacturing is actually taking, and they are quarreling about the kinds of explanations that make the most sense out of particular cases. Robert Z. Lawrence of the Brookings Institute has led the technical counterattack on the deindustrialization thesis. According to Lawrence,[8] there really wasn't any significant change in the aggregate level of U.S. manufacturing employment during the 1970s. And those industries that did suffer, did so not for deep-rooted structural reasons, but in response to normal fluctuations in the economy, like the business cycle and short-term movements in terms of trade. In Lawrence's view, there are no intransigent, systemic forces promoting industrial decay in the United States.

It is here that technical answers take on political and ideological coloration. If familiar macroeconomic processes, like the business cycle, explain manufacturing trends, as Lawrence suggests, then employment loss can be counteracted by the conventional fiscal and monetary policies already in place. If, however, industrial decline is "significantly structural," as Bluestone, Harrison and Matthews have recently reasserted,[9] then the government's standard arsenal of policy tools won't suffice to renew economic growth and employment. Instead, economic regeneration may require national industrial policies targeted at specific economic sectors, regions, and communities. That is a political implication that policy analysts in most Washington think tanks are still loathe to entertain.[10]

We think the insight to be had from analyzing nationally aggregated trend data is often limited.[11] With deindustrialization, as with all aspects of social life, context is important.[12] Deindustrialization may or may not rack up a big economic score on an aggregate national balance sheet; but there is certainly reason to believe it has had a dramatic impact on certain industries, regions, and communities. So even though most Washington-based policy analysts are giving industrial proposals the cold shoulder, these initiatives are receiving serious attention from government officals in economically troubled states and localities.[13] Downriver is a case in point.

The Communities

Rail arteries, emerging like spokes from a central city hub, link the factories of metropolitan Detroit. The Downriver Corridor is the southern spoke, and along it cluster fourteen municipalities and two townships. Ranging in size from 2.4 square miles (River Rouge) to 23.3 square miles (Taylor), all sixteen communities add up to 340,000 people taking up 120 square miles of land south of the central city of Detroit. (See Figure 10.1.)

Downriver dependence on heavy industry is extraordinary, even when gauged against the metal-working Motor City. In 1980, for example, 22 percent of U.S. workers and 33 percent of metropolitan Detroit workers were employed in manufacturing; but the figure for Downriver was 37 percent (and it went as high as 45 percent in Ecorse and 47 percent in Gibraltar). Downriver residents were also more likely to be employed in industrial working-class jobs than their metropolitan and general U.S. counterparts.

Despite cyclical downswings, long-run industrial expansion provided economic security for several generations of Downriver residents. Economic stability reinforced ethnic and family ties and promoted a Downriver ethic of self-reliance. Downriver residents proudly proclaim that it was their advanced steel industry that gave birth to the Ford Motor Company and industrial Detroit. And many families can still trace their Downriver lineage to immigrant kin from Italy, Poland, and Ireland who lived in shanties and worked the steel mills of Wyandotte where the Bessemer steel process was pioneered in 1864.[14]

DETROIT

DETROIT RIVER

DOWNRIVER

ONTARIO

3

5

2

6

4

1 Taylor
2 Allen Park
3 Melvindale
4 Lincoln Park
5 River Rouge
6 Ecorse
7 Wyandotte
8 Southgate
9 Brownstown Township
10 Riverview
11 Trenton
12 Woodhaven
13 Flat Rock
14 Rockwood
15 Gibraltar
16 Grosse Ile

1

8

7

10

9

12

11

16

13

9

15

14

9

RIVER

DETROIT

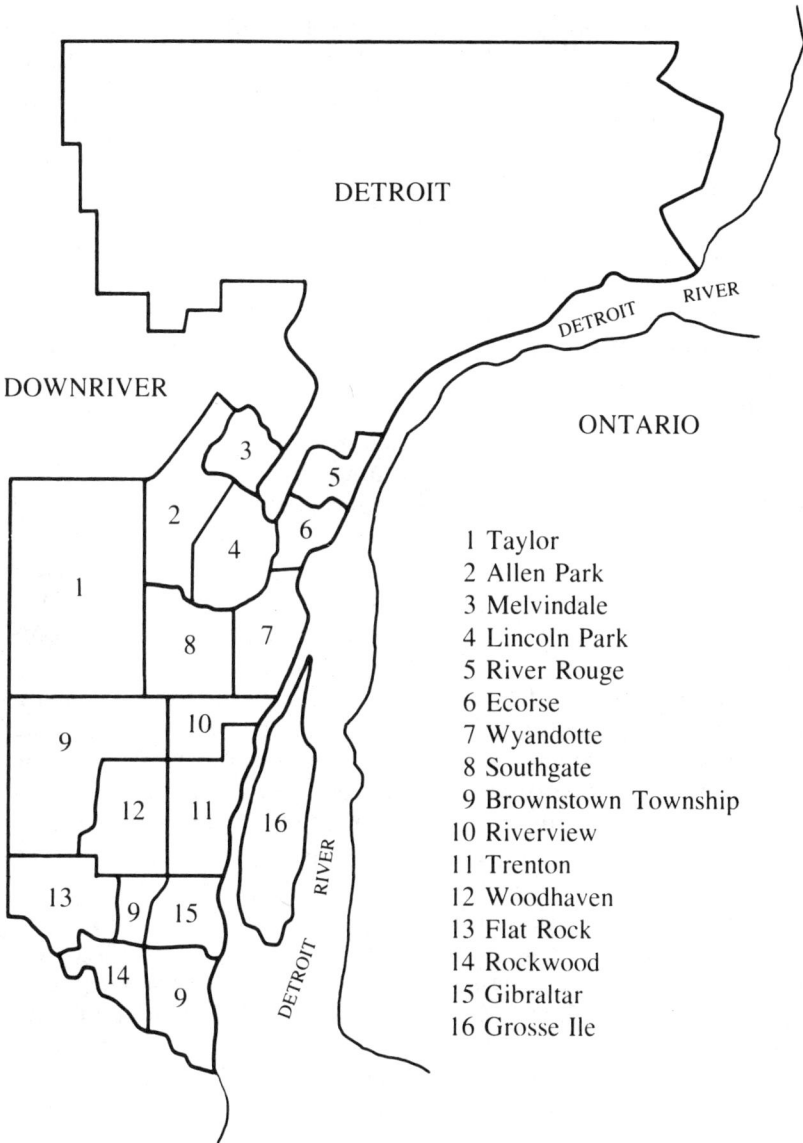

Figure 10.1: Downriver and The Detroit Metropolitan Area

In past years Downriver's youth tended to stay in the area; those venturing outside, for college or travel, usually returned; and those moving up the occupational ladder often just moved further down the river to the region's southernmost communities. Many Downriver youngsters attended the same high school as their grandparents. And when retired residents went to church festivals, they often mingled with childhood chums.

Ethnicity and religion are important ingredients in the lives of Downriver families. German, Irish, and Polish are the cultural identities most often encountered in Downriver, but there are also sizeable concentrations of Italians, Hungarians, blacks and southern whites. Catholicism is the most prevalent Downriver religion, although individual churches manifest the distinctive character of their Irish, Polish, or Italian congregations.[15] In summer, ethnic festivals celebrate Downriver's ethnic abundance with thousands from all over the metropolitan area coming to listen to German marching bands and Hungarian orchestras, to watch Polish dancers, and to dine on kielbasa, stuffed cabbage, chicken paprikash, and Irish Harp beer. Local organizations, like St. Patrick's Catholic Church of Wyandotte and the German Club of Downriver, sponsor these ethnic festivals, and proceeds are targeted for local community projects.

Sense of place, and of ethnic and religious identity are all intertwined with the industrial jobs that brought economic security to the area. Downriver's totem is the industrial smokestack. Wyandotte, the focal point of ethnic celebration, is itself one of the most heavily industrialized communities in the region. Even at play people don't drift far from work; some of the most popular nightspots stand just in the shadows of Downriver's great mills and plants.[16]

Although Downriver participated fully in the nation's early postwar prosperity, by the late 1950s new industry was mostly locating further down the river, bypassing the older, northern Downriver communities. As major plants located further south, clusters of population staked their claim on the new tax base in Brownstown Township, and formed new communities like Flat Rock, Woodhaven, Rockwood, and Gibralter.[17] Although between 1970 and 1980, the whole Downriver area lost 3.3 percent of its population, it was the older, northern, inner-ring industrial communities—like River Rouge, Ecorse, and Wyandotte—that were losing most of the population. (See Table 10.1.) Communities on Downriver's southern rim actually grew considerably during the 1970s; one, Woodhaven, was even the second fastest growing city in Michigan.[18]

Downriver communities seem egalitarian in comparison to the rest of suburban Detroit. White- and blue-collar workers often live on the same block. Many belong to unions, so average income is relatively high and the distribution of community income is relatively even. Although Downriver's older northern half hasn't enjoyed much prosperity in recent years, only River Rouge fell below the median U.S. household income in 1979, and all but three Downriver communities (River Rouge, Ecorse, and Wyandotte) stood above the median for metropolitan Detroit. (See Table 10.1.) Downriver workers tend to commute from their community of residence to a job in another Downriver community, which has cushioned the unequal income effects that usually attend uneven economic growth among communities.[19] Only four Downriver communities have median incomes well above the Downriver average. Grosse Ile, a residential enclave for industry managers, sticks out as the center of Downriver affluence.

But Downriver egalitarianism has never extended across racial lines. Metropolitan Detroit has a black majority central city bounded by a white suburban noose. It is clear wehre the racial line is drawn Downriver. (See Table 10.1.) Ecorse and River Rouge, communities that border the center city, are about one-third black. But one is hard pressed to find another Downriver community with a black percentage as high as one percent. The difference in household income between River Rouge–Ecorse and the rest of Downriver underlines racial inequality in an otherwise relatively homogeneous economic environment. Black communities downriver bear the stamp of segregation,[20] and that racial blockade has been maintained by fierce white resistance to blacks who sought core jobs in Downriver's heavy industries.[21]

The Industry

Downriver's industry is mainly steel, and strong pressures are working to restructure the U.S. steel industry in ways that have torn Downriver communities apart. In 1982, U.S. steel producers lost a colossal $3 billion—their worst record since the Great Depression. The years that followed have brought slight improvement. The forces behind these dismal figures include: (1) a relatively stagnant domestic market; (2) the internationalization of steel production; and (3) new technologies which domestic producers have been slow to adopt.[22]

TABLE 10.1. Population and Economic Characteristics of Downriver Communities, Michigan, 1980

	Population	Change 1978–1980 %	Black %	High School Graduates %	Below Poverty Level in 1979 %	Median Household Income in 1979 $	Unemployment Rate %	Manufacturing %	Operators Fabricators Laborers %	Precision Production, Craft, Repair %
Allen Park	34,196	−16.1	0.4	71.9	2.1	$26,897	8.5	31.6	15.3	14.5
Brownstown Twp	7,040	na	0.4	74.1	na	na	10.1	43.9	20.1	22.4
Ecorse	14,447	−17.5	39.3	47.4	13.3	16,906	19.8	44.9	35.4	13.1
Flat Rock	6,853	21.4	0.4	73.2	7.5	23,158	14.2	38.0	25.6	18.2
Gibraltar	4,458	16.0	na	69.1	2.9	27,797	13.7	46.3	21.9	23.1
Grosse Isle Twp.	9,320	12.2	na	92.1	3.3	36,570	4.8	29.5	8.4	10.6
Lincoln Park	45,105	−14.9	0.5	59.0	5.0	21,244	13.0	37.0	25.6	15.5
Melvindale	12,322	−11.1	0.4	53.6	9.5	20,440	14.1	38.4	28.7	16.3
River Rouge	12,912	−19.0	32.6	51.1	16.4	14,242	19.4	38.5	28.0	16.3
Riverview	14,596	28.5	0.4	71.1	3.6	27,725	8.5	37.3	17.6	16.5
Rockwood	3,346	3.8	na	70.5	4.4	24,291	11.0	39.9	22.5	21.7

Southgate	32,058	−5.5	0.6	65.7	3.1	25,227	10.1	37.2	22.2	17.8
Taylor	77,568	10.8	1.6	60.6	8.5	22,380	13.9	36.4	27.5	16.6
Trenton	22,762	−5.7	0.1	75.4	3.9	27,622	8.2	32.1	13.4	16.7
Woodhaven	10,902	205.7	0.4	79.5	3.3	27,614	11.8	40.1	19.3	20.1
Wyandotte	34,006	−17.2	0.1	56.4	7.7	19,433	11.6	38.9	25.7	17.3
Downriver	341,891	−3.3	3.6	n.a.	n.a.	n.a.	11.9	36.7	22.9	16.5
Detroit SMSA	4,353,413	−1.8	20.5	67.1	10.2	21,222	11.7	31.5	19.3	12.9
U.S.	226,500,000	11.4	11.7	68.6	11.7	16,830	7.1	22.4	18.3	12.9

Source: U.S. Bureau of the Census, 1983

n.a.: not available

Market Saturation

There is less relative and absolute demand for steel today than there used to be. In 1950, the United States consumed 64 tons of steel for each one million dollars of gross national product; by the mid-1980s that ratio had fallen by half, to 31 tons. Steel is by nature a cyclical industry, but even so, steel consumption keeps dropping by about 10 million tons from the peak of one recovery to the peak of the next.[23]

There are several reasons why the demand for steel has declined in the United States. For one thing, fast-growing sectors of the economy no longer use much steel. Compare today's computers and video games to yesterday's washers and dryers, and contrast the rise in services to the decline in manufacturing. Companies are also substituting other materials for steel. There is more plastic in cars and more concrete in bridges, and beverage cans are now made from aluminum. Finally, U.S. manufacturers are importing larger quantities of processed steel from abroad in the form of West German machine tools, Toyota cars, and the like.

The Realignment in World Steel

The world steel industry is also going through a structural realignment. Semi-peripheral countries in the Third World—particularly Brazil, Argentina, Venezuela, Mexico, Taiwan, and South Korea—now have modern steel plants, built and financed by Japan and West Germany, and are emerging as prime international suppliers of raw steel. Some data help make this point. The leading industrial countries (the United States, the European Economic Community nations, and Japan) increased their raw steel-making capacity by 12 percent during the past decade; but raw steel-making capacity in the Third World increased by 100 percent. Although they increased their capacity, the leading industrial countries actually produced 28 percent less steel during the decade; developing countries, on the other hand, increased production by 100 percent. So the Third World's share of total crude steel production increased from 7 percent in 1970 to 17 percent in the early 1980s.[24]

The current realignment in world steel began with the oil shocks of the early 1970s. That energy crisis led to the first of three major world recessions during the decade. Economic slump upon slump forced U.S. and European producers to dismantle millions of tons of excess capacity. Big steel corporations in Europe and Japan (like Mannes-mann in West Germany and Nippon Steel in Japan) tried to compensate for declining demand by helping to build huge, integrated, "turnkey" steel complexes abroad. And Western bankers, awash in petro-dollars, willingly bankrolled those ventures.[25]

Third World turnkey projects were meant to fill local demand. And Third World demand went up from 42 million tons in 1973 to 107 million tons in 1983. But capacity outstripped domestic demand in several semi-periphery nations and they became major steel exporters. They placed millions of tons of low-priced, high-quality steel on the world market during a deep recession, and that helped trigger a realignment in the world industry.

Domestic Competition: The Mini-Mills

New technologies are now sustaining a strong domestic rival to the traditional, integrated (mine-to-market) steel companies. Refinement in the electric furnace and new continuous casting techniques enable companies to produce low-cost steel in smaller plants with less overhead. "Mini-mills," mostly in the South, melt down scrap into simple steel products for regional markets. Mini-mills now dominate certain lines of production, like bars and rods, and are expanding into new product areas and geographical markets. Often non-union, they usually pay lower wages, and their technology is better matched to the products they make than are the methods of the big integrated steel companies.[26]

Overproduction

By all accounts, the major U.S. steel producers were over optimistic about steel consumption in the early 1970s, and they made production capacity and modernization plans accordingly. By the early 1980s, their share of the market dropped precipitiously—from 81 percent to just over 50 percent of a much smaller market.[27] About one-quarter of the U.S. market is now supplied by imports, and another quarter by the mini-mills. But the overproduction crisis is not limited to the United States. In West Germany, for example, imports now capture 40 percent of the domestic market. And only 39 of Japan's 65 blast furnaces were operating in 1983. Steel production in Japan fell below 100 million tons for the first time in a decade; imports reached 10 percent of the domestic market, and Japan lost a large share of the Southeast Asia market to producers in South Korea and Taiwan.[28]

The Restructuring of the U.S. Steel Industry

The United States Steel Corporation has been synonymous with the American steel industry since it was first put together by J. P. Morgan in 1901. Then, "The Company" controlled 65 percent of the U.S. steel market and was the largest enterprise in the world. From the beginning, government anti-trust action worried U.S. Steel more than any threat its competitors might mount. In 1920, the Supreme Court decided U.S. Steel was a "good monopolist"—one that would refrain from using its singular power to drive out competitors or charge exorbitant prices—and for most of this century the behavior of just about everyone connected with steel business was governed by U.S. Steel's special status. The Company set the industry's prices; it set the industry's wage pattern; and it set the performance standards for other firms. And U.S. Steel's objective, above everything else, was to maintain price discipline and stability in its marketplace.[29] This is the system that has come apart and is now being put back together in a different way.[30]

In a market where competitive standards are increasingly set by foreign producers and domestic mini-mills, the majors are following several restructuring strategies. First, they are retrenching and consolidating operations and demanding concessions from workers. U.S. Steel has cut its steel-making capacity by 18 percent, reduced its steel division employment from 93,000 in 1981 to 49,000 in 1984, and obtained a 9 percent wage concession from the United Steel Workers. That added up to $1.5 billion, or a 30 percent cut in the company's labor costs.[31] Armco and National have even discarded profitable plants—for example, National's Weirton plant in West Virginia was recently purchased by its workers.[32]

Secondly, the majors are combining forces through mergers and joint ventures. Jones-Laughlin, a division of the LTV conglomerate, is a case in point. Jones-Laughlin has been trying to improve its prospects by buying out large but weak competitors. In 1978 it bought Youngstown, and it recently purchased Republic, to become the industry's third-largest firm.

And Big Steel is diversifying. Here U.S. Steel stands out. The Company sold raw materials properties to bolster its cash reserves. Then, with the further aid of big bank loans, it acquired Marathon Oil in January 1982. By the end of 1983, steel was accounting for just 31 percent of the Company's sales, compared to 53 percent for oil and gas.[33] And it seemed to critics as though U.S. Steel might be opting out of the business altogether.[34]

But perhaps the most significant turn of events is now unfolding on a global scale. What seems to be emerging there is a dual or two-tiered division of labor in the world steel system. Third World producers in the semi-periphery with comparative advantages in labor, energy, raw materials, and transportation costs, account for an increasing share of the world's raw steel. Companies in the advanced capitalist nations, on the other hand, are modernizing by building continuous casters and are concentrating more on sophisticated speciality steel products.[35]

Third World producers continue to play their traditional role of commodity supplier, but this time by providing basic steel (like reinforcing bars used in construction). Companies in the advanced capitalist countries, on the other hand, focus upon high technology, speciality products (like seamless pipe for the oil industry, and speciality steels that are alloys of steel and rare metals like nickel and molybdenum). The two-tier system splits the formerly integrated industry into steel-producing and steel-processing segments, with steel processors concentrated in the center and steel producers concentrated in the semi-periphery. Some analysts envision a growing "symbiosis" between steelmakers in the industrial center and the developing semi-periphery as more major corporations import crude steel products from Third World producers even against strong opposition from organized labor.[36] Others see Third World producers playing a more familiar role—that of carrying the burden of cyclical downswings in the world market for steel.

The Corporations

Corporations develop strategies to combat economic crises of overproduction and international competition. And it is to those corporate strategies that we must look if we are to understand the ways global economic change forces wrenching transitions in community life. A profile of Downriver's major employers helps connect the reorganization of the world steel industry to Downriver's blue-collar communities.

McLouth Steel was the nation's tenth-largest steel company and Downriver's third-largest employer in 1983. McLouth's headquarters is a four-story brick building settled amid a jumble of plants and warehouses belonging to Fisher Body and to Jones & Laughlin in downtown Detroit. But McLouth's main factory is eighteen miles downriver in Trenton,[37] a city dependent upon the company for 12 percent of its tax revenues. Founded in 1934, McLouth rebuilt its entire production apparatus in the early 1950s with the help of a $25 million loan from General Motors.[38] After that, McLouth became a "most favored" GM supplier. Sales to the auto industry accounted for as much as 75 percent of McLouth's orders, and GM by itself regularly consumed half the company's production. But by 1982, the Trenton plant was running only one of two blast furnaces, the mills rolling finished steel were under 60 percent capacity, and the work force had dwindled from a peak of 5,000 to a mere 1,600.[39]

McLouth lost $56 million in 1980, and another $19 million in 1981. In December 1981, McLouth sought protection from its creditors under Chapter 11 of the Federal Bankruptcy Code. The steelmaker listed debts above $300 million, including $45 million to Prudential Insurance, $37 million to Metropolitan Life, $18 million to New York Life, and millions more to a handful of banks, including Manufacturers Hanover and the National Bank of Detroit. McLouth had secured $25 million a year in wage concessions from its unions and price concessions from its suppliers, but when the company filed bankruptcy it owed over $100 million to some 2,000 suppliers (including $11.8 million to Detroit Edison); it owed $16 million in acquired pension liabilities to the United Steel Workers union; and it was in arrears to some workers for as much as $1,600 in back wages.[40] And, of course, thousands of jobs were on the line—jobs in the company's own plants and in firms supplying and servicing McLouth.[41]

McLouth paid Lazard Freres a $300,000 retainer to look for a buyer.[42] But contacts with domestic and foreign steelmakers yielded no solid prospects. Then, in November 1982, McLouth was acquired by Cyrus Tang—a reclusive industrialist based in the Chicago suburb of Elk Grove Village. Cyrus Tang owns Tang Industries, a metal-processing conglomerate composed of 15 companies, with estimated revenues of $200 to $300 million in 1982.[43]

Cyrus Tang's move to turn McLouth around was premised upon the quality of existing facilities and on concessions from organized labor. McLouth is a modern steel mill—one of only three built in the United States since World War II. The company's Trenton plant is considered one of the best in the industry. All of Trenton's steelmaking capacity comes from the advanced basic oxygen process (compared to only 65 percent worldwide), and all of its finished goods are produced by continuous casting (compared to only 60 percent of finishing capacity in Japan, for example).[44] Tang negotiated a contract with the United Steel Workers in advance of buying McLouth. He offered workers 15 percent of the company in return for a cut in wages to $18 per hour—$7 less than the national average for unionized steel workers. Tang also received concessions from environmentalists and McLouth's debtors.[45]

Rouge Steel, founded in 1920, ranks among the nation's top ten steel producers and employs 4,300 hourly and salaried workers at its complex near River Rouge. Rouge Steel is a wholly owned subsidiary of Ford Motor Company. Apart from the steelmaking operations, Ford owns iron ore and coal mines, and a fleet of ore boats, giving the company control over every phase of steel production. And Ford's Rouge plant ships much of its flat rolled steel down the road to Ford's Dearborn stamping plant where it is molded into Ford cars.

Rouge Steel possessed a number of advantages in the steel industry. It has a wealthy parent in Ford Motor Company. It has the newest hot-strip mill in the domestic industry. And it has the lowest shipping costs among U.S. steel producers.[46] Yet steelmaking has been a losing proposition for Rouge since 1979. In September 1983, Ford announced that Rouge Steel was hopelessly behind the competition. Wages were too high, Ford management argued, and too little capital was available for modernization. Ford threatened to shut Rouge down, and the company began looking for a buyer.

Rouge Steel was courted for a time by Nippon Kokan, Japan's number two steel producer; but negotiations fell through, and Ford put into effect a two-pronged restructuring plan instead. First, Rouge workers approved a new contract with big concessions in incentive pay, paid time off, and other benefits amounting to nearly $4.50 an hour. All told, Rouge workers turned over $40 million a year in concessions to the Ford subsidiary. Then the Rouge Steel company embarked upon a modernization plan. The company is now installing a continuous casting machine; restoring blast furnaces to full capacity after years of disrepair; and putting in new equipment to produce galvanized steel to meet the rising demand for auto rust protection.[47]

Ford's Casting Plant at Flat Rock was less successful. This 2.7 million-square-foot foundry was built to produce cylinder blocks and other castings for V-8 engines. At its peak, the Flat Rock facility employed 5,500 workers. But Ford closed the casting plant for good in January 1982, when rising gasoline prices had halted demand for larger engines. This plant closing, and its repercussions, cut the city of Flat Rock's property tax base almost in half. Revenues plummeted from $150 million in 1981 to $87 million in 1984.[48]

Great Lakes Steel in Ecorse is the largest employer in the Downriver area. Until recently, Great Lakes Steel was a branch of National Steel, itself a subsidiary of National Intergroup, Inc. National Steel ranks seventh among steel producers in the United States and second or third in the flat rolled steel market.[49]

National's steel production started in 1929 as a small operation that grew into Weirton Steel. The firm then acquired companies in the Detroit area and renamed itself National Steel. National has been a big supplier of flat rolled steel and tin plate products to auto producers. But in the mid-1960s, National started to diversify, first into metal services, then into aluminum production. In 1980, the company bought a savings and loan association and moved into financial services. By 1983, National had dropped steel out of its new name, National Intergroup, Inc. By then National Steel had become just one of six business groups, which included financial services, aluminum, distribution, and diversified operations. National was, in fact, in the process of divesting itself of its steel operations; first through cutbacks[50]; then by selling its Weirton, Va., division to its employees. In February 1984, National Intergroup, Inc., accepted a bid from the U.S. Steel Corporation to buy its entire steel division and was about to leave the steel business altogether. But anti-trust objections from the Justice Department stifled U.S. Steel's urge to merge with National. Then in June 1984, the Justice Department approved Nippon Kokan's $292 million offer to buy half of National Steel. Nippon Kokan's move into U.S.-based manufacturing is the biggest by a foreign steelmaker. The Japanese steel giant now owns half of National's Great Lakes Steel plant in Ecorse, and steel plants in Portage, Indiana, and Granite City, Illinois. It also owns half of National's iron ore and coal operations.[51]

Deindustrialization Downriver

By the early 1980s, the ripple effect from worker concessions, corporate cutbacks, plant closings, mergers, diversification, and the world realignment in steel threatened to swamp Downriver. The impact on communities defies calculation, but the loss of thousands of jobs and millions in tax revenues left few lives untouched. The job trends from 1976 to 1983 among Downriver's sixteen largest industrial plants suggests something of the magnitude of deindustrialization Downriver. (See Table 10.2.) By 1983 the official unemployment rate was above 12 percent.[52]

Downriver's economy centers on steel and other closely linked industries that "begin at the furnace," like auto producers and suppliers, and manufacturers of industrial chemicals. In 1979, just as the economy was sliding into the worst recession since The Great Depression, Downriver's major factories included Great Lakes' and McLouth's rolled steel mills (15,500 workers in Ecorse, Trenton, and Gibraltar); Ford's casting, parts, and stamping plants (10,900 workers in Flat Rock, Brownstown, and Woodhaven); Chrysler's engine and chemical plants (3,250 workers in Trenton); Firestone's wheel rim plant (1,200 workers in Riverview); DANA Corporation's truck frame plant (900 workers in Ecorse); Whitehead & Kales metal fabricating plant (1,200 workers in River Rouge); and BASF's chemical plant (1,700 workers in Wyandotte).

In 1980, DANA Corporation closed its Ecorse plant, and BASF shut down its Wyandotte factory. By 1981, Downriver's major factories employed 13,435 fewer workers than in 1979, a 36 percent decline. And the downward slide continued. By 1983, four more major plants had closed: Firestone, Ford Casting, McLouth Steel in Gibraltar, and Whitehead & Kales. Job loss in Downriver's major factories now came to 14,750, a 40 percent decline since 1979.

Because each of these major plants was connected to a myriad of smaller firms that supplied or serviced them, the secondary impact of disinvestment was considerable, especially in communities where major plant closings took a multitude of machine shops and tool-and-die shops in their wake. Take McLouth's suppliers, for example: 75 percent of the business of Petroleum Specialities, Inc., of Trenton consisted of oil and storage tank production for McLouth; Stroble Metal Company made an aluminum product that entered every sheet of metal that emerged from McLouth's furnaces; and Riverside Mobil Service Station in downtown Trenton pumped one thousand dollars worth of gas into McLouth company cars each week. Between 1977 and 1983, Ecorse lost 50 percent of its manufacturing establishments, Flat Rock lost 38 percent, River Rouge lost 43 percent, and Riverview's manufacturing concerns dropped 40 percent.[53]

The loss of thousands of manufacturing jobs cut deeply into

TABLE 10.2. Employment by Major Employers in the Downriver Area, Michigan, 1976–1983

Company	City	Product	Employment Levels			
			1976	1979	1981	1983
American Sunroof	Southgate	Automotive trimmings	1,600	900	300	500
BASF Wyandotte	Wyandotte	Chemicals	2,500	1,770	800	2,200
Chrysler Engine	Trenton	Motor vehicle engines	3,400	2,700	2,700	1,900
Chrysler Chemical	Trenton	Motor vehicle bodies	300	550	280	402
DANA Corporation	Ecorse	Truck frames	905	900		0 (plant closed)
Fabricon Auto Products	River Rouge	Textile & canvas goods	—	210	80	250
Firestone Steel	Riverview	Truck & bus wheel rims	1,040	1,200	578	0 (plant closed)
Ford Casting	Flat Rock	Engine, axle castings	4,700	4,800	2,821	0 (plant closed)
Ford Parts	Brownstown	Motor vehicle parts	1,500a	1,500	907	907a
Ford Stamping	Woodhaven	Automotive metal stampings	3,800	4,600	2,768	4,300
Great Lakes Steel	Ecorse	Cold rolled sheet metal	9,000	10,500	7,500	5,500
Karmazin	Wyandotte	Fabricated plate work	300	300	225	250
McLouth Steel	Gibraltar &	Finished rolled steel	1,000	0	(plant closed)	
	Trenton		3,500	5,000	4,023	5,000
Pennwalt	Wyandotte	Industrial chemicals	825	762	566	950
Vulcan Mold & Trim	Trenton	Grey iron	260	277	186	260
Whitehead & Kales	River Rouge	Metal fabricating	800	1,200	na	0 (plant closed)
Total Employment			35,430	37,169	23,734	22,419
Number of Jobs Lost since 1979					13,435	14,750
Total Employment as % of 1979 Employment					64%	60%

a estimate

na: not available

Sources: Michigan Manufacturers Industrial Directory: Cleveland: Harris Publications, 1977; Michigan Manufacturers Directory, Detroit: Pick Publications, 1984; U.S. Senate. Committee on Labor and Human Resources. Washington. DC: U.S. Government Printing Office, 1982a.

purchasing power, and a number of large and small retail stores folded. Perhaps the most visible case in point was the Kresge Store in River Rouge; until it folded, Kresge had served as the anchor for the city's business district. Downriver lost 1,639 retail jobs between 1977 and 1982.[54] But the impact of industrial decline cannot be gauged by higher unemployment totals alone. The reality is harsher than that. Disinvestment is a social process that tears at the fabric of community life. The Kresge Store in River Rouge, for example, was the traditional social hub for the town's senior citizens. When Kresge's closed, the town's older residents lost part of their taken-for-granted social world.

Even the economic activities that prosper during business crises indicate the disruption of community life. For example, as one business after another retrenched or folded, the Wyandotte Record Exchange experienced a mini-boom. People unloaded their record collections before they moved. Those who stayed behind had a lot of time on their hands and could spend a dollar on a used record for cheap entertainment. A new discount theatre, selling tickets for $1.25, arose to cater to that demand, too. And bars, like WJ's Pourhouse across the street from the McLouth plant in Trenton, also managed to retain their clientele.[55]

But it is Downriver municipal fiscal crises that most visibly indicate the public effects of private disinvestment. A few large plants accounted for much of the tax base in many Downriver communities. Ford's casting plant yielded 67 percent of Flat Rock's tax base. Great Lakes Steel generated 65 percent of the tax revenue in Ecorse. McLouth accounted for 42 percent of Gibraltar's taxes and 12 percent of Trenton's. Since 1980, Downriver communities have cut back services and laid off 10 percent of their municipal workers. Especially hard hit communities, like Flat Rock and Ecorse, laid off a quarter of their city employees.[56] Municipal workers remaining on the job faced concessions and wage freezes.

With big losses in industrial tax revenue, local schools experienced chronic fiscal problems. McLouth's closing cost the Riverview school district $3.4 million, and forced district administrators to shut down one school and reduce programs and school hours in others. Downriver school districts laid off teachers, imposed wage freezes, cut services, and threatened worse in the absence of new tax levies. Facing a $5.7 million deficit, Taylor's school board pressured the community to pass higher school district property taxes by eliminating bus service in a district where 75 percent of the students took the bus to school. Taylor's school board also threatened to close 12 of 24 schools, lay off 100 teachers and school workers, eliminate school athletics and the cafeteria.[57] The Woodhaven school district couldn't open a newly completed $6.2 million school because it lacked the operating money. The political fallout over troubled public finances and reduced services led to the ouster of five Downriver mayors in 1983 alone.

The security taken for granted in Downriver communities dissipated with the smoke of the region's abandoned factories. Reports from social service agencies and community groups testified to the social and psychological ramifications of disinvestment. To make it from day to day, many people required assistance with the basic necessities—food and shelter. Although churches and public organizations attempted to help, they were ill-equipped to restore what had been lost as proud people became dependent. At the Wyandotte Salvation Army, they put plastic flowers on the tables to give the soup kitchen a restaurant atmosphere for the new poor, whose cuisine now featured hot dogs and macaroni.[58] A new emergency hot line averaged 30 calls a day as alcoholism, emotional problems, family violence, and suicide increased. Still, less than half of those eligible for social services in Downriver's communities actually applied for assistance.[59]

Cycles of boom and bust set the rhythm of life in industrial communities like those Downriver, but deindustrialization is of a different order of magnitude. Unemployment benefits and belt tightening do not suffice when months of unemployment turn into years. As they awaited the reports of friends scouting for jobs elsewhere, some laid-off workers worried that they would be the first in their family to leave Downriver. Others were anchored to houses they couldn't hope to sell. Caught between their belief in the sanctity of the individual and the realization they were snagged in forces beyond their control, Downriver's striken residents faulted themselves for failing even as they blamed their companies and government for betraying them. As one Downriver mayor remarked before a Congressional committee, "they had followed all the rules of the American Dream . . . —suddenly, not only the rug, but the whole house has been pulled out from under them."[60]

Deindustrialization and Public Policy

Downriver residents share a regional consciousness born of three generations of experience with heavy industry's booms and busts. But persistent crisis in the metal industries has compelled local governments, businesses, unions, and social service agencies to translate that collective identity into a collective organization, the Downriver Community Conference (DCC).[61] The DCC's mission is to combat industrial decline and the attendant social crises that beset the entire region. The DCC is an interesting regional organization in its own right; but the DCC has also served as something of a proving ground for federal crisis intervention policies during the Carter and Reagan administrations. So the DCC also conveys much about the federal response to local traumas born of global economic change.

The Downriver Community Conference, founded in 1977, is an intergovernmental planning and development organization. The DCC is organized like a corporation, governed by a board of directors made up of the mayors and supervisors of the 16 Downriver communities, and it is run by a paid staff.[62] City officials in the Detroit area like to call themselves entrepreneurs in the public interest, and the DCC has been quite successful in putting together the kinds of coalitions among diverse community interests required to obtain grant money from private foundations and public agencies.

The Downriver Community Conference's most important programs fall into three areas: (1) economic development, (2) employment and training, and (3) community services. DCC's initial foray into *economic development* included public relations campaigns promoting the Downriver image and lobbying for changes in state legislation to improve Michigan's business climate. A DCC task force also set up "business retention teams" to forestall store and plant closings.[63] Lush DCC brochures now entice business investment with promises of tax abatements and other sorts of financial assistance.[64] DCC circulates community profiles, and information on industrial facilities and commercial properties. It has an ombudsman service to assist businesses with permits and zoning.[65] DCC provides assistance to businesses wishing to procure government contracts[66] and runs a "business incubator center," where new businesses can reduce operation costs by sharing office machines, secretarial help, and a conference room.[67]

Most of DCC's economic development efforts are directed at smaller businesses, but the organization has also served as an intermediary in the allocation of federal development grants to major corporations. In 1984, for example, the DCC funneled a $4 million federal Urban Development Action Grant to McLouth so that the steelmaker could replace its high-cost electric-heated steel rolling furnace with a lower-cost gas-fired furnace. McLouth claimed the renovation would eventually enable it to expand production and add several hundred jobs.[68] The DCC played a similar role in coaxing Mazda to choose Ford's abandoned casting plant in Flat Rock for its first U.S.-based assembly operations.[69]

The aim of DCC's *employment and training* program is to return workers as expeditiously as possible to quality jobs in the labor market. To that end DCC has built a "labor exchange network" by which the DCC mediates between "supply employers" (those who fire) and "demand employers" (those who hire). DCC now touts a network of 200 demand employers, most of whom (185) are in Michigan.[70] Workers judged to have "transferable skills" are sent to job developers, hired from the private sector, who match them to appropriate employers. The others are candidates for DCC retraining in robotics, building-operations management, drycleaning, computer programming, word processing, and other fields.[71] Workers who are disqualified from the classroom because they are not high school graduates, or have poor reading skills or low test scores, DCC tries to place in employment where they can receive on-the-job training.

The Downriver Community Conference also helps coordinate several *community services* through the Downriver Human Services Coalition, which includes the Department of Social Services, hospitals, and agencies dealing with mental health, substance abuse, aging, information and referral, and domestic violence.[72] The DCC offers a "Hotline" referral system to help workers cope with the stress of losing their jobs. DCC's Hotline services also include a "Health Referral Network" through which local doctors offer some appointments, hospitals offer bed space, and pharmacies offer some prescriptions free or at reduced prices to the unemployed.

The Downriver Community Conference is very good at forging alliances among community groups around programs that are sustained by foundation and government grants. However, the key issue is whether organizations like the DCC have the clout to combat crises whose origins lie in global economic contradictions and the investment strategies of multinational corporations. The DCC effort falls within parameters set by a national policy that encourages communities and states to compete against one another for private capital investment.[73] That means business support is critical for the DCC, and it must be solicited through every phase of the organization's activities. The redevelopment maxim is: if you want to create jobs, you must offer public incentives to increase private profits. So the fate of Downriver's communities continues to ride on the shifting sands of corporate strategies.

Although the DCC works mainly with small businesses, Downriver's dependence on major corporations is likely to continue. As of 1983, the DCC had generated $20 million in contracts for local companies, and had created several hundred new jobs.[74] But deindustrialization of Downriver threw thousands out of work.[75] And even should DCC's most ambitious development plans come to pass, they will fall far short of that required to restore Downriver's economy.[76]

The DCC has been most successful in meeting the hiring needs of smaller businesses through subsidizing their training and labor recruitment activities. A recent study suggests that workers helped by the DCC do better than those who seek work on their own. Participants in the DCC program are likely to stay re-employed longer and receive higher wages in their new jobs than workers going it alone.[77] Interestingly enough, though, successful retrainees are most likely to find jobs doing semi-skilled industrial work as machinists, welders, and pipefitters. Even with special DCC training, few Downriver workers are finding "high tech" jobs.[78]

A renewed emphasis on labor discipline has been institutionalized in the DCC training and placement program. Downriver's unemployed industrial workers must now market themselves to employers as if they were pursuing a professional career, and they must place their fate in the hands of job brokers who speak about having "a wealth of information on a person" and about knowing "very well if they show up or if they are motivated" to work.[79] These residents are lucky just to be in the program, as demand for services far exceeds the DCC's resources. In 1985–1986, the program was able to take in only 2,076 of 8,200 applicants interviewed.[80]

DCC's public entrepreneurs know the limitations under which they work. It takes nothing away from their own sense of commitment or their programmatic accomplishments to suggest that something more is needed. It's obvious that localities can't by themselves solve globally produced problems. What then is to be done with declining industries like steel, and the workers and communities in areas like Downriver that are dependent upon them?

Big Steel has its own answers. The industry will turn around, the steel majors argue, if the government erects further barriers against foreign imports; if the government reverses the tax policies and environmental regulations the companies hold responsible for drying up the capital they need for modernization; and if the government exempts steel corporations from antitrust prosecution so they can merge with one another.

But it is hard to muster much confidence in Big Steel's program. For one thing, past government assistance to the industry has not brought notable success. Protection proposals seem premised on the idea that if imports are controlled, the domestic majors will once again control the U.S. steel market. Pricing power, the traditional prerogative of U.S. Steel, could then be recaptured and the old system reconstituted. But as critics have noted, controls won't protect the majors against weak demand or against competition from domestic mini-mills. And since import controls will raise U.S. prices, they will raise costs for consumers and companies purchasing U.S. Steel products.[81] Price increases give billions in extra profits to the major steel companies. But is it capital shortage or choice of investment projects that underlie Big Steel's woes? The U.S. majors haven't modernized their steel plants as much as they have diversified into other industries, and they still seem overly attached to massive, integrated facilities.[82]

The issue is not whether the government should intervene or not, since the steel industry is already organized around government tariffs, pollution regulations, depreciation allowances, and the like. And only ideological points can be made by totally opposing import protection, and precious few at that, since the Reagan administration's free marketeers have already put quotas on autos, sugar, motorcycles, and textiles. Rather, the choice is between government assistance without much in the way of reciprocal commitments from Big Steel, or government assistance tied to an industry agreement to reorganize the way it does business so as to be more responsive to the needs of workers and the communities in which they live.

But how should government intervention be organized, and what forms should industrial restructuring take? Certainly many industrial policy advocates would agree that reviving basic manufacturing should rank high on the federal agenda. And troubled industries like steel that are central to the provision of basic needs, and linked to many other key industries, should be targeted for restructuring. Most would also agree that government support should be contingent upon industry performance measured by criteria that can be annually reviewed, verified, and enforced.[83]

But there is little agreement over how deep and how wide-ranging government-industry relationships should become. For example, industrial policy advocates like Garten and Altman[84] would limit government steel assistance to trade, anti-trust, and tax policy, and rule out even federal loans or guarantees. Analysts like Markusen,[85] on the other hand, envision the government's promoting a transition toward community and worker ownership along the lines laid out by the Youngstown Coalition.[86]

The United Auto Workers has forwarded a proposal that illustrates how national industrial policy could be connected to local community development.[87] Four principles govern the UAW's vision of industrial policy. First is the principle of *coordination*—the economy must be viewed holistically, as made up of linked parts. When one part suffers, so do many others. Second, industrial policy should be the consequence of *democratic decision making*. Labor, management, and government must come together to bargain over direction for the economy and for specific industries. Third, there should be a *strong role for government* in the formulation of industrial policy. Only government has the tools—tax, credit, trade, manpower programs—to accomplish the task. The federal government should set the economic ground rules in such a way as to ensure the public interest is served. Fourth, reindustrialization strategies must be evaluated by *social accounting* principles, that is, by evaluating social costs and benefits, not just profit and loss. The costs to society in unemployment benefits, lower tax revenue, idle factories, and worker and community dislocation must be taken into account in making decisions about assisting troubled companies and industries.

The UAW has blueprinted how an industrial policy like this might be organized. The first step would be to establish *Strategy Committees* for each major U.S. industry. Made up of representatives from business, labor, and the government, these committees would meet to analyze the strengths and weaknesses of each industry and come up with a plan for rejuvenation.

Next, the strategic industry plans would be sent to a *National Strategic Planning Board* for study and possible certification. Representatives from business, labor, state and local government, and public interest groups would join together with cabinet-level federal officials to comprise this top board. The National Strategic Planning Board would evaluate and act upon plans from industry strategy committees in light of social accounting principles and the board's own national targets for employment, taxes, credit, and trade.

A *Bureau of Conversion Assistance* would be linked to the Planning Board. The objective of the bureau would be to keep factories going by assisting doomed plants to convert to alternative product lines or production processes. The bureau would also arrange for retraining and assistance for displaced workers, and for help to affected communities.

A *National Strategic Development Bank* would make board-approved loans or take equity in companies being restructured under a board-approved loan. The development bank would have a number of branches, including those for national and regional projects and a branch to assist industrial development in local communities, and one to make loans to workers to buy out firms abandoned by private owners.

Finally, the top board would also be linked to a *National Civilian Technology Administration,* which would provide aid for exploring new technologies that could save industries or create new ones. The agency would be empowered to apply a long-term horizon to risk-taking and to keep social benefits in mind—that is, to take the kind of risks (like neutralizing toxic waste, for example) that commercial banks usually shun.

How might this work in the steel industry? First, a steel industry strategy committee would bring together representatives from unions that have steel contracts, steel company management, the federal government, and state and local governments with large concentrations of steel plants. The committee would conduct a thorough study of the steel industry, looking at factors shaping the trajectory of the industry. The committee could then draw up a steel restructuring plan, based upon social accounting principles, which addresses the industry's situation and dovetails with similar plans from other linked industries. The committee would also assess likely labor and community effects of the restructuring proposal, including the need for worker retraining and financial support for communities in transition. The plan would then go to the National Strategic Planning Board for certification, for recommendations for necessary investments by the National Strategic Development Bank, for provision of help from the Bureau of Conversion Assistance, and for research assistance from the Civilian Technology Administration. The strategy committee's proposal might also prompt the top board to recommend new legislation concerning tariffs, tax location incentives, consumer interest rates, and the like.

Whatever one makes of the UAW's industrial policy concept, one thing seems certain: the United States government needs to develop its own perspective on the steel industry's predicament, and it needs to do so in the context of a broader industrial policy. There are public choices yet to be made that could vitally affect the future of the steel industry, steelworkers, and steel communities. For example, the United States needs to rebuild its infrastructure—roads, rail lines, bridges, sewers— and a far-reaching program of this kind could help revitalize the domestic steel industry (as could a national commitment to build a modern public transportation system). The task of an industrial policy should be to tie government support to industry restructuring in ways that further the public interest. To fail to do so is to perpetuate conglomerate power, industrial decay, and community malaise at public expense. Downriver and her sister communities throughout the United States deserve better than that.

Notes

1. Business Week Team, *The Reindustrialization of America.* New York: McGraw-Hill, 1982.

2. Lester Thurow, *The Zero Sum Society.* New York: Basic Books, 1980; Martin Carnoy and Derek Shearer, *Economic Democracy,* New York: Simon & Schuster, 1979; Ira Magaziner and Robert Reich, *Minding America's Business.* New York: Random House, 1982; Robert Reich, *The Next American Frontier.* New York: Times Books, 1983; Samuel Bowles, David Gordon, and Thomas Weisskopf, *Beyond the Wasteland.* New York: Times Books, 1984; Michael Piore and Charles Sable, *The Second Industrial Divide.* New York: Basic Books, 1984.

3. Barry Bluestone and Bennett Harrison, *The Deindustrialization of America.* New York: Basic Books, 1982.

4. Frank Blackaby (ed.), *Deindustrialization.* London: Heinemann, 1979.

5. Bluestone and Harrison, Ch. 1.

6. Candee S. Harris, "The Magnitude of Job Loss from Plant Closings and the Generation of Replacement Jobs: Some Recent Evidence." *Annals of the American Academy of Political and Social Science.* September 1984, pp. 15–27.

7. See for example, David Smith, "The Public Balance Sheet", in Pat McGuigan and Bob Schaeffer (eds.), *Developing the Public Economy.* Cambridge, Ma.: Policy Training Center, 1978, pp. 3–15.

8. Robert Z. Lawrence, "The Myth of Deindustrialization." *Challenge,* November/December 1983, pp. 12–21.

9. Barry Bluestone, Bennett Harrison and Alan Matthews, "Structure vs. Cycle in the Decline of American Manufacturing Employment." Paper presented at a Conference on the Urban and Regional Impact of the New International Division of Labor, Hong Kong, August 20, 1985.

10. See William Branson, "The Myth of De-industrialization." *Regulation:*

The American Enterprise Institute Journal on Government and Society, September/ October 1983; Richard B. McKenzie, *Fugitive Industry.* Cambridge, Ma.: Ballinger, 1984; Charles Schultze, "Industrial Policy—A Dissent." *Brookings Review,* Fall 1983, pp. 3–12.

11. For a demonstration of this point, see Michael E. Bell and Paul S. Lande (eds.), *Regional Dimensions of Industrial Policy.* Lexington, MA: Heath and Company, 1982.

12. Sheldon Wolin, "Political Theory as a Vocation," in M. Fleisher (ed.), *Machiavelli and the Nature of Political Thought.* New York: Atheneum, 1972.

13. See William Schweke and Lee Webb, "A National Industrial Policy? States Seize the Initiative." *Ways & Means,* vol. 7, number 1, 1984, p. 6.

14. Deborah Kaplan, "Wyandotte: A Mouse That Roars." *Detroit Free Press,* June 7, 1985.

15. August Gribbin, "Suburbia Paces Sharp Upsurge in Religious Interest." *Detroit News,* February 6, 1982.

16. Ann Cohen, "Company Shutdowns Shatter a Lot of Lives." *Detroit News,* March 23, 1982.

17. One hundred and sixty years old, Brownstown is Michigan's oldest township. In the late 1970s, Brownstone experienced a mad scramble among several communities to secure more tax base: Rockwood coveted a mining operation to the south, Gibraltar and Riverview eyed concentrations of high-value housing in the township's midsection, and Taylor desired jurisdiction over a Ford warehouse in the north that carried with it a $60-million tax base. Melvindale, landlocked on Downriver's relatively stagnant northern edge, proposed to merge with neighboring Dearborn in the hopes of garnering more federal and state revenues. See Mary Ellen Kirby, "Brownstown Takes Action." *Detroit News,* June 9, 1978; and Robert Wells, "Melvindale Wants to Merge with Dearborn." *Detroit News,* October 9, 1978.

18. David Verway (ed.), *Michigan Statistical Abstracts, 1980 and 1983.* East Lansing, MI: Graduate School of Business Administration, Michigan State University, 15th and 17th editions, 1980, 1983.

19. In 1980 the percentage of workers employed outside their area of residence ranged from 67.5 percent in Trenton to 92.7 percent in Gibraltar. See U.S. Bureau of the Census, *1980 Census of Population, Vol. 2, Subject Reports, Place of Work.* Washington, DC: U.S. Government Printing Office, 1984.

20. For example, in 1981 the courts found the Ecorse school district guilty of racial segregation and ordered the system's administration to desegregate its elementary schools. Milton Hospital in River Rouge also suggests racial isolation downriver. Blacks have taken their families for medical care to this small,

black-owned hospital since 1937. See Denise Crittendon, "Born Again: Family Hospital Finds Its Niche." *Detroit News,* September 30, 1982.

21. Wyandotte is the industrial and cultural heartland of Downriver and it is also a white barrier against black migration from the north. In 1984, the Michigan Civil Rights Commission awarded a $1.5 million judgment to a black man formerly employed at a Firestone Steel Products plant in Wyandotte for the harassment and dirty tricks he endured from co-workers and supervisors. According to the Commissioners, it was the worst civil rights violation they had ever seen. As of 1980 only 29 blacks had settled among Wyandotte's population of 34,006.

22. Louis Schorsch, "The Abdication of Big Steel." *Challenge,* March-April 1984, pp. 36–37.

23. Steven Greenhouse, "Steel Moves Off Center Stage." *New York Times* May 9, 1984.

24. John Tagliabue, "The Realignment in World Steel." *New York Times* September 11, 1983.

25. A case in point is the Pohang Steel Works in South Korea, one of the largest and most efficient integrated steel mills in the world. Pohang, built by a joint South Korean and Japanese consortium, turns out 9 million tons of raw steel a year.

26. Schorsch, p. 36.

27. Greenhouse.

28. Tagliabue.

29. Schorsch, p. 37.

30. The Company, accustomed to being a price-setter, not a price-taker, was poorly prepared to control costs and meet the new competition. U.S. Steel's share of the market fell from 30 percent in 1950 to 20 percent in 1970 to 18 percent in 1982. (See Schorsch, p. 36.)

31. Steven Greenhouse, "U.S. Steel's Long Road Back." *New York Times* June 5, 1984.

32. As workers become embroiled in the competition among firms, labor relations are fragmenting along with the market. Wage concessions at medium-sized plants like McLouth, Wheeling-Pitt, Rouge, and Weirton suggest industry-wide bargaining may soon be a thing of the past.

33. Greenhouse, "U.S. Steel's Long Road Back."

34. Schorsch, p. 38.

35. Tagliabue.

36. Agis Salpukas, "A Restructured Steel Industry." *New York Times* February 2, 1984.

37. McLouth also has plants in further downriver Gibraltar, and in Detroit.

38. "McLouth Steel Corporation," *Moody's Industrial Manual,* vol. 2, 1982, p. 5698.

39. Winston Williams, "A Steel Company Fights for Its Life." *New York Times,* May 2, 1982.

40. Ibid.

41. Cohen.

42. Needless to say, not everyone suffers from major bankruptcies. An army of lawyers, accountants, and investment bankers receive high fees, but these legions dwell elsewhere in the metropolis.

43. Winston Williams, "Attempting to Save a Steel Producer." *New York Times,* December 29, 1982.

44. Continuous casting eliminates the intermediate step of making ingots.

45. Williams.

46. James V. Higgins, "Ford to Spend $200 million on Rouge Steel." *Detroit News,* October 2, 1983.

47. Ibid.

48. James V. Higgins, "Flat Rock Prime Candidate for Mazda Site." *Detroit News,* March 16, 1984.

49. Daniel Cuff, "New Emphasis for Intergroup." *New York Times,* February 2, 1984.

50. During 1982, National's manufacturing plants operated at less than half capacity. The corporation laid off almost one-third of its total work force (almost 10,000 employees), and cut back salaries, employee benefits, and dividends. "National Steel Corporation," see Moody's Industrial Manual, vol. 2, 1983, pp. 3208–3210.

51. "Japanese Firm Can Buy Half of National Steel, U.S. Rules." *Minneapolis Star and Tribune,* June 13, 1984.

52. Data released by the Detroit office of the Michigan Employment Security Commision.

53. U.S. Bureau of the Census, *1977 Census of Manufacturers, vol. III, part 1,*

General Summary. Washington, DC: U.S. Government Printing Office; *Michigan Manufacturers Directory.* Detroit: Pick Publications, 1984; *Michigan Industrial Directory, 1977.* Cleveland: Harris publications, 1978.

54. U.S. Bureau of the Census, *1977 Census of Retail Trade, vol. II, part 2;* U.S. Bureau of the Census, *1982 Census of Retail Trade, Geographic Area Series, Michigan.* Washington, DC: U.S. Government Printing Office.

55. Denise Crittendon, "Troubled Times Peril Spirit of Togetherness." *Detroit News,* March 22, 1982.

56. Roger Martin, "34 Payrolls in County Trimmed by 470 Jobs." *Detroit News,* February 2, 1984.

57. Roger Martin, "Bus Cutoff Strands Students." *Detroit News,* February 2, 1984.

58. Sally Nelson, "Pride Steps Aside." *Detroit News,* August 4, 1982.

59. Committee on Labor and Human Resources, U.S. Senate, Subcommittee on Employment and Productivity, *Examination of the Automotive Industry's Problems of Unemployed Workers and What Alternative Measures Might be Adopted to Improve Overall Employment, January 11, 12, 1982.* Washington, DC: U.S. Government Printing Office.

60. Ibid, p. 25.

61. Prior to the late 1970s, the strongest intergovernmental link among Downriver communities was the 1967 Mutual Aid Pact through which fire and police services were organized and distributed on a regional basis.

62. "Downriver Community Conference." Southgate, MI: Downriver Community Conference, no date.

63. Subcommittee on Employment and Productivity.

64. "Classroom Training." Southgate, MI: Downriver Community Conference, no date.

65. "Downriver Comprehensive Jobs and Economic Development Programs." Southgate, MI: Downriver Community Conference, April 1, 1983.

66. DCC hopes to create jobs by helping small and medium-sized firms bid on government contracts. DCC's business assistance center holds 1.6 million pages of government specifications, drawings for 71,000 different federal items, manufacturers' catalogues, and lists of government suppliers. Center personnel can also "help interpret a bid description and its codes and terms, and explain inspection, packaging, and shipping requirements." See "Senator Reigle Speaking on the Downriver Community Conference Job Center." *Congressional Record,* vol. 128, May 3, 1982.

67. Joe Hoshaw, "Business Venture: DCC Incubator Nurtures Budding Companies Along." *The Mellus Newspapers,* March 14, 1984.

68. DCC helped route the federal grant to the city of Wyandotte, which was eligible as an "economically depressed area" because it was the place of residence for hundreds of McLouth workers. From there funds passed through Trenton, location for the McLouth plant, and then to the corporation itself in the form of a low-interest loan which McLouth is to pay back to Wyandotte and Trenton. See Walter B. Smith, "U.S. Grant to Help McLouth Steel Save 2,000 Jobs." *Detroit News,* November 1, 1984.

69. When the federal government balked at a Mazda request for a low-interest loan, the Japanese automaker warned it was reconsidering its Flat Rock venture. DCC mounted an intense lobbying effort and squeezed a $2.5 million interest-free loan out of Washington. The state of Michigan then came up with a $21 million low-interest loan. See Marcia Stepanek and Jon Pepper, "Mazda Delays New Plant at Flat Rock." *Detroit Free Press,* March 29, 1985.

70. Subcommittee on Employment and Productivity, pp. 57–73.

71. "Classroom Training."

72. "Downriver Community Conference and the Downriver Human Services Coalition." Southgate, MI: Downriver Community Conference, no date.

73. The state of Michigan offered Mazda a $120 million incentive package. Apart from the low-interest loan, the package included funds for labor training and improvements in transportation and sewer services around the Flat Rock site. The single largest item was $80 million in reimbursements to local school districts for money lost due to Mazda's 12-year property tax abatement. See Susan Benkelman, "Mazda Gets $21-Million State Loan." *Detroit News,* April 4, 1985.

74. "The Dislocated Worker: There Are Answers." *Showcase,* vol. 5, no. 3, April 1983.

75. For example, DCC helped Eagle Bob Trail Tractors, of Grosse Isle to win a contract from the U.S. Air Force. The contract had grown to $16 million by 1985, but it still has added only 20 new workers to the payroll. See Crista Zivanovic, "Dealing with Defense Requires Lots of Savy." *Detroit News,* March 31, 1985.

76. For example, the DCC hopes its Michigan Investment Fund Project will generate 2,300 new jobs over the next five years and bring a return of $15 million in twelve years.

77. A Labor Department study of 767 workers laid off between June 1979 and December 1980 (half of whom were former Dana Corporation and BASF workers) reported that "seventy-two percent of the Downriver participants

found jobs within two and a half years of being laid off, compared to 50 to 60 percent of those not in the program." The average pre-layoff wage was $9.25 per hour, DCC program participants were re-employed at an average of $8.20 per hour, and nonparticipants who found new jobs earned $6.20 to $7.70 an hour. See Charles Green, "Retraining Program Passes Test." *Detroit Free Press,* May 25, 1983.

78. Richard Koening, "Detroit-Area Retraining Program Being Emulated as Funding Grows." *The Wall Street Journal,* March 30, 1983.

79. Subcommittee on Employment and Productivity, p. 58.

80. "Annual Report, Fiscal Year 1985–1986." Southgate, MI: Downriver Community Conference, 1986.

81. It was estimated at the time that enactment of the ITC recommendations would have raised steel prices 10 percent, or $50 a ton, right away; after that, prices would climb more slowly. That added up to an estimated $2 billion in additional profits for Big Steel. See Clyde Farnsworth, "Panel Asks for Protection for Steel." *New York Times,* June 13, 1984.

82. Schorsch, p. 39.

83. These agreements could bear upon a range of concerns, including productivity, right to organize, affirmative action, and environmental preservation.

84. Jeffery Garten and Roger Altman, "U.S. Offers Big Steel a Deal." *New York Times,* March 16, 1984.

85. Anne Markusen, "Can Steel Be Saved? It's Not Dying of Natural Causes." *Dollars & Sense,* November 1983, pp. 9–13.

86. The knottiest problems come into play on the international plane. Protecting "American Steel" against producers in other countries is hardly a progressive trade policy. International agreements need to be reached on matters that go beyond export subsidies and market barriers, to relations of production—including wages, working conditions, and organizing rights within the national steel industries themselves.

87. United Auto Workers, "Blueprint for a Working America." *Solidarity,* May 16–31, 1983.

Chapter 11

Disinvestment and Economic Decline in Northeastern Pennsylvania: The Failure of a Local Business Elite's Growth Agenda

Thomas J. Keil

Introduction

Much of Neo-Marxist theory dealing with the interests of local business elites posits that thay have the power to shape and dominate local growth agendas. Local business elites, however, often face severe constraints that limit their capacities to control political and economic processes, even in their own backyards. This chapter examines the efforts of local capitalists, organized into various "factions" or subelites, to build and maintain a smoothly functioning "growth machine" in Luzerne County, Pennsylvania, and its principal city, Wilkes-Barre.[1]

The Wilkes-Barre area presents a situation where the local business elite has been seriously weakened (although not rendered impotent) in implementing a growth agenda by three historical/economic factors: (1) their dependence on national capitalists and capital; (2) their inability to dominate a strong and militant working class; and (3) their impotence in the face of national and international patterns of capital migration out of the local economic arena. All three of these factors have limited the abilities of the local business elite to create conditions of sustained economic growth, and hence have limited the local business elite's prosperity and its political fortunes. Each of these forces

will be described briefly before showing how they affected the fortunes
of the local elite.

The Age of Growth: The Anthracite Era

As the nineteenth century began, a small group of prosperous farm
families in Luzerne County began to achieve the social, economic, and
political pre-eminence that marks an upperclass. Some prosperous
farm families began branching out into other economic endeavors,
such as milling, wholesale and retail trade, banking, the professions, especially law, and later into newspaper publishing, and small-scale
manufacturing. Under their auspices, Wilkes-Barre was transformed
from a small settlement of less than one thousand people in 1810 into
the major metropolitan center of a vast trading area covering all of
northeastern Pennsylvania.[2]

Because of their position in the county's leading economic institutions, these families, eventually numbering close to one hundred,
achieved a position of dominance over the entire regional economy.[3]
Their investment decisions defined the terms under which other entrepreneurs functioned. These families not only were economically
dominant, they were also a political ruling class. They supplied Wilkes-
Barre and Luzerne County with municipal and county officials, judges,
militia officers, and state and national representatives.

In the 1840s anthracite coal began to be mined in large quantities
for export from Luzerne County. Almost from its inception in Luzerne
County, the anthracite industry was controlled by corporate capital. At
first, several of the major corporations were in the hands of local investors, but they soon gave way to national corporations headquartered in
New York, and to a lesser extent in Philadelphia.[4]

By the early 1870s, under corporate auspices, Luzerne County's
production far outpaced the older, locally owned Lehigh and Schuylkill fields to the south. As national capital assumed more importance in
the anthracite industry, there was a dramatic shift in the economic
position of Luzerne County's upper class. It was no longer a dominant
class in the sense that its investment decisions determined the course of
local economic development and set the parameters within which other
local capitalists made their investment decisions. Economic dominance passed to the extra-local corporations. Corporate investment
decisions were the prime determinant of overall growth in the county
economy, and of differential growth rates within the county.

While the local upper class lost economic dominance as a result of corporate penetration of the local economy, corporate investment created a broad range of new profit opportunities linked to the maintenance and expansion of the anthracite industry. The greatest opportunities that mining created for local profits came from its effects on population growth rates. The county's population explosion (56,000 to 257,000 between 1850 and 1900)[5] created vast profit opportunities in real estate speculation and sales, housing construction and building, materials, construction of roads and bridges, the development of utilities, construction and operation of local rail systems, and in merchandising, banking, insurance, and the professions.

Growth created new opportunities for upward economic mobility into the ranks of the wealthy. Many of the new fortunes that came into being between 1865 and 1900 were built up by Welsh, Irish, German, and Jewish immigrants. As a result, the dominant business elite, in which 95 percent of the members were related through descent or intermarriage,[6] came to be increasingly divided into class factions organized along both economic and ancestral lines. It was not until late in the nineteenth century that the old-stock families' extreme social exclusiveness gave way to a more socially inclusive network of upper-class institutions.

Davies has shown that between 1865 and 1875, members of the old-stock upper class held 42 out of the 52 possible elected city offices in Wilkes-Barre.[7] Similarly, they held a number of county offices, including judicial posts, and they had a virtual strangle hold on the county's congressional seat. Members of Wilkes-Barre's upper class also held important posts in Pennsylvania government and in the Republican and the Democratic parties in the state. At one point, Luzerne County politicians simultaneously held the governorship, leadership positions in both houses of the state legislature, a seat on the state Supreme Court, and leadership positions in both political parties.

Several of its members also sat on important statewide commissions, including the Canal Commission, which authorized the building of a river canal along the North Branch of the Susquehanna River from the New York state line to the Pennsylvania Main Canal. This not only provided for the expansion of the local coal trade, but also provided for a general expansion of the merchant trade network, controlled by Wilkes-Barre capitalists, in northeastern Pennsylvania. If it could be said that, "The capitalist class's business is business,"[8] then given Wilkes-Barre businessmen's political involvements, it is safe to say that for most of the nineteenth century "part of the business of business was political rule" in Luzerne County.

The business elite used its political position to ensure that the needs of the mining industry for a particular type of urban space would be met, especially in ways that allowed the members of the business elite themselves to gain the largest profits. Development decisions were designed to produce an urban infrastructure meant to foster the maintenance and expansion of the coal industry.

Class Conflict in the Nineteenth-Century Anthracite Industry

Control of local political life was used not only to guarantee that the physical needs of the mining industry would be met; it also was used to meet anthracite operators' needs for a pacified working class. This last function brought the local business elite into direct conflict with the county's mine workers.

Because of the anarchy of competition within the coal industry, mining, throughout most of the nineteenth century, was unable to achieve any degree of stability. It oscillated between periods of relative prosperity and troughs of deep depression. Chronic instability made it impossible to construct a "social system of accumulation"[9] that secured labor peace in return for decent wages, good working conditions, and stable employment. Even during prosperous times, the lot of the mine worker and his family was hard. Typically, prosperity only brought marginal improvements in miners' economic well-being. Given the overall economic condition of the mine workers, it is not surprising that the industry's history was marked by an almost continual conflict between labor, on one side, and the corporations and their local allies, on the other. In 1848, the first miners' union appeared. It was called the Bates' Union, after its founder. The union was not able to spread beyond a few production points and soon disappeared.

Between 1848 and 1868 mine workers tried on several different occasions to organize a union, but with little success. Because the mine workers lacked organization, mine strikes usually ended in quick and total defeat for the workers in the face of the combined power of the state and the coal operators.

In 1868, mine workers in the three major production regions, the Wyoming, Schuylkill, and Lehigh fields, came together to form the Workingmen's Benevolent Association (WBA). The WBA managed a successful strike in 1869 and it had modest success in electing sympathetic public officials and in having a number of mine safety bills enacted by the Pennsylvania legislature. The WBA was the first successful instrument that the mine workers developed for placing some effective limits on the mining companies' powers of accumulation. The union, which had renamed itself the Miners' and Laborers' Benevolent Association (MLBA), was defeated in the so-called "Long Strike of 1875" by the combined power of the operators and the state. After six months, it surrendered to the companies.

Between the collapse of the MLBA and the emergence of the UMWA (the United Mine Workers of America) in the late 1890s, the strongest organized force that represented Luzerne County's miners was the Knights of Labor. The Knights continued the MLBA's tradition of political activism. The Knights were broken in the strike of 1888.[10] Over much of the next decade the mine work force was unorganized. UMWA organizers first appeared in the anthracite region in the mid-1890s. Between 1894 and 1900, the UMWA made substantial strides in organizing the anthracite region. By 1900, the UMWA was in a position to carry out a successful strike that shut down all but the smallest operations. They struck again in 1902. After a strike in which the miners endured incredible deprivation, the corporations acceded to federal arbitration and the strike was settled.

During this long period in which the miners struggled to overcome their own internal divisions[11] and the power of the corporations, state coercion, under the control of the old-stock business elite, was continually used against the workers to suppress dissent and break worker organizations. This sometimes led to bloody massacres, such as that at the Lattimer Mines in the 1890s, when a sheriff's posse killed six unarmed miners and wounded thirty-nine others.[12] In other instances, it led to military occupations of the region.

Public and private power were so closely intertwined that it often was impossible to tell where one ended and the other began. For example, in the Molly Maguire trials of the 1870s, Franklin B. Gowen, the President of the Reading Railroad and the man who had hired the Pinkertons to gather evidence on the Mollies, served as a state prosecutor. In another example, in 1865 the Pennsylvania legislature granted the infamous Coal and Iron Police, the private police force of the mine owners, powers of investigation and arrest anywhere in Pennsylvania. This was greater power than that held by any public police agency in the state.

Given the role that the state played in conflicts in the anthracite industry, it is small wonder that the UMWA, like the WBA, the MLBA, and the Knights of Labor before it, was an activist union politically and contested the old-stock business elite's direct rule. The UMWA, working largely through the Democratic Party in the county, backed candidates drawn from its own ranks or the ranks of other unions, or supported candidates who were sympathetic to its cause, for a variety of municipal, county, and state offices. But, while the UMWA had some limited successes in helping to elect candidates for minor offices in the county and in municipalities, and while it did succeed in electing some candidates to the state legislature from districts where miners made up the overwhelming majority of the electorate, its political power was not great enough to displace the old-stock business elite from its position as a ruling class in the county or in the city of Wilkes-Barre. Therefore the union was unable to effectively restrain the business elite from deploying state power against the union and the workers whenever it felt the need to do so, or whenever it was called upon to do so by the corporations.

In looking at Luzerne County at the end of the nineteenth century, it is not hard to see that as the century closed the region had been converted into an enormously profitable growth machine that integrated the economic and political needs of the mining companies with those of the old-stock business elite. The growth machine had succeeded in transforming the county into one of the nation's leading centers of energy production. In the process of doing so, the institutional arrangements that the old-stock elite and the corporations had built not only enriched both parties but also enhanced the elite's local and statewide political power and provided some of the families with an opportunity to become part of the national upper class.

This system of accumulation was built and maintained only through brutal practices of economic exploitation and political repression. In order for the wealth to flow out of the mines, the workers were kept in an almost chronic state of impoverishment. Except during the relatively brief flurries of prosperity that swept the industry from time to time, the average mine worker was poorly paid and chronically underemployed. He had to face long periods of unemployment; if he was among the fortunate and kept his job, he often had to make do on a shortened work week. As a result, few mine families were able to survive on the basis of one worker's wages. Grinding poverty and constant economic uncertainty, coupled with the nearly total situation of repression, especially in the company towns, helped keep alive the workers' drives for effective organization in the face of so many defeats by the companies, their local business allies, and the state.

As the century ended, the mine workers had finally achieved their goal: they had built a union strong enough to fight the company and the state in defense of their interests. Yet while the UMWA had proven its mettle in 1900 and, again in 1902, the local business elite and the coal companies could look to the future with the confidence that the system of accumulation that they jointly had constructed would continue bringing them profits in the decades ahead. The local accumulation system had survived worker challenges in the past and there was no reason to expect that it would not continue to be able to do so for the indefinite future, and in the process, enrich both the local business elite and the mining corporations. This, however, was not to be.

The Demise of Anthracite and the Erosion of the Local Elite's Class Rule

As the twentieth century began, the anthracite industry was organized into an oligopoly controlled and policed by the Morgan banking interests.[13] This arrangement ended anarchistic competition among operators and brought stability to the industry. But just when the anthracite industry had finally managed to achieve effective internal integration, it began facing serious competition from the rapidly growing bituminous fields in West Virginia, Kentucky, and Tennessee. Bituminous operators had several competitive advantages over the anthracite industry: first, the bituminous fields were located closer to the rapidly expanding Midwest markets; second, because of the geomorphology of the coal beds, capital costs for opening and operating mines were lower than they were elsewhere. Third, new bituminous mines were non-union.[14]

World War I brought unparalleled prosperity to the anthracite region. During the war, wages rose, men worked a full work week, and production soared to an all-time high. The war-induced prosperity proved to be short-lived, however. With peace, the industry and the region plunged into a deep economic depression. From 1914 to 1929 production in the three major anthracite fields fell by 25 percent.[15] While its decline was partly a function of decreasing demand, more important was capital flight. Corporate producers withdrew capital from the industry, while increasing their investments in the bituminous fields (where higher profits were to be had) and in the development of the Texas oil fields.

As production fell, the levels of misery among mining families in-

creased sharply. The UMWA, weakened by layoffs and company at
tacks, found it next to impossible to protect its members' economic interests. It lost several important strikes in the 1920s. And the UMWA
faced internal threats to its organizational integrity. Throughout the
Great Depression of the 1930s, there were sometimes violent wildcat
strikes, mass popular expropriation of coal lands, and other ex-
pressions of worker discontent. In the case of coal land seizures, the
coal companies were unable to get state and local authorities to act
against the miners.[16]

Prosperity briefly returned to the anthracite region with the beginning of World War II. Luzerne County's anthracite mines raised their
production by about a million tons per year,[17] but the number of
workers in the industry continued to decline. After the war, corporate
disinvestment accelerated and tens of thousands of men were thrown
out of work. Symbolically, deep mining around Wilkes-Barre ended
with a disaster when, in January 1959, an ice-swollen Susquehanna
River broke through the roof of the Knox Mine, just outside of Pittston,
killing several men and flooding all area operations south of that point.
But by that time, the industry had already become merely a shadow of
what it once had been.

As mining wound down, unemployment skyrocketed and became
pandemic in the region. Mass outmigration began. Job seekers replaced coal as the county's principal export. Between 1930 and 1970, the
county's population decreased by roughly 23 percent.[18] One of the
major factors responsible for migration was that during the mining
years, Luzerne County's capitalists had made few investments in productive activities that were not directly or indirectly related to the
anthracite industry.[19]

As the economy worsened, almost all sectors of local capital, including the old-stock business elite, saw the value of local investments
plunge and their prospects for future profit seriously threatened. The
Chamber of Commerce, dominated by the old-stock elite and the up-
wardly mobile local businessmen who had been incorporated into its
ranks, began a furious scramble to attract new investors into the region.
Between 1945 and roughly 1959, the Chamber had a difficult time finding companies that were willing to locate production facilities in the
county. According to Chamber officials, the principal obstacle to attracting new investment capital was the nature and reputation of the
county's work force. Potential employers supposedly were reluctant to
come into the county because of the workers' reputation for militant
trade unionism, the high wage rate to which the former miners had

become accustomed, and the belief that the mine workers would not be able to adjust to the rhythms and routines of modern industrial production.

The only industries interested in relocating to the area were low-wage, labor-intensive manufacturing, a typical example of which were garment manufacturers, who came in search of cheap female labor. Unlike other manufacturers who felt that the region's history of militant class conflict was an obstacle to investment, the garment manufacturers, as well as the owners of other low-wage, labor-intensive industries such as shoe manufacturing, tobacco products, and the like, believed that they would be able to escape the "negative" effects of unionism by virtue of the fact that the local population was in desperate need of jobs and the fact that these manufacturers would be relying on a labor pool much different from that in the mines. In a short time, garment manufacturing became the county's largest industry.[20]

Low-wage employers had not counted on the way in which trade unionism had become part of the local scene. Even though the demise of anthracite wiped out the UMWA as an effective presence in the region, trade unionism had not been eliminated from people's lives. Militant trade unionism, both as ideology and as social practice, remained a deeply ingrained feature of the local culture, influencing not only the men who had worked in the mines and their families, but almost all sectors of the local working classes. Therefore, it was not long before the garment manufacturers and other low-wage employers had to contend with union organizing drives and strikes for union recognition, higher wages, and improved working conditions and benefits.

Business Elite Reorganization

Just as the local union movement reconstituted itself along new lines in the postwar years, so, too, did the local business elite. On an economic level, the major change that took place in the business elite was its transformation into a regionally integrated stratum of finance capitalists. It was this fraction of local capital that played the leading role in trying to rebuild the city and the county into an effective growth machine.

The emergence of a well-defined stratum of finance capital that is centered in Wilkes-Barre has been the result of a gradual and uneven process of bank consolidation, merger, and buy-outs that has been stretched out over 70 years or more.[21] The process began with gradual bank consolidation within the city of Wilkes-Barre, as various small, weak banks were bought out by or merged with larger and stronger ones. Next, came a period during which the banks in Wilkes-Barre began absorbing the smaller independent suburban banks, consolidating bank capital county-wide. Only a handful of these smaller banks managed to retain formal independence from the Wilkes-Barre banks. Finally, the Wilkes-Barre banks began to integrate themselves regionally, establishing operations in surrounding counties and, most important, integrating themselves with their counterparts in Lackawanna County and Scranton, the other major metropolitan area in northeastern Pennsylvania.

By the late 1960s, three banks had emerged as the dominant centers of financial power in Luzerne County. While different individuals served on the boards of each of the banks, all three banks included the same broad categories of local capital. In addition to the fact that each of the banks fused similar sectoral interests in the local economy, the myriad direct and indirect links between and among them allowed for a more inclusive economic fusion of those local capitalists who had organized themselves around individual banks. For example, different banks have members from the same families or have corporate officers from one or more local companies sitting on their boards.

An especially important interlock comes from the joint representation of the Wilkes-Barre and the Scranton banks on the board of the county's major locally owned utility company, Pennsylvania Enterprises, Inc., a highly diversified utility company that supplies gas and water to households throughout northeastern Pennsylvania. Pennsylvania Enterprises also has substantial forestry holdings, coal leases and coal lands, and is active in real estate development, especially in the Pocono Mountains, which lie just to the east of Luzerne County.

In addition to their economic ties in and through the banks and their ties with other corporate boards, including charities, educational institutions, and the Chamber of Commerce, Wilkes-Barre's finance capitalists display high levels of social integration. A large number of them have memberships in one or more of the upper-class organizations in the region: the Wyoming Valley Country Club, the Westmoreland Club, the Wyoming Historical and Geological Society, and/or Masonic Lodge 61, F & AM. In addition, bank capitalists have a high level of residential concentration in the semi-rural "Back Mountain" suburban region of the county. Socially, finance capital is more broadly based than was the old-stock business elite, as it also includes Irish, German, Italian, and Jewish businessmen and professionals. The only major ethnic groups that seem to be underrepresented in local finance capital are the various Slavic populations and other Eastern Europeans.

The organization of the upper echelons of the business elite into finance capital represents a new level of local upper-class consolidation. The integration of diverse investors around and through the local banks, and the multiple ties among the banks, has enabled the business elite to achieve a degree of economic consolidation and coordination that it has not had since the days when the old-stock business elite was integrated by kinship and marriage. Because of their substantial collective and individual power, especially to control the levels and directions of local investments, the local finance capitalists have been able to achieve hegemony over other parts of local capital and build a consensus that the interests of finance capital are the interests of all business strata in the county.

Political Realignment and the Loss of Direct Rule by Local Business

While the local banking stratum has been highly successful in dominating other strata of capital and creating a general capitalist consensus as to its leading role in the local economy, its attempt to rebuild the region as a growth machine has been continually frustrated by its inability to achieve the same control over the local unions and, equally important, the state. With the deepening economic crisis that set in after the Second World War, the coalition of professional Democratic politicians, trade unionists, ethnic leaders, small entrepreneurs, less well-established professionals, and others who had finally consolidated themselves on a local level during the Depression, was able to displace the old-stock business elite from its position as a ruling class in the county.

This coalition had achieved some limited political success prior to the Depression. It had won control over local government offices in a number of the small municipalities surrounding Wilkes-Barre, had elected several candidates to Pennsylvania's General Assembly, and, in 1906, it had wrenched control of the county's congressional seat from the hands of the old-stock elite when Thomas D. Nicholls, the militant and radical president of District One, UMWA, won the office, running as an "independent" Democrat. Nicholls served until 1911. Between 1913 and 1930, John J. Casey, an official in the Plumbers and Steamfitters Union, served six terms in Congress, although defeated twice in bids for re-election. Since the 1940s, the county's congressional seat, with rare exception, has been held by the Democrats. For most of this time, the seat was held by one man, Daniel J. Flood.

Despite these political victories, the Democratic coalition could not consolidate its political position and break the business elite's control over public offices in Luzerne County's government or in Wilkes-Barre city until the late 1950s. The Republican Party dominated by the local business elite, controlled the mayor's office in Wilkes-Barre from 1933 to 1944 and from 1948 to 1960. Since 1960, however, the city and county, as well as many of the small municipalities in the county, have been largely controlled by the Democrats. While the Republicans have been able to win an occasional election, they have not been able to mount a serious challenge to the Democrats.

The loss of direct rule over local government has seriously compromised the ability of the business elite to reconstitute the growth machine of the past. It has not been able to command government resources so as to build and maintain those physical and social arrangements that would make the region attractive to outside investors. The business elite has responded to its loss of direct rule with a variety of political initiatives designed to limit the possible threats and damages to its interests that it feared would come as a result of the assumption of power by the Democratic coalition. In the late 1950s, the business elite led a drive to consolidate local government. This was rejected overwhelmingly by suburban voters. In the early 1970s, as part of a proposed program of regional recovery from a flood, the local business elite formulated a proposal to amend the county government charter. The proposal's aim was to consolidate local government services, while leaving local government structures intact.

The business elite wanted consolidation in one form or another for both political and economic reasons. On a political level, they recognized the value of consolidating services as a way to weaken the Democratic patronage system. On an economic level, the business elite saw the presence of over 70 municipal governments in the county, each empowered to offer a broad range of services, as a major cause of what it took to be excessive tax rates and public expenditures, especially in the city of Wilkes-Barre, where the business elite members, both individually and collectively, had substantial property holdings. Service consolidation was seen as a way to partially resolve Wilkes-Barre's growing financial difficulties by spreading the costs of government more "equitably" in the county. Finally, the business elite saw government fragmentation as an obstacle to economic development. The presence of so many jurisdictions, each with its own tax rate, zoning ordinances, housing and building codes, and the like, made it difficult to plan and implement development on a county-wide level.

Like the 1950s consolidation proposal, this referendum was defeated in a county election. Local voters proved unwilling to surrender control over what was left of their municipal political autonomy to a centralized structure. The business elite had a bit more success with its drive to reorganize Wilkes-Barre's government. In 1967, it was the major force behind a referendum to change Wilkes-Barre's government from a mayor–commission to a manager–council form. This referendum passed, partly because of voter discontent with the recent enactment of a city wage tax proposed by the Democrats.[22] According to Wolensky, a group identified here as the business elite handpicked the first city manager. In 1976, the city abandoned the managerial form and amended its charter to allow for a strong mayor–council form of government. Democrats took control of the council and the mayor's office and have retained control for most of the time since then.

In addition to proposing structural changes in government as a way to possibly minimize the political damage it feared from its loss of direct control over state offices, the business elite began to change the Republican Party's candidate-selection process. The Republican Party began nominating small businessmen, ethnics, and, in some cases, workers as candidates for public office. This was a marked departure from the party's earlier practice of mainly nominating successful businessmen and professionals of English, Welsh, or German Protestant background for office. The business elite, however, continued itself to maintain control over county party offices.

Seeing the political winds shifting, the business elite began taking steps to reach accommodation with the county's new political forces. It began to incorporate Democrats and trade unionists into an expanded pro-growth coalition. Individuals from both of these groups were given seats on various Chamber-sponsored groups dealing with economic development. Democratic office-holders reciprocated. They appointed members of the business elite to important government commissions, authorities, and boards that dealt with economic development issues. They relied on business–elite-dominated policy formulation groups, such as the Pennsylvania Economy League and the Chamber of Commerce, to design and implement economic development policies. And they put together generous government subsidies for firms expressing an interest in locating in the city and county.

With respect to labor, the key group was a "Citizens–Labor-

Management Committee," composed of eight community members, eight trade unionists, and eight business people. The business elite hoped that by bringing these groups into an alliance organized around a growth agenda they could allay potential investors' fears about the region, especially with respect to its reputation for labor militance, and would retain control over the largest part of the county's economic development agenda. Union leaders are unwilling to discuss the concessions they made to participate in the coalition. However, given the county's low wage rates in manufacturing compared to other metropolitan areas in Pennsylvania, even during the prosperous 1960s, it seems a safe bet that one major concession the unions made was to act "responsibly" with respect to wage demands in order to help "create" new jobs in the county, which may partly explain why wages across almost all sectors are lower than statewide averages.

While the business elite continued to be the dominant force in this coalition, and while elected officials and trade unionists were forced to make concessions, elected officials and the trade unions were not without some degree of influence. Acting together, the Democrats and the trade unions were able to force the Chamber to move toward recruiting higher-paying, unionized industries, rather than the low-wage, non-union firms that had been brought into the county during the late 1940s and the 1950s.

Helped by the national prosperity of the 1960s, the coalition achieved considerable success in attracting new manufacturing industries to the county. As the decade ended, on the surface it appeared that Luzerne County had finally turned the economic corner and was beginning to rebound from decades of economic depression. All parties in the pro-growth coalition seemed to be doing well as a result of their alliance. Trade unions saw the unemployment rate drop, wages rise, and union membership increase. Claiming that their economic development program had helped bring jobs, the Democratic politicians were able to strengthen their hold on public office. The business elite was able to take advantage of the new prosperity to begin a massive program of real estate development in the rural parts of the county, especially the "Back Mountain" area, to the northwest of Wilkes-Barre.

Parts of the business elite had begun moving their homes from Wilkes-Barre into the rural Back Mountain in the 1930s and 1940s.[23] Outmigration accelerated in the 1950s. By the decade's end, the old upper-class neighborhoods along South Franklin and South River Streets in Wilkes-Barre were bereft of their former residents. The huge homes once occupied by the business elite were converted to other uses.

Almost from the moment they arrived in the Back Mountain, the business elite began priming the district for residential and commercial development. They acquired utility rights in the area and began buying up vast tracts of land. But their plans for the area would have to remain just that—as plans—as long as the county's economy was in the doldrums. The prosperity of the 1960s, fueled by the growth in manufacturing employment, brought the business elite its chance to put into effect its plan to develop the Back Mountain and other parts of the periphery into suburban housing developments and commercial subcenters. These development efforts eventually expanded to include residential and commercial development of the Pocono Mountain resort area. The development of the Poconos was a joint effort of Wilkes-Barre and Scranton bank capitalists.

But it was Wilkes-Barre bank capitalists who reaped the primary benefits from the development of Luzerne County's periphery. They owned the land, the construction companies, the building supplies companies, construction equipment businesses, utilities, home furnishings stores, trucking and automobile dealerships, insurance agencies, and the banks that controlled the mortgages. They also lent the money to the municipalities that were required to expand their services to keep pace with the mushrooming populations of the suburbs.

The heavy flow of capital to the periphery helped to accelerate the decline of the Wilkes-Barre central business district (CBD). The combination of years of economic decline and heavy capital investment in the periphery had turned the once thriving commercial and retail center into a "marginal" area filled with cheap restaurants, taverns, pool halls, hotels for transients, rooming houses, discount stores, and small shops catering to low-income customers who lived in the surrounding neighborhoods. Matters were even worse in the smaller cities in the county, where central business districts were completely wiped out due to the long years of economic decline and the consolidation of capital into the hands of the Wilkes-Barre banks.

In 1972 the Wilkes-Barre business elite got a chance to partially rectify the growing imbalance between investment in the CBD and in the periphery when the city and its inner suburbs were struck by a flood that was, until that time, the costliest natural disaster in U.S. history. According to Wolensky,[24] shortly after the flood struck, a small group of individuals met and took steps to form what would become the Flood-Recovery Task Force (FRTF). They called a meeting that brought together representatives from 13 financial institutions in the county. The FRTF eventually had 34 members, 17 of whom Wolensky[25] classified as "core group" members. Fifteen of the 17 core group members had held office in the Chamber of Commerce, and over 90 percent belonged to the city's prestigious urban men's club, the Westmoreland Club. The 17 non-core members were drawn from a slightly different pool; although 82 percent were Chamber of Commerce members, only slightly more than half belonged to the Westmoreland Club.[26]

When the FRTF was still an ad hoc group, its members worked closely with Pennsylvania's influential congressional delegation to help draft and secure Congressional passage of legislation that provided extensive emergency relief to flood victims. Among other things, this bill gave flood victims a $5,000 cash grant and authorized the Small Business Administration to make personal and business recovery loans at 5 percent interest. By covering personal and business losses in this way, the bill helped guarantee, among other things, that the local banks would not have to face the spectre of massive defaults on existing loans, and it also ensured that capital would be available to finance recovery.

FRTF members used their extensive political contacts with the national Republican administration to have the Economic Development Council of Northeastern Pennsylvania, Inc., a private group closely tied to the Chamber of Commerce, named as the official coordinating agency for disaster recovery. While it placed substantial control over redevelopment in the hands of local capital, this Economic Development Council (EDC) included representatives of social groups and economic strata, including business groups, whose interests were not entirely compatible with those of the banks and other large Wilkes-Barre capitalists.

The FRTF also was able to secure for itself an important independent role in the recovery process. The FRTF received a $240,000 federal grant to help it plan for what needed to be done to rebuild the area. It used this money to carry out three studies. One dealt with housing, the second with "public services," and the third with the quality of life in the county.[27] In addition to the research grant, the U.S. government awarded the FRTF a review authority over all redevelopment proposals that would be making use of federal money, which meant that, along with the EDC, it had review power over all local government redevelopment proposals and quite a few private sector proposals as well.

The business elite used its powers to push for redevelopment of the central business district and for a number of other programs that benefitted its interests. The total package of programs was aimed at restoring land values and rental prices in the CBD, while at the same time expanding development opportunities on the periphery. While its program for county political change through municipal service consolidation eventually was defeated by the electorate, the business elite, through the FRTF, was able to implement an ambitious plan to redesign the CBD, create a county public transportation authority, and secure financing from the federal government for a limited-access highway that connected the Back Mountain to the CBD.

Using federal funds and local government's right of eminent domain, the business elite and the city government presided over the demolition and rebuilding of the entire CBD and blocks of adjacent parcels of land. A new hotel was built, new office towers were constructed, and the run-down shops and taverns were replaced with new businesses designed to cater to a more up-scale clientele. As part of the redevelopment process, large numbers of cheap housing units were torn down and their former residents forced to move into public housing or to seek more expensive private housing elsewhere in the city or the metropolitan area.

The FRTF saw creation of a public transportation authority as essential to CBD revitalization. Private transit companies were under extreme profit pressures. They had a hard time making a reasonable profit, especially on non-peak–hour service. In order to improve accessibility to the CBD for shoppers and workers, the FRTF proposed and had put into operation a public transportation authority which, for a time, was able to provide better service at cheaper rates into and out of the CBD. Less attention was paid to improving radial service in the metropolitan area, as the transit system primarily was conceived as a way of providing a subsidy to CBD businesses. The first chairman of the transit authority was a member of the business elite who had chaired the FRTF subcommittee that had proposed forming the authority.

For over a decade, the business elite had been trying to have the state build a limited-access highway to connect Wilkes-Barre to the Back Mountain. Plans for the highway always floundered because of the enormous financial costs and because of political resistance to the proposed route. The highway required the construction of a new bridge across the Susquehanna River, and the road would have to be built through densely populated inner suburbs. The suburban governments were not anxious to see taxable residential property lost to highway construction, to have hundreds, if not thousands, of houses and businesses demolished, neighborhoods destroyed, residents forcibly relocated, and the other costs generated from building the highway. Under the FRTF, the business elite was able to overcome these obstacles and get its highway.

In looking at the response by the business elite to the flood, several points need to be made. First, the business elite was able to respond as quickly as it did because of its high level of integration as a class faction. Second, because of the hegemony that it exercised over other factions of local capital, there was little opposition from other capitalists to the FRTF's agenda. Third, because of its extensive extra-local political connections, the FRTF was able to subordinate local governments to its power and ensure that the flood-recovery policy process would remain in private hands. Had a different national administration been in office, or had the flood taken place in a metropolitan area where the business elite was not as well connected with the Nixon Administration as was Wilkes-Barre's, it is an open question whether such powers would have been assigned to it. Fourth, there was virtually no organized local opposition to the federal government's giving substantial public power to the county's business elite. While the Democratic governor, Milton Shapp, and the former Garment Workers' Union leader, Ms. Minn Matheson, denounced the federal government's decision to assign control over redevelopment to the Chamber and the FRTF, their opposition seems to have been the exception rather than the rule.

The community consensus seems to have been that there was nothing problematic about ceding public power to private groups who, in turn, used it to benefit their financial interests. The community grassroots did not press for an alternative, such as empowering county government to take on the task of recovery. That there was no substantial local popular opposition to the FRTF and the CED's having taken over public power shows the degree to which the business elite exercized ideological hegemony within the region. But ideological hegemony is only part of the reason for the lack of opposition to the FRTF and its recovery agenda. Had local government and the trade unions not seen that the FRTF's proposals matched their perceived interests and had they not been incorporated into the pro-growth coalition, it is likely, given the history of the region, that they would have mobilized against both the FRTF and its agenda. But as matters stood, the massive construction projects that were proposed held out the promise of new jobs for the unions and an increased tax base for city and county government. So it was in their perceived interests to support both the

FRTF and its recovery program. The only serious resistance to what was being done with recovery money came from various neighborhood groups that sprang into being.[28] But these groups organized against the governments, not the CED or the FRTF, claiming that they were not responding quickly enough to neighborhood needs for clean-up and repair.

In hindsight, the flood could not have come at a more opportune time for the county's pro-growth coalition. It staved off, for a short time at least, the effects of the national recession. Shortly before the flood, there were signs that the decade-long prosperity that Wilkes-Barre and Luzerne County had enjoyed was coming to an end. When the 1960s began, the county had an unemployment rate of 12.1 percent; by 1970, this had fallen to 5.2 percent, one of the lowest rates since the end of World War II. But in 1971, the county's unemployment rate started rising once again as the region began to feel the effects of the national recession. Matters became worse as the 1970s progressed. Jobs in the industries that the county had recruited since the end of the war proved to be especially vulnerable to the effects of foreign competition, plant relocation, and technological displacement. Thousands of manufacturing jobs were lost in the local economy, as a second wave of deindustrialization swept through the region. Total employment, however, increased. New jobs were created in the service sector, retail trade, and the like. But those sectors that grew rapidly in the 1970s paid lower wages, on the average, than the sectors that were contracting.

As economic conditions deteriorated, local employers demanded that their workers make substantial contract concessions. Some workers went along with employer demands and protected their jobs; others made concessions only to find out in a few years that their plants were shutting down anyway. Still others chose to resist and went on strike. It was just such a strike in 1978 that led to local labor's withdrawal from the county's coalition, producing serious strains between local Democratic officials and the county business elite.

In May 1978, the local owners of the Wilkes-Barre Publishing Company sold their newspaper to Capital Cities Communications, Inc., a top-20 newspaper, radio, and television conglomerate. Capital Cities and the four newspaper unions began negotiating new contracts almost immediately after the company took control of the paper, but the newspaper's employees soon went on strike. The strikers set up their own newspaper in direct competition with Capital Cities. This paper, the Citizens' Voice, continues to publish and has a larger circulation in the county than does the company paper.

The first months of the strike were marked by exceptional violence. Strikers fought company guards in the streets in front of the publishing company, and company vehicles and property were subjected to hit-and-run attacks almost everywhere in the metropolitan area. Company officials were shocked to find that the local police and judiciary were not willing to take any actions against the strikers and that the vast majority of the county's professional politicians and elected officials sided with the strikers, even to the point that many of the politicians participated in an informal boycott of Capital Cities. Elected and appointed officials refused to grant Capital Cities' reporters interviews and often failed to inform them of press conferences or send them news releases.

While the county's trade unions, politicians, and grassroots citizenry lined up behind the strikers and their newspaper, the business elite supported Capital Cities. The local business elite initially had been elated with the company's decision to purchase the paper. They believed that a company with its size, reputation, and national and international connections would be extremely helpful in attracting new investors to the region. The local business elite also hoped that Capital Cities would be able to help them in their drive against union contracts and in their increasing demands for reductions in local government taxes and spending. These last expectations were based on the company's reputation for taking an aggressive stand with its own unions and for favoring conservative economic policies.

The local business elite used every means at its disposal to try to defend the company. They applied political pressures on government officials and they refused to place advertisements in the strikers' paper. The appeals to local politicians fell on deaf ears, and after the strikers' paper demonstrated its power to mobilize consumer boycotts against merchants who would not advertise in it, many of the merchants abandoned their advertising boycott and began purchasing space in the Citizens' Voice. At the same time, however, they continued buying space in the company's paper.

The strike demonstrated to potential investors that despite the business elite's claims to the contrary, Luzerne County's long tradition of militant labor conflict, its unions' capacities to mobilize broad public and political support, and their ability to inflict heavy financial costs on companies with whom they are fighting (Capital Cities has lost well over $30 million in Wilkes-Barre since the strike began) have not disappeared to be replaced by some new spirit of labor-business cooperation. Moreover, the fact that the business elite could not get the local governments to intervene on behalf of the company raised serious questions about the overall political capacities of the local business elite. If they could not get the state to intervene to suppress worker violence and other perceived "excesses," there was little hope they would ever be able to secure their other objectives, such as rolling back government expenditures and business taxes. Furthermore, given the way the local population had responded to the unions' pleas for help, participated in the call for a consumer boycott of Capital Cities and its advertising supporters, and supported the politicians who backed the strikers, there appeared to be little likelihood that the business elite would be able to capture public office and consolidate their control over local government any time in the near future.

What was left of the pro-growth coalition eventually broke apart when the Chamber supported changes in the state's unemployment and workers' compensation programs. The unions resisted the changes supported by the local and statewide Chambers. The Chamber's program eventually was passed by Pennsylvania's legislature. Therefore, even had this particular strike not taken place, it is likely that the progrowth coalition that had been built up in the 1960s would have broken apart in any event, if for no other reason than that local politicians would not have been able to accede to the business elite's ever-increasing demands for reduced state expenditures without jeopardizing their offices, and local union leaders would not have been able to continue making concessions without having to face an angry rank-and-file.

In 1982, four men, all of whom were personally and/or institutionally connected to the business elite, worked with the Wilkes-Barre Industrial Fund, an offshoot of the Chamber of Commerce, to establish a nine-member Economic Revitalization Task Force as a means for coping with economic contraction. The group renamed itself the Committee for Economic Growth, and went on to establish two task forces charged with various research and planning activities.

In 1983, the Committee became an independent group, with a full-time executive director. In 1984, it took control of the Wilkes-Barre Industrial Fund, completed its studies, and the next year raised over $2 million dollars in contributions for its programs.

Among the major recommendations the study groups produced was one to establish a new labor-management committee. This was done. However, it has met with limited success. The primary obstacle has been union resistance to establishing in-plant labor-management committees. These committees serve a variety of purposes across the country. However, all share a common goal of 'harmonizing' the interests of workers and managers. Labor leaders in the Wilkes-Barre area feared that they would be used by management to evade union work rules and to weaken the position of the unions. At most, local unions want the labor-management committee to serve as an informal mediation and conciliation service. Business, on the other hand, continues to press hard for the in-plant organizations.

The 1986 board of directors of the Committee for Economic Growth includes, among its 27 members, two elected officials, namely the mayor of Wilkes-Barre and the Chairman of the County Commissioners. Most of the remaining members are from the county business elite. There are no union members on the board, reflecting the continuing split between labor and capital in the county.

The collapse of the inter-class, inter-party growth coalition, coupled with the changing investment patterns of national and international capital and the widespread job loss through technological displacement, has made it increasingly difficult for the local business elite to attract to the region new investors in production facilities and to maintain the levels of industrial investment it already has. Given that other metropolitan areas are able to offer potential investors physical infrastructures the equal of, or even superior to, Luzerne County's, while also offering a more subservient and compliant local government and labor force, the business elite has been unable to attract sufficient capital to prevent the second major wave of deindustrialization in fifty years. As a result, Wilkes-Barre and Luzerne County once again are experiencing severe industrial decline; as they do so, the quality of life for the local working class is beginning to show signs of serious erosion. Public services are coming under increasing fiscal stress, the infrastructure outside the flood zone is in serious need of repair, and the jobs available in the region offer low wages, few fringe benefits, and little chance for advancement.

Discussion and Conclusions

Evidence from the history of Luzerne County and the city of Wilkes-Barre reveals the failure of a local business elite to build and maintain a metropolitan area as a growth machine. The organization of the county into a growth machine in the nineteenth century had been predicated upon an alliance between a sector of national capital and a well-organized, integrated sector of local capital. The latter was able to use its economic power to serve the interests of anthracite investors. It also used its political power to control local class relations so that they were brought into line with the accumulation imperatives of the anthracite industry.

Throughout the nineteenth century, the growth coalition held together, even in the face of numerous national and industry-specific economic crises and of industrial conflict between the mining companies and their workers. The growth coalition finally collapsed after World War I under the cumulative and interacting pressures of (1) corporate disinvestment, (2) trade union economic militance, and, (3) the increasing political success of a broad-based Democratic coalition that included trade unionists, non-elite capitalists and professionals, and other parts of subordinate classes. Eventually this coalition succeeded in displacing the business elite from its position of direct class rule in the county and in Wilkes-Barre.

Following the growth machine's collapse, the county was characterized by a 10- to 15-year period of development "anarchy" (1945–1960) during which time the local business elite, now constituted as finance capital, was unable to convince most national investors that the region was a potentially profitable place in which to put their capital. The region's past reputation as a place of militant class conflict, and its union organizing drives and strikes, deterred many investors from locating production facilities in the region.

Matters threatened to become even worse for the local business elite as the Democratic coalition's political successes became more pronounced. The business elite responded to its increasing loss of control over the local political system by mounting a number of offensives. For example, it tried to revitalize the Republican Party and open up its candidate selection process, and it tried to alter local government structures so that the political victories of the Democratic coalition would be rendered harmless to its interests. Using its own private institutions, it also tried to build a pro-growth coalition that, in addition to itself, would include other sectors of local capital, government officials, Democratic politicians, and trade unionists.

For a time the business elite achieved some degree of success in putting together and maintaining this development coalition. As a result, it was able to capitalize on the national prosperity of the 1960s to attract a better quality of investment than it had during the earlier postwar years. However, during this decade of prosperity, forces were at work that once again would devastate the county's economy and make it increasingly difficult to keep the pro-growth coalition together.

As the post–World War II long-wave expansion began to falter in the early 1970s, the county's manufacturing sector began to contract and thousands of industrial jobs were eliminated through layoffs and plant closings. Local business groups estimate that the county is likely to lose another 5,000 to 6,000 jobs in the garment industry alone within the next decade. In addition, employers made demands for major contract concessions from their unions in the hope that this would permit them to restore their profit rates. These demands often met with widespread resistance, as workers were unwilling to peacefully accept the erosion of their wages and benefits and/or the possibility of seeing their unions destroyed or rendered completely ineffective. Recently, a major pencil manufacturer threatened to move a substantial part of its manufacturing operation to Mexico unless workers accepted a 25 percent wage reduction; the unions refused and are now awaiting the company's reaction. The newspaper strike at the Wilkes-Barre Publishing Company, which was but the most spectacular example of worker resistance to increasingly aggressive employers, provided a fitting punctuation to mark the final collapse of the development coalition assembled in the heady years of the 1960s.

At the same time that workers were resisting employers' economic demands, the trade unions and their allies in the Democratic coalition were attempting to fight the business elite's demands for political concessions. These were sought in the form of reductions in expenditures for social services, public-sector layoffs and wage and benefit freezes, substantial reductions in business taxes, and increased police repression of striking workers.

As a result, the Wilkes-Barre business elite is caught in the midst of a global economic crisis and is locked in a hyper-competitive struggle with business elites in other urban areas and with capitalists in other countries for investment capital. They must contend with not-always-reliable local government that is often unwilling and/or unable to act in ways that benefit business elite interests (let alone maximize them), and confront a politically active trade union movement that has deeply penetrated both the public and private sectors. The union movement has not been willing to sacrifice its commitment to the culture of militant trade unionism; as a result the local business elite has found it difficult to realize its ambition of creating conditions it finds favorable to local economic development: low taxes, a "neutral" police force committed to protecting business interests, a compliant and controlled work force, stable government expenditures, and a government devoted to promoting a "good business climate."[29] Lacking a good business environment and the power to produce one, the Wilkes-Barre business elite once again has seen the local economy plunge into a disinvestment crisis which, before it ends, has the potential to be as devastating as the one generated by the withdrawal of mining capital.

The findings presented in this general overview of the Wilkes-Barre area's economic development history illustrate Molotch's contention earlier in this volume that local elites sometimes face severe constraints on their ability to implement a growth agenda. In the case of Wilkes-Barre and Luzerne County these constraints, to reiterate, were the disinvestment decisions of mining capital, the presence of a militant and politically active and effective trade union movement, and the investment decisions of contemporary national and international manufacturing capitalists.

Notes

1. Harvey Molotch, "The City as a Growth Machine: Toward a Political Economy of Place." *American Journal of Sociology,* September 1976, pp. 309–332.

2. Edward J. Davies II, "Elite Migration and Urban Growth: The Rise of Wilkes-Barre in the Northern Anthracite Region, 1820–1880." *Pennsylvania History,* October 1978, pp. 291–314.

3. Edward J. Davies II, "Wilkes-Barre 1870–1920: A Study in the Evolution of Urban Leadership during Industrialization." Unpublished manuscript, no date.

4. Clifton K. Yearley, Jr., *Enterprise and Anthracite: Economics and Democracy in Schuylkill County, 1820–1875.* Baltimore: Johns Hopkins Press, 1961. Donald L. Miller and Richard E. Sharpless, *The Kingdom of Coal: Work, Enterprise, and Ethnic Communities in the Mine Fields.* Philadelphia: University of Pennsylvania Press, 1985.

5. U.S. Bureau of the Census: *Characteristics of the Population, 1850 and 1900.* Washington, DC: Department of Commerce, 1853 and 1903.

6. Davies, "Wilkes-Barre 1870–1920."

7. Edward J. Davies II, "Class and Power in the Anthracite Region: The

294 THOMAS J. KEIL

Control of Political Leadership in Wilkes-Barre, Pennsylvania, 1845-1885."
Journal of Urban History, May 1983, pp. 291-334.

8. Anthony Giddens, *A Contemporary Critique of Historical Materialism.*
Berkeley and Los Angeles: University of California Press, 1981, p. 281.

9. David M. Gordon, Richard Edwards, and Michael Reich, *Segmented
Work, Divided Workers: The Historical Transformation of Labor in the United
States.* New York: Cambridge University Press, 1982.

10. Victor Greene, *Slavic Community on Strike.* South Bend, IN: Notre
Dame Press, 1968, Miller and Sharpless.

11. Greene; Thomas J. Keil, "Capital Organization and Ethnic Exploitation: Consequences for Miner Solidarity and Protest (1850-1870)." *Journal of
Political and Military Sociology,* Fall 1982, pp. 237-255.

12. Michael Novak, *The Guns of Lattimer.* New York: Basic
Books, 1978.

13. Ernst von Halle, *Trusts or Industrial Combinations in the United States.*
New York: Macmillan and Co., 1895; Peter Roberts, *Anthracite Coal Industry.*
New York: Macmillan and Co., 1901.

14. David Alan Corbin, *Life, Work, and Rebellion in the Coal Fields: The
Southern West Virginia Miners, 1880-1922.* Urbana: University of Illinois
Press, 1981.

15. Morris L. Ernst, *Anthracite Coal Commission Report.* Harrisburg, PA:
Commonwealth of Pennsylvania, 1937.

16. Jeremy Brecher, *Strike!* Boston: South End Press, 1972.

17. Robert P. Wolensky, *Power, Policy, and Disaster: The Political-Organi-
zational Impact of a Major Flood,* Final Report, National Science Foundation,
Grant Number CEE 8113529. Stevens Point: University of Wisconsin–Stevens
Point, 1984.

18. U.S. Bureau of the Census: *Characteristics of the Population, 1930* and
1970. Washington DC: U.S. Government Printing Office, 1931 and 1973.

19. Burton W. Folsom, Jr., *Urban Capitalists: Entrepreneurs and City Growth
in Pennsylvania's Lackawanna and Lehigh Regions, 1800-1920.* Baltimore: Johns
Hopkins University Press, 1981.

20. *Pennsylvania Abstract.* Harrisburg, PA: Pennsylvania Bureau of Statistics and Planning, 1974.

21. Materials on the history of bank consolidation are taken from *Moody's
Bank and Finance Manual.* New York: Moody's Investor Services, Inc., 1984.

22. Wolensky.

23. Ibid.

24. Ibid.

25. Ibid.

26. Robert P. Wolensky, "Power Structure and Group Mobilization Following a Disaster: A Case Study." *Social Science Quarterly,* March 1983, pp. 96–110.

27. Wolensky, *Power, Policy, and Disaster.*

28. Ibid.

29. Harvey Molotch, 312-313; Fred Block, "The Ruling Class Does Not Rule: Notes on the Marxist Theory of the State." *Socialist Revolution,* May–June 1977, pp. 6–28.

PART FOUR
Downtown Prosperity and Neighborhood Poverty

Chapter 12

Urban Democracy and the Power of Corporate Capital: Struggles over Downtown Growth and Neighborhood Stagnation in Hartford, Connecticut

Kenneth J. Neubeck and Richard E. Ratcliff

Introduction

Hartford is a city of striking contrasts. Since the mid-1970s, the city's downtown skyline has changed constantly as new buildings have been pushed upward. The prosperity of the major insurance companies and banks that dominate Hartford's economy has meant increasing numbers of well-paid white-collar and professional employees. On weekdays the downtown resembles the new service-oriented, post-industrial society often proclaimed to be the bright future of the United States. However, the close of the business day brings another side of Hartford into view. As downtown workers pour out of buildings, most heading for homes in the suburbs, left behind is a central city whose residential population is disproportionately poor and minority.

Most Hartford city residents live in neighborhoods that have experienced little if any of the apparent economic boom that has transformed the downtown. Instead, they live in the midst of the ongoing decline of the old manufacturing economy of the Hartford area and the disappearance of the types of jobs that once offered working-class families a promise of relatively decent and secure incomes. Residential Hartford today is heavily afflicted with poverty and near-poverty. While the processes of rampant decline that raced through Hartford's neighborhoods in the 1960s and early 1970s have largely subsided, and some vigorous efforts at neighborhood rehabilitation are under way, most poor sections of the city are, at best, just holding their own. In recent years this juxtaposition of lavish corporate growth in downtown Hartford and economic deprivation in the city's neighborhoods has been the central factor in a series of local political struggles.

Our study of Hartford focuses on three issues that have generated conflicts between the interests of corporations and large property owners and those of low-income residents. The first is the tax burden in Hartford; who will pay how much to the city government to finance its activities. The second concern is which groups and which priorities will shape the nature and impact of development in Hartford. The third issue concerns efforts by both the city's corporate leadership and the city government to change the city in ways that would lessen the built-in confrontations between wealth and poverty.

Before examining these issues in detail, it is useful to consider the broader context of the interconnections between urban change and urban politics.

Urban Democracy and the Power of Capital

One of the great sources of tension in American political economy exists in the contrast between the concentrations of capital found in cities and the roles the same cities have played as centers of working-class politics. While the highly visible concentrations of downtown business wealth symbolically underscore the basic economic inequalities in our society, the political structure of cities, numerically dominated by working-class and poor groups, embodies a real, if imperfect, form of class civic equalization that persists in the same society.

The odd juxtaposition of wealth and poverty in American cities is paralleled by the very different orientations that large corporate interests and working-class and poor residents take to questions of urban policies. Corporations locate in downtown areas because of the advantages associated with the concentration of management functions, support services, and channels of communication that modern corporations require. Real estate developers and investors follow the interests of corporate capital in order to seek their own profit oppor-tunities. For all such interests, the desired role of city government is to provide public services and development assistance to help maintain the downtown as an attractive place to do business. For working-class and poor people, city government has a quite different character, that of the provider of such services as education, public safety, housing, job training and jobs themselves, and health care. The strain on cities to provide these services has become even greater in recent years because middle- and upper-income taxpayers have relocated to the suburbs.

The role of cities such as Hartford as service providers to their lower-income citizens poses the question of whether city government, with its taxing authority and its electorate dominated by lower- and working-class voters, might serve as a mechanism of economic redis-tribution. In fact, since the emergence of ethnic machine politics in the late nineteenth century, there has been an uneasy co-existence in urban politics between the potential use of democratic forms by the property-less to bring some economic redistribution and the interest of the pro-pertied in avoiding or limiting such tendencies.[1]

U.S. urban history demonstrates that despite its potential, success-ful attempts to use control over city government to redistribute wealth in favor of the poor have been rare. The reasons range from the peculiar absence of class polarization in American working-class urban politics to the hegemonic influences of large corporations and the dispropor-tionate mobilization among those with local property interests.[2] In ad-dition, economic processes are leading constraints on the political sys-tem. In a capitalist economy the general inability of political forces to control investment decisions, markets, and flows of capital greatly limits, and can even preclude, any attempts to gain control over local structures of wealth and property.[3]

Urban Polarization: When the Downward Trickle Dries Up

The contrast in Hartford between the vibrant development of the downtown and the general economic disadvantages visible in residen-tial neighborhoods reflects a major weakness in American capitalism. The often-heralded "trickle-down effect" of the benefits of business prosperity is at best a very uncertain and uneven process. Until re-cently, many older industrial areas had enjoyed a period when a ver-sion of "trickle down" worked reasonably well. For many working-class families and their communities the manufacturing-based economy had supported a pattern of relative prosperity that was directly linked to the employment provided and to the union-led struggles that brought higher wage rates and other benefits to workers. But in the current era of manufacturing decline and "deindustrialization," this system has rapidly fallen apart.[4]

The "new prosperity" represented by development of the sort occurring in downtown Hartford is notable because of its meager and uneven "spread" effects. The jobs produced are either at relatively high white-collar levels, which do little to aid working-class and poverty-level groups, or at clerical or service levels, which carry low wages and benefits. Moreover, as corporations have become more integrated nationally and internationally in supply and support networks, cities are experiencing greatly reduced spin-off or multiplier benefits from corporate investments in local development projects.[5] Similarly, corporate actors and other investors have been able to secure tax concessions and other benefits that greatly limit the local returns from downtown development projects. This lack of beneficial "spread" effects contributes to political conflicts over development.

The tensions between capital and democracy in cities such as Hartford are exacerbated by the fragmentation among relevant government units. As important as the split between federal and state governments and between state and local levels is the independence that local governments have from each other. This balkanized structure of local government, with each central city and its surrounding municipalities standing alone, both as a taxing unit and as service provider, creates special burdens for central cities such as Hartford. Central cities tend to house a disproportionate share of the poor and other groups requiring heavy social service expenditures. These cities also contain and must support many educational, cultural, health, transportation, and other infrastructure components that are used, but little supported, by the surrounding metropolitan region. In addition, the independence of governmental units creates a competitive context in which corporations and other holders of movable capital are able to get local governments to bid against one another, with each unit trying to maintain existing, and attract new, capital investments by lowering taxes and other costs they can impose.[6]

The Remaking of Hartford

Hartford, like many older industrial cities, has experienced reduction of manufacturing and the uneven emergence of a service-oriented economy. But like a number of other older cities, it had moved from spiraling decline in the early 1970s to a substantial boom in downtown construction and employment by the 1980s.[7] However, two features of Hartford have made conflict between the city's corporate sector and its relatively impoverished residential population especially intense. First, historically the boundaries of Hartford were drawn very closely around the central city. Even though the larger Hartford metropolitan area (SMSA) ranks as the 34th largest in the U.S., the city of Hartford is only the 116th largest.[8] As a result, Hartford houses fewer of the middle-class and better-off working-class groups whose presence in other cities often serves to blur the conflicts between wealth and poverty. Second, the economic growth within Hartford has been tied to sectors such as insurance that provide few attractive economic opportunities to lower-class workers. Thus, the downtown boom has done little to lessen the economic consequences of the decline in manufacturing for lower-income groups in Hartford.

In Hartford over the past several decades the combination of manufacturing decline and suburban dispersion has contributed to a profound transformation in the city. By 1980, Hartford's population had dropped by one-fourth from its 1950 peak, to 136,000 residents, and the city's manufacturing base had declined precipitously. The changes in the economic structure have been particularly rapid. While as recently as 1963 some 21 percent of those holding jobs in Hartford were employed in manufacturing, by the early 1980s only 7 percent were so employed. The residential character of Hartford's work force has also changed dramatically. In 1960, some 48 percent of the jobs in Hartford were held by residents of the city; by 1980 this figure had fallen to 23 percent. In effect, the city's population and its labor force are barely synonymous.

Post–World War II housing patterns contributed to the selective movement of better-off residents out of the city. Since Hartford's city limits were drawn around the city as it existed nearly a century ago, in modern times there has been almost no room for extensive new housing developments within the city. In the decades following 1950 those groups well off enough to buy new housing, especially the wealthy and the middle classes but also the economically stable and better-paid blue-collar workers, left the city for the suburbs in large numbers.

The exodus from Hartford to the suburbs was also, for the most part, a "white flight." Between 1960 and 1980, as many whites left the city, the minority population has become the majority within the city. The largest single city group in 1980 remained the whites (45 percent) but these were outnumbered by the combination of blacks (33 percent) and the primarily Puerto Rican hispanic group (20 percent). Along with the depressed economic conditions of minority families, racially restrictive housing patterns in the suburbs that surround Hartford also have played a major role in the shifting racial and ethnic concentration of the city's population. Even in 1980 the suburbs bordering Hartford made up a nearly solid wall of racially exclusive areas. The four suburbs that border Hartford on the west, south, and east, with a population over a third larger than Hartford itself, are less than 2 percent black. Only in two suburbs to the north has any significant integration occurred. But even in these two suburbs the total black population is less than one-fifth the size of the black population in Hartford itself.

As one result of these patterns, the city's social structure has shifted from one that generally reflected the stratification patterns in the larger society to one that is disproportionately poor. In 1960, the median family income of Hartford equalled that of the entire SMSA. By 1980, the city's median family income was only 58 percent of that of the SMSA.[9] Hartford now houses 60 percent of the poor in its metropolitan region.[10] Moreover, the poverty situation is becoming worse. Whereas in 1970, 17 percent of Hartford's residents lived on incomes below the federal government's official poverty line, by 1980 the proportion of poor had climbed to 25 percent. This statistic, almost twice the national level, enabled Hartford to gain the dubious distinction of being the fourth most poverty-ridden city in the nation.

The pervasive poverty among Hartford's residents intensifies needs for services facing the city government. Decent and affordable housing is extremely scarce, a problem worsened by the condominium conversions and other development projects near the downtown. Even the crime- and pest-ridden subsidized housing projects have long waiting lists. Health care available to the poor is very inadequate and in some Hartford neighborhoods infant mortality rates are higher than in a number of seriously deprived underdeveloped nations.[11] The schools also are crowded and resource-starved, their failures reflected in their extraordinarily high dropout rates.[12]

The movement of more affluent tax-paying residents out of Hartford has left the city having to finance, with its tax base further depleted by the decline in manufacturing, a disproportionate share of the service obligations of the entire metropolitan area. But this movement has also created an electorate that is disproportionately low-income. Were the Hartford area to have a metropolitan form of government, the poor and near-poor voters of Hartford would be merely another one of many interest groups represented in each election. But in Hartford city elections low-income groups are a formidable segment of the voting-age population. While corporate actors have many ways to influence city government, their properties cannot vote. And the one clear candidate for carrying an increased tax burden has of course been the growing downtown commercial and office areas. This odd configuration in Hartford of low-income voters and corporate capital owners creates the basis for the kinds of ongoing political struggles that are the focus of this analysis.

Our study examines several features of the conflict between Hartford's business elites and its low-income communities. The issues analyzed are tied directly to the growing economic polarization in the city. Conflict between Hartford's major corporations, wealthy developers and speculators, on the one hand, and its numerous low-income neighborhoods on the other, revolve around property tax issues in the city, the financing of urban services, and the establishment of development priorities in the downtown. The conflicting interests of the downtown business elite and the community groups generate a divisive political dynamic over the course of urban growth and the policies necessary to sustain that growth.

In order to illustrate the struggle over urban development policy in Hartford, we have broken our discussion into three sections. First, we will describe downtown development in the city, and identify the corporate and financial interests shaping its contours. Second, we will examine the various reactions to downtown growth on the part of community and neighborhood groups in the city. In some instances, community opposition immobilized the downtown elite's growth agenda. In other cases, however, community groups were powerless in the face of the strength of wealthy developers and major corporate forces. Third, we will discuss various attempts to export the city's low-income residents to suburban jurisdictions through a series of legal and developmental maneuvers. In our concluding section, we will examine the role of municipal government in mediating class coonflict within the city, and offer some speculations about Hartford's future.

Development in Hartford

Actors in the City's Development Process

The major actors promoting development in downtown Hartford have come from three areas: leaders of the largest corporations; entrepreneurial real estate investors; and elected politicians and the Hartford city government.[13] While other interests have been involved, these three types of actors have made the greatest difference.

CORPORATE LEADERS IN HARTFORD

John Filer, who would head the giant Aetna Life & Casualty Company for twelve years beginning in 1972, came to Hartford in 1958 as a corporate lawyer. He found, as he later reported, a city in which:

> The Chamber of Commerce had more clout than either political party, and the fabric of the city seemed relatively peaceful and unchanging. No one was protesting, the "powerless" were so indeed, and a male, white, Anglo-Saxon Protestant was very much at home everywhere that counted.[14]

The Hartford that Filer found was a city in which a small and cohesive corporate elite was accustomed to having a major voice in policies of both city government and private social and civic organizations.[15]

Much has been made of the ability of the "Bishops," as the most powerful corporate elites in Hartford have been called, to shape what happens in the city.[16] To some extent the Bishops have continued the patterns of the old families that once controlled their corporations and that had long exerted considerable influence in the city. During the 1960s and 1970s the cohesiveness of Hartford's corporate elite was reflected in regular breakfast meetings attended by ten to fifteen Bishops, most of whom were tied to the city's large insurance companies and banks. Also, an extensive pattern of interlocking directorships among the largest firms has worked to merge business and broader policy concerns.[17] The small size of Hartford also facilitates close personal ties among the Bishops. As the long-time head of the local Chamber of Commerce observed in regard to the "unusually high degree of cooperation in Hartford" among the Bishops:

> In New York City, you've got the downtown lower Manhattan group, and the upper Wall Street crowd. There's no other place to go in Hartford. They bump into each other at cocktail parties, luncheons, dinners, civic affairs. . . . God, they might as well be roommates. These guys see each other daily, someplace.[18]

While most of their investments in Hartford have been guided by clear profit motives, Hartford's Bishops have also pursued certain goals in the city that were seemingly guided by elements of an "enlightened self-interest" oriented beyond short-run profit maximization.[19] Most important in this regard have been the corporate reactions to the many indications of urban decline in Hartford. The large insurance companies in particular found themselves in the 1960s with substantial investments and historical commitments in a city in crisis. A series of racial riots in the late 1960s reinforced the threats. The growth of the insurance companies posed the question of whether they would continue to expand and build new facilities within the city, or move elsewhere. For the most part the decision was to stay, with the consequence that firms were drawn into more projects and investments that would help stabilize the city and make it, or at least the downtown area, a secure and attractive place to do business. As one executive of Travelers Insurance Company explained his firm's involvement in city development projects: "We want a community that can recruit employees."[20] Thus propelled by a combination of broadly and narrowly focused motives, Hartford's corporate leaders and their corporations have been centrally involved in its development process. In particular they have taken the lead in shaping large-scale plans and projects.

THE ENTREPRENEURS: REAL ESTATE INVESTORS IN HARTFORD

In contrast to the corporate leaders, the most notable characteristic of entrepreneurial real estate investors is their diversity, both in the projects undertaken and in their lack of unity.[21] Moreover, while large corporations have the resources and the broad interests that allow for long-term projects, real estate entrepreneurs are more focused on specific projects and short-term profits. Nevertheless, the recent history of Hartford suggests that these entrepreneurs are central figures in determining the direction of development in the city.

Entrepreneurial investors are the warlords and the raiding parties, as well as the foot soldiers, of the local "growth machine."[22] In their search for lucrative investment opportunities, they push the development process along, often in directions or at rates that effectively undermine the carefully laid plans of other, supposedly more powerful, actors. For example, some of the neighborhood protest activities, which have caused problems for large downtown projects, have been mobilized in response to office and condominium conversions carried out by small-scale developers in residential areas on the edges of the downtown.

Examples of the most prominent local developers and investors include David Chase and Richard Gordon. Both are self-made millionaires who began as small suburban developers. In recent years each has put together a number of highly speculative projects that taken together, have reshaped the skyline of downtown Hartford. The many other speculative investors and developers active in recent years are an odd assortment, including a former minister who gave up his inner-city church for apartment-to-condominium conversions in areas adjacent to the downtown, and Nicholas Carbone, who gained national fame as a "progressive" Democratic elected city official in the 1970s,[23] and is now involved in developing luxury apartment towers on an old factory site. Despite the modest scales on which most operate, real estate entrepreneurs do much to propel the processes of transformation in the city.

THE CITY GOVERNMENT

The city government has also been a major player in downtown development. The key feature of Hartford's city government is its structural weaknesses. A corporate and middle-class "reformist" assault on old-style ethnic and machine politics in the 1940s produced a fragmented government structure that largely prevents either the Mayor or the City Council from gaining enough power to exert much control over city affairs. The structure combines at-large elections, very low pay for City Council members, a guaranteed minority party (i.e., Republican) representation of three on the nine-person Council, and a largely ceremonial Mayor with no real executive powers. The low pay discourages many of the ambitious and able from running or seeking reelection. Instead, the low pay favors those with jobs in the large corporations that sanction their political activities as "public service" and those with independent financial means. The weak city government structure has had the effect of strengthening the power of downtown business interests.

Even with its weaknesses, the city government has faced a series of challenges in recent years. In the 1960s and 1970s, it was under pressure to take all possible steps to promote economic development in the city. More recently, it has been called upon to resolve the many conflicts inherent in downtown development and the polarization between the corporate and residential sectors of the city.

During the 1970s a group led by Nicholas Carbone was successful in gaining control of the City Council and using that power to make the city a more active force in development issues.[24] This activism led to a number of programs aimed at encouraging development in the city. The Council also fought attempts by Hartford's suburbs to separate themselves from the city's problems. This era of activist city government had broken apart by 1980. Yet it left a legacy of increased expectations among city residents about what the government could do.

Contours of Downtown Development since the 1950s

Over the past three decades, Hartford's corporate elites, in association with local developers and with support from city government, have been able to shape the downtown development agenda. The story begins in the 1950s, when the downtown business district of the city of Hartford was showing unmistakable symptoms of creeping deterioration. Physical decline, coupled with the emerging demographic shifts involving class and race, prompted concern among Hartford's corporate elites who pressured the Chamber of Commerce and city officials to come up with ways to reverse the process of downtown decay and demise.

In 1958 city government, with financial backing from Travelers Insurance Company and federal urban renewal programs, launched its first major downtown development project. The development site encompassed an area of tenement homes and marginal small neighborhood businesses. A working class enclave long populated by Italian immigrants and their children, it was also developing a sizable low-income black community. The protests of the residents that the area should not be destroyed had no effect. The site was leveled and its residents were dispersed to other neighborhoods away from the central business district. Having thus created a piece of prime real estate, Travelers erected three high-rise office towers, a large hotel, a headquarters for local radio and television stations, underground parking facilities, and a set of shops. Completed in 1962, "Constitution Plaza" was portrayed as a decisive response on the part of the corporate community to a downtown in trouble.

Despite this success, no new large projects occurred to spur the development of downtown for a number of years. Finally, another Bishop-inspired plan led in 1970 to a successful vote on a bond issue to finance a large downtown civic center. The civic center was proposed as a venture combining government and corporate investments. The city would finance a coliseum for sports and other events while Aetna Life and Casualty Company would finance an adjacent indoor shopping mall and a large hotel. Opened in 1975, the Hartford Civic Center, which attracted sports and entertainment events as well as conventions, added a new locus of economic and social life to an area of aging office structures and stagnating retail establishments. The Bishops' commitment to a revitalized downtown was further demonstrated in 1978 when heavy snow and structural deficiencies caused the collapse of the civic center's roof. Aetna and others came together with remarkable speed to secure the financing necessary for reconstruction.

Following the successful bond issue for the Civic Center in 1970, and even before its completion, the downtown development boom really took off. Since then a series of large downtown buildings have been built and a multitude of smaller projects have been completed. Older office buildings have been rehabilitated, apartment or old commercial buildings converted to condominiums, public buildings refurbished, and parks and other facilities added.

This development boom reflected important changes in the way things were done in Hartford. Traditionally, major projects were carried out by one of Hartford's leading corporations, and tailored to the specific needs of large firms slated to occupy them. In contrast, the new projects were often directed by entrepreneurial developers operating with financing secured outside of the city. Moreover, many of the new investments were speculative and begun before the space had been leased or sold.

This new approach is exemplified in the activities of David Chase. In 1972 Chase constructed the first major new office building in decades in Hartford as a speculative investment. His gamble paid off when one of the area's largest corporations, United Technologies, took the building for its headquarters. The success of Chase's project, coupled with a rash of new demand for office space by the growing finance, insurance, and real estate sectors of the city's economy, spurred an unprecedented building boom downtown, with both entrepreneurs and large corporations soon playing active and often cooperative roles. Between 1972 and 1984 the volume of office space in the city tripled. Hartford's downtown was transformed in ways that could scarcely have been envisioned when the Constitution Plaza project commenced back in 1958.

There was a bleaker underside to the dramatic revitalization of downtown, however. While the rapid expansion of office space continued, by the mid-1980s it had contributed very little to the city's retail sector and, if anything, had had a negative impact on the city's housing situation. Hartford's retail sector had been in a state of decline since the 1950s, as a result of residential suburbanization, competition from new suburban shopping centers and malls, and the declining economic condition of the remaining city residents. While most development attention was given to the languishing state of downtown retail establishments, Hartford's local neighborhood shopping facilities were undergoing an equally sharp descent. By 1985 eleven of the city's thirteen chain grocery supermarkets had shut down.

The housing situation in the city was also deteriorating while the downtown enjoyed increased prosperity. Despite efforts to build and rehabilitate housing units, between 1970 and 1982 Hartford suffered a net loss of 7 percent of its housing stock. A sizeable share of the loss resulted from units destroyed to make way for offices and from residential buildings being taken over by entrepreneurial developers and converted into gentrified office space convenient to the downtown. In addition to the actual loss of housing units, the conversion of apartments to condominiums has placed many of the remaining residential units out of reach of low-income residents.

Neighborhood Struggles with the Downtown Growth Coalition

As the agenda of Hartford's downtown growth coalition unfolded in the 1970s, a variety of issues brought vocal and at times militant responses from residents of the city's low-income neighborhoods. Neighborhood organizations mobilized to seek some control over the rapid social change emerging in Hartford. Their grievances were numerous, ranging from complaints about city services, to housing deterioration, to the effects of the many redevelopment projects then underway.

The origins of these groups were varied, with some building on earlier involvement in the civil rights movement, and others being linked to the efforts of churches to build stronger ties in poor neighborhoods.[25] By the end of the 1970s, however, the various neighborhood groups had united to fight against pervasive business domination in the city and and the indifference of city government to neighborhood needs. To the surprise of observers accustomed to neighborhood residents' relative passivity, these groups came to have a significant, if limited, impact on how development was to proceed in Hartford. The militancy of some groups' tactics, such as the mobilizing of poor demonstrators at the homes of corporate leaders, led to special tensions since some of their financial support came from the local corporate-supported United Way.

One issue which consistently divided business interests and neighborhood groups in Hartford was local taxation and the financing of city services. In the mid-1980s the annual budget of Hartford was about $250 million, with about half coming from property taxes. The largest share of the rest came from state and federal funds.[26] Property taxes are important to the city budget and represent a sizeable expense for property owners. Due to Hartford's restricted city boundaries, its few affluent neighborhoods, and the relatively small size of residential neighborhoods in general, only about one-sixth of the city's property taxes are paid by residential properties with less than four units. Commercial properties pay about half, and the final one-third comes from assessments on motor vehicles. Nevertheless, the levies paid by individual low- and moderate-income homeowners are heavy. Hartford's tax rate is from one and a half times to over twice as high as that of the more affluent suburbs that surround it.[27]

The polarization of Hartford's residents around extremes of wealth and poverty has manifested itself in conflict over financing city services. Local tax policy is directly related to the downtown growth agenda in a number of important ways. We will review three controversies over local tax policy in order to illustrate the conflict of interests between Hartford's low-income neighborhoods and downtown development proponents.

The first controversy centered on a short-lived policy that had businesses pay a higher tax rate than did residential owners. The second concerned the city policy of using tax abatements as a means to stimulate downtown development. The third involves a still-continuing struggle over whether downtown projects could be made subject to a special tax that would help pay for housing and other services aimed at helping the city's low-income residents.

Tax Differentials

In 1978 a rather unusual political compromise was struck in Hartford. The city's dominant business interests agreed to pay, for a two-year period, a higher property tax rate than that paid by residential owners. This peculiar arrangement was short-lived, and in 1980 and again in 1982 major battles were waged over attempts to pass state legislation to extend this tax differential.

The origins of the tax differential are found in the failure of the city to reassess property at the state-prescribed ten-year interval. As a result, in 1978 Hartford was collecting taxes based on assessments done in 1961. Since 1961 much had happened to change property values, including the racial explosions of the 1960s that had contributed to major drops in market values in black areas and the general decline in retail business values. Due to these changes, the revaluation forced by the state legislature in 1978 had a potential for creating great political divisiveness. A study done in 1978 indicated that despite new downtown construction, the revaluation would bring a substantial decline in taxes on commercial property and an increase for residential properties. In addition, the decline in property values in minority neighborhoods meant that much of the new burden on residences would be borne by white neighborhoods. One estimate was that tax bills in such areas could go up by nearly half.[28]

Faced with the possibility of contentious political battles between white and minority groups, city political leaders sought a temporary solution. The relief came in the form of state legislation that created a temporary tax differential until 1980. The special law allowed the city to assess residential property (one- to four-family residences) at lower rates than commercial property. The cost to business of this tax differential would be $6 million per year.

The basis on which business agreed to this measure was never fully clear to most participants. Some of the "enlightened self-interest" of the Bishops seemed to be at work. Faced with the prospect of a major battle with sides drawn along racial lines, some corporate leaders saw a compromise as necessary. However, many business interests remained opposed. The City Council was able to create pressure on business by holding up funding needed for the new roof of the Civic Center.[29] Neighborhood groups also pressed hard for the differential. Ultimately business agreed to the change but, in their view, only on a temporary basis.

The 1978 legislation was due to expire in 1980 but neighborhood groups got active and, together with some support from city officials, won a two-year extension. In 1982 the scene was quite different. Neighborhood groups took on the tax differential as a major campaign while city officials, still outwardly supportive, were less involved. Busi-

ness interests lobbied fiercely. The heads of both the Hartford Insurance Group and the Connecticut Bank and Trust were personally
active, visiting legislators, and even obtaining a meeting with the governor.[30] While neighborhood groups again picketed and demonstrated,
the commercial interests won. The only concession allowed was for
phasing out the tax differential over five years.

In this case, then, neighborhood mobilization had an impact, but
not one great enough to overcome a concerted corporate reaction. The
large corporate interests, including the Bishops with their "enlightened
self-interest," showed no willingness to give, on a permanent basis, an
added measure of financial support to city services through somewhat
higher property taxes.

Tax Abatements

Large corporate interests as well as entrepreneurial real estate
developers have shown great support for property tax differentials of a
different sort. Beginning in 1972, using special powers granted by the
state legislature, Hartford city officials offered tax breaks to entice
developers downtown. Such breaks helped facilitate the building of the
Civic Center and David Chase's initial office building project, as well
as a large number of subsequent projects. City tax breaks were aggressively defended as critical, not only in attracting developers, but in
keeping existing institutions from pulling out of Hartford.

As it became obvious that the level of office space development
going on in the city was likely to be self-sustaining and market-
sensitive, and as arguments around the tax differential made residents
especially aware of tax distribution issues, a chorus of protest against
such tax breaks emerged. In 1981 neighborhood groups—focusing on,
among other things, the contradiction between these breaks for the rich
and rising tax burdens on homeowners—successfully pressured the
City Council to clamp down on them. For the most part, such tax advantages ceased being negotiated with developers of office space by
1982. Instead, they were to be limited to other kinds of projects, such as
ones involving retail trade, said still to be risky and in need of added incentives.[31] On this issue, then, Hartford's neighborhood organizations
were effective, at least as a veto group, in limiting some of the city
government's inclinations to lavish benefits on large corporate and entrepreneurial developers.

"Linkage" to the Benefits of Corporate Prosperity

The defeat of the tax differential led neighborhood groups to consider other strategies to get the prospering downtown to bear more of the costs of services for low-income residents. The proposals that emerged, known as "linkage" after similar policies adopted in recent years by several cities, including San Francisco, Santa Monica and Boston, called for special taxes or payments from developers of downtown commercial property. The monies thus collected would then be channelled directly toward increasing housing and job opportunities for city residents.

By late 1983 neighborhood groups were pressuring the City Council to adopt a linkage ordinance. Under increased pressure on a range of issues involving the split between the downtown boom and the depressed conditions in residential neighborhoods, the Council sought to deflect this new challenge by creating and funding a "Linkage Task Force." The Task Force, with representatives of the neighborhoods and other citizen groups, city officials, and business representatives, functioned for a year and a half before it dissolved. The history of this effort reveals important aspects of the current conflicts between neighborhood and downtown interests.

For the neighborhood groups the establishment of the Task Force represented an important, if only partial, victory. Linkage was an issue they had placed on the city policy agenda. Through their active mobilization they had forced the city government and business interests into "negotiation." However, participation in these negotiations also appears to have weakened the positions of these activist groups. For one thing, in exchange for participation in the Task Force, neighborhood groups largely deferred the political mobilization around the linkage issue that had been begun in 1983. Militant confrontational tactics that had gotten notice, as well as enraged the corporate targets, mostly ceased. The Task Force drew neighborhood leaders into numerous meetings but did little to sustain citizen political activity.

In addition, during the course of negotiating the linkage issue there appears to have been a significant drop in just how much the activist groups felt they could demand from downtown developers. Even though the rhetoric used in mobilization campaigns called for forcing corporations to address seriously the shortages of housing and jobs in the city, by 1985 neighborhood-backed proposals called for payments of only two million dollars a year or less. In a city with a budget of a quarter billion dollars a year and with the serious social problems that Hartford has, another one to two million dollars each year from downtown developers would hardly have represented any significant redistribution of wealth in the city. In fact, a consultant's report on linkage indicated that such an amount, if devoted entirely to housing, would only meet about one-third of the needs resulting each year from displacements directly linked to the expansion of the downtown.[32]

The timidity of activists' demands contrasted sharply with the fervor with which many spoke regarding the issue.[33] The source of this timidity apparently exists not in open political assaults from the business side but rather in the fear that heavier demands on developers "would force construction out of Hartford into the suburbs."[34] Repeatedly, the issue has not been what is just or reasonable given the level of prosperity in corporate Hartford, nor the level of need in the neighborhoods, but rather whether new taxes or payments would put Hartford at enough of an increased cost disadvantage to seriously affect the downtown development boom. For example, the consultant's report on linkage that was highly favorable to the approach, nevertheless referred to its recommendation as being limited to what was "feasible in terms of market absorption."[35] Stressing the same theme, one political columnist argued: "Make the linkage tax high enough, and commercial geese will find some suburban nest in which to lay their golden taxable eggs. Even a minimum tax may deter some."[36] Neighborhood activists acknowledged that they felt unable to call for taxes above a fairly low level.

In critical ways, larger market forces impose severe limits on the redistributive inclinations of Hartford's low-income groups, even though they appear to exercise considerable political power. The mobility of Hartford's capital certainly creates the strong impression, and to some extent the reality, that no one political contingent could act aggressively to divert some of the wealth located within city borders unless it was also willing to risk considerable capital flight and the resulting economic consequences.

The Linkage Task Force efforts collapsed when business participation was withdrawn. The manner of this withdrawal suggests a change in the nature of corporate involvement in Hartford's problems. As the linkage controversy grew, leaders of the Chamber of Commerce had assumed the central role in meeting with community groups and politicians. Based on the active role of the Chamber, Task Force participants assumed that business support for a linkage policy would result. As one neighborhood representative reported: "We thought that

Herb [the Chamber President] and the Chamber were behind it, and that there was serious involvement and commitment by the higher-ups in the corporate world in Hartford."[37]

These expectations were shattered when business support for a linkage policy was suddenly withdrawn in the spring of 1985. The collapse of the Linkage Task Force revealed a split in the business community between the Chamber, which seemed to be pursuing the old model of corporate "enlightened self-interest," and a new generation of corporate leaders who were unwilling to accept any programs that would impose new burdens on downtown corporate and development interests. This new mood was reflected in a private memorandum, subsequently leaked, in which a top Aetna lawyer called upon government relations officials at six other large Hartford corporations to pay "serious attention to a developing debacle." This "debacle" was described as "the potential call for a 'linkage fee' or 'lease tax' to help pay for low or moderate income housing in Hartford."[38] The clear implication of the memo was that the Chamber representatives on the Task Force were conveying the mistaken impression that the "business community should acquiesce in some form of linkage fee or lease tax," and that these representatives should be reined in.[39] After the withdrawal of business participation it was reported that the proposal for a linkage tax was "rejected by the task force's business caucus because any mandatory fee would create a perceived barier to development." As one business representative stated, while a modest linkage tax of the sort being discussed "would not make or break a deal, . . . the perception would be far more reaching."[40]

The linkage debate is not totally dead. In late 1985, the victorious slate of Democratic candidates for City Council campaigned on a platform supporting linkage. The defeated slate had publicly opposed the linkage tax concept.[41] In early 1986 the City Manager was instructed to develop proposals for implementing a linkage policy. However, his proposals rejected taxation and instead stressed voluntary business contributions at an even lower level than that discussed by the Task Force.[42] Through the summer and fall of 1986 the City Council members not only voted down all attempts to legislate linkage but also even disavowed their earlier support for the concept.[43] It appeared unlikely that any real redistributive thrust would emerge from the linkage approach, even with apparently strong political support.

The picture that emerges from our review of conflicts over tax policies in Hartford suggests in general the failure of either side to win major new advantages. However, it also shows that the status quo operates very much in favor of private-sector interests. While transformation of the Hartford downtown continues at a fast pace on terms controlled by private developers, low-income residents in Hartford have not been able to gain any real benefits from this process of growth.

The Search for Alternative Forms of Linkage

Throughout the 1980s there has been broad public agreement that the city should do more to ensure that downtown development occurs in ways that spread the benefits beyond just each individual project. The agreement does not specify, however, what the benefits should be. City officials have been most concerned about what happens downtown. In 1983, the City Council passed a new zoning ordinance in which the approval of new building designs, especially in regard to height, would be made contingent on public amenities included in the designs. This rather weak measure encouraged downtown developers to include arcades, art exhibition areas, small parks, and other such features in their building plans.

These sorts of enhancements did little to meet the strong demands from residential groups for the spread of benefits to their neighborhoods. The city thus was pressured to pursue modified "linkage" agreements that would do something to meet the demands for housing and employment assistance for city residents. An ordinance was finally passed requiring developers who destroy housing units to provide some form of replacement. In the employment area, the city has also made some moves. One recent example, that of Northeast Plaza, reveals how the political conflicts in Hartford have affected the relationship between developers and the city.

Northeast Plaza is a $96 million office and retail development located in the central downtown business area. It is controlled by a partnership between an entrepreneurial developer and Travelers Insurance. The plan includes office towers as well as a "festival marketplace" containing numerous restaurants, shops, and related amenities. The marketplace was promoted by city officials and downtown corporate interests, with the idea that, much in the style of Boston's Faneuil Hall Marketplace, it would give the center of the city new life and uplift the stagnating retail scene. The commitment of local corporate interests to the project was indicated in January 1985, when the city learned that an expected federal grant for financing the marketplace was to be cut by over $8 million to $3.3 million. Within days the amount cut was guaranteed by Travelers and other local corporations, and the project stayed on schedule.

The developers were encouraged to incorporate the marketplace in their design in exchange for a substantial seven-year tax abatement. With the abatement and other financing benefits, retail rents in the marketplace were to be kept low. In return for the abatement, half of the 700 jobs created in the retail part of the complex were to go to city residents, and 20 percent of the shops would be occupied by female- or minority-owned businesses.

Neighborhood groups, learning of the proposed abatement agreement, objected. They argued that much stronger guarantees on hiring and business opportunities had to be in place before the City Council gave the tax abatement, if the abatement were to be granted at all. The protests against the abatement became rather lively. At one meeting, a neighborhood activist reportedly complained that the Council was giving away the shirts off residents' backs, whereupon members of the audience threw shirts at members of the Council. Under heavy pressure from neighborhood groups, the Council gave the neighborhoods a modest victory. While the abatement was approved, the developers not only provided the job and business opportunity concessions but also agreed to penalties for noncompliance. They would, for example, have to pay cash fines if they did not meet hiring goals in any given year. And the developers had to provide a modest fund, $100,000, for job training.

The Northeast Plaza case indicates that even a powerful group of corporate actors are not invulnerable to neighborhood mobilization when open political approval is needed for their plans. While the costs imposed on the developers in this case were not great and their basic plans won approval, the case does reveal the uneasy power balance that currently exists in Hartford between downtown interests and neighborhood groups. The neighborhood groups were unable to win a comprehensive linkage policy that would tie all downtown development to benefits for city residents, but they have shown that they can mobilize in individual cases and win significant concessions.

Neighborhood groups' mobilization did play a central role in stopping one development initiative by downtown business interests. In the late 1970s, neighborhood opponents fought a proposal to build a "skywalk," or enclosed and elevated pedestrian walkway connecting a number of downtown buildings that city planners envisioned as tying downtown Hartford together in a unique and attractive way. The first section of the skywalk was proposed in conjunction with a project to be funded by one of Hartford's insurance giants. Connecticut General Life Insurance Company had tentatively agreed to finance the renovation of an historic downtown building, then owned by the city, into expensive apartments and a new commercial mall. However, the company made the project contingent on support for the skywalk. Initially they received that support, both from other major downtown corporate actors and from city officials who developed a plan for funding the skywalk from a federal grant that was to be combined with unused highway funds and local corporate contributions. Supporters argued that the renovation and the skywalk were important to maintain the momentum of downtown development.

Neighborhood opponents challenged those who claimed that the skywalk, like other downtown projects, would send trickle-down benefits to the city's residents. They pointed to the growing city property tax burden for residents and the declining conditions in residential areas as evidence that benefits were not being spread. As one opponent stated, "We keep hearing about the trickle-down effect and we haven't seen it work with this or other downtown projects. If we had seen the trickle-down effect work, believe me, there'd be no tax increase."[44] Some street-level shopowners in Hartford were also opposed, on the practical grounds that the skywalk would divert potential customers away from sidewalk entrances. More generally, neighborhood groups claimed the skywalk was symbolic of a larger plan by downtown interests to fence off some of the unpleasant aspects of the city. By using skywalks, office workers and shoppers in up-scale downtown stores would be able to avoid contact with the less affluent on city streets.

The skywalk was initially approved by the federal government and by the City Council, despite the controversy. However, active neighborhood opposition continued and the project was ultimately shelved. Nevertheless, the issue is one that could always re-emerge, as it did in 1986 when a major redevelopment proposal included a limited section of such a walkway.[45] Still, the skywalk controversy shows again, as with tax abatements, that neighborhood groups can be effective in blocking projects that include what appear to be particularly one-sided concessions to corporate interests.

Exporting Hartford's Problems to the Suburbs

The cases reviewed thus far indicate that political struggles have done little to reduce the disparities between wealth and poverty in

Hartford. While political mobilization in Hartford's low-income neighborhoods has forced some limits on the prerogatives of downtown business interests, in reality the direction of downtown development has been little affected to date and there has been no notable redistribution of benefits to Hartford's residents. The current situation, which promises little relief to the city's neighborhoods, contrasts with efforts that were undertaken in the 1970s to bring about rather substantial transformations of the social, economic, and political realities of Hartford. One of these was a corporate effort on a grand scale. The second was carried out by city politicians. The ultimate failure of these efforts has left the city caught in seemingly unresolvable tensions.

Hartford Process and the "New Town" in Rural Connecticut

In the late 1960s, Hartford seemed caught in the web of neighborhood and central city decline, race-related violence, poverty and a myriad of other urban ills. It is within such a context that the corporate leaders of Hartford launched a major initiative to direct the processes of change in the metropolitan area. Viewed from the hindsight of the 1980s, they seemed to possess startling audacity in their approach to urban decline.

In 1969, the leaders of Hartford's largest corporations, in conjunction with the Chamber of Commerce, formed an organization, later to become Greater Hartford Process, that was pledged to find solutions to the major problems facing the Hartford metropolitan region. By 1972, now funded by corporate commitments of $1 million per year, Hartford Process revealed a comprehensive plan that included a set of projects that, according to its own statements, would affect the lives of some 670,000 persons living in 29 communities in a 750-square-mile area. Key elements included the total rebuilding of Hartford, beginning with the most blighted and minority-populated northern half of the city, and then proceeding to the less blighted, predominantly white southern half. The plan also called for the construction, from scratch, of an entire "new town" somewhere out in Hartford's more rural suburbs. Meanwhile there were also to be new regional approaches to solution of problems in such areas as housing, transportation, health care, education, law enforcement, and social services.

The Hartford Process proposal was hailed as bold and visionary, "as the most ambitious 'total approach' to urban problem solving in America," and as a possible model for future metropolitan development processes across the nation.[46] Although some leaders of Hartford's black community claimed that the new-town idea was an attempt to dilute their power in the city, and others objected to the lack of citizen input into Hartford Process plans, the basic local reaction was positive.[47]

While the Hartford Process plan was most detailed on projects in the city, intense interest was immediately stimulated by the proposal for a "new town" in the suburbs. This town was not only to provide opportunities for enhanced lifestyles for suburban dwellers, but would also enable some low- and moderate-income people to move out of the city. The prospect of such movement was not warmly received in the suburbs. One suburban official commented," I don't see the problems of the central city as my responsibility."[48]

Nevertheless, Hartford Process, while refusing to reveal the location of the proposed new town, was soon secretly buying up land. In January 1973, the location was discovered to be Coventry, a quiet rural community of 8,500 some fifteen miles from the city. Hartford Process then energetically publicized and defended its ambitious plans for a community with a population of 20,000 that would include not only houses and apartments but also commercial and industrial areas. The suburban reaction to this plan was largely shaped by Hartford Process's concept of dispersing Hartford's poor population. Since 15 percent of the housing units would be set aside for low-income families, it was acknowledged that Coventry, then nearly all white, would gain some blacks and other minorities. The response to concerns on this issue by Hartford Process officials reveals the rather remarkable audacity with which this corporate-led effort operated. Coventry residents were told not to worry about any large-scale movement of blacks into their community since the Hartford Process plans for north Hartford would soon make the city so "livable" that few would want to leave.[49]

A major vulnerability of the new town idea was its dependence on the cooperation of Coventry public officials and townspeople in granting zoning changes and in developing a formal plan. Coventry officials' refusal to cooperate and the townspeople's mounting public efforts to block the new town ultimately led to its being shelved. Pressured also by rising interest rates and other changes in investment markets, the Coventry plans were dropped two years after they were announced. Whatever the power of corporate Bishops and their servants in Hartford, these forces had little sway out in Coventry. The successful resistance of the town to Hartford Process's overtures turned out to be costly for the organization. An estimated $8 million had been invested in land acquisitions and related costs before the project was dropped.

Hartford Process's loss of the Coventry new town project was to prove costly in another way. While planning had meanwhile been going on for the rebuilding of blighted areas in Hartford's northern half, the actual implementation of these ambitious plans rested heavily on the ability of the Hartford Process development corporation to generate profits on projects such as a successful "new town" that could be channelled back to the city. No profits meant a serious setback for the plans for promoting development in the city.

The failure of Hartford Process to carry out its bold plans to re-structure the metropolitan region apparently made it turn to more ex-pedient approaches to solving Hartford's problems. This was indicated by an internal memo by the staff of Hartford Process which was leaked to the press in January 1975, shortly after the announcement of the can-cellation of the Coventry plans. That memo laid out policy proposals calling for the containment of poor areas and their isolation from the downtown area. The memo appeared to build on the then-popular "triage" approach, which suggested that the poor and lower-income areas of cities should be written off and available resources for housing and other neighborhood services concentrated on moderate-income areas that still could be "saved."[50]

Gone from this memo were the earlier ambitious aims of ending blight in Hartford's minority areas. Instead, guided by what its authors called a "'geopolitical' or demographic strategy," it was asserted that "the ghetto will remain" and should be "planned for."[51] One problem noted was that the ghetto was too close to downtown, both in its actual proximity and in occupying land needed for other purposes. Thus the memo argued that "the ghetto should be moved away from Down-town—at least one stop away," while certain areas were targeted to be "cleared and landbanked if necessary." Housing projects adjacent to downtown "should come down" and another nearby area "recycled as a mixed to upper income residential area." One proposal that was to prove particularly controversial when made public stated that "Puerto Rican in-migration must be reduced" and "efforts should be made to consolidate the welfare dependent elements of this population" in two already depressed neighborhoods.[52] The memo then discussed the need to "concentrate school resources" and "immediate spot rehab" efforts in the city's better-off single-family areas.

The revelation of the Hartford Process memo caused major tur-moil in Hartford, with politicians and even some business leaders quickly disassociating themselves from its recommendations. Neigh-borhood residents, particularly in black and Puerto Rican areas, were outraged. The controversy cost Hartford Process further legitimacy and provided evidence as to how far the large corporate interests had re-treated from their ambitious goals of a few years before. Hartford Pro-cess existed for a few more years before it was absorbed into the Cham-ber of Commerce.

Hartford's Suit Against the Suburbs

As the controversial plan to build a new town was slipping into a tailspin, and Hartford Process regional planning efforts were faltering, a new and different effort to disperse and share some of Hartford's problems emerged. In 1975 the City Council voted to file a federal suit against seven neighboring towns to bar them from receiving federal community development grants. The longer-term goal was to force these towns to build low-income housing and thus take some of the pressure to shelter the region's poor off the city. The suit was a result of the continuing frustration Hartford city officials felt at seeing how resistant local towns were to making low-income housing available. They recognized that Hartford was destined to continue as the pre-dominant center of poverty in the region as long as so few housing openings existed in its suburbs.

The legal opportunity for the lawsuit was created in 1974 when the Community Development Act was enacted. This federal law provided Community Development Block Grants (CDBGs) for communities. Monies were to be used to address housing and related needs of low- to moderate-income citizens, especially minorities. The CDBG program was intended to provide positive inducements for suburban areas to open themselves up to more low-income housing. In this regard, the 1974 legislation represented an attempt to overcome some of the met-ropolitan fragmentation that allowed suburbs to fence themselves off from problems of the central city.

The Hartford suit was brought against seven suburban towns which were eligible for, and had applied to receive, $4.4 million in CDBG funds. Hartford, which was to receive its own $10-million CDBG grant, was not claiming the suburbs' grants for itself but rather was demanding that federal funds be denied them until the suburbs had moved to increase low-income housing within their own borders.[53] The suit noted that some of the towns had indicated in their grants that they actually had no unmet low-income housing needs. Instead the CDBG funds were to be spent by these towns for new parks, sewers, roads, urban renewal projects, and other public works. Hartford city officials argued that such uses, in the absence of programs to meet low-income housing needs, not only violated CDBG regulations but would also amount to using federal subsidies to help make the suburbs even more attractive places for better-off families to live.[54]

The suit, which immediately drew harsh criticism from the suburbs, had a substantial initial impact. Shortly after the suit was filed, a federal court judge issued a temporary injunction that prevented the seven towns from receiving their CDBG grants until the suit was settled. The various projects the towns had planned, some of which had been started, were thrust into limbo. In early 1976, a federal judge issued a permanent injunction against the grants for the seven towns. His decision noted that the CDBG program "intended to create a lessening of concentration of low-income groups in the region" and ruled that the grants should be withheld until the towns had submitted acceptable applications. The decision also found that the U.S. Department of Housing and Urban Development (HUD) had been too lenient in its enforcement of the law's requirements.[55]

Subsequent to this decision several of the towns did submit new applications and, more significantly, HUD revised its regulations to put more emphasis on the requirements for low-income housing. Hartford's suit, however, was ultimately unsuccessful. In 1977, the U.S. Court of Appeals reversed the lower court decision and dismissed Hartford's suit.[56]

The dismissal was based largely on a narrow procedural issue—that the city "lacked standing" to intervene in the grant-giving relationship between HUD and the suburban towns. Regardless of the legal issues or even of the political wisdom of launching a legal assault on the city's suburbs, Hartford officials were certainly correct in terms of urban processes that the city was very much affected by the housing policies of its suburban neighbors. The ultimate court decision was regarded in Hartford, as by observers in other cities across the country, as a major defeat in the efforts to force suburbs to take a more responsible view of their position in regard to urban problems.[57]

The ultimate impact of the suit is difficult to judge since, despite its legal failure, it moved HUD to enforce the regulations more tightly. However, in Hartford's suburbs there has been little evidence of any significant new openness to low-income housing. In fact, pressure from HUD on one Hartford suburb to meet low-income housing needs led to a referendum election in which the voters overwhelmingly chose to stop applying for CDBG funds.[58] This vote showed again the strength of the sentiments in suburbs against any "metropolitization" of the problems of central cities.

Conclusion

The sources and direction of Hartford's downtown growth and its continued contrast to the economic stagnation of the city's neighborhoods are difficult to sort out and explain. No single theory of urban political economy adequately captures the rich complexity, tensions, and dynamics that are involved.

Clearly much of what happens in Hartford is shaped by forces tied to the ownership and control of private capital. The city's large corporations and their leaders remain centrally important factors in what occurs. However, downtown development has also been influenced by the mixed collection of entrepreneurial developers and other components of the urban "growth machine." Viewed in the aggregate, the actions of such real estate interests have often been as important as the larger plans of the corporate actors in determining the direction of change in the city. In addition, the impact of property interests on the city is a complex mixture of direct and indirect effects. Due to the real and the perceived importance of capital and investment decisions in the economic life of the city, property interests can shape the policy process even without the active participation of specific business actors. For example, city officials in seeking to encourage development will form policies that they think will be attractive to investors and will even defend such policies against political attacks, all without any direct intervention from the economic interests who are the intended beneficiaries. Nevertheless, in Hartford such indirect manifestations of economic power are continually mixed with instances where corporate actors aggressively seek to win political advantages through active participation. The fight over the tax differential was but one example of how large economic interests get their way only by direct participation.

At the same time, attention to the role of corporate elite participation must be tempered by the fact that all activities undertaken by corporate and other private sector actors are embedded in larger economic and political contexts. These contexts impose certain structural constraints that shape the parameters within which local change occurs.

For example, the general process of "deindustrialization" that is now evident (albeit unevenly) across the U.S. urban scene, is not something readily controllable from the corporate suites of Hartford. Likewise, federal policies bearing on aid to cities and in particular to their low-income populations is outside direct local corporate control, even while such policies may play a crucial role in reducing or masking the disparity between concentrated capital. and squalor within city boundaries.

Those who would look to the evident class polarization and class struggles in Hartford as the primary forces shaping events in the city need to recognize the limits imposed by both the private control of capital and the larger economic system. A predominantly lower-to working-class population, largely black and hispanic, has a democratic system of city governance nominally in its hands. Yet this population's ability to make the political system work on behalf of changes in the capital/squalor ratio is offset by the fact that capital is eminently movable today. If class-based challenges to capital arise in Hartford, the threat and the reality of "capital flight" emerge as powerful disciplining forces. This situation breeds a timidity such that original demands are often abandoned and settlements made for less than felt needs. Thus, even when aggressive political mobilization occurs, neighborhood groups are often cornered into accepting relatively minor political and economic concessions. Community groups who do extensive organizing can become successful in blocking some of the specific tax-paid projects that are most visibly self-serving for business interests. However, getting the city to give serious attention to their own agendas for change is much more difficult.

City officials, when pressured to address redistribution issues prompted by downtown growth, are caught in the pincers of metropolitan fragmentation. Again the mobility of capital is an unspoken threat to progressive public policy, as the continuing loss of more parts of Hartford's shaky tax base to the surrounding suburbs is seen as something that must be resisted. The activities of government officials thus must also be seen as embedded in a context. Campaign rhetoric out in the neighborhoods, even when well meant, rarely matches deeds when victors assess the situation from the vantage point of the City Council chambers. Thus, even though the democratic political system does provide a setting in which disputes between downtown and neighborhood interests inevitably will emerge, the system does not actually allow for the resolution of most of these disputes.

What will become of Hartford? One hesitates to speculate. The population of the city is becoming poorer, and more and more unlike the population of its surrounding suburbs not only in economic terms but in racial terms as well. The pressure to keep providing needed city services will continue, even while Hartford officials must somehow deal with the specter of more cutbacks in federal social spending. The city government is in a situation where social service needs will certainly grow but also where too many additional demands upon the corporate sector may well generate more movement out of Hartford. Metropolitan-area solutions to the city's troubles do not seem to be on the horizon.

Perhaps the Hartford Bishops will make at least one more grand effort to gain control of the direction in which matters are going. There is little reason to expect that they will succeed. One of the central contradictions of capitalism is that even as the power of capital continues to grow, the ability of corporate actors to shape events in ways that deviate from the central directions of economic change is limited. Moreover, no matter how well-intentioned and enlightened the motives of corporate Bishops might seem at times, their necessary preoccupation with profit means that they can never truly pursue the goal of ensuring human well-being.

Thus, one is left with a vision of Hartford moving on in the same general direction defined by the combination of local investment decisions and larger economic forces. The economic crises of its neighborhoods create the prospect of ongoing political turmoil and perhaps even of periodic disruptive upheavals. But there are few apparent means by which any real resolution of the city's divisions seem likely to be achieved.

Notes

1. David M. Gordon, "Capitalist Development and the History of American Cities," in William Tabb and Larry Sawer (eds.), *Marxism and the Metropolis,* 2d ed. New York: Oxford University Press, 1984, pp. 21–53; Martin Shefter, *Political Crisis/Fiscal Crisis: The Collapse and Revival of New York City,* New York: Basic Books, 1985, ch. 2.

2. Ira Katznelson, *City Trenches: Urban Politics and the Patterns of Class Conflict in the United States,* New York: Pantheon, 1981; Harvey Molotch, "The City as a Growth Machine: Toward a Political Economy of Place," *American*

Journal of Sociology, September 1976, pp. 309–332; Edward Greer, *Big Steel: Black Politics and Corporate Power in Gary, Indiana,* New York: Monthly Review Press, 1979.

3. Fred Block, "The Ruling Class Does Not Rule: Notes on the Marxist Theory of the State. " *Socialist Revolution,* May-June 1977, pp. 6–28; Roger Friedland, "The Politics of Profit and the Geography of Growth." *Urban Affairs Quarterly,* September 1983, pp. 41–54.

4. Barry Bluestone and Benjamin Harrison, *The Deindustrialization of America,* New York: Basic Books, 1982, ch. 3.

5. Harvey Molotch and John Logan, "Tensions in the Growth Machine: Overcoming Resistance to Value-Free Development." *Social Problems,* June 1984, pp. 483–499.

6. Todd Swanstrom, "Tax Abatement in Cleveland." *Social Policy,* Winter 1982, pp. 24–30.

7. Bluestone and Harrison; Norman I. Fainstein and Susan S. Fainstein, "Restructuring the American City: A Comparative Perspective," in Norman I. Fainstein and Susan S. Fainstein (eds.), *Urban Policy under Capitalism, Urban Affairs Annual Reviews,* vol. 22, Beverly Hills, CA: Sage Publications, 1982, pp. 161–190; Richard Child Hill, "Fiscal Crisis, Austerity Politics, and Alternative Urban Policies," in Tabb and Sawer, pp. 298–322.

8. *The World Almanac and Book of Facts: 1986,* New York: Newspaper Enterprise Association, 1986, pp. 262, 267–313.

9. Pierre Clavel, *Progressive City,* New Brunswick, NJ: Rutgers University Press, 1985, p. 20.

10. Suzanne Bilello, "Hartford's Poverty Line: Threshold of Desperation." *Hartford Courant,* February 27, 1983; Kevin Thomas, "Burgeoning Progress Leaves Legacy of Lost Opportunity." *Hartford Courant,* February 28, 1983.

11. Connecticut Association for Human Services and Junior League of Hartford, *Growing Up at Risk in Connecticut,* 1984, p. 31.

12. Ibid., p. 82.

13. Our overview of the development process was aided by a series of interviews with city officials, neighborhood group representatives, and other individuals active in the city's political and economic affairs.

14. John Filer, "Hartford Reflections." *Northeast Magazine, Hartford Courant,* March 17, 1986.

15. Everett Carll Ladd, *Ideology in America: Change and Response in a City, a Suburb, and a Small Town.* New York: Norton, 1972, p. 323.

16. Antoinette Martin, "The Powerful in Hartford: 'Bishops' of the Board Rooms Set City's Course." *Hartford Courant,* January 23, 1983.

17. David Lieberman, "The Power Elite." *Hartford Advocate,* June 4, 1980.

18. Martin.

19. Ladd, pp. 322–330; see also Kenneth J. Neubeck, *Corporate Response to Urban Crisis.* Lexington, MA: Lexington Books, 1974.

20. Barbara French, "Budd Knows Travelers Can't Live on Past Glory." *Hartford Courant,* January 27, 1983.

21. Joe R. Feagin, "Urban Real Estate Speculation in the United States: Applications for Social Science and Urban Planning." *International Journal of Urban and Regional Planning,* March 1982, pp. 35–60; Matthew Edel, Elliott Sclar, and Daniel Luria, *Shaky Palaces: Home Ownership and Social Mobility in Boston's Surburbanization,* New York: Columbia University Press, 1984, pp. 195–223.

22. Molotch.

23. Clavel; Harry Boyte, *The Backyard Revolution: Understanding the New Citizen Movement.* Philadelphia: Temple University Press, 1980, pp. 154–183.

24. Clavel.

25. Boyte.

26. "Comprehensive Plan of Development: Economics and Employment Component, 1984." Hartford: Commission on the City Plan, City of Hartford, 1984, p. 48.

27. Ibid., p. 55.

28. Bettina Edelstein and Gary Nielson, "No Easy Way Out." *Hartford Advocate,* May 4, 1983.

29. Eve Bach, Nicholas R. Carbone, and Pierre Clavel, "Running the City for the People." *Social Policy,* Winter 1982, p. 18.

30. Marc Gunther, "Thomas Runs a Taut Ship at Work, in City." *Hartford Courant,* January 30, 1983; Steve Grant, "Connolly a Man of Contrasts." *Hartford Courant,* February 3, 1983.

31. Mark Pazniokas, "Northeast Plaza Developers Awarded Tax Break." *Hartford Courant,* July 2, 1985.

32. "A Linkage Policy for Hartford: A Report Submitted to the Hartford Linkage Task Force." Boston: Stockard and Engler, Inc., June 1986, p. 2.

33. See Bill Hagan, "The Corporations' Hold on Hartford," Letter to the editor. *Hartford Courant,* April 4, 1986.

34. D. J. Shea, "The Missing Link: How Hartford Can Bridge the Gap between Downtown and the Neighborhoods." *Hartford Advocate,* January 11, 1984.

35. "A Linkage Policy," p. 2.

36. Don O. Noel, "Hartford Already Has Linkage—Development." *Hartford Courant,* February 2, 1986.

37. Mark Pazniokas, "Memo Casts Doubt on Commitment to City Residents' Needs." *Hartford Courant,* May 22, 1985.

38. Ibid.

39. Ibid.

40. Ibid.

41. "Questions to the Candidates." *Hartford Courant,* September 5, 1985.

42. Mark Pazniokas, "Gatta Plan Hinges on Voluntary Linkage Payments." *Hartford Courant,* February 25, 1986.

43. Larry Williams and Mark Pazniokas, "City Council Hears Chorus of Midterm Criticism." *Hartford Courant,* November 30, 1986.

44. Bruce Kauffman, "Here Comes the Skywalk." *Hartford Advocate,* August 2, 1978.

45. Mark Pazniokas, "Pratt Street Renovation Is Planned." *Hartford Courant,* May 29, 1986.

46. Monroe Karmen, "Businessmen, Politicians Seek to Renew a City and Help Suburbs Too." *Wall Street Journal,* July 26, 1972.

47. Aron Hall, "It's Bold, It's Big, Tomorrow Starts Now." *Hartford Courant,* May 7, 1972; *Hartford Courant,* January 23, 1973; *Willimantic Chronicle,* March 13, 1973.

48. Karmen.

49. J. Hubert Smith, " 'New Town' Cost Told." *Hartford Courant,* January 31, 1972.

50. See S. Jerome Pratter, "Strategy for City Investment," In *How Cities Can Grow Old Gracefully.* Washington, DC: Committee on Banking, Finance and Urban Affairs, U.S. House of Representatives, 1977, pp. 79–90.

51. Quotes in this paragraph are drawn from a copy of the unpublished

"Confidential Addendum" to the Hartford Process memorandum released in January 1975.

52. Elissa Papirno and Bill Grava, "Process Head Rejects Puerto Rican 'Cutback'," *Hartford Courant,* January 18, 1975.

53. Thomas D. Williams, "City Wins Lawsuit Blocking U.S. Funds." *Hartford Courant,* January 29, 1976.

54. Lawrence Fellows, "Hartford Battles Suburbs for Federal Aid." *New York Times,* November 17, 1975.

55. Williams.

56. Arnold H. Lubasch, "Ban Lifted on U.S. Aid to Hartford Suburbs," *New York Times,* August 16, 1977.

57. Lawrence Fellows, "Hartford vs. Suburbs: Case Closed." *New York Times,* January 22, 1978.

58. Bruce Kauffman and Cliff Schechtman, "Keeping Out the Poor People." *Hartford Advocate,* June 13, 1979.

Chapter 13

Fiscal and Developmental Crises in Black Suburbs

John R. Logan

On the nights of November 20 and 21, 1985, in the predominantly white Elmwood section of Philadelphia, local residents demonstrated the importance of race in the city. Angry gatherings of two to four hundred people massed outside two homes, shouting "We want them out!" and "Beat it!" The occupants of those homes, a black couple and an interracial couple, had recently purchased them through the Veterans Administration. Neighbors believed that the Veterans Administration had given preference to minority buyers, or had been manipulated by realtors engaged in systematic blockbusting in the area.

Philadelphia's Mayor W. Wilson Goode declared a state of emergency in the neighborhood, banning groups of four or more persons from gathering on public property. The City's Human Relations Commission and the Philadelphia Board of Realtors imposed a ban on real estate solicitations, hoping to quell rumors of blockbusting. The black couple moved out, frightened of violence, and soon afterward their home—with their furniture, clothing, and other possessions—was burned.[1] An anonymous letter mailed to local residents in December called on them to organize a "White Residents Association":

> Most of the old white neighborhoods are gone now—you've even watched them die. And you know what killed them. So when the first non-whites showed up in your neighborhood (courtesy of the Federal Government), you knew it was time to act. Southwest Philly's last white enclave decided to fight for its life.[2]

Racial incidents in American cities, not just Philadelphia, are an old story. Between 1982 and 1985, the Philadelphia Commission on Human Relations investigated 49 cases of ethnic or racial tension arising from a move into an inhospitable neighborhood.[3] These cases do not much surprise us. They match our image of entrenched ethnic working-class neighborhoods, under siege in cities with growing black, hispanic, and Asian minorities, engaged in a last rear guard action before joining white flight to the suburbs. New York City, for example, lost 1.4 million whites between 1970 and 1980, while its total minority population increased by 570,000. Philadelphia experienced a similar change but on a smaller scale, losing 283,000 whites and gaining 23,000 minority residents.[4]

These movements of population have their roots in the profound economic transformation of metropolitan centers in the post–World War II era. Central cities have shed their former roles as centers of manufacturing, losing industrial jobs to their suburbs, to newer regions of the country, and to foreign competition. This process, which many now refer to as deindustrialization, has radically changed the structure of opportunities in the city. In place of union jobs at moderate hourly wages, cities now offer a more polarized job market: increasing opportunities in highly rewarded professional and technical occupations associated with finance, producer services, and corporate management, and even greater expansion in low-wage clerical, sales, services, and non-union manufacturing.

This shift is obvious in the neighborhoods. From one perspective, Philadelphia is a city on the rebound. Its downtown is taking on a new look with high-rise office buildings and hotels looming over Independence Hall. Townhouses have become fashionable again for a younger and more affluent crowd, and the neighborhoods renovated by these people are also drawing a new variety of shops and restaurants. Philadelphia is prosperous. But the more deeply entrenched ghettos, the slow abandonment of working-class areas, and the struggles of growing minority populations to improve their standing in the city reveal another Philadelphia. Racial incidents of the type described above reflect a competition for resources, for both jobs and neighborhoods, in an environment which has less and less to offer less affluent people.

The phenomenon of "downtown prosperity and neighborhood decline" is described clearly elsewhere in this volume, in the Hartford study by Neubeck and Ratcliff. In this chapter, I will broaden the discussion beyond the boundaries of the central city, to show that similar processes of uneven development—of prosperity in some privileged areas alongside enclaves of deepening poverty—also occur in the suburbs. I believe that suburbanization has always been a stratifying process, separating rich from poor, black from white. The suburbs have even marketed themselves this way—leave crime behind, place your children in schools where you can count on the right kind of classmates, invest in a house where your neighbors will protect their investment and yours in the bargain.

Recently the inherent inequalities among suburbs have been intensified by fundamental changes in their metropolitan role. "The city" has been moving to some suburbs in the form of luxury condominiums, office centers, regional shopping malls, and industrial parks. It has been moving to other suburbs in the form of disinvestment in older factories, dilapidation of older housing, increasing numbers of people dependent on public assistance, and increasing crime. What could be understood in a redeveloping central city as "downtown" prosperity and "neighborhood" decline shows up in suburbia as a competitive development game in which there are big winners and equally big losers. And similar to the central city situation, the competition for resources has an important racial component.

Black and White Suburbs in the Philadelphia Metropolitan Area

Indeed, blacks, too, have joined the flight to the suburbs. Philadelphia's overall increase in minority population was due to growth in its hispanic and Asian communities. It lost 13,000 blacks in the 1970s, while the proportion of blacks in Philadelphia's suburbs jumped from 12.4 percent to 15.4 percent during the decade.[5] Social scientists who have investigated this phenomenon generally agree that the move is fraught with problems. While most suburbs have remained nearly all-white, the suburban black population has been resegregated into a small number of communities. These black suburbs are much like the central city neighborhoods which blacks left behind—poor, densely populated, and deteriorated in comparison to other suburbs. And they have one additional defect: their local governments, and by and large their schools, are cut off from the central city treasury that previously supported their public services. They are on their own in a competitive environment, with little to tax but their homes, going deeper into debt and increasingly dependent on federal and state assistance.[6] As a result, black suburbs face serious constraints in their efforts to pursue community or neighborhood development.

Black suburbs are the necessary result of a dual housing market. In a dual housing market, a variety of agencies, including realtors and financial institutions, "steer" or "contain" blacks in suburbs that whites no longer find desirable.[7] Banks and insurance companies deny blacks mortgages in white areas and "red-line" interracial and black areas as unsuitable for further investment.[8] Suburban governments themselves restrict black access to housing through exclusionary zoning.[9] Realtors use their monopoly over housing information to direct blacks and whites to appropriate "black" and "white" communities.[10] In a tight housing market, this practice is highly profitable. One study found that blacks in St. Louis paid 15 percent more for similar housing than whites in the same neighborhood, while housing costs were over 25 percent more in black neighborhoods than in white neighborhoods.[11]

In this context, another Philadelphia story takes on special relevance, this one suburban. Mrs. Patricia Bailey moved into Darby Township, in suburban Delaware County just west of the city line, in 1981. "My nerves were almost shattered during the first six months. It's the worst feeling to lay your head down and not be able to sleep—or to hear a pin drop and jump up and say, 'What's that?' " Mrs. Bailey's house suffered 27 broken windows in the first week. Then a hatchet was thrown through her front window, a cross was burned on her lawn, her car's gas tank filled with dirt, the car splattered with black paint, and a fetal pig left on her front steps.[12] Darby Township was a small town of 3,500 in 1950, with a 78 percent black population. But suburban subdivisions in the northern part of town created a large area that is now 97 percent white, while the southern end has become 99 percent black.

Pennsylvania's Human Relations Commission reported in 1981 that blacks "in Delaware County have experienced terroristic acts of violence and other forms of harassment when they tried to move into or live peaceably in eastern Delaware County."[13] More recently Philadelphia's Inter-Agency Task Force on Civil Tension counted 19 racial incidents in Philadelphia during 1985, nearly matched by the 18 in Delaware County. These included 6 cross-burnings at the homes of blacks and interracial couples.[14]

Such incidents are only the most dramatic evidence of racial problems in suburban areas which generally parallel the situation in large central cities. My purpose in this chapter is to document the more routine issues in black suburbanization. It begins with a general overview of the kinds of communities in which Philadelphia's black sub-urbanites live. The chapter then turns to specific areas of concern: discrimination in housing, job discrimination, the segregation—and desegregation—of schools, and prospects for urban renewal and community development.

Philadelphia's suburban ring gained 55,000 black residents between 1970 and 1980 (the number increasing from 190,000 in 1970 to 245,000 in 1980). But the suburbs were highly segregated in 1970 and remained so. The U.S. Bureau of the Census recognizes more than one hundred communities in the metropolitan area around Philadelphia. One of every five blacks in this ring lives in just one of these communities; namely, Camden, New Jersey (53% black in 1980). Another one in every ten lives in Chester, Pennsylvania (57% black in 1980). One small town in the New Jersey portion of the metropolitan area, Lawnside, was 98.5 percent black in 1980.

These suburbs into which blacks have been moving are different from other suburbs in important ways, all of which lead to the conclusion that blacks are steered to areas of less opportunity, and that such areas are no longer desired by whites. There are some illustrative comparisons between suburbs which were more than 10 percent black in 1980, those that had between 1 percent and 10 percent black population (referred to as "mixed"), and those which had less than 1 percent black residents (designated "white"). (See Table 13.1.)

The data on income and housing in each community are taken from the 1980 Census of Population. (See Table 13.1.) "Median family income" is the income of the family that falls right in the middle of the

TABLE 13.1. Comparison of black, mixed, and white suburbs Philadelphia (1977-1982)

	Black	Mixed	White
Median family income	$19,850	$23,300	$21,900
% Poor	47%	34%	35%
% Rental housing	43%	34%	30%
Property tax base/capita	$10,590	$13,550	$13,150
Debt/capita	$103	$64	$44
Burglary rate	1991	873	805
Larceny and theft rate	3618	2381	1901
Assault rate	591	125	117

income distribution in the community, and that thus might be considered the "typical" family. The average for black communities was $19,850—$2,000 to $4,000 less than the average for mixed or white suburbs. The "proportion poor" is the proportion of families whose incomes were less than 80 percent of the average in the Philadelphia metropolitan area; it therefore tells us the percentage of families in the given community who are at the bottom end of the income distribution. In the average black suburb, nearly half of local families had incomes this low, compared to only about one-third in other suburbs. Finally, the "proportion of rental housing" tells us to what extent residents of the community live in apartments or other housing that they do not own. This measure is often believed to reflect not only people's socioeconomic status, but also their stake in the community and their sense of permanence. Again, black suburbs have a much higher proportion of rental housing than mixed or white suburbs. (See Table 13.1.)

The 1977 Census of Governments and state reports on municipal finances provide information on communities' taxes. (See Table 13.1.) The "property tax base" is the total value of real property that municipal governments and school districts can tax in order to support public services. Property taxes are the principal source of revenues for most local governments in the United States. Divided by the number of residents to yield a per capita figure, this figure is the best single measure of each suburb's governmental wealth. Suburbs with a high property tax base can supply more services at a lower tax rate than can suburbs with a poor property tax base. Black suburbs have an average tax base of about $10,000 per capita, which is 30 percent less than mixed or white suburbs. (See Table 13.1.) One result of this governmental poverty is high municipal indebtedness. Black suburbs are more likely to run a deficit and to borrow funds in order to make improvements in local roads, parking, and the like. Their total municipal debt per capita is just over $100, nearly double that of mixed and white suburbs. In the long term, such debt threatens fiscal crises for the communities, a possibility that will be considered in more detail below. Even when there is no threat of municipal bankruptcy, a weak tax base undermines the community's ability to provide basic services, especially public education.

As for crime rates, three types of offenses have been selected for which the Federal Bureau of Investigation published data in the 1982 *Uniform Crime Reports* series (See Table 13.1). These are burglary, larceny/theft, and aggravated assault. For many people, crime and the fear of crime constitute an important motive for moving to the suburbs, where crime rates are typically less than half that of central cities. But it appears that this advantage does not accrue to residents of black suburbs. The larceny and theft rate in Philadelphia's black suburbs is more than 50 percent higher than in mixed suburbs. For assault, the difference is even greater: the assault rate in black suburbs is more than four times the rate in mixed or white suburbs.

The "average" black suburb is poor, fiscally stressed, and crime-ridden compared to other suburbs. Behind the averages, however, are some interesting differences. (See Table 13.2.) Data have been assembled for three black suburbs whose experiences are reported in more detail in the following sections. Chester, Camden, and Yeadon have in common the fact that all have uncommonly high proportions of black residents, proportions which have increased in the last twenty years.

Camden, New Jersey, just across the river from Philadelphia, is the largest of the black suburbs; with over 80,000 residents, it is larger than many U.S. central cities. Camden was formerly a prosperous industrial town with a variety of middle- and working-class neighborhoods. It housed the corporate headquarters and factories for several product lines of RCA and Campbell's Soup Company. Its docks were an important transshipment center, supporting a thriving warehouse complex and many related businesses. Today, Camden is among the most distressed communities in the country, suffering the losses of deindustrialization without any of the compensating gains that continue to make cities like Philadelphia economically viable. In 1982 Camden's last department store closed, along with Van Sciver's Furniture Store, the largest surviving retail business.

TABLE 13.2 Community characteristics of selected black suburbs

	Chester	*Camden*	*Yeadon*
Median family income	$14,214	$10,607	$21,240
% Poor	60%	73%	38%
% Rental housing	46%	46%	32%
Property tax base/capita	$4,571	$5,395	$8,284
Debt/capita	$226	$217	$8
Burglary rate	2948	4304	895
Larceny and theft rate	3915	5330	2174
Assault rate	2166	1100	222

"The city no longer has any supermarkets, movie theaters, automobile dealers, or restaurants, except fast food outlets. . . . Nearly half the housing stock is substandard, and some blocks are rows of rickety vacant houses. Schoolchildren here are outscored in every other city in New Jersey in reading and mathematics skills. . . . More than half of Camden's population is on some form of public assistance and the unemployment rate is 19 percent.[15]

Camden is by far the poorest of the black suburbs, with a median family income of only about $10,600. (See Table 13.2.) In fact its median family income is barely half that of the average *black* suburb; its property tax base is no better, and it has double the crime rate of other black suburbs.

Chester, Pennsylvania, is in little better shape. Chester is like many of the aging industrial satellites that ring central cities in the Northeast and Midwest—suburban in location but industrial in function. During World War II, the town's shipbuilding industry was at its peak, producing Liberty Ships for the nation's wartime merchant marine. But employment in shipbuilding is way down, as are the numbers of jobs in other local firms, such as the Scott Paper Company. Chester has an even weaker property tax base than Camden. (See Table 13.2.) Like Camden, but less extremely so, Chester is poorer than the average black suburb, and suffers from higher crime rates. By 1983, about 5 percent of its total housing stock lay vacant and abandoned, a situation reflected in the description of one street: "On its lower end, Potter Street is deteriorating, its vacant buildings left to the vandals and vagrants, the rodents and roaches; its residents, left to their own devices to keep one step ahead of decay."[16]

Furthermore, it is estimated that hundreds of people are living in abandoned buildings without heat. A local newspaper reported on one homeless woman:

Lillian Robinson, 26, is one of those who lives in a house the government says is unfit. . . . Although the unheated house is two stories, she stays in only the front room on the first floor. There are gouged-out places in the wall where someone has dug out electrical plugs, wiring, hunks of insulation. She keeps a twin bed propped vertically against the door separating the front room from the kitchen. The kitchen is unusable because there is no hot water, no stove and no refrigerator. . . . The bed helps block the cold air from the front room.... Why doesn't she leave? "Where am I going to go?"[17]

One of the few predominantly black suburbs in the United States that has remained middle class is Yeadon, Pennsylvania. It was never an employment center, and owes its existence to the outward migration of middle-class homeowners who continued to work in nearby Philadelphia. Its median family income of over $21,000 is nearly equal to that of the average white suburb, and its homes are mostly owner-occupied. (See Table 13.2.) Because it is a dormitory suburb with few local businesses, Yeadon has a weak property tax base, which is an indicator of potential fiscal problems. But its debt is negligible, and crime rates are comparable to most white suburbs.

The 1980 census figures actually understate Yeadon's relative prosperity. Most of the borough's poor black residents once lived in a 1,000-unit low-income apartment development, Park View Court, built in 1972. According to the borough manager, Dan Fox, as many as 40 percent of all local police calls used to be to that complex. But Park View Court was sold in 1981 to a Cleveland management firm, which has since evicted most welfare tenants and converted it to private market housing. Yeadon seems to be proof that black suburbanization is not necessarily ghettoization. Its experience, then, is especially interesting as a test of what race relations in the suburbs can be like under the best of conditions.

Let us turn now to to some of the concrete manifestations of racism in suburban development, starting with discrimination in housing in Yeadon.

"You'll Be More Comfortable with Your Own Kind"

Yeadon is a small borough, or municipality, bordering on southwestern Philadelphia, and it is near Darby Township where Mrs. Bailey experienced such trouble in 1981. The borough has traditionally been divided into separate white and black sections. Few blacks had bought homes in "white Yeadon" until there was a sudden increase in sales volume in early 1978. Yeadon was thrown into an uproar; rumors of blockbusting and racial steering led many whites to put their homes up for sale before it was too late.

According to Dr. William H. Harris, one-time head of the borough's Human Relations Council, "Real estate people were trying to turn Yeadon into an all-black enclave. They were steering just blacks to the borough."[18] The borough's official response was to forbid the use of for-sale signs, as was done more recently in Elmwood. Again in Dr. Harris's words, "It gives the borough the appearance of stability and cuts down on panic selling."

Racial steering and blockbusting are hard to prove. There is some evidence from a report of the audit of the practices of one real estate firm, conducted during July and August of 1978 by the Landsdowne–Upper Darby Area Fair Housing Council.[19] The Council used a standard method of testing for discrimination. Four teams of testers were sent to the real estate broker over a 17-day period, each team including one white couple and one black couple, who gave similar stories of their backgrounds and housing needs. For example, both couples in the first team said that they were married, and were seeking a duplex or row house in the $25,000–32,000 price range. Others were similarly matched, looking in various price ranges.

The results of these tests are surprisingly strong. In three of the four cases, no houses were shown in Yeadon to the white pair and no houses outside Yeadon were shown to the black pair. In the fourth case, the white pair was shown one house in Yeadon, but outside its "sensitive" area, whereas the black pair was shown one house in Yeadon, but inside the "sensitive" area. Altogether, white pairs visited or were told about 16 houses, of which 15 were outside Yeadon. Black pairs visited or were told about 18 houses, of which 14 were inside Yeadon. This disparity came about despite specific comments by two of the white pairs that houses in Yeadon were "a good buy," or that they were indifferent as to the racial composition of the neighborhood. One black pair "was repeatedly told they would be taken only to places where they would feel comfortable. [The] salesperson commented that he could tell them this 'as long as the Human Relations Commission wasn't listening.'"[20]

For black homeseekers, being shown a house in Yeadon meant that they weren't shown homes they could afford in adjacent white suburbs. The extremes to which some realtors would go are demonstrated by a case cited in a previous audit report by the Council. A black homeseeker asked to see a house in Havertown which was advertised through the Multiple Listing Service. The salesperson who attempted to arrange a showing was told by her broker that "the listing agent... took the house off the market upon learning the prospective buyer's race," and that "the listing agent's representative had come to the office to warn that 'no one had better show blacks his listings again.' "[21]

Such behavior is patently illegal but common, and hard to pin down without systematic testing. Most individuals have no way to know for sure that they are being treated differently because of their race. A more recent newspaper story describes the treatment experienced by a 71-year-old black woman who applied for an apartment unit:

> What sticks in Mary Armstrong's mind, she says, is how politely she was treated. The manager of the Long Lane Apartments in Upper Darby was warm and ingratiating. He made small talk and showered her with unsolicited advice about the real estate market and how to get the best price for a home. Despite his seeming good will, the manager lied to Armstrong. . . . when he told her that no units were available.[22]

These are not isolated cases. Testing by the Pennsylvania Human Relations Commission in 1983 found the minority tester was given false or incomplete information or otherwise discriminated against in 26 percent of cases.[23] Testing on a national level by the U.S. Department of Housing and Urban Development suggests an even higher level of discrimination, finding that a black homeseeker who makes three contacts with a realtor or apartment complex is virtually certain to be discriminated against at least once.[24]

There is further evidence that racial discrimination is not perpetrated only in the private sector: public housing in the United States, even in the suburbs, is often racially segregated. One clear case is found in Chester, where the public housing authority was brought to court by the Pennsylvania Human Relations Commission (HRC) in the early 1970s *(Pennsylvania Human Relations Commission V. Chester Housing Authority)*. This case went as far as the U.S. Supreme Court before the Chester Housing Authority consented to a desegregation order.

The HRC suit alleged racial segregation of four housing projects administered by Chester Housing Authority, and charged that the Authority's actions promoted school segregation in Chester. The following figures cited for the summer of 1969 suggest a strong prima facie case of discrimination:

| Lamokin Village | 0 whites, 346 blacks |
| Ruth L. Bennett Homes | 0 whites, 385 blacks |

William Penn Village	20 whites, 257 blacks
McCaffery Village	347 whites, 0 blacks

The HRC investigation revealed multiple cases of black prospective tenants' being denied housing until a unit became available at a "black" project, even though a vacancy existed in the "white" project and vice versa for whites. For example, Larrie Ellis, a black woman, applied for a 3-bedroom unit in August 1970. Eleanor Hayes, a white woman, applied for a 3-bedroom unit in November 1970. Ms. Hayes was rented a unit in McCaffery Village on December 18, and Ms. Ellis was rented a unit in Ruth L. Bennett Homes on February 1, 1971. Ms. Ellis applied three months earlier, but was forced to wait until six weeks after Ms. Hayes received an apartment. Clearly the Chester Housing Authority maintained two waiting lists, one for blacks and another for whites.

The Human Relations Commission ordered the Housing Authority to cease renting to blacks in the black projects, and to whites in the white projects, until desegregation was achieved. This order was affirmed by the Pennsylvania State Supreme Court, and allowed to stand by the U.S. Supreme Court in 1975. At this writing, however, the projects remain largely segregated. Blacks who moved into McCaffery Village were subjected to vandalism, and most whites refused apartments in the three black projects. The Human Relations Commission, charged with enforcing the order, is only now conducting a compliance review on the case.

At one level, discrimination in housing is a personal tragedy for people who are unable to choose freely a community within the metropolitan housing market which suits their own family's needs. Systematic racial steering has consequences also for whole communities. It places the futures of communities into outside hands, disrupting the efforts local people have made to establish a positive reputation. Businesses, especially retailers, avoid investing in black suburbs just as they avoid black neighborhoods in central cities. Residents must increasingly work and shop outside the community, thereby contributing to the economic base of their more affluent white neighbors and undercutting their own development chances. All suburbs are already involved in a destructive competitive struggle. Adding racial steering and residential segregation to the picture tilts the development game one more notch against disadvantaged people.

How Many Years?

In 1954, the U.S. Supreme Court held that segregated schools are inherently discriminatory and unconstitutional *(Brown v. Board of Education)*. School desegregation is still a hot issue in Philadelphia. It has also been a volatile concern in the suburbs. Let us begin with an example in Chester.

The 1963–64 school year in Chester witnessed a series of protest demonstrations by black residents on school segregation. At this time, the city was about 40 percent black. Demonstrations began in November 1963, when an organization called the Freedom Now Committee demanded that the School Board relieve overcrowding at predominantly black Franklin Elementary school. This school was designed around 1910 to hold 500 pupils, but had an enrollment of over 1,200 in 1963. One class, the superintendent had acknowledged, was being conducted in a basement coal bin.[25] A total of 240 demonstrators were arrested in November before the district agreed to transfer some of these students to other schools. Again on March 27–28, 1964, scores of arrests were made during the course of massive demonstrations, this time directed at the whole pattern of segregation among local schools. In the intervening period, the Mayor had appointed a Chester Commission on Human Relations, which recommended integration of schools and faculties; its recommendations were rejected by the School Board. During the next four weeks, more than 600 persons were arrested and another 24 injured in daily demonstrations; at one point state police were called in to reinforce local police.

By mid-April, Governor William Scranton was under pressure to resolve the situation. Scranton was preparing a challenge to Senator Barry Goldwater's bid for the Republican Presidential nomination in the party's upcoming convention. At a time of national furor on civil rights issues, and given Scranton's political base in his party's liberal wing, the Governor had to be sensitive to charges of police brutality by state troopers. He met personally with representatives of the School Board and the Freedom Now Committee, and requested the Pennsylvania Human Relations Commission to intervene.

After holding hearings through the summer, the HRC reached the following conclusions:

(1) Respondent maintains segregated, all-Negro and substantially all-Negro public schools within its school system, (2) re-

spondent has established public school zones which confine the
Negro pupils to all-Negro schools, (3) respondent has failed to
make available kindergartens in sufficient number to accommodate the children of Negroes living in Chester, (4) respondent
assigns only Negro teachers and only Negro clerks to the all-
Negro schools, (5) respondent has permitted the physical condition of the all-Negro school buildings to be inferior to that of
other school buildings in its system, and (6) respondent has
failed to accept or adopt any affirmative plan whereby the public
schools it administers will be effectively desegregated within a
reasonable time *(Pennsylvania Human Relations Commission v.
Chester School District).*

HRC ordered desegregation of one junior high school (of four in
the district) and five elementary schools (of eleven in the district) whose
enrollments were either all-negro or substantially all-negro. The HRC
action was affirmed by the Pennsylvania State Supreme Court in 1967
(Pennsylvania Human Relations Commission v. Chester School District).
This case clearly was the major step toward state action on de facto
segregation, overturning the argument that since school segregation
resulted from discrimination in housing, civil rights legislation did not
make school boards responsible for school desegregation.

Chester is not the only suburban school district to face official ac-
cusations of segregation. The HRC has also taken action against
Coatesville, Norristown, William Penn School District in Delaware
County, and Darby Township in Delaware County. Reaching acceptable desegregation plans in these cases has often been a tedious process, involving negotiations between the school boards, the Human
Rights Commission, local parent groups, and federal courts. According
to one superintendent of schools, the problem is how to desegregate
without losing large numbers of white students to private and parochial
schools.[26]

In many cases, school segregation becomes an issue because
blacks who move into a community are steered into black enclaves. In
other cases, the question is how a school district draws attendance
boundaries. In the state of Pennsylvania, many small school districts
were consolidated in 1972 into larger districts for reasons of administrative efficiency and cost. In one such case, the Darby Township
School District, which had a high proportion of black students living
in only one portion of the district, had desegregated in 1968 under court
order. In 1972 Darby was merged with the predominantly white

Collingdale, Folcroft, and Sharon Hill districts. The administration of the new Southeast Delco School District decided to maintain the prior attendance areas. As a result, Darby Township Elementary School had a black enrollment of 88 percent in 1977, while the district's three other elementary schools ranged from only 0.5 percent to 3.8 percent black. Because Darby Township students were all assigned to schools within Darby, many were bused past white schools closer to their homes, even though those schools had unused capacity. Following a complaint by the Human Relations Commission, the U.S. District Court found in 1980 *(Velma Mitchell, et al. v. Mark A. McCunney, et al.)* that the school board had "intentionally maintained a segregated school system."

School desegregation means more than changing student enrollments. Another important issue is faculty and administration, and both civil rights groups and school boards are sensitive to the racial implications of personnel actions. In 1982, the Pennsylvania State Chapter of the NAACP censured the West Chester Area School District for changes in job titles of three black administrators (from Assistant Superintendent to Director of Pupils and Personnel, from High School Vice Principal to Supervisor of Specially Funded Programs, and from Supervisor of Federally Funded Programs to High School Guidance Counselor). NAACP members from West Chester drafted the resolution. One member, Charles Melton, said concern for job security had kept the black administrators from complaining: "There's a plantation system where they are afraid to speak out . . . [District officials] don't want black administrators and they're doing what they can to get rid of them."[27]

Another perhaps more emotional issue in many districts has been the claim for recognition of black history and cultural heroes. The demand to include Dr. Martin Luther King, Jr.'s birthday on the calendar of school holidays became a central rallying point for a reviving NAACP chapter in Kennett Square.[28] "We're 100 years behind the times here," a local NAACP officer was quoted as saying. Another officer suggested that the public march of about sixty persons to a local church to commemorate Dr. King's birthday "made history in Kennett."

In Coatesville, where about 28 percent of the students are black, a racial slur used by a school board member ignited two months of protests and hostility. In February 1983, more than three hundred people (in a town of about ten thousand), attended a school board meeting to demand the board member's resignation. At the meeting were representatives of the teachers' association, the NAACP, YWCA, and parent-teacher groups.[29] By mid-March, both local newspapers and the Chamber of Commerce had urged the board member to resign. "People here feel that as long as he's on the board, he's completely lost his credibility, irredeemably so," said the Rev. Charles Willis, pastor of the Tabernacle Baptist Church. Paul Johnson, City Council president and its only elected black, added, "It was gradually getting to be a stable situation—I don't know if you'd call it 'harmonious'—but now [the slur] has polarized some segments."[30]

Coatesville—Race in a Factory Town

The heat generated by racial issues in the schools and in housing cannot be understood in isolation from events in other sectors of the community. In Coatesville we can see how racial tensions are linked to deeper economic development trends.

Coatesville has in fact witnessed a long series of public controversies involving race. While the school board member's racial remark was being openly aired, other problems were brewing beneath the surface in the Coatesville Police Department. The town's first black police chief, Chief John Griffy, promoted through the ranks, was involved in a struggle within the police force. It has been alleged that trouble started from his first week in office, with notes slipped under his door saying, "Nigger go home." By mid-1984, a public petition signed by 23 of the department's 30 officers, charged that he "has alienated all the police officers of the City . . . and has acted in a manner inconsistent with the public welfare" by fixing tickets, setting arrest quotas, and hiring or promoting on the basis of favoritism. Dr. Charles Butler, chair of the Pennsylvania NAACP and vice chairman of the national organization of NAACP, countercharged that "Griffy is a black police chief and the police department is predominantly white. The white officers don't like him. If he was white, this wouldn't be happening."[31] Chief Griffy resigned.

These issues have their roots in more fundamental problems of racism in the community, clearly linked to the processes of industrialization and deindustrialization that have transformed the metropolis as a whole. Like Camden and Chester, Coatesville is a declining industrial center, in this case a steel town dominated by a single company, Lukens Steel. Blacks moved into the steel mill after the early

1950s, in a period of expansion; between 1967 and 1984, about 1,500 blacks worked at the mill. Black workers chronically complained of racial discrimination and harassment at Lukens, and in 1973 filed a federal lawsuit against Lukens Steel, United Steelworkers of America, and two Lukens Union locals. After a trial that began in 1980, U.S. District Judge John Fullam ruled that the defendants had discriminated for years against blacks at the Coatesville plant, and had given tacit encouragement to racial harassment by individual workers.

Judge Fullam found that the company had intentionally discriminated against black workers in initial job assignments, in promotions and transfers to better-paying jobs, in denying incentive pay in certain areas, in promoting workers to salaried positions, and in tolerating racial harassment.[32] He noted the massive amount of incontrovertible evidence of historical discrimination on account of race at Lukens. He went on:

> For decades the races at Lukens were segregated as a matter of official company policy. It was not until 1966 that segregation in locker room facilities was eliminated.... It is apparent that Lukens management preferred to avoid confronting racial issues if at all possible.... The net results were too-frequent toleration of continued harassment of blacks by whites on racial grounds, passive encouragement of the belief that individual acts of racial discrimination would go unpunished, and a tendency to presume that any charge of racial discrimination was, almost by definition, either totally unfounded or quite trivial.[33]

Coatesville's experience gives weight to those who argue that racial conflicts are usually tied to struggles over jobs and resources. Race relations in the 1980s are directly linked here to a history of job discrimination, reinforced by residential and school segregation. Many people have come to believe that advancement in any one area depends upon gains in all three.

One vision is that black communities must take control of their own futures, using political tools of autonomous local government to seek adequate social services and education, housing, and economic opportunity. Many cities have found that plans to improve their economic base rise or fall on their ability to offer a trained work force and a positive living environment. Improvements in these social dimensions in turn depend upon marshalling the existing economic resources in the community. In this view, the future depends on community control of a comprehensive program of urban redevelopment. Is this possible?

Tripping over Your Own Bootstraps

The first lesson in urban redevelopment is that depressed communities cannot pull themselves up by their own bootstraps. When Camden's former Mayor Angelo Errichetti was convicted in the Abscam bribery cases in 1981, his successor, Melvin Primas, found the city in such bad financial condition that he raised property taxes 88 percent in his first week in office. Nonetheless, after one month the city was bankrupt and the New Jersey Department of Community Affairs had to take over its financial affairs. In 1982 the state backed a Camden bond issue for debt consolidation and the city got its bond rating and formal financial independence back.[34]

Since that time, Camden has been involved in extensive planning for economic rejuvenation, bidding to reverse the long-term deindustrialization of the city. Nearly half of the city has been declared an "enterprise zone," eligible for special state assistance for new employers. Lacking prospects for major private developments, Mayor Primas sought a medium-security prison for North Camden, and the $30–$40 million project began in 1982. Part of the deal negotiated with the state was a commitment of $250,000 for improving the neighborhood around the prison, and $450,000 annually to local firms outside the state bidding process. The prison will create 300 permanent jobs, and pay $1 million to the city in taxes.

The prison is part of an $194 million plan for waterfront redevelopment, which includes a new site for the Campbell Soup Company's corporate headquarters, an engineering plant for RCA, and a 23-acre park including a marina and an aquarium. Besides the prison, funds from the county, state, and federal governments have supported a new transportation terminal and four county office buildings. Such projects are being pushed by the Greater Camden Movement, which includes the city's major employers: Campbell Soup Company (350 jobs), RCA (4,000 jobs), the Camden branch of Rutgers University, the southern headquarters of New Jersey Bell, and Cooper University Hospital.

But it is clear that redevelopment is dependent upon continued state and federal assistance, which is very much in doubt at the start of 1986. So far there is little evidence that the massive flow of private development funds into downtown Philadelphia has reached across the river to Camden. And in the meantime there are social costs of Camden's development strategy. In particular, the emphasis on the waterfront, close to corporate offices, is perceived to be at the expense of housing and neighborhood preservation. Michael Norman reports that Mayor Primas has decided in his second term to concentrate less on economic development and more on strengthening neighborhoods. But, he notes, "spokesmen for the poor have so far been excluded in the planning for the new Camden. The city was once strong with community and neighborhood groups. While many still function, their influence has waned."[35] Most concretely, these groups have been cut off from the community development funds which they previously administered, with decision making now highly centralized in City Hall.

A similar situation, and similar conflicts, are found in Chester, which lost 9,000 jobs between 1979 and 1983. As a long-time Republican stronghold, Chester has been well placed to seek federal development assistance. The U.S. General Services Administration opened a major new office center in 1983, and the ailing Pennsylvania Shipbuilding Company has recently received a $10 million contract from the U.S. Navy. Using federal grant funds, the city has subsidized two major private developments, a chemical plant ($5 million grant) and a computer facilities center for a major bank ($1.8 million grant). More recently the city has discussed locating a new medium-security federal prison within its borders.

Once again, these developments are dependent on federal assistance, which is likely to decline in the near future. In fact, federal revenue sharing in 1986 provides $2.5 million to the city treasury, supporting the full cost of Chester's police department. But revenue sharing is expected to end in 1987. It is unclear how the city will police its streets by then, much less how it will subsidize development projects.

Chester's location adjacent to a major interstate highway (I-95), the Chester Amtrak station, the Delaware River, and Philadelphia International Airport gives it some development potential. This potential depends largely, however, on displacing the current residents of the deteriorated East End. Housing prices in the area are so low that a 3-bedroom row house could be bought in 1982 for $5,500. This means that paying people for their properties, or providing moving expenses for renters, would not be sufficient to ensure that they can find alternative housing in another location.

In 1982, a planning study by a consortium of local businesses backed by Pennsylvania Shipbuilding and Scott Paper proposed large-scale housing redevelopment using vacant and tax-delinquent units. A neighborhood group in the city's East End expressed fears that any project would be designed for affluent outsiders. A spokesperson for local residents agreed "that this area needs to be rehabilitated. But when this study was done, the community was not aware of it, nor were we consulted. . . . We have nobody to fight for us, and that's why the people in this neighborhood are up in arms."[36]

More recently, the McLaughlin Development Corporation of Philadelphia has proposed a $120-million light industrial development on 60 acres of partially occupied land. One local resident, Josephine Hood, says the developers regard Chester as a Monopoly board. "But the pieces aren't the red and green houses on that Monopoly board that don't give any resistance. . . . They're going to find out that while they're playing the game of Monopoly, we're playing the game of Life."[37]

Some local groups have acted aggressively to take control over redevelopment on behalf of poor residents. In 1983 the Chester Welfare Rights Organization seized eight abandoned houses to shelter people who had been removed from the welfare rolls by the state. Symptomatically, Chester's Redevelopment Authority had been planning to demolish the houses for a parking lot.[38] Such brash actions and tough rhetoric show that people are aware of their dilemma. But independent community organizations have little influence over development policies in a town which many observers consider to be dominated by a county-wide Republican Party machine,[39] where the first black mayor was installed only in January 1986, and where there is still a white majority in the City Council.

Conclusion

Black suburbs illustrate a broader phenomenon of urbanization: that the organization of space is a means of organizing inequality. Racial inequality is an enduring reality in American society and has found expression in many forms. Space is an important form because so many resources are tied to location: access to schools, to jobs, to social services, and to networks of sociability depend partly upon where you live. Space then, is a resource, and is therefore not only an arena but also a reason for conflict between social groups. Protecting "turf" means protecting capital, prestige, and power.

The deindustrialization of American cities has provided a fertile setting for racial conflict over issues of turf. The urban white working class has been trapped between the outward movement of jobs and the very real costs of following those jobs—particularly in an era of high interest rates and unemployment. Those who remain in the city have neither the resources nor the control of their futures which they once enjoyed. At the same time, gentrification and urban renewal, and the growth of the city's minority population press on their borders.

Social scientists interested in the community dimension of racial inequality and conflict have traditionally focused on the central cities. The very scale of black migration to Northern cities earlier in this century, combined with the exclusion of blacks from the suburbs, justified this focus. This tradition is so strong that even now some social scientists use black suburbanization as an indicator of progress in race relations.

The cases described in this chapter show that the racial problems of the central cities are not solved by the opening up of the suburbs. In several related forms—especially discrimination in housing, school segregation, and job discrimination—the same problems arise in the suburbs. Because the majority of black suburbs are former industrial satellites that have themselves suffered from deindustrialization, blacks and whites tend to meet in the suburbs in the most volatile situations.

The suburban case thus parallels what has been taking place in the central cities. Downtown office development has its counterpart in suburban shopping malls and industrial parks. The wealth of some exclusive suburban enclaves is more than matched by the gentrification of some inner-city neighborhoods. And the status of black suburbs in relation to the rest of suburbia is very much like the status of black ghettos in relation to the rest of the inner city. Conflicts over housing and schools between blacks and working-class whites are embedded in and aggravated by the patterns of uneven development which operate to the disadvantage of both.

In three ways the suburban situation is even worse than in the central city. The first is that we have a tendency to think of all suburbs in terms of an outmoded stereotype, as privileged islands of relative affluence. The stereotype masks problems and helps us to avoid dealing with them. Second, suburbs operate under different legal imperatives than central cities. In central cities, segregated housing is not an acceptable excuse for segregated schools. But when a suburban school district experiences racial change, there is officially no segregation if schools within the district have a similar composition. It does not matter under current law that white students are in white districts and black students are in black districts, except when (as in the Darby case) those districts are consolidated. Finally, predominantly black communities like Camden and Chester have the governmental authority to take control of their own futures, in a way that no central city black neighborhood can. But black suburbs are on their own, in their present or impending fiscal crisis, without the broad corporate tax base of the great central cities, and are ultimately more dependent on state and federal largesse to balance their budgets. As a result, black suburbs face increasingly serious problems of community development in the coming years.

Notes

1. Howard Goodman, "Racism in the City of Brotherly Love." *Albany Times Union,* December 22, 1985, sec. E., p. 1. See also Julia Cass, "Reality Limits Imposed in Elmwood." *Philadelphia Inquirer,* November 28, 1985, sec. B, p. 6.

2. "Philly Police Investigating Racial Letter." *Albany Times Union,* December 25, 1985, sec. A, p. 9.

3. Tom Infield, "Racial Tension Is Not Limited to S. W. Philadelphia." *Philadelphia Inquirer,* December 8, 1985, sec. D, pp. 1, 4.

4. John D. Kasarda, "Urban Change and Minority Opportunities," in Paul Peterson (ed.), *The New Urban Reality,* Washington, DC: The Brookings Institute, 1985, pp. 51–53.

5. John R. Logan and Mark Schneider, "Racial Segregation and Racial Change in American Suburbs, 1970–1980." *American Journal of Sociology,* January 1984, p. 877.

6. Mark Schneider and John R. Logan, "Suburban Municipalities: The Changing System of Intergovernmental Relations in the Mid-1970s." *Urban Affairs Quarterly,* September 1985, pp. 87–105.

7. Donald L. Foley, "Institutional and Contextual Factors Affecting the

Housing Choices of Minority Residents," in Amos H. Hawley and Vincent P. Rock (eds.), *Segregation in Residential Areas,* Washington, DC: National Academy of Sciences, 1973, pp. 85–147.

8. Peter J. Leahy, "Are Racial Factors Important for the Allocation of Mortgage Money?" *American Journal of Economics and Sociology,* July, 1985, pp. 185–196. Also Karen Orren, *Corporate Power and Social Change: The Politics of the Life Insurance Industry,* Baltimore: Johns Hopkins University Press, 1974.

9. Anthony Downs, *Opening up the Suburbs: An Urban Strategy for America,* New Haven, CT: Yale University Press, 1973.

10. Robert Lake, *The New Suburbanites: Race and Housing in the Suburbs,* New Brunswick, NJ: Center for the Urban Policy Research, 1981. See also Diana M. Pearce, "Gatekeepers and Homeseekers: Institutional Patterns in Racial Steering." *Social Problems,* February 1979, pp. 325–342.

11. John Yinger, George Galster, Barton Smith, and Frederick E. Eggers, *The Status of Research into Racial Discrimination and Segregation in American Housing Markets.* Washington, DC: U.S. Department of Housing and Urban Development, 1978.

12. Sandra Long, "Finding the Courage to Live in Harmony." *Philadelphia Inquirer,* December 5, 1982, sec. N, p. 1.

13. Ibid.

14. Infield.

15. Donald Janson, "Camden Gets Grant." *New York Times,* May 22, 1983, sec. 11, pp. 16–17.

16. Mary Jane Fine, "Chester's Vacant Houses Challenge City in Decline." *Philadelphia Inquirer,* June 30, 1983, sec. B, p. 6.

17. Jan Pogue, "Deep Down among the Down and Out in Chester City." *Philadelphia Inquirer,* January 24, 1982, sec. A, p. 12.

18. Long.

19. "Audit of John E. Wallace Real Estate—Century 21." Unpublished report, Landsdowne-Upper Darby Area Fair Housing Council, 1978

20. Ibid., page 3.

21. "Real Estate Practices in Eastern Delaware County: An Audit." Unpublished report, Landsdowne-Upper Darby Area Fair Housing Council, 1976. p. 14.

22. Marc Duvoisin, "Housing Bias, 1980s Style: It's Covert Now." *Philadelphia Inquirer,* November 19, 1984, sec. A, p. 1.

23. Ibid.

24. Ronald E. Wienk, Clifford E. Reid, John C. Simonson, and Frederick J. Eggers, *Measuring Racial Discrimination in American Housing Markets: The Housing Market Practices Survey.* Washington, DC: U.S. Department of Housing and Urban Development, 1979.

25. William G. Weart, "Demonstrations Halted." *New York Times,* November 15, 1963, p. 22.

26. Suzanne Gordon, "Delco Desegregation Plan Includes 2 Magnet Schools." *Philadelphia Inquirer,* February 12, 1982, sec. B, p. 6.

27. Mark Butler, "NAACP Assails School District for Job Changes." *Philadelphia Inquirer,* October 29, 1982, sec. B, p. 1.

28. Janet McMillan, "NAACP Re-emerges in Chesco." *Philadelphia Inquirer,* March 12, 1982, sec. B, p. 1.

29. Chris Conway, "Outcry Follows Report of Racial Slur by School Official." *Philadelphia Inquirer,* February 19, 1983, sec. B, p. 4.

30. Chris Conway and Mark Butler, "Remark Reheats Racial Tension in Chester County Factory Town." *Philadelphia Inquirer,* March 13, 1983, sec. C, p. 1, 4.

31. Chris Conway and Henry Goldman, "Petition Brings Probe of Coatesville Chief." *Philadelphia Inquirer,* June 5, 1984, sec. B, p. 6.

32. Chris Conway, "Judge: Lukens Steel and Union Discriminated." *Philadelphia Inquirer,* February 14, 1984, sec. B, p. 2.

33. Chris Conway, "Blacks Believed for Decades What Lukens Ruling Confirms." *Philadelphia Inquirer,* February 20, 1984, sec. B, pp. 1, 4.

34. Janson.

35. Michael Norman, "The Sparks of Renewal Are Glimmering in Camden." *New York Times,* December 27, 1985, sec. B, pp. 1, 6.

36. Mark Wagenveld, "Housing Plan Draws Opposition." *Philadelphia Inquirer,* February 9, 1982, sec. B, p. 4.

37. Mary Jane Fine, "Chester's East End Is Wary of Revival Plan." *Philadelphia Inquirer,* July 29, 1985, sec. B, p. 5.

38. Mary Jane Fine, "Chester's Vacant Houses Challenge City in Decline." *Philadelphia Inquirer,* June 30, 1983, sec. B, p. 6.

39. Homer Bigart, "Hope for Racial Peace in Chester, Pa., Rests with State Inquiry." *New York Times,* May 3, 1964, p. 75.

Chapter 14

The Limits to Neighborhood Power: Progressive Politics and Local Control in Santa Monica

David S. Daykin

Introduction

Soon after a new progressive City Council majority took office in April 1981, in Santa Monica, California, it appointed a citizen's task force to develop policy recommendations for strengthening the city's neighborhoods. This task force endorsed independent grassroots neighborhood organizations for increasing Santa Monica residents' participation in decisions that affect their lives. The task force identified the purpose of neighborhood organizations for the people of Santa Monica:

> Neighborhood organizations can organize, educate and empower those who have not previously been involved in local government. Such participation is essential to a healthy democratic society and will keep government accountable to the people it serves.

> Neighborhood organizations can provide a sense of community for residents of the neighborhood, reducing the fear of crime and the feeling of isolation so prevalent in major urban areas.[1]

This chapter is a case study of neighborhood organizations during that progressive political administration in Santa Monica. The significance of neighborhood-based planning for local residents, municipal government, and the private sector is evaluated. The chapter considers the innovative strategies that the newly elected City Council members in Santa Monica developed in collaboration and in conflict with the city's neighborhood organizations. Finally, this chapter analyzes the barriers to local control encountered by Santa Monica's neighborhoods.

The City of Santa Monica overlooks the shimmering Pacific Ocean to the west, and is surrounded on three sides by the City of Los Angeles. In 1980, the city held 88,314 residents within an eight-square-mile area. Santa Monica's population is projected to grow slowly to 92,899 by the year 2000, an increase of only 5 percent, or 4,000 residents.[2] The racial/ethnic composition in 1980 included 78 percent non-hispanic white, 13 percent hispanic, 4 percent black, 4 percent Asian, and 0.5 percent other groups.

Essentially, Santa Monica is a middle-class city. The median income in 1980 was $16,604, close to the national average.[3] By 1985, the median income had increased to $22,650 and the proportion of households with less than $10,000 had declined (from 28.4% in 1980 to 18.3% in 1985). Households with incomes of $40,000 or more increased slightly, from 12.8 percent of the population in 1980 to 23.4 percent by 1985.[4] However, taking into account inflation and more slowly rising incomes nationally, the actual changes in the upper and lower income groups are slight. Although certain neighborhoods have rapidly gentrified, a recent study concluded that the population of Santa Monica remains relatively unchanged in its diversity since the pre-rent control days of 1979.[5]

Even more prominently than its middle-income character, Santa Monica is a city of renters. Major urban change occurred with the completion of the new freeway connecting Santa Monica to downtown Los Angeles in 1966. As land use became more intense, hundreds of small bungalows were torn down and replaced with low-rise apartment buildings and condominiums. The population of renters grew substantially. Renters now comprise a dominant part of the city's population: 78 percent, according to the 1980 census, while only 22 percent are homeowners. By comparison, tenants comprise only 60 percent of the residents of Los Angeles and 50 percent nationally. The rent control issue was a major factor in bringing the progressive City Council members into office in Santa Monica.

Economic development and changes in the labor market in the Los Angeles region heavily influence the growth of Santa Monica. According to a county regional planning agency, Santa Monica is one of

the nineteen growth centers in the Los Angeles region.[6] Major shifts in
the composition of the labor market in Santa Monica will occur as the
office sector increases more rapidly than the traditional manufacturing
section. (See Table 14.1.)[7] Non-governmental office employment is projected to grow from a current 33 to 41 percent of the work force by the
year 2000.[8]

Trends suggest that in Santa Monica, manufacturing-sector employment will not decline as in "Gray Belt" cities in the East and Midwest. However, employment projections indicate an increase by the
year 2000 of only 9.2 percent in manufacturing. Since 1978 there has
been a net loss of acreage dedicated to industrial use.[9] The industrial
corridor in the Pico neighborhood experienced more than a 50 percent
decline of traditional manufacturing firms, from 161 in 1978 to 75 in
1982. Small firms suffered the greatest losses. Only high-technology
firms increased their space, from 10 percent of the total acreage in 1978
to 16 percent in 1982.[10] In general, Santa Monica's labor force will
follow the national pattern, with a relative decrease in the manufacturing sector and an increase in the service/office/sales sector of the
economy. The manufacturing that survives will shift from traditional
industries to high technology.

These labor market changes directly influence Santa Monica's
neighborhoods in several ways. The largest minority population in

TABLE 14.1. Employment in Santa Monica

Economic Sector	1980	Year 1982	2000	Increase from 1982	Percent Increase (1982-2000)
Government	4,680	4,700	4,905	205	4.4%
Office	16,470	17,790	34,223	16,433	92.4
Retail	11,636	12,101	17,221	5,120	42.3
Manufacturing	6,906	6,974	7,616	642	9.2
Wholesale	1,814	1,929	3,356	1,427	74.0
Services[a]	10,970	11,288	15,431	4,143	36.7
Total	52,476	54,782	82,752	27,970	51.1

Source: City of Santa Monica, General Plan Land Use and Circulation Elements—
Background to the Issue Papers. Santa Monica, CA: March, 1983, p. 21.
[a]Includes communications, construction, transportation, utilities, non-office-based
services, hotels, and hospitals.

Santa Monica is located in the Pico neighborhood, an area containing the industrial corridor. If present land-use policies continue, this neighborhood's job base will be dominated by office development. Office space will increase from 21 percent of the industrial corridor to 41 percent.[11] Locally owned small businesses will be driven out by the demand for office space. A shift in the gender of the new labor force will occur, as demand icreases for more female than male workers.[12] In addition, employers estimate that 30 to 40 percent of their industrial workers are Santa Monica residents, in contrast to 18 percent of the office workers. In all, the minority population in the Pico neighborhood will be more directly affected by these macro-level changes than will the population in other neighborhoods.

Santa Monica does not have a long history of political movements or widespread neighborhood struggles. However, some organized protests did begin in the 1970s. During the late 1960s and early 1970s, young activists moved into the Ocean Park area of Santa Monica. Focusing on the protection of the coastal environment and the maintenance of affordable housing, Ocean Park residents organized against expensive high-rise development in their beach community.[13] During an unsuccessful 1976 campaign for a state assembly seat to represent Santa Monica, Venice, and West Los Angeles, local activists learned the technology of modern electoral politics: computer-aided voter targeting, direct-mail literature appeals, and major fund-raising. Still, these separate forms of organized political action did not result in a community-wide movement.

A single issue, rent control, carried the progressive local activists into the City Council chambers.[14] The first effort in 1978 by a group of senior citizens to bring rent control to Santa Monica ended in defeat. At the same time Howard Jarvis's statewide local-property-tax-reduction initiative, Proposition 13, passed by a substantial majority. Jarvis had promised renters across the state that if they supported his property tax-reduction measure, apartment owners would pass some of the savings on to them as lower rents. When apartment rents increased substantially after the elections, renters reacted in protest. In addition, condominium conversion was pushing out an increasing number of middle- and lower-income tenants from their homes. From 1977 to 1979, over two thousand units of rental housing in Santa Monica were demolished or converted to condominiums.

A city-wide coalition, Santa Monicans for Renters' Rights (SMRR), was founded in the fall of 1978 to place strong rent control on the ballot for the April 1979 elections. SMRR was an electoral coalition of three groups: the Santa Monica Democratic Club; the Santa Monica chapter of Campaign for Economic Democracy, a statewide organization founded by Tom Hayden; and the Santa Monica Fair Housing Alliance, a local organization concerned about affordable housing. The SMRR coalition was victorious in April 1979; the rent control proposition passed with 54.3 percent of the vote. The rent control initiative provided for an elected five-person board. The rent control law developed its own active constituency.

SMRR began to build a broader progressive alliance for the next elections scheduled for June 1981. Anti-rent-control forces solidified behind the Santa Monica Citizens Congress. Yet SMRR's four candidates swept all contested seats on the City Council. Now, with five seats on the City Council, SMRR held a majority. The progressive city council members then selected as mayor a consumer activist, Ruth Yantatta Goldway. SMRR considered city funding for neighborhood organizations to be an important element in its general goal of democratizing local government through citizen empowerment. SMRR's political agenda also included support for local rent control laws; support for planned growth while protecting neighborhoods from overdevelopment; an increase in the amount of affordable housing within the city for low- and moderate-income residents; increased public participation in government by funding community organizations; improved and increased open spaces; improvements in social services and the election of progressive candidates to office.

SMRR's string of electoral victories came to an end in April 1983, when the coalition lost the city council seat held by the mayor. SMRR also failed to unseat two incumbent city council opponents, and did not achieve a majority on the school board. Still, the SMRR coalition maintained a four-to-three edge on the City Council. However, SMRR maintained control of the elected Rent Control Board and defeated a real-estate–backed initiative. This 1983 local election demonstrated a slight city-wide shift in voting away from SMRR's slate of candidates.[15] Moreover, the opposition was able to mobilize an unusually high voter turnout in homeowner areas of the city, while SMRR either maintained the usual voter participation or even experienced a slight drop in turnout in its strong districts. Although the progressive coalition did not mobilize its expected support for this election, it did force its conservative opponent, the All Santa Monica Coalition, to run on a pro–rent-control platform.

In April 1985, SMRR lost majority control of City Council. However, this loss was not due to a lack of voter support. Three SMRR candidates were elected. A defeated SMRR incumbent had to run as a write-in candidate after failing to collect enough signatures to be placed on the ballot. The death of another progressive City Council member reduced SMRR's power in Santa Monica even further. The November 1986 City Council elections failed to return an SMRR majority: only one of the three SMRR candidates won a seat. Now the City Council is evenly balanced between the progressive coalition of SMRR and its opposition, the All Santa Monica Coalition, with three council members a piece. A seventh City Council member was elected as an independent to fill a special two-year position. To the chagrin of SMRR, the All Santa Monica Coalition again ran on a strong pro–rent-control program. Low voter turnout among tenants weakened SMRR's strength at the polls. However, SMRR maintained completed control of the elected Rent Control Board.

During the 1980s two neighborhoods were most active in local planning and politics: the Ocean Park Community Organization (OPCO) and the Pico Neighborhood Association (PNA). A third neighborhood among those most frequently mentioned in this chapter was the most recent one to organize, the Mid-City Neighbors (MCN). The three neighborhoods are briefly described here.

Ocean Park is a relatively densely populated neighborhood of small California bungalows and low-rise apartment buildings. The area is populated by retired people, artists, young professionals, and a strong counterculture. Conservation of the environment is a major component of Ocean Park residents' conception of a human-scale neighborhood. The residents are relatively young, in single (36.7%) or two-person households (36%).[16] They are quite mobile. Ocean Park has the smallest proportion of residents who work in Santa Monica or shop in the City. Yet the neighborhood is well organized. OPCO had closer political ties with the progressive City Council than the other neighborhood organizations. Residents of Ocean Park sat on City Council, held powerful positions in the city administration, and were leading activists in the powerful renters coalition of SMRR. Among the neighborhood organizations, Ocean Park has the longest history of organizing, beginning with the state senatorial races of local candidates.

The Pico neighborhood has the most diverse ethnic and racial mix in Santa Monica.[17] Over half of the blacks, Asians, and latinos who live in Santa Monica reside in the Pico area. The neighborhood is also one of the most stable, with 77 percent of the residents having lived in Santa Monica for five years or more. Compared to the other neighborhoods in the city, the Pico area is a family-based community. Few people in the Pico neighborhood live alone. Pico residents have the lowest incomes in Santa Monica, with 43 percent reporting household incomes of less than $15,000 per year. In a recent neighborhood needs assessment, residents of the Pico neighborhood considered jobs as the greatest need, especially for young people.[18] Compared to other neighborhoods, more residents in Pico work in Santa Monica.

The most recent neighborhood to organize formed the Mid-City Neighbors organization. Mid-City residents consider the ethnic mix of their neighborhood important in their lives.[19] There are fewer families living in the Mid-City area compared to other neighborhoods. The neighborhood is second to the Pico area in proportion of households earning under $15,000 a year (28%). Mid-City residents report the highest mobility rate in the city, with 37 percent of the population having lived at their current residence for less than two years, and the district has the lowest proportion of residents who have lived in the city over five years (53%). A major issue among Mid-City residents is the number of office buildings and the parking problem. The area reports the highest percentage of condo and co-op apartment buildings in the city. Unlike the Pico and Ocean Park neighborhoods, the Mid-City area lacks the physical boundaries that help create a unique neighborhood identity.

Santa Monica's Strategy for Reform: Neighborhood Empowerment and Progressive Change

When the progressive City Council came to power in 1981, the role of the urban neighborhood suddenly took on particular importance in the development and implementation of the city's social and economic policies. City government and neighborhood organizations pursued several strategies as each began to work out its conception of citizen empowerment. These strategies included (1) the negotiation of development agreements, (2) the establishment of neighborhood coalitions, (3) neighborhood participation in electoral politics, (4) the cultivation of neighborhood plans, and (5) exploration of a new distributive policy. Each of these initiatives will be described briefly.

Development Agreements: Negotiating New
Business-Neighborhood Partnerships

The Santa Monica case raises a number of questions about the ability of neighborhood organizations and a progressive city council to negotiate with wealthy developers and real estate brokers in pursuing a political agenda based on local participation and egalitarian ideals. Since the 1981 electoral victory, Santa Monica's progressive coalition has strongly supported strategies to defend the local autonomy of the city. The progressive majority in the City Council recognized the rapid penetration of non-locally owned businesses and capital into Santa Monica's economy. Neighborhood planning and local control were part of a more comprehensive urban policy to democratize city life and define the limits of outside investment.

The progressive majority on the City Council, supported by the neighborhood organizations, succeeded in halting high-rise development and encouraged mixed-use commercial projects and housing for low- and moderate-income residents. The new City Council in 1981 placed a six-months' moratorium on all construction in the city, a move intended to prevent the massive destruction of rental units and the explosive condominium conversion taking place. Sixty-one projects were held up by the moratorium.[20]

For a period of three years until the new land use regulation was adopted in 1984, development agreements guided the city's commercial growth. These development agreements reached among a private developer, City Hall and neighborhood organizations were a key part of the progressives' strategy to control capital investments within Santa Monica and to benefit the neighborhoods. According to the City Manager, John Alschuler, the city administration reviewed these projects, utilizing a public balance sheet that weighs the benefits of development against the costs to residents of the neighborhood where these changes occur.

State law permits cities to enter into agreements so that developers are assured that policies in effect will continue should the city council or city administration change. In return for assurances of policy continuity, cities may require developers to provide various facilities serving the public as part of their contractual responsibilities. With the adoption of the general plan for land use in 1984, it is now the City's policy to negotiate development agreements only for: (1) projects whose construction progress exceeds the normal time period for which use permits are granted; (2) projects in which public/private partnerships are contemplated and the City plays a role in the development and financing of the new projects; and (3) large complex projects.[21]

Between 1981 and 1984, the City Council allowed development of the Greenwood Center, a $90 million office condominium complex, on the condition that the developers, Campeau Corporation and Greenwood Development Corporation, include 30 residential apartments for low- to moderate-income Santa Monica residents working for firms in the Greenwood Center, and a day-care center with a playground and community room. Similarly, the City Council reached an agreement with Welton-Becket Associates for its office-hotel development (Colorado Place) to provide an on-site child care center; a three-acre park; 100 units of low-to-moderate-income rental housing on other sites in the City; job training and local affirmative action hiring programs; and an arts and social services fee equal to 1.5 percent of the cost of the project.[22] Although similar development agreements are becoming more common in other parts of California and in other states, the nature of the Welton-Becket deal was unprecedented. By March 1986, the child care center was completed at the site. About one-half of the affordable housing was built in the Pico neighborhood. However, according to the Pico Neighborhood Association, the job training and neighborhood hiring program was not successful.

Originally, development agreements were intended, in part, to assure the developers continuity in planning long-term projects in an environment fraught with political uncertainties. Yet the City and its neighborhoods have a few assurances of continuity if the developer sells its interest to another firm. In 1986, Southmark Pacific acquired 70 percent control of the $225 million office-restaurant Colorado Place from the Welton-Becket Investment Corporation. Now Southmark wishes to renegotiate the 1981 development agreement that Welton-Becket signed with the City. Attorneys for Southmark filed suit in Superior Court in Santa Monica to change the building height for a new hotel from nine stories to fifteen. Such height is unacceptable to local residents. In addition, the Mid-City Neighbors organization has been renegotiating with Southmark Pacific concerning the company's intention to relocate the 3.3-acre community park originally planned for the site. The new developers plan to build a six-story office building on the original park site and locate the new park in another neighborhood. However, Southmark has agreed to complete the second phase of low-to moderate-income housing construction as planned in the Welton-Becket agreement. Both the City administration and neighborhood organizations have come to appreciate the difficulty of gaining compliance with development agreements under conditions of fluctuating ownership of a long-term project.

In 1983, one neighborhood organization in Santa Monica, the Pico Neighborhood Association, directly negotiated an agreement with a private developer. Previously, development agreements to benefit neighborhoods were reached through negotiations betweeen city hall and the private developer. This was the first time a neighborhood organization assumed responsibilities as the main negotiator for the city. In a memo of understanding, the developers of the $43 million 2140 Colorado Boulevard project agreed to an up-front payment of $1.3 million to the PNA, 2 percent payment of the hard costs of construction and 2 percent PNA ownership of the building. The funds were to be used for a variety of purposes including housing rehabilitation and a job advocacy program for local residents. For various reasons, some not related to the development agreement, the developers, in the end, did not follow through with the project.

The PNA negotiated with city hall for complete control of the revenue accumulated through partnership in the Colorado Development Corporation project. The PNA asked the developers to establish a trust fund for the neighborhood. The fund would be distributed following a democratic process based on neighborhoods' needs. Such an agreement with the City would have significantly reduced the annual uncertainties neighborhood organizations experience about continued City funding. Reliable funding for neighborhood organizations remains a formidable barrier that Santa Monica's City Council has not been able to resolve.

However, City administrators opposed a neighborhood's exclusive control over such funds. Even the most progressive City Council members want City Hall to maintain control of the development funds. Their argument holds that the City Council is legally responsible for the overall welfare of Santa Monica and that the industrial corridor of the Pico neighborhood is a city-wide concern, not solely a neighborhood issue. The progressive coalition felt strongly the City Hall was now accessible to all neighborhood organizations to clearly make their interest heard. This form of democratic centralism practiced by the city administration and the progressive City Council critically limited the extent of local neighborhood power and decision-making.

All neighborhood organizations in Santa Monica did not demand the right to negotiate directly with private developers to reach agreements. The Ocean Park Community Organization, for example, only wanted to act as a mediator in the process, as the City administration negotiated directly with the developers on its behalf. City administrators allowed neighborhood organizations to choose whether to take on the burden of direct negotiations with a developer or to allow the City to act for them. As a matter of City policy, all developers were told to first talk with neighborhood organizations before approaching the City administration for development permits.[23]

The new housing and land use elements require that both commercial development and housing projects provide public benefits to mitigate their impact on the neighborhoods. While earlier, these public benefits were acquired through development agreements, the new housing and land-use elements now regulate the specific public provisions to be made by developers. The City has adopted an inclusive zoning program for housing, commercial, and industrial development. For every free-market housing unit a developer constructs (excluding single-family homes), there must also be provision for low- or moderate-cost housing.[24] The housing may be either rental or ownership units.

New office developments are also required to provide specific numbers of units of affordable housing.[25] A study of office development in Santa Monica demonstrated that in current office buildings of over 10,000 square feet, 82 percent of the workers are not residents of Santa Monica; 22 percent of this group would be eligible for affordable housing; 56 percent would move to Santa Monica within the next two years if they had the opportunity; and 32 percent said that the price of housing is the most important factor now determining where they live.[26] In addition, the developer must provide certain amounts of open public spaces (e.g., parks). A developer may choose to meet the housing requirements by agreeing to contribute funds to a City-approved non-profit housing developer.

The housing requirement for new office developers may strengthen sentiments for neighborhood solidarity, since workplace and residence are brought closer together. In fact, recognizing the problems created by the separation of residence and workplace, the City Council encouraged new development plans that combine commercial and residential use in neighborhoods. One private development corporation agreed to the City Council's demand that employees be allowed first priority in renting the residential units to be built as part of the commercial project. The City's new housing plan encourages residential structures in commericial zones and the consideration of housing in industrial zones.

With the adoption of the new land use policy, also in 1974, neighborhood participation is encouraged in the following areas: the development of neighborhood impact statements for large projects; neighborhood needs assessments; and participation on advisory committees established by the City.[27]While the new City housing and land-use regulations set the neighborhood entitlements for housing and public space, neighborhood organizations may approach developers for agreement on other issues. Currently, the Pico Neighborhood Association is negotiating with a prospective developer for the inclusion of a supermarket and local job hiring in a new shopping center within the neighborhood.

The PNA seeks to convince developers to hire local residents for both skilled and unskilled jobs to be created by projects. However, agreements to provide local jobs are difficult to achieve. The earlier development agreement with the Welton-Becket Colorado Place failed to deliver the local jobs and training expected. Moreover, without the development of local job training programs, the poorer, unemployed residents of the neighborhood are not able to meet the skills demanded for employement in the new high-technology office development projects. Neighborhood small business training and local job creation depend on forging stronger ties between private labor demand and the public/private-sector job training programs.[28]

The City's location within a high-growth region allows its neighborhoods to achieve agreements with private developers which are unlikely within neighborhoods in economically depressed cities. Although the Chamber of Commerce and other conservative business organizations in the city claimed that the development agreements and other restrictions on commercial/industrial growth cause the local economy to stagnate, industries are not leaving Santa Monica. In fact, the City's businesses continue to generate sales taxes higher than the state average.[29]

Neighborhood Networks: An Escape from Localism

Localism continues to limit Santa Moncia's neighborhood organizations. Yet community networks are beginning to develop. The oldest grassroots neighborhood organization in Santa Monica, OPCO, assisted the Pico area residents to form their own neighborhood organization. However, both organizations are quite protective of their own territory and different goals. The PNA-OPCO relationship is particularly conflictive since racial, ethnic, and class divisions also separate the two neighborhoods.

The networking of neighborhood organizations with semi-autonomous nonprofit corporations such as the Community Corporation of Santa Monica provides distinct advantages. The Community Corporation provides housing rehabilitation and new housing acquisition within the confines of its capacities. Santa Monica's neighborhoods are too small to develop efficiently and productively their own separate housing development corporations. In 1984, the Pico Neighborhood Association achieved strong representation on the Community Corporation. The PNA joined on the condition that (1) the PNA representatives in the Community Corporation will be accountable to and under the control of the PNA Board; (2) the PNA will have control over project monies generated by the PNA; (3) the PNA will have the right to negotiate with other community development corporations; and (4) the PNA will have equal representation with OPCO and the Board of the Community Corporation. So the Community Corporation utilized $583,000 in community development block grant funds (Pico Neighborhood Housing Trust Fund) to purchase dwelling units within the neighborhood as a strategy to preserve affordable rental housing.[30] In addition, the PNA maintained its partnership with a Los Angeles-based community development corporation to continue a housing rehabilitation program for low- and moderate-income tenants.

The new housing regulations adopted by the City mandate the Community Corporation to continue to develop City-owned affordable housing; to lease housing to tenants and non-tenant cooperatives; and, to provide technical assistance to non-profit housing organizations. In addition, the Community Corporation is required to develop job training programs and affirmative action hiring in the course of its work with housing construction, management, and maintenance.[31]

The PNA has networked with national organizations such as the Center for Community Change in Washington, D.C., and the Lower-Income Housing Coalition. As a result of the PNA and City Hall's affiliation with the Working Group for Community Development Reform (part of the nationally based Center for Community Charge), Santa Monica passed an ordinance, in September 1983, reinstating targeting of CDBG funds in poor neighborhoods, something the Reagan adminstration had dropped at the federal level.

The Lure of Electoral Politics

Some community organizations adopt electoral strategies to achieve local control. In Santa Monica, the Pico Neighborhood Association threatened the progressives on the City Council with running its own candidates if the City Council did not make PNA appointments to City commissions such as planning and personnel. According to an executive board member of PNA, "PNA activists are put in a bind by the Council's resistance to sharing power.... Until the PNA can wield autonomous power in electoral politics, the Pico neighborhood will not secure the political power necessary to save itself."[32] Similarly, in other cities, Heathe Booth's State and Local Leadership Project, Massachusetts Fair Share, and the Ohio Public Interest Campaign (OPIC) have recently adopted electoral strategies.

Even though there is movement toward electoral politics, Alinsky-style community organizations are still uncertain about electoral participation. According to organizer John Judis, "Community organizations have historically stood outside the system and attacked it. Anyone who gets into office has to sell his soul so many ways there is no way to hold them accountable."[33] Some community organizers feel that neither conservative nor liberal/progressive politicians on city councils can adequately serve the needs of the majority during times of severe federal cutbacks. Accordingly, by this argument progressive neighborhood-based planners should remain out of power and in opposition until more favorable national changes occur.[34]

The problems raised for neighborhood organizations by electoral involvement are directly related to their financial dependence on federal and city government. The survival of OPCO was seriously threatened by its loss of federal CDBG funds because of its alleged political work in the spring 1983 municipal campaign. Similarly, federal funding for the other major neighborhood organization, PNA, was also in doubt, this time for using the organization's equipment to produce fliers opposing an anti-renter initiative on the spring ballot.

In an attempt to avoid funding conflicts, some neighborhoods created political clubs, legally separate from the organizations receiving federal grant money. In Santa Monica, the Ocean Park neighborhood created the Ocean Park Electoral Network (OPEN), and the Pico electoral organization (PEP) was developed for the Pico neighborhood. These neighborhood political clubs directly supported the statewide reform movement, Santa Monicans for Renters' Rights (SMRR), but operated separately from city-wide organizations like the Santa Monica Democratic Club. Neighborhood political clubs varied in strength according to their closeness to the main neighborhood organizations. OPEN and the Ocean Park Community Organization were strongly supportive of each other and had considerably overlapping membership. In the Pico neighborhood, there were weaker ties between PEP and Pico Neighborhood Association. Leadership in PNA considers the political club to be a closed group, unwilling to cooperate in broader electoral debate.

Both of the neighborhood-based political clubs dissolved within two years. OPEN's leadership was absorbed back into the SMRR coalition. Learning from the vulnerability of OPCO to charges of partisanship because of its close membership association with the local political club, the Pico Neighborhood Association never closely allied with its local political club. Neither the SMRR coaltion nor its progressive Council members moved to change City Council elections from a city-wide to a district basis.[35] To maintain power centralized in City Hall, SMRR decided not to empower neighborhoods by switching to district City Council elections.

Cultivating Grassroots Participation

Although neighborhood organizations are unable to mobilize proportionally large numbers of residents, there are strategies for increasing citizen participation in the planning process. In April 1983, the Pico Neighborhood Association completed a neighborhood plan with relatively widespread participation of local residents.[36] The PNA, in collaboration with a community advocacy planning organization, the Los Angeles Community Design Center, conducted a participatory planning process that involved over 200 residents and 24 neighborhood meetings during a period of four months. The Pico Neighborhood Plan examined five crucial areas, including housing, commercial/industrial development, youth, city services, and crime. Five committees composed of neighborhood residents met over several months assessing the issues and proposing strategies to resolve them. The neighborhood plan is advisory; it has no legal authority within city government. As part of the planning process, the PNA and OPCO also hold annual congresses to establish community priorities for the following year's work.

The newly adopted Land Use Element formally requires the City's support for neighborhood plans to assess local needs and problems. Moreover, proposed major development projects must include neighborhood impact statements. While neighborhood participation is required to conduct these studies, the City plan does not specify the extent of involvement by neighborhood organizations. The City's strategy appears to follow the liberal model of inviting neighborhood participation in the planning process without a transfer of decision-making powers to neighborhood organizations.

Neighborhood organizers in Santa Monica were confronted with weak minority participation. The Latino Resource Organization in Santa Monica focuses on the need for more culturally relevant personnel and bilingual information.[37] This view emphasizes building cultural unity among latinos before moving toward participation in neighborhood organizations. This cultural nationalist perspective rejects neighborhood-based organizations as vehicles for mobilizing latinos. The Pico Neighborhood Association considers this separatist strategy a barrier to its approach. The PNA emphasizes the common problems of class oppression experienced by all ethnic minorities within the neighborhood. Its focus is on economic class barriers to mass participation rather than on cultural impediments to activism.

A Santa Monica latino household survey reports that church organizations are the dominant community link outside the family.[38] Also, a number of Mexican hometown associations (e.g., Club Pegeros, Club del Valle de Guadalupe) are important informal family-related organizations for locating jobs and for social support. In Los Angeles, churches form the core of the city's largest neighborhood organization, the South Central Organizing Committee (SCOC). The SCOC, formed early in 1983 with the assistance of the Alinsky-founded Industrial Area Foundation, represents 22 churches, 7 denominations and 42,000 families. Similarly, the largest latino neighborhood organization on the Los Angeles East Side, the United Neighborhood Organization, is principally supported by Catholic parishes. Neighborhood organizations in Santa Monica, however, have not yet cultivated these religious and cultural organizations as a means of increasing neighborhood participation.

Distributive Policy

A concern raised repeatedly at public hearings conducted by the Santa Monica Task Force on Neighborhood Planning was that neighborhood empowerment might lead to increased inequalities and conflict among neighborhoods. For this reason, some members of the City Planning Council wanted assurances that the Council-appointed Task Force would allow neighborhood organizations advisory powers only. The City Council voiced concern for equal protection for all neighborhoods. Council members thought that more affluent, better-organized neighborhoods might obtain more and better services than the less organized, poorer areas of the city. Moreover, as municipal resources were reduced by fiscal problems and taxpayer revolts, they felt conflicts would increase among neighborhood groups contending for scarce resources.

Historically, most cities distribute services unequally among neighborhoods, with the less powerful areas receiving the least. In Santa Monica, until 1981, City Councils favored the more affluent neighborhoods with federal Community Development Block Grants (CDBG) monies more than the predominantly minority-populated Pico neighborhood. While an English bowling green was constructed in one middle-income neighborhood, numerous streets in the poorer Pico neighborhood were still unlighted. Before the Pico Neighborhood Association was created, the neighborhood received less than 2 percent of the City's CDBG funds.[39]

In 1983, after two years of neighborhood organizing and with the progressive majority in City Council, the Pico neighborhood received 80 percent of the CDBG funds. While neighborhood organizers claim that their efforts were responsible for the redistribution of CDBG funds, the SMRR coalition asserts that their progressive majority on the City Council was principally responsible for the shift of funds, regardless of the pressure from the neighborhood organizations.

In Santa Monica, neighborhood leaders expressed concern that policies promoting more jobs in one neighborhood would conflict with the priorities for lower density, and higher environmental quality in other neighborhoods. Generally the poorer, minority neighborhoods are concerned more with the maximizing of jobs and affordable housing in their neighborhoods. For example, Pico residents ranked affordable housing and jobs as the two most important issues in their neighborhood.[40] From another perspective, residents of the more affluent neighborhoods demonstrated greater interest in the preservation of low-density development, clean air, and open sea views from the apartments.

Originally, the City's citizen task force on commercial and industrial land use proposed a new policy that would have been more restrictive of job development in the city than the current land use regulations. In response, the City asked private consultants to propose alternative land use strategies that did not restrict job growth but also conserved the environment. The City Council's revision of the land use regulations demonstrates concern for controlling the larger forces of economic growth influencing the City's neighborhoods, and for balancing the expressed needs of different neighborhoods.

Barriers to Neighborhood Control: Dilemmas in the Reform Agenda

Despite an impressive list of accomplishments, the barriers to neighborhood control severely constrain the Santa Monica experiment in egalitarian reform. To what extent is progressive social change limited by the neighborhood movement? Or, to what degree is local control limited by tendencies within a progressive coalition to centralize its decision-making power? In the conclusion to this chapter, I will examine several problems which have frustrated the progressive agenda in Santa Monica: external dependency, low participation, social control, localism, electoral politics, legal restrictions, and inadequate funding. Each problem is discussed and explained with examples drawn from the Santa Monica experience.

"External Dependency"

Much of the neighborhood movement is based on beliefs in self-reliance, local economies, political autonomy, decentralized administration, and a general grassroots populism.[41] At the same time, there is a common recognition by neighborhood activists of the importance of extra-local economic and political forces in determining neighborhood conditions. Local groups increasingly see their chances of achieving economic development tied to changes in the international flow of labor and capital. Some observers recognize that national labor markets and investments mostly determine the viability of neighborhood jobs, not local efforts toward job creation.[42]

After World War II Santa Monica experienced substantial changes in its economy. Traditional small businesses, family businesses, and local entrepreneurs were joined in the 1960s by corporate developers with regional, national, and international interests. In 1986, the Chamber of Commerce listed Santa Monica's major employers as two major hospitals, a computer software firm, the city of Santa Monica and its service providers, an aerospace company, an insurance company, a military-government policy research organization, and a light manufacturing company. These national and international corporations have become as much a part of the business environment as the local businesses. More important, it is the corporate actors who are negotiating most of the development agreements with the Santa Monica city government and neighborhood organizations. The local government does not control national economic trends or the strategic planning of large corporations. These macro-level forces will continue to influence and limit local planning efforts.

Lingering Neighborhood Sentiments and Weak Incentives: Low Participation

Community studies show that residents who rely most on their neighbors are also those with few resources outside the neighborhood, those not working at all or working part-time, those new to the city, and those committed to their homes by marriage or ownership.[43] Modern cities allow people to build more personally rewarding relationships than can be achieved through local neighborhood networks. These wider networks decrease residents' dependence upon the neighborhood and their need for local organizations to provide an improved quality of life.

As long as districts of consumption (residential neighborhoods) are separated from districts of production (workplaces), urban residents are less likely to participate in neighborhood-centered networks. In Santa Monica, the division of workplace and residence is extensive. Without changes in land use policy, economic development will produce a decrease in the proportion of jobs held in Santa Monica by its own residents—from 29 percent in 1982 to 26 percent by the year 2000.[44] The scarcity of moderate-priced housing in Santa Monica is a major factor limiting the movement of the non-resident work force into the city's housing. As previously mentioned, according to one survey of existing office buildings, 39 percent of the non-resident employees indicated a willingness to move to Santa Monica given the opportunity.

Low participation rates in neighborhood organizations dampen their claims to legitimacy. Despite lengthy attempts to mobilize the Pico and Ocean Park neighborhood residents, paid membership in the neighborhood organizations remains at 300 to 400, 1 or 2 percent of the neighborhood population. Still, some 800 to 1,000 residents participate in neighborhood activities throughout the year. Nevertheless, opposition groups claim that the neighborhood organizations do not represent their neighborhoods because of their low levels of citizen participation. The issue of nonrepresentation or misrepresentation is continuously raised, mainly by organizations representing the commercial sector of Santa Monica.

A more serious issue concerning participation in neighborhood organizations is representation by class and ethnicity. Neighborhood organizations are more vulnerable to criticism of legitimacy on this issue. The latino population participates little in the Pico neighborhood organization, the neighborhood holding the largest number of latinos in the City. Latinos compose 40 percent of the Pico neighborhood's population. While latinos have recently occupied one-third of the PNA board of directors, it is generally recognized that blacks are much more active in the organization. The higher black participation is consistent with national trends where black activism draws support from organizations developed during the civil rights struggles of the 1960s. Interviews with latino community leaders in Santa Monica show serious alienation of latinos from neighborhood associations.[45] These latino community leaders do not feel that the neighborhood-based organizations in the city are addressing the problems experienced by this constituency.

Social Control: Cooptation and Institutionalization

Neighborhood organizations are vulnerable to cooptation. Local community organizations in Santa Monica fear that their activist members will be coopted by participation in neighborhood councils if they become extensions of city government. If neighborhood councils are not independent from city government and do not hold major decision-making power, participation on these councils will only take time away from their neighborhood advocacy work. The numerous citizen task forces and commissions created by the City Council since 1979 depleted participation in local chapters of the Campaign for Economic Democracy, the PNA and OPCO neighborhood organizations. Earlier, some members of the progressive City Council opposed the idea of neighborhood councils because they felt they would destroy or compete with existing neighborhood organizations. Mainly, neighborhood organizations like OPCO and PNA fear losing their adversarial position toward city government if they are absorbed into an official role of governance. Some city planning commissioners in Santa Monica are critical of City sponsorship of neighborhood organizations for fear that they might become instruments of political patronage.

The Santa Monica city administration considers it too problematic politically for the City Council to certify the legitimacy of groups as formally representing a specific neighborhood. The Citizen's Task Force on Neighborhood Planning developed a criteria of legitimacy to determine eligibility for city funding.[46] However, the City Manager's office and the City Council decided to avoid the issue of certification altogether. The city administration felt that a policy requiring formal criteria for the recognition of neighborhood organizations would also prevent it from funding new organizations that, in the beginning, may not represent the neighborhood as a whole.

From the start of discussions about neighborhood planning in Santa Monica, OPCO, in particular, resisted proposals for official City recognition and delegation of responsibilities to neighborhood organizations. OPCO's strong concern for democratic process made members wary of the effects of institutionalizing a relationship with City Hall. Neighborhood organizations expressed a strong interest in maintaining a position of informal advocacy as the best strategy for representing its local residents. Proposals developed by the Task Force on Neighborhood Planning also strongly resisted institutionalizing responsibilities for planning and service delivery. The Task Force recommended voluntary roles for neighborhood organizations.

Localism

A major criticism of the Alinsky-style neighborhood organizations is that these organizations remain too localistic, never forming wider coalitions among themselves. Small is not necessarily beautiful. Localistic decision-making is not any more virtuous than centralized decision-making.

The formation of the non-profit Community Corporation of Santa Monica illustrates the tension between two neighborhood organizations. The new community development corporation, established to facilitate the development, rehabilitation, and operation of housing for low- and moderate-income people, was closely associated with OPCO, sharing the same office space. OPCO activists first developed the idea of a community development corporation for Santa Monica. But the first reaction of the PNA was to reject participation in a development corporation associated with the Ocean Park neighborhood. PNA activists considered the development corporation a mechanism for coopting their neighborhood organization. Later the PNA became supportive of the community development corporation, once specific guidelines were created to allow for equal representation on the board of directors and to allow each neighborhood organization to directly appoint representatives to the board.

Localism of neighborhood organizations continues to disrupt the city-wide efforts of the Community Corporation to provide affordable housing. Recently, in 1985, the PNA sponsored a neighborhood community development corporation, the Neighborhood Resources and Development Corporation (NRDC), to provide housing rehabilitation services to the Pico neighborhood. The NRDC was created to compete directly with the Community Corporation. Later the NRDC broke away from the Pico Neighborhood Association, taking the City-funded housing rehabilitation program and staff along with it. The Pico Neighborhood Association's distrust of city-wide community development efforts led to the sponsorship of a community development corporation that lacked the capability of a city-wide organization like the Community Corporation. The Community Corporation maintains a precarious balance between encroaching on the separate power bases of the neighborhood organizations and serving a larger public good.

Issue-oriented groups frequently come into conflict with the localistic interests of neighborhood organizations. Recent efforts by the issue-oriented Campaign for Economic Democracy (CED) to organize in Santa Monica's neighborhoods led to conflict with one of the neighborhood's organizations, the PNA. The PNA wanted to focus more on its own neighborhood problems and resented attempts by outside groups to take control of the issue agenda. Class differences between the predominantly middle-class, white CED and the lower-class, minority population of the PNA neighborhood partially explain the conflict. Moreover, the statewide perspective of the CED membership saw a danger in neighborhood diversion of organization and resources needed to launch programs for reordering national priorities.

Electoral Politics and Neighborhood Organizing

Electoral politics pose a serious challenge to neighborhood organizations. If neighborhood organizations follow the Alinsky tradition of political mobilization, community organizations would remain non-partisan. In Santa Monica, this has not occurred. The Pico Neighborhood Association was criticized by its opponents on City Council for having used the organization's equipment to copy letters opposing an anti-rent control proposition in April 1983 municipal elections. The PNA was threatened with suspension of its federal Community Development Block Grant funds because of this type of electoral participation.

Finally, in 1985, the close political ties between two of Santa Monica's neighborhood organizations (OPCO and Mid-City Neighbors) and Santa Monicans for Renters Rights contributed to their loss of City funds. Within a year after the progressive majority lost control of City Council, the new City Council ended CDBG for both OPCO and the Mid-City Neighbors organization. The City Council stated that scarcer CDBG funds required that all these monies go to the neighborhood with the largest low-income population, the Pico neighborhood. Throughout the period when the progressives controlled the city administration, the PNA identified the least with them. Maintaining a non-partisan, opposition strategy, the PNA survived the political transition within City Council. In 1986, the PNA remains the only neighborhood organization with a professional staff funded by the City. OPCO and Mid-CityNeighbors have voluntary part-time staff.

In all, the forays of the neighborhood-based political clubs into city electoral politics were nearly disastrous for the neighborhood movement in Santa Monica. Only one neighborhood organization, the PNA, survived intact after the SMRR coalition lost its majority in the City Council. Participation in local electoral politics remains a very real barrier for the continuity of neighborhood organizations dependent on city funds.

Legal Barriers

The law is a frequent barrier to the empowerment of neighborhood organizations. Some state legislatures prevent the devolution of local services from the city to neighborhood agencies.[47] In many states the power to tax or police cannot be shifted from the state or city to the neighborhood without new state enabling legislation. Federal regulations have restricted this mode of delivery of various types of local services. For example, in Santa Monica until 1981, CDBG monies could not be used for neighborhood organizing. Now small amounts may be applied to these as social services. In Santa Monica, CDBG funds used by one neighborhood organization for citizen participation were tied to particular capital improvements within the area. Some federal crime prevention funds must be managed by City Hall.

As long as neighborhood organizations hold advisory powers concerning city planning and delivery of services, there are no legal constraints. But once these organizations begin to advocate decision-making and implementation powers, then legal barriers to local control arise. Some states encourage more power sharing with community organizations. Article 34 of the California State Constitution allows charter cities to delegate power to subunits of government. Thus the precedent exists for a greater devolution of decision-making power to Santa Monica's neighborhoods.

Funding: The Struggle for Independence

With growing federal, state, and municipal austerity, public funding for neighborhood organizations is one of the most critical barriers to local control. Existing neighborhood organizations are hard pressed to find funds for staff salaries and the maintenance of other services. Cities known for their support for innovative neighborhood planning (e.g., Seattle, Denver, Atlanta, Salem, Portland, and St. Paul) have significantly cut back funding for their neighborhood programs.[48]

In Santa Monica, the City Council once provided start-up funds from CDBG monies for new neighborhood organizations in the Pico and Ocean Park communities. And, in 1983, Mid-City Neighbors received City funding to implement crime prevention and neighborhood improvement programs in an unorganized area. However, Santa Monica's neighborhood organizations have not fared well recently. A City Council vote denied $164,000 in federal funding to the Ocean Park organization.[49] Later, the Mid-City Neighbors organization also lost its funding. These two neighborhood organizations lost CDBG monies, in part, because of sharp reductions in federal support. In addition, when the All Santa Monica Coalition gained control of the City Council, it decided these organizations were politically allied with its opposition, SMRR.

In 1986, the only remaining City-funded neighborhood organization, the PNA, received funding from several sources. Most funds come from the city government's federal Community Development Block Grants, General Revenue Sharing, and City funds. About 15 to 20 percent of the neighborhood organizations' funds must be raised privately. Private funding of neighborhood organizations is also problematic. It is limited, in part, by the amounts larger corporations allocate to community development. Corporate contributions will not replace a significant part of the federal/state cuts in social spending. Corporate contributions are directed toward local ventures that focus on neighborhood organizations with strong track records in management of local development programs. The Pico Neighborhood Organization received seed funding from the Local Initiatives Support Corporation, a Ford Foundation project to help fund the housing acquisition program. Besides the quantitative limits to corporate philanthropy, there are serious restrictions on the kinds of ventures that are likely to be funded in programs guided principally by profit maximization.[50]

Conclusion

The barriers to progressive political movements for neighborhood control are substantial. Still, neighborhood organizations can help cities seek innovative solutions to urban problems. Whose interests will the neighborhood organizations serve? Santa Monica's more affluent, less organized neighborhoods have not gained city services disproportionately. The poorest neighborhood in Santa Monica, the Pico neighborhood, gained more of the CDBG money between 1981 and 1984 than any of the other neighborhoods. The progressive City Council majority and the strengthened neighborhood organizations redistributed these city funds rather than create more inequality among neighborhoods.

Will Santa Monica's tenant movement confront the macro-economic forces shaping its neighborhoods or will the City's neighborhood organizations adopt a reformist strategy, gradually to be assimilated into conventional urban development? There are indications that much stronger local empowerment will be necessary for Santa Monica's neighborhood organizations to avoid being swept away by assimilationist currents. Recent analyses of Santa Monica's radical coalition suggest a weak foundation of support for long-term radical change.[51] The Santa Monica progressives came to power by supporting local economic control and a strong rent control program. However, beyond these issues, there is little agreement within the radical coalition of Santa Monica for Renter's Rights for the development of a more comprehensive political agenda. Moreover, a survey shows that tenant consciousness is as conservative in Santa Monica as elsewhere in the United States.[52] Heskin encountered a basic lack of egalitarianism in the attitudes of Santa Monica's activist tenants. This new urban populism attacks large landlords and the dominance of outside speculators. However, tenants support the ideology of the small, entrepreneurial landlords and small-scale economic growth. This position is reflected in the City's rent control law, which exempts resident owners of three or fewer units.

Support for Santa Monica's progressive coalition is based mainly in consumer issues like improved air quality, cleaner water, better housing, and environmental preservation. The coalition has accomplished much less in terms of production issues, such as control over public investment, workplace democracy, and the creation of a progressive system of health care.[53] Without increased local mobilization behind workplace democracy issues, the neighborhood movement does not appear able to link local organizations to national coalitions. Few urban movements in the United States or Western Europe have successfully unifed their workplace and community experiences.[54] Instead, many urban movements oppose rather than support state controls of capital. Similarly, in Santa Monica, the politics of economic democracy remain only loosely connected to the struggle for neighborhood control.

Issues of class and race, although generally hidden from public debate by the City Council and SMRR, are not far below the surface in discussions on neighborhood economic development. The Pico Neighborhood Association's efforts toward empowerment raised considerations of class and race most distinctly. The issue of PNA's struggle for an autonomous trust fund based on the neighborhood's development agreement indicated the City's reluctance to allow power to develop within a minority, working-class neighborhood. Studies of other city governments conclude that few progressive city administrations have coped well with minority neighborhood organizations.[55] In fact, none of the neighborhood organizations in Santa Monica gained substantial power that was autonomous from City Hall. A recent study of Santa Monica politics suggests that SMRR was unwilling to allow significant decentralization of power to any neighborhood organizations, regardless of the class or ethnicity of neighborhood.[56]

The neighborhood movement in Santa Monica is still quite young. External dependency, weak resident participation and social control, localism, electoral politics, and inadequate funding all limit the growth of the neighborhood organizations and progressive local control. However, the neighborhood organizations have shown considerable innovation in dealing with these common barriers to neighborhood control. The earlier intense negotiating of numerous development agreements among the neighborhood organizations, City Council, and the developers has been institutionalized, in part, by the City's adoption of new housing, land-use, and circulation elements of the General Plan. Both the SMRR coalition and the neighborhood organizations played major roles in formulating and implementing these plans.

In theory, all cities can impose conditions on capital in exchange for access to their urban space. However, certain cities are strategically located to drive harder bargains than others. Cities such as Santa Monica, San Francisco, and Santa Barbara have the power to require developers to offset the demands their projects create on the environment with public services and amenities. Santa Monica and other cities have succeeded in requiring developers to provide affordable housing for low- and middle-income residents, as well as public parks, day-care centers, funding for cultural programs, and job training programs. The barriers to achieving progressive social change through the neighborhood movement are formidable. However, Santa Monica's experiences suggest that innovative solutions are still to be found in grassroots movements where neighborhood organizations work with progressive city administrations to improve the quality of urban life.

Notes

1. My interest in neighborhood-based planning flows from observation of a citizens' task force on neighborhood-based planning appointed by the new progressive City Council in Santa Monica. The Task Force on Development Permit Processes and Neighborhood Planning met weekly from October 1981 to May 1982. The Task Force was appointed to develop proposals for neighborhood planning for the city (Resolution No. 6270). I conducted interviews with members of the city administration and the neighborhood organizations. The current neighborhood organizations include: Ocean Park Community Organization (OPCO), Pico Neighborhood Association (PNA), Sunset Park Community Planning Coalition, Douglas Park Homeowners Association, Palisades Beach Property Owners, and the Mid-City Neighbors.

2. *Land Use and Circulation Element (Final Adopted).* Santa Monica, CA: City of Santa Monica, 1984.

3. *General Plan Land Use and Circulation Elements, Issue Paper: The Industrial Corridor Summary.* Santa Monica, CA: City of Santa Monica, 1983.

4. Daniel Barber, "The Analysis of the Population Diversity of the City of Santa Monica, 1979 to 1985." Santa Monica, CA: Rent Control Board, City of Santa Monica, 1985, p. 16.

5. Ibid.

6. *Revised Growth Forecast.* SCAG-82: Southern California Association of Governments, Los Angeles, 1983.

7. These employment projections assume the continuation of current land use policies to the year 2000.

8. *General Plan Land Use and Circulation Element, Background to the Issue Paper.* Santa Monica, CA: City of Santa Monica, 1983, p. 21.

9. General Plan Land Use and Circulation Element, Issue Paper, The Industrial Corridor Summary. p. 4.

10. Ibid., p. 7.

11. Ibid., p. 5.

12. Ibid., p. 4.

13. Derek Shearer, "Santa Monica: How the Progressives Won." School of Architecture and Urban Planning, University of California, Los Angeles, 1982.

14. After World War II Santa Monica reformed its government and adopted a city manager arrangement. Currently, the city is governed by a City Council and manager. The seven City Council members are elected at-large to four-year terms. In other cities, council members are elected from specific districts within the city.

15. Allan Heskin, "After the Battle is Won—Political Contradictions in Santa Monica." School of Architecture and Urban Planning, University of California, Los Angeles, 1984, p. 3.

16. *1983 Community Needs Assessment Survey.* Santa Monica, CA: City of Santa Monica, 1983, p. 7.

17. Ibid., p. 2.

18. Ibid.

19. Ibid., p. 3.

20. William Fulton, "On the Beach with the Progressives." *Planning,* May 1985, p. 6.

21. *Land Use and Circulation Elements,* p. 150.

22. Fulton, p. 7.

23. *Guide to Property Development.* Santa Monica, CA: City of Santa Monica, 1983.

24. *Housing Element Policy Report (Adopted).* Santa Monica, CA: City of Santa Monica, 1983, p. 33.

25. *Attachment B (Land Use Element), Project Mitigation Measures for Accessory Housing and Parks Program.* Santa Monica, CA: City of Santa Monica, 1984.

26. *Office Development in Santa Monica: The Municipal Fiscal and Housing Impact.* Santa Monica, CA: Hamilton, Rabinovitz and Szanton, Inc., 1982.

27. *Land Use and Circulation Elements,* p. 156.

28. Richard Moore, "Job Training Networks: A Tool for Economic Development." Santa Monica, CA: Training Research Corporation, 1985.

29. Mark Kann, "Radicals in Power: Lessons from Santa Monica." *Socialist Review,* May–June 1983, p. 81.

30. Pico Neighborhood Association, *4th Annual Assembly Bulletin,* 1984.

31. *Housing Element Policy Report,* p. 27.

32. Richard Moore, "Is There a Place for the Pico Neighborhood in Santa Monica Politics?" *Santa Monica Democrat,* November 1982.

33. David Moberg, "Gail Cincotta Is Out to Reclaim America." *In These Times,* September 8–14, 1982, p. 17.

34. Eva Bach, Nicholas Carbone, and Pierre Clavel, "Progressive Planning: A Report from the Berkeley and Hartford Working Papers." Unpublished manuscript, Cornell University, 1981.

35. Heskin, p. 26.

36. Gary Squier, Anita Landecker, and Paul Zimmerman, *Pico Neighborhood Plan.* Santa Monica, Pico Neighborhood Association, 1983.

37. Alfredo Ortiz and Marie Fastiggi, *A Model for Community Organization, Outreach and Research in the Latino Community: Final Report for 1981–82 to the City of Santa Monica.* Santa Monica, CA: City of Santa Monica, 1983, p. 109.

38. Ibid., p. 83.

39. Squier, Landecker, and Zimmerman, p. 25.

40. Ibid.

41. Harry Boyte, *The Backyard Revolution*. Philadelphia: Temple University Press, 1980.

42. See Harvey Molotch and John R. Logan, "Urban Dependencies—New Forms of Use and Exchange in U.S. Cities." *Urban Affairs Quarterly*, December 1985, pp. 143–169; Susan Fainstein and Norman Fainstein, "Economic Restructuring and the Rise of Urban Social Movements." *Urban Affairs Quarterly*, December, 1985, pp. 187–206. Stephen Weissman, "The Limits of Citizen Participation: Lessons from San Francisco's Model Cities Program." *Western Political Quarterly*, March 1978, pp. 32–47.

43. Claude Fischer, *To Dwell among Friends—Personal Networks in Town and City*. Chicago: University of Chicago, 1982, p. 102.

44. *The Industrial Corridor Summary*, p. 6.

45. Ortiz and Fastiggi, pp. 15–23.

46. According to the Task Force report, the elements for a legitimate neighborhood organization include the following: the neighborhood organization carries on advocacy for and is accountable to the neighborhood; membership is open to all residents of the neighborhood; dues are not required; the organization is multi-issue oriented; it is democratic and participatory; it is non-partisan; and it is independent of city government.

47. Anthony Downs, *Neighborhoods and Urban Development*. Washington, DC: The Brookings Institute, 1981, p. 180.

48. Joel Werth, "Look for Fewer Neighborhood Plans." *Planning*, February 1983, pp. 38–42.

49. The progressive majority on the City Council was weakened by the loss of three members in the April 1983 elections. A conflict-of-interest problem prevented a fourth progressive council member from voting on OPCO funding. The conservative council members argued that OPCO was too political to continue to receive federal CDBG funds.

50. Woodstock Institute, *Evaluation of the Illinois Neighborhood Development Corporation*. Georgetown, MD: U.S. Department of Housing and Urban Development, 1982, p. 26.

51. See Allen Heskin, *Tenants and the American Dream*. Philadelphia: Temple University Press, 1983, and Mark Kann, *Middle-Class Radicalism in Santa Monica*. Philadelphia: Temple University Press, 1986.

52. Heskin, *Tenants and the American Dream*.

53. Mark Kann, "Radicals in Power: Lessons from Santa Monica." *Socialist Review,* May–June, 1983.

54. Manuel Castells, *The City and the Grassroots: A Cross-Cultural Theory of Urban Social Movements.* Berkeley, CA: University of California Press, 1983. Also, see Manuel Castells, "Review of I. Katznelson's *City Trenches." International Journal of Urban and Regional Studies,* September 1982; pp. 447–449.

55. Pierre Clavel, *The Progressive City—Planning and Participation, 1969–1984.* New Brunswick, NJ: Rutgers University Press, 1986.

56. Kann, 1986.

Index